# British Film

This book explores British cinema in relation to its social, political, and cultural contexts. Each chapter deals with a specific topic and includes close readings of key films from different historical periods. Topics include realism, expressionism, popular cinema, film and theater, sexuality and gender, comedy, class and ideology, heritage film, and diasporic cinema. Demonstrating the richness and variety of a national cinema that has traditionally struggled to define itself between the paradigms of Hollywood popular film and European art cinema, *British Film* also addresses the problematic concept of "national character," as it has been applied in studies of national cinemas and cultures, and the increasing pressure on all of these ideas in the age of globalization. Designed for the general reader, this volume is suitable for use as a textbook, providing comprehensive coverage of British cinema and detailed discussion of specific films that can be used in tandem with screenings.

Jim Leach is a professor in the Department of Communications, Popular Culture, and Film at Brock University, St. Catharines, Ontario. The author of a volume on Canadian filmmaker Claude Jutra, he has published widely on Canadian and European cinema and cultural theory.

# National Film Traditions

*General Editor*
David Desser, University of Illinois, Urbana–Champaign

*National Film Traditions* examines the cinematic heritages of Great Britain, Italy, Russia, India, China, Japan, and Australia, from their origins in the silent film era to the present. Relating film production in these countries to the changing social, political, and cultural contexts in which they were created, volumes in this series will also analyze the problematic concepts of nation and nationalism, and their impact on cinema. Designed for use in undergraduate and graduate courses, volumes in this series will include in-depth readings of paradigmatic films, as well as filmographies, videographies, and selected bibliographies.

# BRITISH FILM

**Jim Leach**

*Brock University*

CAMBRIDGE UNIVERSITY PRESS

PUBLISHED BY THE PRESS SYNDICATE OF THE UNIVERSITY OF CAMBRIDGE
The Pitt Building, Trumpington Street, Cambridge, United Kingdom

CAMBRIDGE UNIVERSITY PRESS
The Edinburgh Building, Cambridge CB2 2RU, UK
40 West 20th Street, New York, NY 10011-4211, USA
477 Williamstown Road, Port Melbourne, VIC 3207, Australia
Ruiz de Alarcón 13, 28014 Madrid, Spain
Dock House, The Waterfront, Cape Town 8001, South Africa

http://www.cambridge.org

First published 2004

Printed in the United States of America

*Typeface* ITC Garamond Book 10.25/13 pt.    *System* QuarkXpress®   [MG]

*A catalog record for this book is available from the British Library*

*Library of Congress Cataloging in Publication Data*
Leach, Jim
British film / Jim Leach
p.    cm. – (National film traditions)
Includes bibliographical references
ISBN 0 521 65276 6    ISBN 0 521 65419 X (pb.)
1. Motion pictures – Great Britain – History.    I. Title.    II. Series.
PN1993.5.G7L38 2004
791.43´0941–dc22
2004040683

ISBN    0 521 65276 6    hardback
ISBN    0 521 65419 X    paperback

# Contents

# Acknowledgments

I would like to thank David Desser, the editor of the "National Film Traditions" series, for the invitation to write on British film and for his support and enthusiasm for the project. I am also grateful for the comments and suggestions made by Beatrice Rehl, Fine Arts and Media Editor for Cambridge University Press. As always, I am thankful for the support of the faculty in the Department of Communications, Popular Culture, and Film at Brock University, and especially to the department's media technician, Rob MacMorine. Michael Gnat, free-lance production editor and typesetter, has offered numerous corrections and improvements to the manuscript, and I am very grateful for his care, his patience (most of the time), and his humorous asides.

# Introduction

At the beginning of *Strapless* (1988), written and directed by David Hare, a woman (played by American actress Blair Brown) meets a man (played by Swiss actor Bruno Ganz) in a Catholic church somewhere in Europe (the sequence was filmed in Portugal) (Figure 1). This chance encounter leads to an obsessive relationship in which Lillian, a doctor in a cash-strapped London hospital, finds her life turned upside down by Raymond's unpredictable comings and goings dictated by his dubious financial activities. In a key sequence, Hare uses the American doctor to express his own dismay at the state of contemporary Britain, in a speech to her colleagues that blames the crisis at the hospital on the abandonment of national traditions by a government that places economic restraint above human need. However, her lucidity and independence are deeply disturbed by the personal needs that attract her to Raymond.

As in much of Hare's work for theater, television, and film, social and political beliefs come up against the irreducible, and often destructive, power of passion and desire (see Chapter 6). His characters also often feel uncomfortably out of place, and the casting of foreign actors in this film reinforces the disorienting effect of Lillian's affair with Raymond. At the same time, the presence of well-known European and Hollywood actors (Bridget Fonda also appears as Lillian's sister) conforms to the commercial logic of the contemporary global media environment in which producers have to sell their films in different national markets. Yet, ironically, the presence of foreign actors and characters is itself a sign of the film's "Britishness."

From the beginnings of British cinema, foreign actors have figured prominently for a number of reasons, including the political turmoil in Europe during the 1930s that led many actors to seek exile in Britain, the commercial motives of producers who sought success in the international market, and the desire of filmmakers to exploit the stereotyped exotic appeal of certain countries. After the coming of sound, the accents of these actors provided a rich counterpoint to the already complex interplay of "standard" English and class-based and regional accents.

The politics of accents, domestic and foreign, is a vital part of British cultural life and figures in many chapters of this book. Foreign actors provide alternative models against which to measure British actors and the versions of national identity that they represent, although these distinctions become much less clear when foreign actors assume a British identity or when British actors masquerade in foreign roles. However, their presence also attests to a sense that the British national identity is rather less easy to define than is often claimed, and this insecurity informs a widespread and persistent critical tradition that depicts British cinema as occupying a kind of no-man's land between the two major modes of international film production.

The confidence and energy of Hollywood filmmaking in the "golden age" of the 1930s and 1940s reflected the emergence of the United States as a world power, at a time when Britain's status was in decline. For those who rejected what they saw as the lowering of standards brought about by mass culture, the British documentary movement offered one alternative, but another was provided by foreign-language films from other European nations that came to be identified as "art cinema." As we shall see, British filmmakers have sought to emulate both the popularity of Hollywood and the cultural status of art cinema, but critics often feel that their films do not fit comfortably into either category.

To cite just a few characteristic examples of this tradition: "as, geographically, Britain is poised between continents, not quite Europe, and very far from America, so . . . the British cinema seems to hover between the opposite poles of France and Hollywood" (Lindsay Anderson, 1949); "artistically, as well as geographically and economically, Britain's cinema belongs somewhere between America and Europe" (Penelope Houston, 1963); "British film-making is caught between Hollywood and Europe, unconfident of its own identity, unable to commit or develop strongly in either direction" (Christopher Williams, 1996).[1]

As these quotations demonstrate, the sense of being in between is a symptom of larger concerns about British culture, and it lies behind François Truffaut's notorious claim that there is "a certain incompatibility between the terms 'cinema' and 'Britain.'"[2] One of the leading figures in the French New Wave and a great admirer of the Hollywood auteurs, Truffaut made this remark in 1962 during a long interview with Alfred Hitchcock, as part of his argument that the director's Hollywood films were superior to his earlier work in Britain. His assessment seems to have touched a nerve and, by 1986, Charles Barr was complaining that Truffaut's comments had become so "tediously familiar" that it was virtually impossible to write about British cinema without quoting them.[3]

It is quite reasonable to ignore Truffaut on the grounds that "this linking of national characteristics with a capacity for contributing to the cinema is inane."[4] Yet the frequent repetition of this inanity shows that it tapped into deeply ingrained responses to British cinema. Rather than ignore this phenomenon, we need to look more closely at Truffaut's claims to discover how he envisages the relations between cinema and nation.

**Figure 1.** A romantic encounter: Lillian (Blair Brown) is attracted by the charm of Raymond (Bruno Ganz) when she meets him in a European church at the beginning of *Strapless*.

According to Truffaut, the futility of British cinema is the result of "national characteristics – among them, the English countryside, the subdued way of life, the stolid routine – that are anti-dramatic in a sense." He even added that "the weather itself is anti-cinematic."[5] His argument depends on a particular view of cinema (he equates "cinematic" and "dramatic") that conflicts with the moderation and inhibition often seen as basic attributes of the British national character. Implicitly, he contrasts British filmmakers with those from other nations who are more in tune with the needs of the medium: In the context of the interview, we are likely to think of dynamic Americans (who welcomed Hitchcock to Hollywood) and passionate Frenchmen (like the New Wave filmmakers).

The persistence of this view of British cinema suggests that, on the one hand, it is has a good deal of truth to it and, on the other, that it is a rather too convenient way of describing – and often denigrating – a complex and "messy" national cinema.[6] It also tends to ignore the difficulty of distinguishing clearly between popular and art cinema. While the distinction is useful as a critical tool, these are not mutually exclusive categories: Popular cinema is an art form as well as an industry, art films may become popular, and many films include significant elements from both models. The boundaries between popular and art cinema were never as clearly drawn as critics sometimes try to make them seem, and these distinctions are becoming increasingly blurred everywhere.[7]

It is also becoming increasingly difficult to define the boundaries of national cinemas. Many British films have been made with 100 percent U.S. financing, and a recent issue of the American journal *Literature/Film Quarterly* illustrates the uncertainty that this situation can create. A reviewer casually refers to *Shakespeare in Love* (John Madden, 1998), a film hailed in

Britain as a triumph for the national cinema when it was chosen Best Picture at the 1999 Academy Awards, as a Hollywood film. In the same issue, an article discusses *Shadowlands* (Richard Attenborough, 1993) and asks, "how true to life should a Hollywood movie be?"[8] The production of these films, like many others, was dependent on U.S. funding, but both have their roots in, and engage, with British cultural traditions. Both are also examples of popular films that incorporate features more usually associated with art cinema.

Since Britain formally joined the European Community in 1973, the European context for British culture has become more important, but Britain's place in Europe remains an ambiguous one. John Hill has suggested that economic and technological developments in the 1980s pushed British filmmakers toward the art-cinema model traditionally associated with other European nations.[9] Certainly, European investment has been a major factor in the careers of British filmmakers as diverse as Peter Greenaway and Ken Loach, and their work is often discussed in terms of the director's personal vision. At the same time, the European Community has sought to compete with Hollywood by encouraging large-budget coproductions, often described as "Europudding films" because "the need to satisfy so many producers, as well as different audiences, from different cultural contexts often ends up denying the film any clear identity at all."[10]

The hybrid character of such productions is indeed a characteristic of contemporary media in the age of globalization. The diasporic migration of many ethnic groups throughout the world, often caused by attempts to purify the nations from which they come, only renders more visible the cultural diversity in most modern nations. If the definition of "nation" is thus rendered more complicated, "cinema" is at the same time becoming increasingly subsumed into a "global multimedia marketplace" dominated by the new electronic media.[11] We will examine all of these issues, but we need to look more closely at the ways in which the relations between cinema and nation have been traditionally defined.

In one of the first attempts to analyze a national cinema systematically, Siegfried Kracauer argues that "national characteristics are effects rather than causes – effects of natural surroundings, historical experiences, economic and social conditions."[12] As the title of his book *From Caligari to Hitler* (1947) suggests, Kracauer studied German cinema in the period before World War II and discovered patterns of imagery and narrative that, he argued, explain why the German people supported Hitler. Although Kracauer explicitly rejected "the concept of a fixed national character," it is often difficult to avoid thinking in such terms when reading a book in which he sets out to uncover "a secret history involving the inner dispositions of the German people."[13]

Films thus function as symptoms of cultural processes of which they themselves are a product. While some critics have become suspicious of this rather circular argument, others still write as if there were a very direct relationship between films and the nations in which they are made. Thus, in a discussion of British cinema in the 1980s, Harlan Kennedy suggests that "if the eyes are the windows of the soul, the windows of a nation are its movies" and claims that, "almost too easily, Britain's schizophrenia can be glimpsed through the perfect transparency of its cinema."[14]

If movies were "the windows of a nation," the study of national cinemas would be a fairly straightforward undertaking; but there are at least two major problems with this metaphor. It suggests that film style has no effect on what is seen, that we look through rather than at movies, and it implies that nations have "characters" that films simply observe – or reflect, to use another common metaphor. It makes a difference whether "national character" is seen as the cause or effect of historical processes, and this distinction may affect the ways in which national traditions are represented in specific films. With regard to the theorizing of national cinemas, however, both approaches depend on the assumed existence of a shared set of characteristics that produce the distinctive qualities or limitations of a body of films identified by national origins.

This assumption has been challenged by a growing awareness that subjectivity and identity are far more complex and unstable than earlier cultural theorists believed and that class, ethnic, gender, and other differences deeply affect the experience of national identity. It is thus tempting simply to dismiss "national character" as a myth that obscures the diversity and contradictions in the nation and in the films produced in that nation. While this may true, however, the myth can have powerful effects on filmmakers, on government policy, and on the response of spectators to the films.

In his influential discussion of cultural "mythologies," Roland Barthes insists that myths are not untrue but depend on a selective perception that comes to stand for the whole truth: Their familiarity makes them seem like natural rather than cultural phenomena. In one essay, for example, he argues that each nation has a "totem-drink," and that a Frenchman who does not drink wine is likely to have "minor but definite problems of integration."[15] National cinemas thus provide a good site for exploring the relations between the coercive effect of cultural myths and the diversity that they seek to organize and conceal.

From this perspective, what matters is not so much whether the critics are right to define British cinema as an in-between cinema as that they have been widely perceived to be right. As Andrew Higson has pointed out, national cinemas are constructed by "critical discourses" that do not "describe an already existing national cinema, but . . . produce the national cinema in their utterances."[16] It is these discourses that produce the distinction between popular and art cinemas and then the idea of British cinema as falling in between the models thus constructed.

Discourses and myths often take the form of stories. If the stories are successful, they often come to stand in for the reality that they are apparently designed to explain. In telling the story of British cinema, critics tend to privilege certain kinds of film and, in this respect, the story has changed in recent years. Whereas the old story stressed a tradition of realist films, opposed to vulgar Hollywood cinema, a new version emerged in the 1980s that insisted on the need to take into account the full range of films produced in Britain. The success of this story has led to a surge in publications on British cinema, often drawing attention to forgotten or neglected films. It remains to be seen what effect this academic work will have on the well-established myths, but it does point to the need to rethink the implications of the earlier accounts.

At the same time that critics are rehabilitating British cinema, the idea of studying national cinemas is itself coming under increasing pressure, not only from a growing awareness of the hybridity of personal identity and national traditions, but also from political and technological developments that call the relevance of national boundaries into question. The argument against the study of national cinemas takes two slightly different, but not necessarily incompatible, forms. One insists that national identities *ought to* matter less (given the harm that they have caused); the other claims that they *do* matter less (in an increasingly global cultural environment). For better or worse, however, nations continue to play a role in the way most people define themselves, and the trend toward multinational political and commercial institutions has been accompanied by the emergence of many new nations.

Obviously, I am not raising these questions at the beginning of a book on British cinema to convince my readers that studying national cinemas is a waste of time. Rather, I want to establish at the outset that the relations between "nation" and "cinema" are complex and unstable and that we need to pay close attention to the ways in which cinematic texts are shaped by, and interact with, their national contexts. As John Orr suggests, "while there is much discussion about how cinema can reinforce national identity, it can also very effectively challenge national identity: far from confirming it, film can point out contradictions or the frailties of perception; it can unveil discord or division."[17] Preconceived notions of the national character cannot explain how specific films work, but we do need to attend to the ways in which myths of the national character are represented, examined, reinforced, and/or contested.

What matters about discourses, myths, stories is less that they are true than that they function. To do so, they must have the authority to impose themselves as truth, which means that they must serve the interests of those with cultural power but also that they must be plausible. An open-minded assessment of as many films as possible, and of the cultural contexts in which the films were made and received, enables us to test the veracity of the existing stories and to create more informed stories; but we should never claim to have access to a truth that somehow lies beyond discourse.

In his study of literature, politics, and culture in Britain after World War II, Alan Sinfield notes that he chose the texts for analysis "because they seem to focus key issues, and discussion of those texts is meant to be symptomatic rather than exhaustive."[18] My approach is rather similar. While I have chosen films to demonstrate the range and variety of films produced by a national cinema often accused of lacking imagination and inventiveness, I focus on a relatively small number of films so that I can explore them in some detail rather than provide a lengthy list of films touched on only superficially. In the process, I have been forced to ignore many fine films that I would like to have been able to discuss.

My goal is not to evaluate the films I discuss, and I have tried to avoid the twin temptations to disparage previously admired films just because they were part of the old story or to replace the denigration of all British films with an equally indiscriminate adulation. I have also avoided the practice of ticking off the "progressive" features of a film and then taking it to task for falling short of the critic's standards in other areas. In many cases, I cite the objections of earlier critics and suggest alternative ways of responding to the films. This usually means taking the films on their own terms, at least initially, to discover how they work and why they take the forms they do.

One of the pitfalls involved in studying a national cinema is the risk of dealing with the films in isolation from other products of world cinema that may reveal similar features. In this study of British cinema, I have made use of a number of theoretical contexts and have occasionally referred to films from other nations where they seemed relevant to the topic under discussion. While the emphasis is certainly on issues of national cinema, there is no claim that this is the only, or even the primary, context in which the films are of interest.

This book is not a history of British cinema. Each chapter is devoted to a topic that raises important issues regarding British cinema, but the films discussed are treated more or less chronologically within the chapters. There is a sort of progress, too, in that the topics discussed in the later chapters lend themselves to the use of more recent films as examples. To avoid too much duplication in the chapters themselves, I briefly describe below the structure of the book and, at the same time, outline some of the key historical moments in terms of the industry and government policy.

In dealing with British cinema, defining the nation is an especially tricky task, for reasons that are discussed in Chapter 1. This chapter explores the idea of national identity and the pressures on the idea of nationhood, and examines some of the ways in which the British "nation" has been conceived and named. The main focus is on how these issues play out in two films – *The Captive Heart* (Basil Dearden, 1946) and *Chariots of Fire* (Hugh Hudson, 1981) – in which the tensions and contradictions in the concept of "national characteristics" become very apparent.

Chapter 2 deals with British filmmaking in the 1930s, when some of the main traditions of the national cinema emerged. Most historical accounts refer to the pioneer work of British filmmakers in the early years of cinema when, as Andrew Higson puts it, "British film-makers were among the most enterprising in the world," competing especially with the French and Americans in technical and storytelling innovations.[19] The first of many crises for the British film industry came during and after World War I, which placed a huge strain on the national economy at a time when the Hollywood studios were rapidly expanding, with the result that, during the 1920s, production declined to alarmingly low levels.[20] A quota system, introduced in the 1927 Cinematographic Act, rescued the industry by requiring British exhibitors to show a certain percentage of British films each year. Although the initial quota was set at the modest figure of 5 percent, the act provided for an annual increase until the figure reached 20 percent in 1936, by which time, despite a number of setbacks and abuses, cinemas were showing more British films than the legal requirement.[21]

The more stable situation allowed British studios to establish long-term production strategies. Chapter 2 focuses on three such strategies that had a major impact on the subsequent development of British cinema: the realist project associated with the documentary-film units established by John Grierson, the prestige pictures advocated by Alexander Korda, and the popular genre films that were produced by almost every studio but most influentially represented by the thrillers directed by Alfred Hitchcock.

Despite the economic revival, the subject matter of British films was restricted by a rigid censorship system. As well as regulating depictions of sexual behavior and violence, the British Board of Censors rejected any projects liable to arouse social or political controversy. It was only with the disruptions caused by World War II that the reins of censorship were loosened, and the films discussed in Chapters 3–5 show the effects of the new possibilities on the three traditions discussed in Chapter 2.

The relative relaxation of censorship allowed filmmakers in the realist tradition to deal with topics that would have been too disturbing or controversial under the previous rules. A "golden age" of British cinema emerged in the "quality" films of the 1940s, although these were not always as single-minded in their realism as critics often claimed. Chapter 3 begins with an account of the critical debates on realism in general and in British cinema in particular. It continues with an analysis of the kinds of realism found in British

New Wave films like *Room at the Top* (Jack Clayton, 1958) and *Saturday Night and Sunday Morning* (Karel Reisz, 1960), in the social-realist films of Ken Loach and Mike Leigh, and in some contemporary films that extend the tradition in new directions.

Chapter 4 identifies a countertradition, loosely descending from the spectacle and fantasy in Korda's films, that I have labeled British expressionism. All of the films discussed in this chapter defy traditional conceptions of the national culture and push the limits of censorship, through their exploration of the unconscious mind and sexual desire. They include the popular Gainsborough melodramas and the excessive "art films" of Michael Powell and Emeric Pressburger from the 1940s, the films of Ken Russell, Nicolas Roeg, and John Boorman that often produced scandal in the 1970s, and the "avant-garde" feature films directed by Peter Greenaway and Derek Jarman in the 1980s and 1990s.

Chapter 5 investigates the relations between popular cinema and national cinema, using Antonio Gramsci's concept of the national-popular. It begins with a discussion of *The Third Man* (Carol Reed, 1949), a film that draws on and responds to Hitchcock's thrillers of the 1930s. The James Bond phenomenon provides an instance of the ways in which popular success can raise questions about national identity, and some popular films of the 1990s, including *Brassed Off* (Mark Herman, 1996) and *The Full Monty* (Peter Cattaneo, 1997), are examined for their attempts to combine the realist tradition with the "utopian" qualities of popular cinema.

Chapter 6 deals with the close relationship between theater and the film industry in Britain, drawing attention to the theatrical basis of role-playing and stereotypes in the construction of national identity. As examples, the chapter focuses on performances by Laurence Olivier and Diana Dors in the 1950s, the contribution of playwrights like Harold Pinter, David Hare, and Stephen Poliakoff to British cinema, and the cultural meanings of Shakespeare in contemporary British films.

In exploring issues of sex and gender in British cinema, Chapter 7 deals first with the new "liberated" sexuality of the 1960s, as illustrated by *Darling* (John Schlesinger, 1965) and *Alfie* (Lewis Gilbert, 1966). These films draw on the image of swinging London, which proved highly attractive to international audiences and thus to the Hollywood studios, who invested heavily in the British film industry at this time. When Hollywood withdrew its support in the 1970s, a major crisis ensued and, for a brief period, the sex film became the most prolific and profitable British genre, testing the limits of the "permissive" society, before being replaced by home videos. These soft-core films are so far removed from the standards set by the "quality" films that most critics prefer to ignore them, but they are part of the overall story of the national cinema. After examining the sexual codes at work in these films, the chapter turns to some recent films by women directors, whose explorations of female sexuality address the implications of feminist theory in this area.

Chapter 8 examines the idea of a national sense of humor, dealing with the relations between comedy and national traditions in the celebrated Ealing comedies, the rather less respectable Carry On films, and the grotesque absurdity of the Monty Python team.

The films discussed in Chapter 9 disturb myths of national identity by depicting "monsters" whose excessive behavior is out of keeping with the inhibition and moderation usually associated with the British character. A discussion of Hammer horror films is sandwiched between sections on British crime films after World War II and more recent contributions to the genre.

The issue of social class figures in most of these chapters, as it does so prominently in British society, but it is addressed directly in Chapter 10. Since the education system is a dominant ideological apparatus, charged with promoting national traditions, this chapter focuses on the school movie, with particular attention to *If. . . .* (Lindsay Anderson, 1968) and *Kes* (Ken Loach, 1969), two films that deal with schools at opposite ends of the social spectrum at a time when the system was supposedly undergoing radical change.

The topic of Chapter 11 is the emphasis on history in British cinema, as in the culture at large. The first section deals with the idea of "heritage" that became highly contentious in the 1980s through its association with the cultural policies of Margaret Thatcher. While her government enacted legislation to encourage the development of the "heritage industry," it eliminated the protective measures, subsidies as well as quotas, that had long sustained the film industry. In the "free market" conditions thus created, one of the major successes was the heritage films, usually adapted from classic English novels. This chapter discusses a number of such adaptations, from novels by Jane Austen, E. M. Forster, and Henry James, as well as some recent history films, to determine the extent to which they support or question Thatcher's ideological agenda.

Finally, Chapter 12 explores the pressures on traditional ideas of the national culture caused by the collapse of the British Empire, the presence of growing diasporic communities, and the impact of globalization. During the 1980s, the intervention of a new television service, Channel 4, helped to sustain a socially conscious British cinema that often challenged the objectives of Thatcherism. While television continues to play a major role in the British film industry, the government of Tony Blair boosted production in the 1990s through a system of tax relief and funding from the National Lottery, although many of the films thus produced have not found distribution. In this context, the future of British cinema is once again very uncertain, but the Britain that is represented onscreen is even more varied than in the past. This final chap-

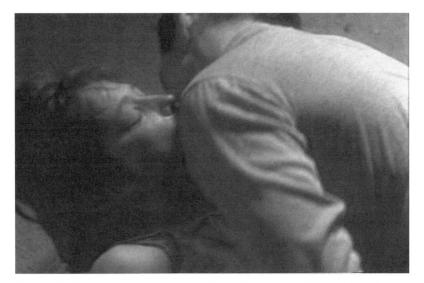

**Figure 2.** There is no romantic meeting in *Intimacy:* Jay (Mark Rylance) is surprised when Claire (Kerry Fox) arrives at his apartment, but they quickly renew their frantic and anonymous sexual affair.

ter deals with films about new Britons, with emphasis on films from the diasporic cultures formed by immigration from the Indian subcontinent.

In an editorial published in the June 2003 issue, *Sight and Sound* warned of yet another crisis facing the British film industry. Of the thirty "British" films reviewed in the journal in the first six months of the year, only twelve were set "substantially in a UK landscape," and just five were "UK-only productions."[22] The dominance of coproductions raises the question of what counts as a British film and further complicates the complex mixture of national and international influences that has always been a feature of British cinema.

Just over a decade after Hare's *Strapless,* another film about an obsessive relationship that eventually becomes destructive illustrated the pressures that the new situation places on the idea of national cinema. Patrice Chéreau's *Intimacy* (2000) was a French–British coproduction based on two stories by Hanif Kureishi, with a screenplay by Chéreau and Anne-Louise Trividic, and set entirely in London. It achieved some notoriety because of its sexual content and was often discussed in relation to a trend in recent French cinema toward films involving "real" sex (Figure 2).

The film was released uncut despite the British censors' concern that the graphic sexuality might prove especially disturbing because it was "in English, with people you recognise and bus routes you recognise."[23] The publicity surrounding the film dwelt on the involvement of two respected actors: New Zealand–born Kerry Fox and Mark Rylance, artistic director of the new Globe

Theatre. The film's premise, in which a couple meet once a week for anonymous sex in a basement apartment, inevitably led to comparisons with Bernardo Bertolucci's *Last Tango in Paris* (1972), and the sexual explicitness could be seen as a sign of the film's lack of the restraint usually associated with British cinema and the national "character."

As we shall see, these myths have never quite corresponded to the diverse range of British films and, by the year 2000, the depiction of British characters in *Intimacy* had obvious roots in the national cinema. Once Jay (Rylance) leaves his apartment to follow Claire (Fox) and intervene in her life, the film relishes the bustle and noise of London celebrated in Kureishi's fiction (see Chapter 12). The film also includes music by artists, like The Clash and David Bowie, frequently evoked by Kureishi, and the cast, apart from a gay French waiter in the bar where Jay works, is English. Timothy Spall, as Claire's taxi-driver husband, is familiar from many Mike Leigh films (see Chapter 3), and Marianne Faithfull, as a member of Claire's acting class, is an iconic figure who carries associations with the social and sexual revolution of the 1960s, which also figures prominently in Kureishi's work.

*Intimacy* can thus be read in a number of contexts, including the earlier work of its director in theater and film and the movement in cinema (European but also global) toward more explicit forms of sexual representation. Yet it is also clearly, in many ways, a British film, in which national traditions interact with influences from elsewhere. If British cinema is still an in-between cinema, this situation takes on a new meaning in a global cultural environment that creates new pressures, but also new opportunities, for British filmmakers. The situation described in the *Sight and Sound* editorial is a serious one, but it is not the first time, or no doubt the last, that the British film industry has been in trouble. Whether it, or indeed cinema as we know it, will survive cannot be predicted in the light of the rapidity of political and technological change, but whatever emerges is likely to have some precedent in the rich and strange conglomeration of cultural traditions and cinematic styles that make up the history of British film.

# CHAPTER ONE

# The National Health

## Great Britain / Deep England

The idea of studying a national cinema depends on the claim that there is a significant relationship between films and the cultural traditions of the nation-state within which they are made. There are numerous obstacles that make it difficult to define this relationship, not the least being the need to determine what exactly a "nation" is. In the influential definition proposed by Benedict Anderson, a nation is "an imagined political community."[1] This formula captures the tension between two interlinked ways of thinking of the nation: as an imaginary structure of myths and traditions that provides a sense of collective identity, and as a political institution.

In an ideal situation, these two senses of the nation will reinforce each other, but both are subject to historical pressures that can pull them apart. These pressures are, to some degree, inherent in the attempt to establish a sense of common, national interests among people whose social status and regional backgrounds are quite different. The experience of national identity has recently been complicated by the emergence of new communities larger than the nation-state (the European Union, for example) and by the disintegration of many established nations into smaller nations on the basis of religious or ethnic differences.

In his analysis of the "new world order," Timothy Luke points out that the "modern nation-state" dates back only to the seventeenth century and suggests that it "proved even in the ideal type models of England and France, to be very limited, fictive and artificial."[2] The choice of "England" to represent one of only two ideal versions of modern nationhood serves to underline Luke's point about the fragility of this institution, but in a rather different way than his apparent intentions. At the time when the ideal of the modern nation-state was supposedly emerging, England became part of the larger national entity known as the United Kingdom. England is often the part that stands for the whole, but the other components of the national culture contest and interact with this sense of a dominant "English" identity.

Officially, the nation is the United Kingdom of Great Britain and Northern Ireland, and it includes Wales, Scotland, and Northern Ireland, as well as England. This political arrangement emerged from a long historical process:

England and Wales were united in 1536, joined by Scotland in 1707 and by Ireland in 1801. During the twentieth century, there were many challenges to the idea of national unity: The southern part of Ireland became independent in 1922 after a bloody struggle, and it seems likely that Northern Ireland will eventually become part of Eire; there are also strong independence movements in Scotland and Wales that have recently led to the "devolution" of some political authority to new parliaments in those countries.

According to Ernest Barker, a classical scholar and historian whose work on "national character" continues to influence discussions of British cinema, Britain is "a multi-national nation."[3] Although Barker himself showed no interest in cinema in his many works on the national culture, Jeffrey Richards has recently endorsed his "view of national character/national identity" as a guide for studying British cinema.[4] It is a view that acknowledges that many people feel as much, or more, attachment to a nation within the nation than to the United Kingdom itself, but it also insists that, underlying this diversity, there are national characteristics that make unity possible.

This argument points to the existence in Britain of dual (or multiple) national identities that are becoming an increasingly common feature in many parts of the world, but it is only the English national character that claims to encompass the others – and often succeeds in doing so, in films as in other aspects of British culture. Because most national institutions, as well as most film companies, are located in and around London, they have tended to reinforce the dominance of English culture.

This historically dominant culture does not represent the whole of England equally. During the 1950s, critic and filmmaker Lindsay Anderson denounced British cinema as "an *English* cinema (and Southern English at that), metropolitan in attitude, and entirely middle-class."[5] Even more narrowly, this cultural formation has its roots in the southeast of England, in the so-called Home Counties around London. Although British films have not always been as restricted in their depiction of the national character as Anderson suggests, the problems involved in naming the nation create numerous pitfalls for writers on the national cinema.

François Truffaut included "the English countryside" in his notorious account of the "national characteristics" of "British" cinema. In a sense, he was simply describing the cultural situation I have just outlined, but this was more likely an example of the familiar slippage that occurs so often in discussions of British culture that it usually passes without notice. Another example is the title of Alexander Walker's book *Hollywood England: The British Film Industry in the Sixties,* which (to add to the confusion) was published in the United States as *Hollywood UK.* More recently, Charles Barr published a study of *English Hitchcock* and justified his title by pointing out that the director was a Londoner whose films were set more often in other European countries than in other parts of Britain.[6] The point is well taken but, while Hitchcock's films may be culturally English, they are still part of a British cinema dominated by English traditions but not confined to them.

## ENGLISH AS IT SHOULD BE SPOKEN

The conflation of Britishness and Englishness is encouraged by the fact that the national language is *English,* and myths of the national character are inextricably bound up with English literary traditions. Barker quotes William Wordsworth, the nineteenth-century romantic poet, to support his claim that the "British way of life" includes all those "who speak the tongue/That Shakespeare spake; the faith and morals hold/Which Milton held."[7] Even though some of the most important authors in this tradition were Scottish, Welsh, and Irish, they wrote in English, and the language tends to take precedence over their national origins. For Barker, language has a cultural and moral force, and the English language has not only shaped the national culture but also spread its values around the world, most notably to Britain's former colonies.

Ironically, of course, one of the legacies of the British Empire is that Hollywood films are made in English, with the result that there is no language barrier to protect Britain's domestic market from American competition. Especially after the arrival of the "talkies" in the late 1920s, the guardians of the national culture became seriously concerned about the effect on the national character. The poster for Alfred Hitchcock's first sound film, *Blackmail* (1929), wittily played on the novelty of sound and the anxiety about exposing audiences to American English in Hollywood films, by inviting audiences to hear "our mother tongue as it should be – spoken!"[8]

Although *Blackmail* was originally planned as a silent film and a silent version was released for those cinemas not yet equipped for sound, Hitchcock used sound in highly imaginative ways in many sequences.[9] Along with the aesthetic and technical difficulties, his ingenuity also had to cope with the problem posed by the star, Annie Ondra, who was Polish. She had starred in *The Manxman,* Hitchcock's previous film made earlier the same year, as the daughter of an innkeeper on the Isle of Man, but this was a silent film. For the sound version of *Blackmail,* it was not yet technically possible to "post-dub" her dialogue to eliminate her accent, so she mouthed her lines while another actress spoke them offscreen – in a refined accent that was just as inappropriate as Ondra's would have been for the daughter of a London shopkeeper who kills an artist when he attempts to rape her in his studio (Figure 3).

The coming of sound meant that the social, regional, and national origins of actors and characters could now be identified by their accents. In Britain as in Hollywood, some actors were unable to make the transition. Whereas, in silent films, casting depended on the actor's appearance, now the voice had to match the appearance. As in the case of Annie Ondra, this was not primarily a question of realism but of social and aesthetic conventions. These conventions, for British cinema at the beginning of the sound era, required that a heroine, even in Hitchcock's morally ambiguous world, speak with the refined accent associated with the upper classes and the West End theater.

Not surprisingly, a Scottish cinema owner complained that the British film industry produced "English films in a particularly parochial sense" and claimed that his audiences found them "more foreign . . . than the products of Hollywood over 6,000 miles away."[10] Yet, as Hitchcock himself pointed out, "the film of chromium plating, dress shirts, and Oxford accents" offered only a very partial representation of "English life."[11] On the other hand, upper-class English accents did not prevent several British stars of the 1930s from becoming extremely popular, and the Hollywood studios supported a large colony of British actors with "English" accents who frequently appeared in literary adaptations and films about the British Empire.

The image of Britain in these Hollywood films was primarily English, upper-class, and situated in the past, making heavy use of traditional stereotypes. Their success only made things more difficult for British filmmakers whose work had to negotiate the class and regional differences that their Hollywood counterparts could afford to ignore. As we will see in Chapter 2, a number of strategies for developing a distinctive British cinema emerged in the 1930s, but it was during World War II that British films developed a national vision that seemed to unify the different traditions that made naming the nation difficult.

This unity was always precarious. In 1944 the critic William Whitebait expressed his confidence that "British films after the war should have their chance of becoming what we want them to be – English."[12] Yet, although such shifts in nomenclature are presumably inadvertent, they do often contribute to a loosely defined system of values. As in the postwar literary traditions discussed by Alan Sinfield, "generally, Britishness is claimed for size and scope, Englishness for core distinctiveness."[13] The wartime and postwar British films developed what Angus Calder has called the "myth of the Blitz," in which the war became a struggle to preserve national values identified with "a Green and Pleasant heartland, 'Deep England.'"[14]

Andrew Higson has also described the persistence of "an essentially pastoral national identity . . . : 'Englishness' as ancient and natural inheritance, *Great* Britain, the *United* Kingdom."[15] As Higson's emphases suggest, to call the multinational nation the United Kingdom asserts a debatable unity, while to refer to Great Britain (as many reference works continue to do) implies a nostalgia for an international status that the nation has not enjoyed since the decline of the empire. For that reason, I use the relatively neutral term "British

**Figure 3.** Sight and sound: Alice (Annie Ondra) compromises herself in the artist's studio in *Blackmail*, while Joan Barry supplies her voice from offscreen.

cinema," except where the context clearly refers to "English" traditions. I do not comment further on the choices made by the critics I quote.

Although the relations between the nation's different names are rather more muddled (and complex) than these theoretical distinctions imply, the distinction between Great Britain and Deep England provides a helpful framework for exploring the tensions involved in an inclusive representation of the nation. In this chapter, I explore these tensions as they appear in a film from the postwar period, *The Captive Heart* (Basil Dearden, 1946), and in *Chariots of Fire* (Hugh Hudson, 1981), a film associated with Margaret Thatcher's efforts to revive the wartime experience of unity in a very different social and political context.

## A LITTLE PIECE OF ENGLAND:
### *THE CAPTIVE HEART*

When he took over as head of Ealing Studios in 1938, Michael Balcon recruited several documentary filmmakers and announced that the Studio would henceforth specialize in realistic representations of the national character. He insisted that "the screen's job is to reflect a country's moods, social conditions and aspirations; and for this reason we try to set Ealing pictures against realistic backgrounds."[16] Looking back over Balcon's career, and shifting the metaphor from reflection to projection, John Caughie notes that he earned a reputation for "projecting an image of Britishness, and particularly of Englishness."[17]

The Ealing films, of the 1940s especially, demonstrate how the uncertainty about naming the nation can be both productive and inhibiting, often at the same time. I discuss the famous Ealing comedies later, but it was the studio's war films, made during and after World War II, that most fully explored the problem of the national community. These films sought to incorporate all classes and all regions in their vision of the war effort, but this placed some strain on their depiction of the national traditions in whose name the war was being fought. Typically, they dealt with a group of men who must overcome their differences to ensure their own survival, as well as for the sake of the nation. In this respect, they are not unlike war films from other nations, but the differences are defined in terms of the British class system and the regional origins of the characters.

These films both reflect and project the idea of World War II as the "People's War," a unified struggle against fascism that would result in a more democratic and less class-bound nation after the war.[18] In *San Demetrio London* (Charles Frend, 1943), for example, the crew of an oil tanker abandon ship when it catches fire under attack in mid-Atlantic, but the occupants of one lifeboat – without senior officers – reboard the crippled vessel, extinguish the fires, and sail it to its destination in Scotland. The men who learn to work together in the common cause include a Welsh and a Scottish sailor, but the inclusive sense of the nation is somewhat undermined when the judge, who awards the crew salvage money, declares that it is "we in England" who will remember their efforts.

As Ealing's first postwar war film, *The Captive Heart* engages with the idea of the People's War at a time when the election of a Labour government in 1945 seemed to confirm that the power of the myth would indeed transform British society. In this case, the male group consists of British soldiers captured early in the war and confined for five years in a German prison camp. Their interaction sets up tensions that expose both the possibilities and contradictions involved in what was supposed to be a new sense of the nation, but the film also incorporates other elements that complicate its treatment of national identity.

The group includes a Welsh and a Scottish soldier, played by Mervyn Johns and Gordon Jackson, the same members of the Ealing stock company who appeared in *San Demetrio London*. Along with the English characters, who come from different classes, they learn to work together against the common enemy. Despite occasional differences, their cooperative attitude contrasts with German regimentation. They are led by Major Dalrymple (Basil Radford), a sympathetic, resourceful English officer whose main peacetime interest was horse racing. He resists German efforts to separate the officers from the men and acknowledges the inevitability of social change, wryly describing himself as "a social parasite, the sort we're fighting the war to get rid of."

**Figure 4.** "Each a little piece of England": Hasek (Michael Redgrave), a Czech refugee, disguised as an English officer, watches as his fellow prisoners work on their garden in *The Captive Heart*.

Much of the film is taken up with the prisoners' efforts to cope with the boredom of life in the camp. As Charles Barr points out, "*The Captive Heart* creates a little England in its prisoner of war camp in Europe," and he refers to a montage sequence illustrating the letters of a prisoner who describes the camps throughout Germany as "each a little piece of England" (Figure 4).[19] In a tribute to Balcon published in 1947, G. Campbell Dixon insisted that "nobody ever made a more English film than *The Captive Heart*" and attempted to relate national character to film style by suggesting that "the pace is deliberately allowed to drag – partly to suggest the slow tempo of prison life, but more fundamentally because the English are the most patient race in Europe."[20]

Slow pacing was indeed a frequent complaint against British films from audiences and reviewers, but the most prominent characteristic of the style of *The Captive Heart* is its generic hybridity. It combines elements of realism and melodrama in ways that raise questions about what it means to call it an "English film." Although the main focus is on the soldiers, the film also deals with the lives of the women they have left behind in Britain. The iconography and narrative structure of the war film, traditionally a "masculine" and "realist" genre, interact with the very different conventions of the domestic melodramas that became extremely popular at the end of the war and were aimed primarily at women.

Like earlier Ealing war films, *The Captive Heart* uses documentary techniques to create a sense of authenticity. Made largely on location in recently vacated German prisoner-of-war camps, it opens with a voice-of-God commentator describing the plight of British soldiers captured in France in 1940 and thus excluded from the possibility of becoming war heroes. During their long march to the camp, documentary "objectivity" gives way to subjective experience as flashbacks present the prisoners' memories of their departures from home. Their relationships with their wives and girlfriends develop through letters received during the five years they spend in the camp, and are then resolved when the men finally return.

During their period of internment, the Welsh soldier learns that his wife has died in childbirth, and he finally returns home to meet his infant daughter; the Scot, who has lost his sight, tries to break off his engagement by letter but finds his fiancée waiting for him; an English soldier receives a letter telling him that his wife has been unfaithful, but they are reunited on his return. These tearful homecomings have the powerful affect expected of melodrama, and the emotion generated relates national unity to personal experience. Yet there is another union that occurs at the end of the film and complicates its effect.

Barr does not mention that the prisoner from whose letter he quotes is not English, nor even British, but a Czech who has assumed the identity of a dead British soldier to save himself from execution by the Germans. Since he speaks fluent German, his fellow prisoners at first suspect that he is a spy, but they help to conceal him once they learn the truth. In order to maintain his disguise, he has to reply to the letters sent by the dead man's wife. Although the marriage was on the point of collapse before the war, now she falls in love again, believing that her husband has come to share her feelings about Deep England. When she finally realizes the truth, she reacts angrily but then recognizes that the fictional performance has created real feelings (Figure 5).

Since Michael Redgrave plays the Czech officer with a perfect English accent, the emotional power of the ending depends on a simultaneous awareness of the actor's and the character's origins (supplemented, for well-informed members of the audience, by an awareness that Rachel Kempson, who plays the widow, was married to Redgrave in "real life"). His accent is explained "realistically" because he lived in London as a child when his father worked at the Czech embassy, but the effect is not unlike that in an earlier Ealing war film, *Went the Day Well?* (Alberto Cavalcanti, 1942), in which the German soldiers in British uniforms who invade an English village are played by British actors.

Some critics were disturbed by "the notion of Germans playing at being British soldiers and unmistakably British actors playing at being German soldiers," and a similar uncertainty about the signs of national identity is at work in *The Captive Heart.*[21] Both films stress the fictiveness of national identity

**Figure 5.** "It was as if you were offering me another world": At the end of *The Captive Heart,* Hasek informs Celia (Rachel Kempson) that her husband is dead and that it was he who wrote the letters from the camp.

through the use of British actors impersonating foreigners whose theatrical skills (uniforms and accents) enable them to pass as British soldiers. In the context of the People's War, it is significant that the accents in question are standard English and that, in the earlier film, the village squire turns out to be a German agent.

The Anglo-Czech prisoner in *The Captive Heart* is a rather more ambiguous figure because his performance eventually earns him a place in the national community. His true identity emerges when he fails to recognize an allusion to "Jane," the popular comic strip, in a casual remark by a fellow prisoner. At first, his ignorance of a curvaceous icon of popular culture seems to confirm the suspicion that he is a "highbrow," which might also explain why he knows German (if he is not a spy). Appearances prove to be deceptive, but this episode illustrates the film's insistence on the popular and inclusive basis of its sense of the national character. Even the major's upper-class background does not prevent him from sharing the jokes and activities of the other prisoners, and the film suggests that the ability to accommodate change is the product of popular cultural traditions that resist dogma and pretense.

The film's use of music reinforces this idea. Although the score is by classical composer Alan Rawsthorne and one of the prisoners is a classical pianist, the diegetic musical performances in the film serve to locate national identity in popular traditions. At the beginning, the men march into the camp defiantly whistling "There'll Always Be an England," and, when the Germans play a recording of a military anthem, the prisoners drown it out by singing "Roll Out the Barrel," a popular song that they call "our national anthem." Later, a choir sings a Welsh folk song, and the prisoners engage in a pub sing-song to cover a raid on the commandant's office. When the men leave the camp at the end, Elgar's *Pomp and Circumstance March No. 1* swells on the soundtrack but soon gives way to a reprise of "Roll Out the Barrel," apparently sung by the men as their ship docks.

The final union of the Czech soldier and the widow of the man he has impersonated implies that, while national identity may be grounded in popular traditions, it is less an inherent attribute than a fictional construction, but one that nevertheless has real effects. Although the film's core image of Englishness is the country house in which the wife lives with her children and her father, this image was already under severe pressure in postwar Britain, both from the progressive aspirations associated with the People's War and from the difficult economic conditions in crowded cities with which most of the people had to cope. *The Captive Heart* ends by affirming a utopian sense of the national character that seeks to combine the traditional and the new and that, while remaining essentially "English," can encompass the rest of the nation, and even sympathetic foreigners.

## ON THE SAME SIDE AT LAST:
### *CHARIOTS OF FIRE*

By the 1980s, when the "postwar settlement" that established the "welfare state" was challenged, and partially dismantled, by the Conservative government of Margaret Thatcher, this image returned in a much more grandiose form in so-called heritage films, in which English cultural traditions again claimed to represent the nation (see Chapter 11). From Thatcher's perspective, the welfare state had spoiled the national character, in the sense that parents who pamper their children supposedly deprive them of the capacity to cope with the challenges of adult life. Her political rhetoric often recalled Winston Churchill's wartime speeches, enabling her to shift the meaning of the People's War away from its associations with social justice to an emphasis on the self-discipline of a nation following the example of a great leader.

In this account, the decline of Britain as a major world power began with the 1945 general election in which the people voted for the Labour Party and against Churchill. At the time, this result seemed to promise a new, more democratic, version of national identity, growing out of the People's War but, as Calder makes clear, the long-established vision of Deep England was a very potent element in the "myth of the Blitz." According to Keith Robbins, the election delivered the message that "'New Britain' should bear a strong resemblance to a 'new Jerusalem' – at least in England's green and pleasant land."[22]

Writing in the late 1990s, Robbins may have been thinking of the much-discussed use of "Jerusalem" in *Chariots of Fire,* although the imagery of William Blake's poem had long been a mainstay of political rhetoric and cultural debate. In any case, this film, made in the early years of Thatcher's regime, aptly illustrates the tensions and contradictions that had accumulated around the idea of the national character.

As many commentators have pointed out, "Thatcherism" was a political platform that combined a progressive orientation, in its aggressive economic policies and encouragement of "enterprise," with an appeal to the past, in its calls for a return to "Victorian" moral values and stress on the national "heritage."[23] Although she often showed impatience with traditional images of rural England, there is little doubt that Thatcher would have approved of *The Captive Heart* as a celebration of British courage and restraint, and many critics saw *Chariots of Fire* as a throwback to that kind of film, thoroughly in keeping with the new times.

The film is rather more complex than the straightforward conservative reading would suggest. It tells the story of two British athletes, Harold Abrahams (Ben Cross) and Eric Liddell (Ian Charleson), who won gold medals at the 1924 Paris Olympics, although the film takes many liberties with the historical record.[24] On one level, the film celebrates their lives, and its narrative builds to a climax in which their individual efforts pay off in an international triumph for Britain. Yet the film's meaning and effect are complicated by its treatment of the politics of national identity.

When *Chariots of Fire* won four U.S. Academy Awards, including Best Picture, screenwriter Colin Welland caused a stir by announcing that "the British are coming!" and the film's success was often compared to that of the athletes in the film.[25] It was certainly a major boost for the British film industry, which had been going through especially difficult times during the 1970s. The film and its narrative could thus be read as an endorsement of the basic principle of Thatcherist enterprise culture: that British products must compete in the international market without government support. David Puttnam, the producer, whose own faltering career was revived by the film's success, encouraged such a reading when he declared that it was about "winning on your own terms."[26]

Yet, as many critics pointed out, the film was not quite the British success story that it seemed to be. Puttnam had great difficulty getting the project off the ground because potential backers thought that the story was "too

British" or even "too English" (the sources differ). Eventually the six-million-dollar budget came from Twentieth Century–Fox and a company headed by Mohammed Al Fayed, the Egyptian shipping magnate. The only British investment was a small amount of development money advanced by Goldcrest Films and paid back before production began.[27]

The ingredients that come together in the film's narrative are also rather more disparate than they first appear. Its basic structure consists of intercutting between the stories of the two runners, who race against each other only once, at a competition in London where Liddell wins and temporarily undermines Abrahams's confidence (Figure 6). Their parallel stories establish that both athletes are outsiders who must struggle not just to win at the Olympics but also to define themselves in relation to the prevailing myths of the national character.

Abrahams, the son of a Lithuanian Jew, arrives at Cambridge University and uses his athletic talent to prove himself to the establishment from which he feels excluded by his ethnic background. He clashes with the college authorities when they learn that he has hired a professional coach. They stress the importance of "games" as part of the education of an "Englishman" but insist on the "way of the amateur" as opposed to the "individualism" encouraged by the "professional attitude." In attacking their "archaic values" and insisting on "the pursuit of excellence," Abrahams speaks for the future – and for Thatcherism – and we are presumably supposed to identify with his position; but the film also suggests that the overt professionalism of the U.S. team violates the Olympic ideal.

Liddell appeals to the other side of the Thatcherist agenda. He is doubly an outsider, as a Scot and as a deeply religious man who places God above country. His first conflict is with his sister, who feels that training for the Olympics will interfere with his religious vocation and distract him from his goal of becoming a missionary in China. Later, he has to defend himself before the national Olympic committee when he decides not to compete in a race scheduled on Sunday. As the head of the committee, the Prince of Wales greets the Scottish runner by saying that it is good to have him "on the same side at last," acknowledging that this is a British team but placing himself firmly on the English side, despite his title. He appeals to their "common bonds" but, when Liddell stands firm, another committee member, the Duke of Sutherland (whose title is Scottish, although the film does not bring this out), reminds them of World War I and argues that they should not demand sacrifices "in the name of guilty national pride."

As the above brief summary begins to suggest, the film tackles, in Puttnam's words, "a whole range of issues, class, race, religion, and the question of gentlemen and players."[28] While these issues are clearly raised in a context that relates them to definitions of the national character, the key question is

**Figure 6.** Running them off their feet: Eric Liddell (Ian Charleson) beats Harold Abrahams (Ben Cross) in their only competitive meeting in *Chariots of Fire.*

how, or whether, the film manages to hold together its various components. Pauline Kael, who disliked the film, thought that it was "held together by the glue of simple minded heroic sentiments."[29] Since its release coincided with the so-called Falklands War, during which Thatcher whipped up patriotic feeling to consolidate her own power, it seems likely that many in the audience indeed read the film as a celebration of Britain's former greatness and an appeal to return to traditional values.

Some critics were less convinced that the film presented a coherent vision. James Park called it "a perplexing mix of anti-establishment rhetoric and panegyric to British traditions," while Sheila Johnston thought that it was "at once iconoclastic *and* deeply conservative."[30] However, such contradictions were very much part of Thatcherism, and it was possible to find coherence by arguing that the film shows that the athletes "have to earn their belonging" and that their success proves that the system can "accommodate outsiders."[31] Johnston refers to the gesture of Viscount Lindsey, who withdraws from his race so that Liddell can take his place, as the act of an aristocrat who recognizes the need for change, thereby demonstrating that "nationhood . . . is a dynamic thing, challenged by the interloper, yet remaining in essence unchanged."[32]

There is little doubt that the resilience of the national character is one of the meanings of the film and, to the extent that this is so, it functions as a fantasy addressed to those who feared that things had changed to the point that national traditions had lost their meaning. As many critics noted, the period setting allows the film to avoid the complications raised by the new diasporic communities in Britain that so disturbed many Conservative politicians (see Chapter 12). Yet "race" is among the issues listed by Puttnam, and there is some ambivalence in the film's treatment of "belonging." After Abrahams triumphs in the one hundred meters, there is a cut to Sam Mussabini, his coach, alone in a hotel room opposite the stadium, from which he has been excluded. He is, as he puts it, "persona non grata," ostensibly because he is a professional, but he is also an outsider because of his ethnic background (Italian and Arab, although played by English actor Ian Holm). As he tearfully listens to the national anthem at the awards ceremony that he cannot see, the effect is far from a simple celebration of nationhood.

The extent to which such moments disturb the film's apparent celebration of the national past is a question often asked of heritage films, but the tensions involved are also apparent in the film's dislocated narrative structure. Despite the changes to the historical events, usually justified in biographical fictions by the need to create dramatic unity, Andrew Sarris complained that there were "three false starts to the narrative and half a dozen anticlimaxes at the end."[33]

The narrative begins in 1978, at a memorial service for Abrahams. Among the congregation are Lindsay and Aubrey Montagu, another member of the Olympic team. Their memories cue a flashback to 1924 that begins with a shot made famous by the film's publicity: the men of the Olympic team running on a beach to the accompaniment of the theme music by Vangelis. A voice-over by Montagu, reading from a letter to his parents, reveals that the athletes will soon leave for Paris and cues a further flashback to 1919, when Montagu arrives at Cambridge and meets Abrahams at the station. Montagu's narration then disappears until the second flashback catches up with the first when the team is on the boat to France.

The rather elaborate temporal regression seems especially odd since it does not introduce Liddell (except as one of the runners on the beach), whose story will soon assume equal narrative importance to Abrahams's efforts to prove himself. By moving from the (almost) present back to 1919, the film sets up its characteristic backward–forward movement, which we have already seen in the confrontation between Abrahams and the Masters. It also introduces, and links, the issues of class, ethnicity, and nation through allusions to World War I: The luggage handlers at the station are disfigured war veterans, and the Master of the college addresses the assembled students on the sacrifice of former students who "died for England and all England stands for" and suggests that "their dreams are now yours."

The film also raises the question of what "England stands for," and how this relates to Abrahams and Liddell, through its use of music. Its original score by Vangelis, a Greek composer, seems to have little relation to the historical period or the national character. Kael commented tartly that the film was "in love with simple values and synthesized music," implying that its technological sophistication exposed the hypocrisy of its apparent nostalgia.[34] There is no doubt that this score was a major factor in the film's success, and that it illustrates the uneasy position of this British film in an increasingly international and market-driven media culture, but it is only one element in a complex musical fabric woven through the film.

Several critics have drawn attention to the singing of "Jerusalem" during the memorial service that frames the narrative. Indeed, the film's title highlights this relatively brief episode, since Blake's poem refers to a "Chariot of fire" that will help to build Jerusalem in "England's green & pleasant Land."[35] Blake's protest against the "dark Satanic Mills" that were changing the landscape and people's lives during the Industrial Revolution was set to music by Hubert Parry during World War I, becoming one of Britain's many unofficial national anthems (adopted initially by socialists rather than conservatives) and a Church of England hymn. As so often happens, the stirring music tended to override the darker aspects of Blake's vision.[36]

In the context of the film, the anthem is heard near the end when Abrahams returns from Paris. He does not leave the train with the rest of the team and thus avoids the celebration of their return. As he embraces his fiancée on the empty platform, "Jerusalem" begins, and a dissolve takes us to the memorial service, where the camera pans across the choirboys singing the anthem (perhaps reminding us of the college porter's snide remark after Abrahams's arrival in Cambridge that he would certainly not be singing in the chapel choir). There would seem to be some irony in the singing of this anthem during a service in a Christian church to honor a Jewish man who became a distinguished member of the British sports community, but the critical consensus seems to be that "the irony is unintentional."[37]

It is, however, notoriously difficult to decide whether irony is intentional or not. The effect of "Jerusalem" in *Chariots of Fire* depends on its relations to the many official anthems that punctuate the film's soundtrack as well to the extracts from the comic operas of Gilbert and Sullivan. On their arrival at Cambridge, the new students are invited to sign up for various clubs, including one devoted to Gilbert and Sullivan. Abrahams shows great interest, and we later see him in the leading role in *H.M.S. Pinafore.* He first sees Sybil, with whom he immediately falls in love, when she appears as a Japanese schoolgirl in a production of *The Mikado* in London.

The Gilbert and Sullivan operas were extremely popular in the late nineteenth century and have become a national tradition. Like that of *Chariots of Fire,* their appeal stems from a strange mixture of conservative and critical elements. David Cannadine has argued that their "ostensibly innocent topsy-turveydom" allows them to "hold out the prospect of the established and political order being overturned and subverted." The endings restore order, but the absurd plot mechanisms simultaneously defuse the satire in laughter *and* undermine the authority of that order. As Cannadine suggests, "in the context of the time, the boundary line between humour and anxiety was very narrow indeed."[38]

The finale of *H.M.S. Pinafore,* which we see in the film, depends on a typical Gilbertian comic inversion that allows the character played by Abrahams, an ordinary sailor in love with the captain's daughter, to become part of the naval establishment. When it is revealed that the sailor and the captain were switched at birth, the sailor simply becomes the captain, and the father, now an ordinary seaman, drops his opposition to the marriage. The opera ends with a stirring mock-anthem celebrating the fact that "he is an Englishman" which is, as Bruce Babington suggests, "balanced between affirmation and irony."[39]

The context in which this sequence appears illustrates the complex effect of music, and its relation to national traditions, in the film. As he walks through the college chapel with Montagu, Abrahams denounces the prejudice in this "Christian and Anglo-Saxon" nation and resolves to "run them off their feet." In the background, a boys' choir is rehearsing, but their "Christian and Anglo-Saxon" music (as Abrahams describes it) gives way to "He is an Englishman," as we see him writing anonymous news reports on his athletic successes as part of a campaign of self-promotion. The source of the music is then traced to the production in which Abrahams is performing, an irony underlined by the song's absurd assumption that "it is greatly to his credit" that, "in spite of all temptations to belong to other nations," he is an Englishman (Figure 7). The next sequence shifts our attention to Liddell, running for Scotland against France, and begins with "La Marseillaise" – played on the bagpipes!

For many of the film's critics, these ironies – whether intentional or not – do not encourage critical reflection but rather allow the audience "to have it both ways: they can guiltlessly adore the reactionary ways of colonial Britain, yet still feel morally superior to its excesses."[40] This comment certainly captures a major aspect of the film's appeal, but it is not clear that all audiences would ignore the tensions involved in its representation of the nation. As John Hill points out, "for a film which is reputedly so nationalist, it is surprising how conscious it is of the complexities of national allegiance."[41]

Like *The Captive Heart, Chariots of Fire* envisages a national character capable of including all classes and regions and even people of "foreign" origins, but it is much less certain about what to call this utopian nation. The Olympic team for which Abrahams and Liddell compete represents Great Brit-

**Figure 7.** *Chariots of Fire:* Abrahams's desire to be an Englishman is temporarily satisfied as he stars in a production of Gilbert and Sullivan's *H.M.S. Pinafore.*

ain – or "*Grande Bretagne,*" as it appears on the placard that precedes the team into the stadium; but a newspaper headline, when Abrahams returns, calls him the "toast of England," and the final caption declares that, when Liddell died in occupied China at the end of World War II, "all of Scotland" mourned.

# CHAPTER TWO

# The Magic Box

## What Is British Cinema?

In the final sequence of *The Magic Box* (John Boulting, 1951), William Friese-Greene, the British inventor, whom the film depicts as an unacknowledged pioneer of motion pictures, attends a meeting of film exhibitors in 1921. He pleads with them to support British producers rather than follow the economic logic that encouraged them to show more popular and less costly Hollywood films. After making his impassioned speech to no avail, Friese-Greene drops dead, creating a powerful allegorical ending that translates the story of an individual who lacks the practical sense to exploit his own invention into the depiction of a national culture that fails to support its own cultural industries.

*The Magic Box* was the film industry's contribution to the Festival of Britain, with many leading actors appearing in cameo roles, designed to mark "the contribution made by the cinema to the life of the nation."[1] It did indeed celebrate the life of a British film pioneer whose work had been overshadowed by other more famous inventors, such as the Lumière brothers in France and Thomas Edison in the United States, somewhat distorting the historical record to make Friese-Greene's work seem more important than it actually was. However, a film about missed opportunity does seem a somewhat odd choice for such a celebratory occasion.

Raymond Durgnat compares this film with *Scott of the Antarctic* (Charles Frend, 1948) to support the idea that "the British could hardly respond to the idea of success without an aura of failure surrounding it."[2] The myth of "gallant failure" is indeed deeply ingrained in discourses about the national character, but the film's box-office failure reminds us that British audiences do not always respond as critics and filmmakers think they will. Still, the way in which *The Magic Box* represents this myth anticipates Truffaut's claim that there is "a certain incompatibility between the terms 'cinema' and 'Britain.'"[3] When Friese-Greene first succeeds in projecting moving images, the film playfully suggests that the cinematic apparatus is a product of illicit desires that run counter to a national culture based on restraint and inhibition.

Working alone in his laboratory in the middle of the night, Friese-Greene rushes jubilantly into the street where he meets a policeman (Laurence Oli-

**Figure 8.** The eyes of the law: A policeman (Laurence Olivier) watches as Friese-Greene (Robert Donat) projects the first moving pictures in *The Magic Box*.

vier) to whom he excitedly describes his achievement. The policeman thinks he is a madman trying to report a crime, especially when he invites him to see Uncle Albert "almost as if he was alive." Only when the policeman looks do we see the images that Friese-Greene has finally succeeded in projecting, intercut with the flicker from the projector playing on his face, an effect that both confirms the reality of the invention and foreshadows its challenge to the law (Figure 8). The anxiety generated by the moving image raises questions about cinema in general, but the film also implies that these questions become especially disturbing in the British context.

Rather than seeing this anxiety as a sign of the impossibility of a successful national cinema, as Truffaut did, we should explore how these tensions work themselves out in the specific forms and themes developed by British filmmakers. As we have seen, the British film industry was often on the verge of bankruptcy and constantly trying to define itself in relation to popular Hollywood cinema and European "art" cinema. These conditions influenced the films in many ways, but the result was a rich, if unstable and hard to define, national cinema.

As a showcase for the British film industry, *The Magic Box* bears witness to the success of the quota system, introduced shortly after Friese-Greene's death in response to the problems he describes in his dying speech. Robert Donat, who plays the inventor, was nearing the end of his career, but he had appeared in many of the key films of the 1930s that helped to build the kind of national cinema for which his character pleads. Although the so-called

quota quickies, cheaply made films intended only to meet the quota require-
ments, were often cited as an abuse of the 1927 Cinematographic Act, even
these films provided experience for young filmmakers, and the steady increase in production created conditions in which it became possible to address questions of national cinema that went beyond its economic survival.[4]

In thinking about these questions, critics and filmmakers could be either
descriptive or prescriptive or both at the same time. They often lamented the
actual state of the film industry and argued for a specific approach that filmmakers ought to adopt if matters were to improve. Only on rare occasions
have critics felt that the films that *were* being produced were the ones that
the national cinema *ought* to produce. One such occasion was the so-called
golden age of British cinema in the mid-1940s, but, even then, the critics who
praised the "quality" films that earned the period its reputation were aware
that most British films did not conform to their criteria for cinematic excellence.

During the 1930s, three filmmakers became associated with very different visions of what the national cinema should be: John Grierson developed
the documentary film movement, Alexander Korda produced "prestige" films
for the international market, and Alfred Hitchcock established a reputation
based on small-budget genre films. By emphasizing these trends, I am inevitably simplifying the complex reality of film production in this period, but they
do represent approaches that continue to influence production and critical
accounts of the national cinema.

They also provided the framework by which audiences outside Britain
judged British cinema. Some of Korda's and Hitchcock's films succeeded in
breaking into the coveted U.S. market, while British documentary filmmakers
exchanged ideas and films with their North American counterparts. These
trends also had an impact in continental Europe. Pierre Sorlin points out
that, while French critics in the 1930s preferred Hollywood films, they also
"praised British documentaries, Hitchcock's thrillers, and some Korda productions."[5]

## THE ENVIRONMENT IN WHICH THEY LIVE: GRIERSON AND REALISM

Grierson was a Scot, brought up according to strict Calvinist traditions, and
he described himself as "more hard-bitten" than the "Englander" who, however, "will be a far better guide to the metropolitan graces." He felt that British cinema was dominated by "the old English film tradition" that produced
films about "a leisure-class that has lost contact with fundamentals."[6] His view
of film as a public service challenged both the aristocratic traditions of British
society and the escapist fantasies of Hollywood cinema.

Grierson argued that British cinema should carve out a distinctive space for itself, not by competing with Hollywood but by specializing in films of fact and public information. He first put his ideas into practice by directing *Drifters* (1929), a feature-length documentary on the Scottish herring fishery, after which he gave up directing and worked strictly as a producer. The film units he established, first at the Empire Marketing Board (1927–33) and then at the General Post Office (1933–9), became a model for state-sponsored film production using documentary cinema to inform and to influence public opinion.

As Grierson and his colleagues repeatedly pointed out, the commercial film industry in Britain paid little attention to the social and political issues of the day. Even if filmmakers wished to tackle such topics, they would have to contend with strict censorship rules that forbade any project with the least hint of controversy. The documentary movement offered itself as an alternative, but its dependence on government or industrial sponsorship also inhibited the topics that could be treated. By operating outside the framework of commercial cinema, Grierson ensured that documentary filmmaking would not depend on box-office receipts, but much of the output of the documentary units was more like public relations than social criticism.

Thus, although *Industrial Britain* (1932) was "made at the height of the depression there is no indication of that fact, indeed, quite the contrary sense is portrayed."[7] Grierson himself did not see this as a problem because, while his sense of the national culture certainly included a resistance to tradition and the class system, he also saw Britain as a bastion of commercial integrity and "public decency" against the shoddiness and exploitation that he associated with U.S. capitalism.[8] As a fairly early work, *Industrial Britain* expresses Grierson's social and political vision clearly, but it also reveals some of the pressures involved in shaping documentary form to the needs of this vision.

The formal and technical problems were heightened by tensions during the production process that led Grierson to fire the director, Robert Flaherty, and to finish the film himself with the help of other members of the EMB film unit. Flaherty was an American filmmaker and explorer who had pioneered documentary techniques in *Nanook of the North* (1922), filmed in the Canadian Arctic, and *Moana* (1925), made during a yearlong stay in Samoa. It was after seeing the latter film that Grierson first applied the term "documentary" to nonfiction cinema and invited Flaherty to work in Britain.

Grierson had reservations about Flaherty's preference for working in remote and exotic locations, but he asked him to direct *Industrial Britain* and persuaded a commercial company (Gaumont-British) to distribute the film, thus making possible a larger than usual budget for a short documentary film.[9] According to Grierson, Flaherty's working methods frustrated him in much the same way as they had the Hollywood producers who backed his earlier films: He consumed most of the budget shooting beautiful images without coming up with a plan about how to organize them. Grierson took over, shot some more material, and edited the final version of the film.

Because this was one of the first documentaries released with a sound-track, Grierson was able to use a voice-over commentary to unify the film and to organize its argument, a method that became a vital component of his approach to documentary in his later films. In describing the efforts to salvage *Industrial Britain,* he noted that "we made a continuity."[10] He was using the term in its technical sense, but "continuity" is the main theme of the film and a key word in the commentary. The opening sequence sets up a visual contrast between the pastoral world of traditional craft workers and the smoky streets of industrial cities, but the commentator assures us that the "spirit of craftsmanship" remains intact even though "the old order changes, giving place to the new" (Figure 9). Later, after a demonstration of traditional glass blowing, we are shown modern "aerodrome lenses" and told that "they stand for the continuity of English craftsmanship."

The other key word in the commentary is "power," and the film fuses together the industrial and political meanings of the word. When the commentator explains that steam is "the sign and symbol of the new order," he adds that "there is power behind it." Later, after a caption (a relic of silent cinema) introduces the topic of STEEL, the commentator describes the use of "British steel" throughout the world and concludes that "there would be no modern world without it." In the ostensible argument, the pronoun refers to "steel," but the rhetoric suggests that the "modern world" is a British product and that Britain remains the dynamic hub of the empire.

The film insists that technological progress poses no threat to traditional values, but the soundtrack exposes the tensions involved in making this claim. Grierson later regretted that the commentator was an actor whose voice "sounded very very West End actory and altogether out of the spirit of Flaherty's shooting and out of the spirit of our film making."[11] The voice lacks the sense of urgency and authority provided by the voice-of-God commentators in Grierson's later films. Although the speaker is male (as God-like authority required), his "theatrical" enunciation does not suit the spirit of documentary realism. It also carries class connotations that accentuate the social distance between the speaker and the workers depicted in the film.

Grierson did not want a commentator who spoke like the workers (whose voices are not heard in the film), because such a voice would be identifiable as belonging to a specific class and region. Instead he wanted a voice that could create the impression of speaking for a nation in which labor and management worked together for the common good. His description of the voice in *Industrial Britain* suggests that not only was it too upper class but also too "effeminate." Apart from a few shots of weavers in the opening sequence, all the workers shown in the film are men, and the film, like Grier-

**Figure 9.** "The old order changes, giving place to the new": An urban landscape in *Industrial Britain,* grimy and enveloped in smoke, but a sign of the nation's power in the modern world.

son's documentary project as a whole, clearly presents working-class masculinity as the driving force of modern industry.

It is also a distinctly "English" voice and thus fails to represent the entire nation, as Grierson wanted. Yet the commentary itself involves the familiar slippage between "Britain" and "England." The film opens with the sails of a windmill, followed by images of craft workers, and the commentator tells us that "half the history of England lies behind these scenes of yesterday." Although there is a later reference to "the coal fields of England, Scotland and Wales," the commentator concludes by claiming that "the products of industrial Britain" depend on "the personal skill of so many first-rate English workers."

This lapse betrays the strain involved in the effort to stress the continuity between tradition and modernity. The basic argument is that "English" traditions still survive in industrial Britain and, by depicting humble cottages rather than aristocratic country houses, Grierson implies that Britain can take full advantage of modern technological developments only by revising traditional views of the national heritage. However, the use of an upper-class English voice, and the apparently casual substitution of "England" for "Britain," leaves the film's vision of national identity decidedly ambiguous.

The choices made during the production show Grierson struggling to develop a form of documentary realism that would serve the nation. He wanted to change the nation but thought that the best way to do this was by modernizing the dominant myths of national identity. Instead of dwelling on past achievements, the films sought to persuade people to "accept the environment in which they live, with its smoke and its steel and its mechanical aids, even with its rain."[12] The documentary movement thus spoke for national institutions but also tried to reform them by stressing the progressive aspects of their operations.

The filmmakers had to balance the claim of realism to show things as they are with the reformer's desire to show how they could be, and the result is that the films often fall into the propagandist mode of conflating the two. In addition, the aesthetic demands of realism were tangled up with the moral sense in which to "be realistic" is to accept the limits of the present situation, an outlook often associated with more conservative views of the national character. These tensions were eventually subsumed into the debate within the movement between filmmakers who stressed the aesthetics of realism and those who were more concerned with the movement's social purpose.

Three short documentaries produced by Grierson in the mid-1930s illustrate some of these issues through their different treatments of the documentary "voice." As we have seen, Grierson used an omniscient, voice-of-God commentator to organize the argument in *Industrial Britain* and made no attempt to record the voices of the workers (which would have been a major technical challenge at the time). This strategy became the hallmark of most of his later documentaries, but there were attempts to experiment with other possibilities.

In both *Coalface* (Alberto Cavalcanti, 1935) and *Night Mail* (Harry Watt and Basil Wright, 1936), the commentary is supplemented by the verse of W. H. Auden and the music of Benjamin Britten, especially written for the films. We do not hear the voices of the miners in *Coalface,* but *Night Mail* does include conversations among the mail workers, although they are clearly performing for the camera (and choosing their words carefully). Even in *Housing Problems* (Arthur Elton and Edgar Anstey, 1935), in which slum dwellers do speak for themselves, their testimony is doubly framed by the words of the commentator and those of an unseen "expert": Councillor Lorder, chairman of the Stepney Housing Committee.

Although the authoritative voice of the commentator in these films claims to tell the "truth" about the reality depicted in the images, there are other elements that cannot be accounted for simply by the need to support the commentator's argument: the visual beauty of the images in *Industrial Britain* and *Coalface,* the music and verse in *Coalface* and *Night Mail,* the working-class accents and colorful idioms used by the tenants in *Housing Problems.* In the last case, the tenants' words may lack the authority invested in the off-screen voices, but it is possible to argue, as does John Corner, that "in *Housing Problems,* the 'ordinary' breaks through directly in the form of testimony, then raising questions about its articulation with the other speech in the film." Corner concludes his analysis of *Coalface* and *Housing Problems* by suggesting that "both films show tensions and contradictions in the documentary project."[13]

Despite these tensions and contradictions, Grierson succeeded in convincing many influential critics that his project offered the best hope for British cinema. The novelist Graham Greene, writing as film critic for the *Spectator,* declared in 1935 that "the only important films being made in England today come from Mr. Grierson's system of film units."[14] The importance of "realism" as a defining feature of British cinema was established, and critical discourses about the national cinema continued to insist on the centrality of the realist tradition until alternative viewpoints began to emerge in the 1970s.

## BIG ONES THAT CAN BE SHOWN TO THE WHOLE WORLD: KORDA AND THE PRESTIGE FILM

Greene's enthusiasm for the documentary movement was reinforced by his distaste for another important trend in British cinema in the 1930s. In a notorious column, published in 1936, Greene argued that "the Quota Act has played into foreign hands," saving "the English film industry from American competition only to surrender it to a far more alien control."[15] The main target of this xenophobic outburst was Alexander Korda, a Hungarian-born producer who came to Britain in 1931 and quickly became a leading producer who frequently employed fellow refugees from the political turmoil in continental Europe.

Korda's films, and their representation of the national character, are the antithesis of those produced by Grierson, although the two men became friends and often dined together in Korda's penthouse suite.[16] Korda had been making films since 1914, first in his native Hungary and then, after he fled the fascist regime there, in Austria, France, and the United States. Shortly before coming to Britain, he affirmed his commitment to filmmaking as an international endeavor: "It is no use thinking about making little pictures. We must have big ones that can be shown to the whole world."[17] Although many critics shared Greene's concerns about the effect of this outlook on the national cinema, Korda followed his own advice and soon became one of the most powerful figures in the British film industry. By the end of the decade, even Greene was working for him as a screenwriter.

At the same time that Grierson was refining his approach to documentary in *Industrial Britain,* Korda produced and directed *Wedding Rehearsal* (1932), his second British film (after a "quota quickie" for Paramount's British studio) and his first for his new company, London Film Productions. Although it was not a critical or commercial success, the film helped to establish the company and to define Korda's project as a British film producer.

The "foreign" origins of the director and many of the creative personnel are not noticeably apparent in this light comedy of manners that, as Karol Kulik suggests, tells "the kind of story that the English upper classes might enjoy telling about themselves."[18] Roland Young, a British stage actor who moved to the United States in 1912 and had recently established himself as a character actor in Hollywood, plays the Marquis of Buckminster, Britain's most eligible bachelor, who sets the plot in motion through his schemes to avoid marrying one of the six upper-class women his grandmother has selected. The marquis engineers marriages for all of them, only to end up realizing that he is in love with his grandmother's secretary.

The film proclaims its national origins in the opening shot, in which the camera pans from the Houses of Parliament to Westminster Abbey to the accompaniment of the "Wedding March" – originally written by Felix Mendelssohn for a production of *A Midsummer Night's Dream*. Among the marital prospects for the marquis are the twin daughters of an aristocratic family, who both have rather dim-witted lovers, and they thus resemble the young couples who defy parental authority in Shakespeare's play. The allusion to the play (and the frequent use of the "Wedding March" in the score) suggests a magical power behind the ludicrously simple way in which the marquis's machinations result in a wedding with no less than six couples (Figure 10).

The film itself is highly "theatrical" and far removed from documentary realism, but whereas *Industrial Britain* ignores the economic and political crises of the time, *Wedding Rehearsal* incorporates them into a curious sequence that follows the opening shot. There is a cut to a printing press, and a chorus of male voices chants newspaper headlines about an eruption of Mount Vesuvius and the threat of war. When news of a "society wedding" drives these stories off the front page, female voices take over, and there is a cut to a working-class man denouncing the upper classes because his wife has gone to see the wedding and failed to prepare his dinner. Despite his outrage, he soon gets drawn into speculation about when Buckminster, the best man at the wedding, will himself be married.

This discussion cues a cut to the marquis himself, and the rest of the film offers the voyeuristic spectacle of upper-class life that the opening has denounced, aligning the spectator with the "feminine" interest in glamour as an escape from world affairs and domestic servitude. The apparent incoherence draws attention to the tensions involved in the stereotypes of "Englishness" on which this and many of Korda's later films depend. His major contribution to the British film industry was to recognize that these stereotypes could be packaged in such a way as to appeal across class divisions and to international audiences, but the films often draw explicit attention to the construction of stereotypes, and to what they leave out.

**Figure 10.** Midsummer marriage: The Marquis of Buckminster (Roland Young) and Miss Hutchinson (Merle Oberon), his aunt's former secretary, are among the happy couples at the end of *Wedding Rehearsal*.

A similar effect occurs in the opening of *The Private Life of Henry VIII* (1933), which seemed to vindicate Korda's policy when it became the first British film to make a major impact in the U.S. market. However, many critics questioned its status as a British film both because of the large number of immigrants involved in the production and because its "keyhole" approach to history seemed to trivialize the national heritage. Characteristically, Korda incorporated allusions to these issues into the beginning of his film.

The opening captions announce that Henry's marriage to his first wife is of no interest because Catherine of Aragon was "a respectable woman," which is why he divorced her. We are then told that his second marriage to Anne Boleyn was also a failure, "but not for the same reason." The film then begins with the preparations for Anne's execution for adultery, which are intercut with those for Henry's marriage to his third wife, Jane Seymour, that is to follow immediately. An eager crowd gathers to watch the execution, including a woman who declares that she feels sorry for Anne, but whose sorrow does not prevent her from making sure that she gets a good view of the block.

The executions of Anne and of Henry's fifth wife, Katherine Howard, and the sexual intrigue that costs the women their lives, easily fit into the "keyhole" approach, and the film's spectators have come for much the same reason as the public comes to enjoy the spectacle at the Tower. Korda also draws attention to his role as a "foreigner" in constructing this historical entertainment through a conversation between the suave French executioner, especially imported for the occasion, and his burly English assistant. The latter asks "what's wrong with English steel" and grumbles that half the English executioners are out of work.

Since the Frenchman points out that English executioners lack the refinement needed to behead a queen, the film seems to address itself to a "feminine" audience interested in upper-class manners. Yet, while the film exploits these stereotypes of gender, class, and national identity, it also disturbs them. The assertive "working-class" masculinity of the English executioner has much in common with the king's crude behavior that frequently scandalizes his court. Drawing on the historical legend of the "bluff" king, Charles Laughton invests enormous energy in the role and, in particular, makes Henry's unceremonious enjoyment of his food function as an extension of his sexual appetite.

Of course, the film does not (and could not) show us what goes on in Henry's bed (just as it denies us the sight of the severing of heads at the public executions). The reliance on innuendo led Kulik to argue that, unlike Ernst Lubitsch, the German director who was then making sophisticated comedies in Hollywood, Korda "relied on the sexual *immaturity* of the audience" in order "to reach the widest possible audience." Kulik seems to view this lack of "sophistication" as a weakness, but he does go on to quote Grierson's appreciative view of Laughton's performance as "a triumph of the native vitality and vulgarity of the English music-hall tradition."[19]

When Henry first appears in the film, he overhears Katherine Howard, who has just arrived at court, telling the other ladies in waiting how she would treat the king who has behaved so badly to his wives. She rescues the situation by telling him that she would treat him "as a man," and their relationship develops through playful exchanges about whether he wants her to respond to him as a king or as a man. Throughout the film, he tries to demonstrate his masculine prowess, but there are strong hints that his need to prove himself covers an underlying sense of inadequacy. In one sequence, he tries to impress Katherine by challenging a wrestler and, although he wins the bout, has to take to his bed to recover. He is outwitted by his fourth wife, Anne of Cleves (played by Elsa Lanchester, Laughton's wife), who makes herself appear so unattractive that he frees her to marry the man she loves, and he ends up in the care of his motherly sixth wife, Katherine Parr.

A concern with men who cannot live up to their own reputations is also a feature of the two later films of the 1930s that Korda chose to direct himself.[20] In *The Private Life of Don Juan* (1934), the aging seducer, played by the aging Hollywood star Douglas Fairbanks Sr., is a victim of his own reputation and pursued by his creditors. When a younger impersonator is killed in a duel and mistaken for him, Don Juan decides to retire. He later seeks to make a comeback, but the audience at a play based on his legend ridicules him for claiming to be the real Don Juan. In *Rembrandt* (1936), with Laughton again in the title role, the artist dies in poverty partly because of his lack

**Figure 11.** *Rembrandt:* "You surely don't expect us to take this as serious art," members of the Civic Guard complain to the artist (Charles Laughton) as they refuse to pay for his celebrated portrait of them.

of business sense and partly because the public fails to recognize the value of his work (Figure 11).

*Rembrandt* is Korda's most accomplished work as a director, but neither of these films achieved the success of *The Private Life of Henry VIII,* perhaps because the national stereotypes in question are not British. The commercial failure of these films and other "big" pictures caused a crisis in the film indus- try in the later 1930s. Many critics blamed Korda for encouraging the produc- tion of films on a lavish scale that the industry could not sustain, but he did have other successes as a producer, including *The Scarlet Pimpernel* (Harold Young, 1934) and the imperial epics directed by his brother Zoltan. Sarah Street has recently argued that "*The Private Life of Henry VIII* became a con- venient scapegoat for the film industry's domestic problems in the 1930s."[21]

The debate over Korda's influence on the national cinema underscored the dilemma for British filmmakers: "Big" pictures could succeed only if they penetrated the U.S. market, but films made on smaller budgets had to com- pete with Hollywood productions even in the domestic market. According to Kulik, Korda's goal was to produce "quality entertainment pictures" that, de- spite their dependence on "existing stereotypes" and their failure to "further the development of the cinema," could provide the resources to make "more audacious, artistic endeavours."[22]

In the 1940s, critics tended to distinguish Korda's "prestige" films from the "quality" cinema that they admired and that typically sought to blend the "theatrical" traditions on which Korda drew with realist techniques adapted from the documentary tradition. The instability of these terms became a key issue in the subsequent development of British cinema. Thus David Lean established himself with "quality" films such as *Brief Encounter* (1945) and *Great Expectations* (1946) but later turned to epic productions, such as *Lawrence of Arabia* (1962) and *Doctor Zhivago* (1965), on a scale far beyond Korda's reach. During the 1980s, similar questions arose from the contrast between "heritage" films that packaged the national past for an international audience and more modest productions supported by Channel 4 television.

## A BLISTERING STYLE OF STORYTELLING: HITCHCOCK AND GENRE

Alfred Hitchcock's thrillers are the best-known examples of a third option for British cinema in the 1930s, between Korda's lavish productions and Grierson's documentary project. Unlike Korda and Grierson, Hitchcock was not a producer, and his emergence as a major director depended heavily on timely interventions by Michael Balcon at critical points in his career. He gave the young filmmaker his first chance to direct for Gainsborough Pictures in the 1920s and, after Gaumont-British took over the company, he produced Hitchcock's *The Man Who Knew Too Much* (1934) and *The 39 Steps* (1935), the first of a series of thrillers that eventually earned the director an invitation to work in Hollywood.

Modestly budgeted genre films were a staple of the British film industry in the 1930s, often with production values only slightly above those of the notorious "quota quickies." At the same time, the pleasures offered by genre films, with their formulaic plots and stereotyped characters, came under attack from critics on both the left and the right of the political spectrum. According to the former, such films distracted the people from urgent political issues, while the latter deplored their failure to meet the standards set by the more demanding works of high culture.[23] Although many of the popular genres had their roots in British literary traditions, many film critics objected to British genre films because they seemed to imitate Hollywood.

In the early stages of his career, Hitchcock directed many different kinds of film, and it was only in the mid-1930s that he was able to put into full and consistent effect his goal of combining an "English idiom" with an "international outlook."[24] There can be little doubt that he succeeded: As Charles Barr notes, "no one could be more obviously, tenaciously English than Hitchcock" while, "at the same time, no one could be more international."[25] Drawing on the thriller genre, he intertwined elements of suspense, romance, and comedy to create films that seemed to function as pure entertainment.

Like Korda, Hitchcock used stereotyped characters and viewed them ironically, but he inserted them into ingenious, fast-paced plots that emulated the rhythms of Hollywood films. A reviewer in the *New York Times* (23 March 1935) declared that, while British cinema was "never notable for its command of pace," *The Man Who Knew Too Much* "goes in for a blistering style of story-telling" with "a fascinating staccato violence." As this remark suggests, the style of Hitchcock's thrillers depends on rapid editing that fragments the action to heighten its impact and to develop his trademark "suspense" situations.

The effect is reinforced by Hitchcock's approach to narrative structure. He insisted that "the key element of any suspense story," which he called the "MacGuffin," is an object or secret of utmost importance to the characters but that need not be "important or serious" in itself and is often "trivial and absurd."[26] The main drawback of this method was that it tended to confirm the view of critics like Grierson, who paid Hitchcock a backhanded compliment by calling him "the world's best director of unimportant pictures."[27] Not surprisingly, Graham Greene also objected to the "inadequate sense of reality" in "the polished fairy-tales of Mr. Hitchcock."[28]

As Andrew Sarris has suggested, "Hitchcock's reputation has suffered from the fact that he has given audiences more pleasure than is permissible for serious cinema."[29] It is fascinating, but futile, to speculate whether Hitchcock would have made British films closer to his dark Hollywood masterpieces, such as *Psycho* (1960) and *The Birds* (1963), if he had been given free rein. *The Lodger* (1926) and *Blackmail* (1929) suggest that he was moving in this direction, but Hitchcock complained that censorship prevented him "from putting on screen authentic accounts of incidents in British life" and forced him to resort to fiction "in order to give utterance to the violent things which I want to express."[30] In the thrillers of the late 1930s, he deftly evaded the censor's watchful eye by becoming a kind of "secret agent" himself, hiding "violent things" beneath a surface of light entertainment.

Even so his films did not entirely escape the censor's attention: There was concern, for example, that the British police were shown using guns at the end of *The Man Who Knew Too Much,* and the ending of *Secret Agent* (1936) had to be changed, with rather confusing results. But the wit and innuendo of all these films allowed Hitchcock to involve the spectator in a play with social and sexual codes that constantly evoked the forbidden without actually representing it. According to Thomas Elsaesser, "Hitchcock's cultivated unseriousness" was also "a moral stance" opposed to the obsolete but still influential "values of Victorian and Edwardian public life."[31]

At about the same time, Graham Greene published a series of novels that he called "entertainments" and in which he challenged "the distinction between serious literature and popular fiction."[32] As a critic, however, Greene felt that Hitchcock did not take the thriller genre seriously enough, amusing rather than exciting the audience in playful films that failed to capture the anxious mood of the period.[33] In his own first thriller novel, *Stamboul Train* (1932), Greene's characters include a naive showgirl, a Jewish businessman, a lesbian journalist, and a disillusioned political activist, whose lives become entangled as their train speeds across Europe. Inevitably, the novel's dark and disturbing vision was largely absent from what Greene called the "cheap and banal" film version made in Hollywood, under the title *Orient Express* (Paul Martin, 1934).[34]

Hitchcock's much lighter handling of a similar situation in his last British thriller, *The Lady Vanishes* (1938), is no doubt partly explained by the strict film censorship that discouraged British filmmakers from adapting Greene's work until the 1940s; but the film deceptively plays with genre conventions to address "serious" issues in ways that seem to have worked below the level of consciousness. They were certainly not apparent to the journalist who interviewed the director shortly after the release of the film and prefaced the story by expressing regret that Hitchcock had wasted his talents on "such a basically trivial story."[35]

The film consistently invites such a reaction, especially in its opening sequences, set in a fictional European country named Bandrika where several English travelers must spend the night at a crowded inn after an avalanche delays their train. Maurice Yacowar notes that "the obvious models of the opening shots give the whole film a fairy-tale aura," and the Bandrikans are depicted using stereotypes borrowed from operetta with no attempt to conceal their artificiality.[36] The opening thus situates the action in a world apparently quite remote from the actual political tensions in Europe at this time. Yet the MacGuffin turns out to be a coded message about a secret treaty between two European powers that uncannily anticipates the soon-to-be-announced treaty between Germany and the Soviet Union.

As in his earlier thrillers, Hitchcock counters the censor's ban on subjects that might give offense to foreign governments by simply not naming the enemy. Once the train leaves Bandrika, it enters a country whose agents work against British interests and that is Nazi Germany in all but name. The apparently fantastic plot thus functions as an alibi that allows the film to disown any disturbing allusions to contemporary politics.

This devious strategy works so well because the film keeps the spectator off balance by its sudden shifts in tone. The enthusiastic reviewer of *The Lady Vanishes* in the *New York Times* (26 December 1938) commented that "if it were not so brilliant a melodrama, we should class it as a brilliant comedy." At the most suspenseful moments, the film veers off into comic episodes that expose the absurdity of its own fictional contrivances as well as the artificiality of social codes, especially those associated with the national character.

The suspense plot deals with the disappearance of Miss Froy (Dame May Whitty), an elderly music teacher who eventually reveals herself to be a rather

**Figure 12.** England on the brink: Miss Froy (Dame May Whitty) attends to Iris (Margaret Lockwood), who is still suffering from a blow to her head, as the train leaves Bandrika in *The Lady Vanishes*.

unlikely British spy. After the lady vanishes, a young woman, Iris (Margaret Lockwood), tries to convince herself and others that she really did see the missing woman on the train (Figure 12). She is assisted by Gilbert (Michael Redgrave), a collector of folk music with whom she has quarreled at the inn and who initially does not believe her. He is eventually convinced and leads the fight against the foreign agents, in the process rescuing Iris from what promised to be a loveless marriage on her return to England.

Meanwhile, a pair of English gentlemen named Caldicott and Charters (Naunton Wayne and Basil Radford) are eager to get home because they have heard news reports about "England on the brink." This phrase evokes the current political situation, but the crisis they are discussing turns out to be the score in the cricket Test Match between England and Australia. They resist becoming involved in the mystery because they do not want to miss the last day of the match, while another English couple, a lawyer and his mistress, also refuse to become involved because of their fear of scandal.

*The Lady Vanishes* was filmed in the fall of 1937, when Hitler's aggressive policies in Europe were causing considerable anxiety in Britain, but it was not released until October 1938, by which time "Europe stood on the brink of war."[37] A few days before the film opened in London, the Prime Minister, Neville Chamberlain, who was desperately negotiating with Hitler, declared: "How horrible, fantastic, incredible, it is that we should be digging trenches and trying on gas masks here because of a quarrel in a faraway country between people of whom we know nothing."[38]

As in many of Hitchcock's thrillers, Iris must convince people who find her story "fantastic" and "incredible" of the reality of her experience. Whereas Chamberlain justified his attempts at "appeasement" by arguing that events in Europe were remote from the experience of ordinary British people, Hitchcock confronts ordinary people (and thus the spectator) with extraordinary events that make it difficult to decide between objective and subjective explanations. Barr effectively captures this aspect of *The Lady Vanishes* when, referring to the blow to the head suffered by Iris just before she boards the train, he suggests that "the whole film proceeds like a fantastic dream from which she intermittently awakes, and into which she then plunges again, just as it is a fantastic adventure for the spectator, who is simultaneously conscious and unconscious of his/her own location in the cinema." He adds that "it is *as if* she . . . is dreaming or hallucinating, but at no point is this made explicit; the double status of the discourse, subjective/objective, is scrupulously maintained."[39]

This dreamlike "double status" also contributes to the way in which the film, like dreams in Freud's psychoanalysis, evades censorship by its apparently insignificant surface. While it makes no pretense of offering an adequate representation of the contemporary political situation, the film strongly implies the need to unify the nation against the threats of foreign dictators. The British passengers have their own selfish reasons for not accepting the truth of the situation, but they also complacently believe that foreigners, despite their strange languages and customs, would not dare to violate the rights of British citizens. Hitchcock manages to convey both the reality of the foreign threat and the fragility of the British sense of national superiority.

While at first the tone seems to be mildly satiric, it becomes darker as the implications of ignoring political violence become clearer, and most of the English passengers eventually prove their worth in a battle of guns and wits with the enemy (Figure 13). The unifying myths here are English rather than British, but the fusion of political and psychological perspectives makes it difficult to pin down the degree to which the film endorses them. Similarly, the romantic plot that brings Iris and Gilbert together both conforms to and unsettles traditional gender stereotypes.

A narrative featuring a female spy and an active heroine seems to end conventionally when the couple return home to the old lady's motherly embrace.[40] Yet the film typically undermines the effect of its ending through absurdity and artifice. Gilbert, who has taken great pains to memorize the secret message in the form of a fragment of music, finds that it has been driven from his mind by Mendelssohn's "Wedding March." The idea that an important message can be turned into a musical code exposes the absurd basis of the plot but also stresses the fragility of the codes and conventions that the characters (like Chamberlain) believe will protect them against the evils of fascism.

**Figure 13.** "I'm half inclined to believe that there's some rational explanation for all this": Caldicott (Naunton Wayne) fires at the enemy during the climactic gun battle in *The Lady Vanishes,* while the lawyer's "wife" (Linden Travers) crouches behind him.

As we have seen, Hitchcock felt an attraction to violence in his own personality, and his films always imply that the spectators share this attraction. *The Lady Vanishes* demonstrates the dangers of myths of Englishness that deny the darker side of human nature. Hitchcock invites us to enjoy the game but also to recognize its serious implications. Of course, the English climate also ensures that the ending is not entirely happy: Caldicott and Charters arrive at the station in London in time for the last day of the Test Match only to be confronted with a newspaper headline announcing that it has been abandoned because of rain.

The screenplay for *The Lady Vanishes* (based on the novel *The Wheel Spins* by Ethel Lina White) was written by Frank Launder and Sidney Gilliat, who would later become a successful writing and directing team, and this was, according to Gilliat, "the only case of Hitchcock taking over a script completed for another director."[41] Although Hitchcock made few changes to the screenplay, the writers may well have been influenced by his earlier films, but it is also true that the characteristics of Hitchcock's thrillers owe much to a rich vein of genre filmmaking already well established in British cinema. His commercial and critical success helped to rescue this kind of filmmaking from its low critical status, and British genre films continue to pose important questions about the relations between national cinema and popular culture.

# CHAPTER THREE

# The Common Touch

## The Art of Being Realistic

Of the three tendencies in British cinema discussed in the previous chapter, the realist tradition was the one most often privileged in critical discourses. There was a virtual consensus that the best, or most distinctive, British films were "realistic" and that the documentary movement paved the way for all important later developments. This version of British film history has come under attack on many counts, and a major shift in critical attitudes has provoked a new interest in previously neglected films, filmmakers, and movements. At the same time, there has been considerable debate over the meaning and effects of "realism," one of the most complex and contested terms in film studies (and elsewhere). As a result of these developments, the realist tradition, once seen as the most important achievement of the national cinema, came to seem more like a liability than an asset.

There is, of course, no single "realist" style but rather a variety of "realisms" that share, according to Terry Lovell, "the claim that the business of art is to show things as they really are," as well as "some theory of the nature of the reality to be shown and the methods which must be used to show it."[1] In Britain, during the 1930s, realism was associated almost exclusively with the documentary movement, and there were many complaints about the lack of realism in British feature films. While most critics thus welcomed the infusion of the documentary spirit into British fiction films during and after World War II, "the wedding of documentary and fiction" led to an unsettled and still contentious relationship.[2]

By drawing on the look and conventions of documentary cinema, fiction filmmakers invoked standards of realism by which their work was to be judged. In most cases, however, the films also drew on other realist traditions, primarily those associated with the nineteenth-century novel and related forms of theater. As John Ellis demonstrates in his survey of critical discourses in the 1940s, "quality" films received praise for their "realism" and "unity," but there was a concern that the observational mode of documentary encouraged a "detachment" that worked against the emotional involvement expected of a fiction film.[3] The effect of these films thus depends less on an assured stylistic unity than on an uneasy tension between what Andrew Higson calls the

**Figure 14.** Tea for two: Laura (Celia Johnson) and Alec (Trevor Howard) become acquainted in the station waiting room in *Brief Encounter*.

"public gaze" of documentary and "the private gaze of individual narrative protagonists."[4]

We have already seen this tension at work in *The Captive Heart* (see Chapter 1), but whereas that film keeps the documentary and melodramatic modes relatively distinct, a more notorious example is *Brief Encounter* (David Lean, 1945), in which they come together to powerful, but controversial, effect. While Jeffrey Richards has recently claimed that the film remains both "documentarily and emotionally true," Robert Murphy points out that, "with its dimly-lit interiors, its hysterical heroine, its threateningly expressive shadows, its theme of doomed love, its creation of a hostile and repressive world, it is difficult to understand how the film fits into an aesthetic of realism at all."[5]

Adapted from a short play by Nöel Coward set entirely in a railway-station refreshment room, the film includes many exterior sequences shot on location, setting up a tension between its theatrical origins and documentary realism. While theater and documentary are often seen as opposing forces in British cinema, both involve an observational distance at odds with the ability of narrative cinema to create a powerful and shifting impression of seeing through the subjective viewpoint of the characters. Coward's screenplay thus not only "opens out" the play to encompass several locations but also interiorizes it by beginning at the end and representing most of the events through flashbacks narrated by Laura (Celia Johnson), the "hysterical heroine" (Figure 14). The departures from realism that Murphy describes express her state of mind, through which our perception of the events and the physical environment is filtered.

Although the location shooting is clearly an important factor, it seems likely that the "quality" film critics accepted *Brief Encounter* as realist for moral rather than aesthetic reasons. As Richard Dyer suggests, the collision between the intense emotions generated by Laura's memory of her meetings with Alec (Trevor Howard) and the banal trappings of everyday life enforces "realism in another sense, namely advocating the necessity of accepting lowered horizons, of 'being realistic.'"[6] Laura's affair unsettles her, defamiliarizing her surroundings and activating fantasies of escape, but she learns to make the best of things and to avoid excessive feelings or extravagant behavior. The couple never actually commit adultery, and Laura returns to the familiar and secure world of the middle-class family. However, there is still a lively critical debate over whether this ending represents the triumph of "a value system centred on decency, restraint and self-sacrifice" or "a tragic victory of conformism over desire."[7]

## THE DOMINANT AESTHETIC OF BRITISH ART: THE TURN AGAINST REALISM

The moral sense of realism accords well with many accounts of the national character in which "not only the temper of compromise, but also the habit of 'muddling through,' is part and parcel of the English habitat."[8] Truffaut was probably thinking of this attitude when he claimed that British filmmakers lacked the "strong emotion" needed to make great films, although other critics have pointed to the danger of confusing restraint with a lack of emotion.[9] Indeed Raymond Durgnat suggested that "the British quieten their lives" because their emotional life is so intense, enabling a cinema in which the audience can be "very emotional in its response to quietly stated emotions."[10]

Just as Truffaut paved the way for the French New Wave by his critical assault on the "psychological realism" of the French "Tradition of Quality," British critics began to question the idea of "quality" cinema and the dominance of the realist tradition.[11] In 1962 a group of young critics launched a film journal called *Movie* with a manifesto deploring the state of British cinema. Like Truffaut and his colleagues at *Cahiers du cinéma,* the *Movie* critics valued films that expressed the personal vision of their directors and insisted that "style is worthy of passionate feeling." They opposed "the traditional British 'quality' picture," which was supposedly impersonal in approach and lacking in cinematic imagination. At a time when many critics had welcomed the films of the so-called British New Wave as a revival of the realist tradition, the *Movie* critics declared that "all we can see is a change of attitude, which disguises the fact that the British cinema is as dead as before."[12]

A similar objection to the British New Wave appeared in Penelope Houston's 1963 survey of *The Contemporary Cinema.* Houston complained that the British filmmakers set out "to investigate a social landscape" rather than to explore the possibilities of the medium and that they "travel as mass observers rather than artists prepared to turn the landscape upside-down if it happens to suit their purpose."[13] Although she made no attempt to explain why investigating a social landscape is less of an achievement than turning a landscape upside down, the implication was that the films rely too heavily on the documentary attitude (evoked by the allusion to the Mass Observation movement).[14]

The status of the New Wave, and of the realist tradition in general, also suffered from a theoretical attack on cinematic realism developed during the 1970s in the radical film journal *Screen*. Like *Movie, Screen* owed a considerable debt to French critics writing for *Cahiers du cinéma*, but, by this time, *Cahiers* had new editors who denounced the earlier focus on personal expression and promoted more radical forms of political cinema. However, this shift of perspective did not rehabilitate realism, which now came under attack not as a constraint on the filmmaker's creativity but as a vehicle for the dominant ideology.

Like their *Cahiers* counterparts, the *Screen* writers used semiotic and psychoanalytic theories to explore the political implications of film language. They rarely discussed British cinema, but the journal's editor, Sam Rohdie, made clear that the argument went to the core of the national culture when he wrote that "the dominant aesthetic of British art, at least since the 1930's, has been realism."[15] According to Colin MacCabe, however, the dominance of the "classic realist text" went far beyond the national culture, and his prime examples were Hollywood films and the nineteenth-century novels that supposedly provided the basic narrative structures for most fiction cinema.

The central problem, according to MacCabe, is that realism "cannot deal with the real as contradictory." Because the realist text claims to reflect reality, it "denies its own status as articulation" and offers the spectator "a point of view from which everything becomes obvious."[16] The only alternative is to "draw the viewer's attention to his or her relation to the screen in order to make him or her 'realise' the social relations that are being portrayed."[17] Citing the drama theory of Bertolt Brecht, *Screen* called for a cinema in which the spectator would not be drawn into the fiction but rather distanced from the images on the screen. In this way, "the transparent immediacy of the film would be broken by analysis," thereby producing "a contradiction which remains unresolved" and must therefore be worked out by the spectator.[18]

In making this argument, MacCabe explicitly rejected the view of realism found in the work of French critic André Bazin, the founder of *Cahiers du cinéma*. While Bazin would have agreed that most fiction films use continuity editing to disguise their fragmentation of time and space and thereby create a "transparent immediacy," he identified and valued an alternative kind of realism that emphasized deep-focus shots and long takes. In films of this kind, the spectator enjoys "a relation with the image closer to that which he enjoys with reality," and this encourages "a more active mental attitude."[19] From Bazin's point of view, "analysis" would close off the spectator's options, but MacCabe argued that it was realist texts that prevented the spectator from thinking, precisely because of their claim to represent reality without subjecting it to analysis.

MacCabe's view of realism has been widely challenged. By 1994, when *Screen* had moved away from its earlier positions under the influence of methods derived from cultural studies, it published an article by Christopher Williams that repudiated the theory of the "classic realist text." Williams argued that "film is not dominated by the forms of the 19th-century novel" but "draws on a wider range of sources and inputs," and, in any case, these novels did not attempt "to deny their own status as writing or articulation."[20]

In the meantime, however, realism had lost its dominant position in British film culture, and critics began to rehabilitate the many nonrealist films previously dismissed as lacking in "quality" (although most would still be covered by MacCabe's conception of the classic realist text) and to stress the nonrealist elements in films, like *Brief Encounter,* previously celebrated for their realism. Nevertheless, the realist tradition continued to thrive, in critical discourses and in film production. In judging its effects, we need to bear in mind Williams's conclusion that "realisms do, necessarily, tangle with conventional ways of seeing the truths and emotions of social and cultural life," but "this involvement does not mean the adoption of fixed positions for the subject, the audience or the medium."[21]

## WHAT DO YOU WANT (IF YOU DON'T WANT MONEY): THE BRITISH NEW WAVE

While many critics welcomed the New Wave films as a shot in the arm for British cinema, they have often come under attack, not only for refusing to turn the landscape upside down but also because they were "essentially parasitic on a literary movement outside the cinema."[22] The nine or ten films, made between 1958 and 1963, that constitute the core of the movement were all adaptations of stage plays or novels, and the argument was thus that British films are less "cinematic" than the formally innovative French *nouvelle vague* films that emerged at the same time.

A few critics have, however, suggested more positive ways of responding to the documentary and literary/theatrical influences on these films. Brian McFarlane finds that the films are "all more interesting than the novels they are derived from, largely because of the way ideological information seeps into every frame," implying a productive tension between location shooting and the cinematic methods used to frame reality.[23] This view of the films' style is supported by Michael Eaton's claim that the New Wave films grew out of "a fruitful conjunction between the polemics of Free Cinema and the actualities of the Royal Court theatre."[24]

"Free Cinema" was the term coined by Lindsay Anderson to describe the films shown in a series of screenings that he organized for the British Film Institute between 1956 and 1959. Not all of these films were documentaries, but the series did include several documentaries made by future New Wave filmmakers: Tony Richardson, Karel Reisz, and Anderson himself. Before moving into the film industry, however, these filmmakers worked at the Royal Court Theatre, the home of the English Stage Company. It was there that Richardson directed the enormously influential production of John Osborne's *Look Back in Anger* in 1956.

Richardson and Osborne established Woodfall Films to produce the 1959 film version of the play, and this company went on to make most of the New Wave films. However, the new working-class realism first came to the screen in *Room at the Top* (Jack Clayton, 1958), based on John Braine's best-selling novel. Produced by a mainstream commercial company (Remus), this film is in many ways a transitional text, but it was a critical and commercial success. Its "realistic" approach to social and sexual themes proved highly (and profitably) controversial, and, in all these respects, it was matched only by Woodfall's *Saturday Night and Sunday Morning* (Karel Reisz, 1960), based on a novel by Alan Sillitoe.

Both films were shot mainly on location in northern industrial cities, although *Room at the Top* includes some exteriors shot in the studio. It was location shooting that most obviously tied the New Wave films to the documentary movement, as Penelope Houston's comments make clear. There were some complaints, however, that the cinematography made the supposedly bleak urban landscape appear visually attractive. In terms that echo Grierson's criticism of Flaherty, Higson insisted that "it is only from a class position outside the city that the city can appear beautiful."[25]

Because these films belonged to the British realist tradition, critics did not interpret "the 'poetic' transformation" of the subject matter in New Wave films as a sign of complexity, as they often did in the case of an acknowledged "art film," like Michelangelo Antonioni's *The Red Desert* (1964).[26] Antonioni was notorious for his willingness to "turn the landscape upside-down," but the unmodified urban landscape of terraced houses and factories in *Room at the Top* and *Saturday Night and Sunday Morning* functions in much the same way, although the effect is much less obtrusive. The tension between the unpleasant reality and the beauty of the images is also matched by the ambivalent effect of characters who are both attractive and morally disturbing.

Like most of the New Wave films, *Room at the Top* and *Saturday Night and Sunday Morning* create an intense engagement with the experiences of an "angry young man" (a term originally coined to describe Jimmy Porter in *Look Back in Anger*). It is possible to provide the same general summary

**Figure 15.** "Don't let the bastards grind you down": Arthur (Albert Finney) works at his lathe at the beginning of *Saturday Night and Sunday Morning*.

of their plots: A young man has an affair with an older, married woman whom he eventually abandons in order to marry a woman of his own age, but only after being punished with a severe beating. The main difference is that Joe Lampton (Lawrence Harvey) in *Room at the Top* uses his sexuality to escape from his working-class origins, whereas Arthur Seaton (Albert Finney) in *Saturday Night and Sunday Morning* has no ambitions to escape and wants only to have a good time.

At the beginning of *Room at the Top,* Joe looks out of a window at the Town Hall, where he has just taken up a position in local government, and sees a young woman getting into a luxury car. He turns to a colleague and says, "I want that." It is not immediately clear whether he is referring to the woman or the car or both, but the colleague makes clear that he thinks Joe is not being "realistic" by aiming so high in a class-bound society. The final sequence depicts Joe's wedding to this woman, but his affair with the older woman, and the shock of her death (in a car accident after he has rejected her), have given him a new sense of reality. Now that his initial goal has become realistic, it no longer satisfies him.

In the precredits sequence of *Saturday Night and Sunday Morning,* Arthur delivers a voice-over monologue in which he insists that he is different from the older workers who were worn down "before the war" and claims that everything besides making money and having "a good time" is "propaganda" (Figure 15). His affair with the wife of a fellow worker comes to a less dramatic end than in *Room at the Top,* although the censors were uncomfortable with a sequence depicting his attempt to arrange an abortion for her. At the end, Arthur and his girlfriend, Doreen (Shirley Ann Field), look down on a new housing estate, where she hopes they will live when they are married. He throws a stone at a billboard and, when she objects, he tells her that this will not be the last stone he will throw.

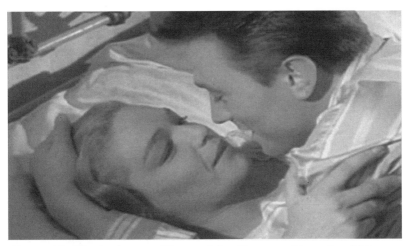

**Figure 16.** "To thine own self be true": Joe (Lawrence Harvey) and Alice (Simone Signoret) enjoy a brief idyllic vacation in *Room at the Top*.

Joe and Arthur are both virile characters who appear in virtually every sequence of the films. Many critics assumed that the films ask us to identify with them in a fairly straightforward way. They certainly do depend on our sharing at least some of the characters' anger at society, but it is far from clear that we therefore have to accept all aspects of their behavior. In particular, their treatment of women is, to say the least, questionable, and critics often accuse the whole working-class realist movement of misogyny.

Sue Harper thus asserts simply that, in *Look Back in Anger,* "Osborne's sympathies are with Jimmy Porter." She feels that Arthur Seaton is "certainly repellent" and suggests that both *Room at the Top* and *Saturday Night and Sunday Morning* are about "the declining marketability of older women."[27] The directors claimed that their films were more complex than this view suggests: Clayton insisted that he wanted spectators to "feel compassion . . . but not sympathy" for Joe, adding that "it would have been morally wrong to make him sympathetic," and Reisz explained that Arthur, like the main characters in all his films, is seen "partly from his . . . own point of view, partly, none too sympathetically, from the outside."[28] In both films, we understand the choices that the characters make, but we also recognize that these choices are severely compromised.

The disturbing blend of identification and detachment is deeply affected by the films' depiction of the mature sexuality of the older women. As many critics, including Harper, have suggested, the casting of Simone Signoret as Alice Aisgill (who is English in the novel) turns the character into the moral center of *Room at the Top.* When Joe and Alice spend a brief vacation together, they pledge their love by jointly quoting Polonius's speech from *Hamlet* in which he advises his son, "to thine own self be true" (Figure 16), but Joe eventually betrays himself as well as Alice. Rachel Roberts's performance as

Brenda in *Saturday Night and Sunday Morning* has a similar effect, but the film is rather less sure about what it means to be true to oneself. After having been beaten up, Arthur defiantly asserts that "I'm me and nobody else," but he immediately adds, "whatever people say I am, that's what I'm not."

The idea of the true self is central to the realism of the New Wave films and to the critical discourses that stressed their documentary "authenticity" (or their failure to achieve it). Along with location shooting, the films' claims to authenticity rest on the characters' northern working-class accents, but the inauthentic attractions of mass culture are an obstacle to being true to oneself. *Room at the Top* is especially concerned with the politics of accents, whereas *Saturday Night and Sunday Morning* stresses the impact of the consumer society on the cultural environment.

*Room at the Top* uses a range of different accents to bring out the implications of Joe's choices. Although some critics questioned Harvey's northern accent, it works well enough to signify his working-class origins. He joins an amateur dramatic society in his pursuit of Susan Brown (Heather Sears), the daughter of a wealthy industrialist, who speaks with a refined "finishing school" accent. Joe sees her performing in a play with Alice, whose accent not only connotes the assumed erotic appeal of "foreign" women but "effectively conceals [her] social origins from Anglo-American ears," so that she becomes "a symbol of honesty and true love."[29]

Susan's mother has an extremely affected upper-class accent, but her father speaks with a broad Yorkshire accent, which he seems to exaggerate to show that he has retained his working-class bluntness. When he invites Joe to dine with him at the Conservative Club, he presents himself as a no-nonsense pragmatist who always speaks his mind. He refers to Alice as an "old whore" and insists that "I use words that fit." If Brown is being true to himself here, it comes at the expense of the woman who most represents this idea in the film.

Northern accents evoked a traditional working-class culture that, according to the influential argument of Richard Hoggart, in his book *The Uses of Literacy* (1957), was giving way to a commercial mass culture, seen as inauthentic and imposed from above. Regional and working-class accents were still officially unacceptable in public institutions like the BBC and were usually confined to comic parts on stage and screen; but they became signifiers of authenticity in the New Wave films in contrast not only to the established cultural norms but also to the new "Americanized" mass culture.

Most forms of popular culture represented in the New Wave films are seen as debased and trivial, in line with Hoggart's analysis. When Arthur comes home from work at the beginning of *Saturday Night and Sunday Morning*, he finds his father staring at the television, and we can just hear the sound of commercials.[30] Rather than watch television, Arthur goes out for a night on the town and takes part in a drinking contest in a pub where a pop group ineptly performs Adam Faith's recent hit, "What Do You Want (If You Don't Want Money)." Arthur takes no notice of the performance, but the song epitomizes the outlook of the affluent society, which he both enjoys and rebels against.

Despite their scathing depiction of most forms of popular culture, the New Wave films did not speak from the point of view of traditional high culture. As far as music was concerned, the filmmakers were on the side of those who advocated jazz as a more authentic form of popular music than rock 'n' roll. Reisz and Richardson had contributed a short film about a jazz club, *Momma Don't Allow* (1956), to the first Free Cinema program, and the film version of *Look Back in Anger* opens with a sequence in which Jimmy Porter (Richard Burton) plays his trumpet with the Chris Barber jazz band. *Saturday Night and Sunday Morning* has a score (by jazz musician John Dankworth) that evokes Arthur's youthful vitality, even though there is no evidence that it represents his own musical taste.

For John Hill, such effects reinforce the "clear distance between observer and observed" in these films, often attributed to the class difference between the directors and the writers of the original works.[31] However, Robert Murphy suggests that *Saturday Night and Sunday Morning,* in particular, was successful because its director was "a middle-class, mid-European Jew" whose "detachment, his position outside the English class system, allowed him to give objective expression to a voice hitherto unheard in British cinema."[32] While this "distance" and "detachment" hardly opens up room for "analysis," in the "Brechtian" manner prescribed by *Screen,* the voices of characters like Joe and Arthur become part of a complex interweaving of discourses.

As Dilys Powell put it in her review of *Room at the Top,* the realist aesthetic in the New Wave films was "married with an emotional directness not often found in a British film."[33] "Directness" was a feature of working-class culture, as traditionally defined and reinforced by Hoggart's analysis, but it also tied in with new sexual attitudes that accompanied social and cultural change in the 1950s (see Chapter 7). The New Wave filmmakers fought several battles with the Board of Censors, which they then exploited for publicity purposes, but the films are far from straightforward celebrations of cultural change.

Because of its melodramatic tendencies, the issues are perhaps clearest in the case of *Room at the Top.* After reading the script, the censor expressed concern about the depiction of sex outside marriage and insisted that Joe's sexual encounters with Alice should not involve nudity. Ironically, it is Joe who expresses this attitude in the film, in a puritanical outburst when he discovers that Alice once posed nude for an artist. The producers insisted that Alice's "violent end" ensured that the film would be "morally right" and noted that they had originally intended to show the car crash and Alice's painful death. As it stands now, the film stresses the impact on Joe who overhears the news of her death (described in graphic language to which the censor also objected) while being congratulated by his colleagues on his forthcoming marriage.[34]

Some critics claim that the moral of *Room at the Top* is expressed by Joe's uncle when he advises him to "stick to your own people." Thus R. Barton Palmer argues that the New Wave was not really new because the realist aesthetic worked to contain the threat of the "'new' discourses . . . to the established social order as usually represented."[35] Similarly, Hill suggests that, while "those films which rely on marriage as a means of conclusion" do not imply "a positive endorsement," they do emphasize the need for "compromise and acceptance of constraint."[36]

However, Hill does also argue that there is "a tension between the energies which the films release and the viability of the solutions they propose."[37] As he indicates, the "solution" in several films is marriage, as it is in *Room at the Top* and *Saturday Night and Sunday Morning,* but these "comic" endings are far from utopian. There is an even stronger awareness of the costs of "being realistic" than in *Brief Encounter,* since the rebellion has gone much further and the relations between sexual drives and social codes are much more complicated. The films provide "happy endings" that seem to satisfy the spectator's desire for closure but also expose the failure to channel the energies unleashed in the film into meaningful social change.

## ESCAPING THEIR OWN STEREOTYPE: MIKE LEIGH AND KEN LOACH

According to most accounts, the demise of the British New Wave occurred in 1963, with the commercial failure of Lindsay Anderson's *This Sporting Life* and the success of Tony Richardson's *Tom Jones,* a colorful and imaginative adaptation of Henry Fielding's eighteenth-century novel. The involvement of United Artists in the production of *Tom Jones* also signaled the beginning of Hollywood's renewed interest in the British film industry, and especially in the "swinging" youth culture that rose to prominence in the 1960s (see Chapter 7). Most of the New Wave filmmakers were soon making films in Hollywood and, for the next twenty-five years, the realist tradition was kept alive mainly in television.

The realist tradition reemerged on the big screen in the late 1980s and early 1990s. In 1993 Michael Eaton welcomed what he called "a comeback of realism from the shadows of cheap television drama" and argued that this represented "not simply a return to a particular style, but a return to value."[38] He attributed this development primarily to the work of two filmmakers,

Ken Loach and Mike Leigh, who had both made their first feature films twenty years earlier and since worked mainly in television. Their names were frequently coupled in discussions of the resurgence of realism, but some critics have argued that their approaches are very different.

It is certainly true that they represent the opposite poles of the realist tradition that we noted in discussing the New Wave, Loach belonging on the "documentary" side and Leigh on the "theatrical." Allowing for this difference, however, their films do share a number of features in common. For example, both develop the "politics of accents" from the New Wave films, although the accents are much more varied. Loach uses accents to suggest the common interests of working-class characters from different regions (with the result that several of his films have been subtitled in the United States), whereas Leigh uses them to suggest the theatrical poses that underlie the class backgrounds of his characters.

Both directors also tend to make it difficult for us to identify with their characters. For George McKnight, "alignment and identification" with Loach's characters "are often at best problematic," and much the same is true of Leigh's films.[39] Several critics noted that Johnny, the verbally inventive and abusive protagonist in Leigh's *Naked* (1993), reminded them of Jimmy Porter.[40] Leigh himself points out that the film confronts the spectator with the problem of whether to like or dislike a character who is on screen almost all the time but is introduced in the "worst possible light," sexually assaulting a woman in a dark alley.[41]

Although *Naked* is perhaps not typical of Leigh's work, a detached perspective is part of the realist aesthetic of his films. However, Loach and Leigh both incorporate elements that work against the realism and further complicate the films' effects. In several articles, John Hill has argued that, although "Loach's films rarely ask us to identify with characters so much as to observe, and understand, their predicaments," their "power to unsettle . . . derives from the apparent impassivity of his cinematic style in relation to the disturbing events in front of the camera." These events evoke "the dramatic machinery of melodrama: impossible choices, misjudgements, coincidences, a foreshortened sense of cause and effect."[42] While Hill acknowledges that Loach's characters are not simply good or bad but molded by economic and social conditions, he comes to the conclusion that his recent films encourage "an increasing sense of political impotence, both in the films' main characters and in their spectators."[43]

Similarly, some critics claim that Leigh is not a realist at all because of the tendency toward caricature in his films. Ray Carney confidently places the films in "the general tradition of English realism, which has been one of the dominant strains of British cinema," and Leigh describes them as "exercises in realism."[44] However, Leigh also acknowledges the "theatricality" of his films and suggests that this produces "a heightened comic quality" and disturbs spectators expecting the social and psychological density associated with realist filmmaking.[45]

As with the New Wave films, critics sometimes complain that both directors have little interest in cinematic style. Leigh's method of developing his films during a long period of rehearsal with the cast, on the basis of which he creates the final screenplay, has encouraged the assumption that the shooting of the film is relatively unimportant. Loach has been taken to task for making "visually boring" films that suggest that "there is nothing interesting to look at in the places where poor people live," an ironic reversal of the charge that the New Wave filmmakers turned bleak urban landscapes into picturesque images.[46]

Loach's films are more overtly political than Leigh's, and Alan Lovell claims that they reaffirm "the critical dimension of realism by giving it a Marxist perspective."[47] In contrast, Carney insists that Leigh's films "carry no political agendas, nor do they offer political alternatives or solutions in the Ken Loach mode," a comparison that, for Carney, works entirely in Leigh's favor.[48] Loach's realism, however, has a rather ambiguous relation to Marxism, and he angrily rejected the Marxist orientation of *Screen* that led to the rejection of "realism as bourgeois."[49] Both filmmakers use realism to question the reductive definitions of reality found in much social and political thought and that create situations in which, as Loach puts it, people have difficulty "escaping their own stereotype."[50]

Loach depicts people who fight to maintain their individuality even though they have been pressured into internalizing social values that define their experience in limiting and demeaning ways. *Ladybird, Ladybird* (1994), for example, depicts the struggle of a single mother, scarred by abusive relationships in her past, to regain custody of her children from a social-service system that she constantly antagonizes by her inability to control her temper. In Leigh's *Life Is Sweet* (1993), Nicola, the anorexic daughter of a working-class family, hides her insecurity behind angry political speeches that are clearly derived from her reading but have little relevance to the messy reality of her family life. As Leigh puts it, Nicola is "a receptacle of received ideas," but "what's important is why she has a need for these ideas and slogans."[51] He suggests that his films address the problem of "being truthfully what we are as opposed to . . . what our received roles are."[52]

Loach's films usually contain what Judith Williamson calls "keynote speeches" that have a more positive function than Nicola's diatribes but that are not simply didactic statements. The ironies generated by the narrative context, of which the speakers are often quite aware, stress the difficulty of applying the political analysis to their everyday lives. As Williamson suggests, these speeches "attempt to speak both of the class struggle *and* of what makes people round and human."[53] In *Riff-Raff* (1991), for example, the most politically aware of the workers on a building site responds to a request for information about a place to live with a long speech on the economics of Thatcherism, punctuated by the groans of his fellow workers who protest that "he only wants a squat." The effect is very funny, but the comedy does not undermine the political analysis.

According to Hill, the main difference between Loach and Leigh is that "Leigh's universe is primarily that of families," and his films suggest that, "if families are flawed, they seem, none the less, to be all that the characters have to hold on to."[54] When there are no families, we get the rootless characters who wander through the arid urban landscape of *Naked*. While Leigh seems to offer a fairly conservative view of gender politics through his recurring female characters who want to become mothers, his films highlight the discrepancy between the ideological emphasis on the importance of the family and the actual social conditions that place external and internal pressures on family relationships.

It was Loach, however, who made a film titled *Family Life* (1971), although the family here offers nothing to hang on to. This early film depicts a middle-class family in which the rigid values of the parents drive their daughter into a schizophrenic state as her own desires conflict with the stereotype they impose on her. In Loach's later films, family life is not usually central to the narrative, but *Raining Stones* (1993) depicts two families struggling against economic conditions in the post-Thatcher north as well as against internalized ideological and religious values that only make it more difficult to cope with their situation.

The apparent pessimism of Loach's films seems to conflict with his Marxist politics but, as Graham Fuller insists, "the idea that Loach's films are depressive or ultimately forlorn is a fundamental misconception."[55] While the endings do not offer Marxist or other solutions to the characters' problems, the "critical" realism of these films demands that "viewers interact with them in a way that is not adequately captured by the idea that we are all made subservient to some dominant ideology."[56] Like the characters, viewers are confronted with the power of the dominant ideology but also with the need to analyze why the alternatives fail to bring about change.

Ironically, the ending of *Raining Stones,* the one film in which Loach comes close to providing a "happy" ending, provoked widespread criticism. The plot has the simplicity of an Italian neorealist fable like *Bicycle Thieves* (Vittorio de Sica, 1948). Bob (Bruce Jones) wants to buy his daughter a communion dress but cannot afford to do so because he is unemployed. His efforts to raise the money are frustrated when the van, on which he depends for his occasional odd jobs, is stolen, and he decides to borrow the money. In a sequence that might seem more appropriate to a Hollywood action movie

**Figure 17.** *Raining Stones:* Bob (Bruce Jones) listens to his father-in-law (Mike Fallon) describe his efforts to change the conditions in which people live on the local housing estate.

than a Ken Loach film, he attacks the loan shark who has terrorized his family and causes an accident in which the man dies. The violence does not solve his problems, however, and Bob fears the worst when a police car arrives during the communion ceremony. It turns out that the police have come to inform him that his van has been found, and the film ends with this (possibly only temporary) reprieve.

In her review, Jenny Turner dismissed this as "a shockingly sentimental ending," and even Michael Eaton, a strong supporter of Loach and realist cinema, argued that "the demands of the storytelling structure contradict the explicit ideology of the piece."[57] Eaton was disturbed that, while the "keynote speech" in *Raining Stones* is made by Bob's father-in-law, a social activist who tries to convince him that he is the victim of an unjust social system and should not feel ashamed that he cannot afford the communion dress (Figure 17), it is a priest who helps Bob and makes "narrative closure" possible. However, the film does not conceal the ironies at work in this ending and certainly does not suggest that it solves the social problems depicted in the film. The effect depends on the dual consciousness generated by our sympathetic identification with Bob in his determination that his daughter should have a new communion dress and our simultaneous awareness of his self-destructive stubbornness.

Despite his reputation for pessimism, Loach's films usually include comic moments, as in the ruses through which the unemployed men in *Raining Stones* attempt to find ways to make money. The rapid shifts in tone are even more unsettling in Leigh's films, which often provoke laughter and tears almost simultaneously. Some critics liken this effect to Brechtian "distancing" devices that prevent stock responses, but Hill rejects this argument. He feels

**Figure 18.** *Secrets & Lies:* "Why can't we share the pain?" asks Maurice (Timothy Spall), in a passionate appeal after a family gathering has given rise to a series of shocking revelations.

that these moments work "not only to inhibit the spectator's emotional identification with the characters but also to encourage a sense of distance from, and superiority to, them."[58] From this perspective, distance does not invite analysis, as the *Screen* theorists wanted; but, if we are made to feel superior to the characters, the films often puncture any possible feelings of complacency.

Leigh defends his approach in realist terms, insisting that, "for me, tragicomic is how life is," but, as Carney puts it, "Leigh's weird mix of moods, tones, and perspectives suspends us in an emotionally unresolved position."[59] The films often involve intense confrontations between characters that tear away the masks and expose the roles that they have been playing. By confronting the *Secrets & Lies* (to quote the title of Leigh's 1995 film) that function as defense mechanisms, they come to a more "realistic" understanding of the limits and possibilities of their relationships (Figure 18). However, as in Loach, there is a strong sense of the difficulty of being "truthfully what we are," or even of establishing what this is in any definitive way.

## AN INTIMATE RELATIONSHIP TO THE FILM SUBJECT: *NIL BY MOUTH* AND *THE WAR ZONE*

The success of both Loach and Leigh in the 1990s, and the international attention that they received, encouraged several younger directors to engage with the realist tradition. Some of their films, such as *Brassed Off* (Mark Herman, 1996) and *The Full Monty* (Peter Cattaneo, 1997), combine the iconography of northern working-class realism with a "tragicomic" blend of depression and comedy, reminiscent of Leigh but also drawing on the "utopian" strain in popular entertainment (see Chapter 5). Other filmmakers sought to renew the realist tradition in ways that cast a new light on the critical debates about the goals and value of realism.

*Nil by Mouth* (Gary Oldman, 1997) and *The War Zone* (Tim Roth, 1998) were the first directorial efforts of two actors who had worked with Mike Leigh at the beginning of their careers, both receiving their first major screen credits in Leigh's television film *Meantime* (1981).[60] Both films start from a premise that links them to Loach and Leigh, a social problem examined in a family context, but the problem is now more extreme – wife abuse in *Nil by Mouth* and incest in *The War Zone* – and both filmmakers refuse to provide a social context that might point to its causes.

Most critics have picked up on this aspect of the films, and several argue that it represents an important development in the realist tradition. Nick James claims that *Nil by Mouth* "marks a change in the *quality* of British realist cinema" because it "acknowledges that British audiences are now more 'in touch with their emotions.'" Although this sounds rather like Dilys Powell on *Room at the Top, Nil by Mouth* pays far less attention to the social environment than the New Wave films, and certainly does not provide the kind of political analysis that *Screen* demanded. Unlike Loach and Leigh who, James suggests, "often maintain, in their desire to show social structures at work, a political distance from their characters," *Nil by Mouth* adopts "an intimate relationship to the film subject, one born from psychotherapeutic models."[61]

These comments suggest a form of realism that stresses the intensity of affect rather than social or political understanding, presumably on the assumption that contemporary culture tends to desensitize viewers who must be shocked out of their apathy. *Nil by Mouth* is certainly a grueling experience for audiences: The intense emotional life of a working-class family is presented in close-up, filmed in cinéma-vérité style with a constantly moving handheld camera, while the soundtrack is dominated by characters who give vent to their frustrations in a torrent of words of which "fuck" is probably the most frequent. The main focus is on Ray (Ray Winstone), who physically and verbally assaults his wife and is a monstrous figure with whom it is virtually impossible to identify, despite the close-ups and his considerable onscreen presence.

*The War Zone* works very differently. Roth acknowledges that "some viewers consider the film's lack of social context to be a failing," but he also points out that the film does not use the "hand-held, grainy, in-your-face photography" often associated with realism (as in *Nil by Mouth*) and instead places the characters in a "classical, David Lean–type landscape."[62] Instead of the desolate urban setting of Oldman's film (described by *Sight and Sound*

**Figure 19.** *The War Zone:* Tom (Freddie Cunliffe) is shocked by what he sees through a window of his home, but there is no reverse shot: For a while it seems as if he has imagined his father's abuse of his sister.

as "the real London"), Roth situates his family (displaced from London for some unstated, but presumably economic, reason) in the beautiful, if often rain-swept, moors of north Devon.[63] The composed, picturesque images of the landscape create a tension with the horrifying narrative in which an adolescent boy discovers that his father is abusing his sister (Figure 19).

Ray Winstone again plays the monstrous father but, for the most part, he presents the character as a troubled but reasonable man, concerned for his family. In only one sequence, after his son denounces him to the mother, does he give vent to his rage in the manner of *Nil by Mouth,* in a speech full of obscenities. When he tries to persuade his son, with the daughter looking on, that the incest that he (and we) have witnessed is the product of his imagination, he is almost convincing, to the point that the film appears to be losing its contact with reality.

Roth explains that he chose to conceal what Tom sees when he first becomes aware of the relations between his father and sister "because I wanted to almost suspect that he was wrong."[64] The strategies of both films thus seem to be responses to the contemporary experience in which the distinction between reality and fantasy (personal and media-driven) seems to be increasingly vulnerable. Whereas *Nil by Mouth* seeks to construct an experience whose emotional impact will convince us that what is shown is real, the visual style and the plausibility of the father in *The War Zone* provoke doubts about whether what we see is actually happening. Both films seek to disorient the spectator and, in so doing, push the realist tradition toward the excesses of the horror films or thrillers in which Oldman and Roth made their names as actors. The impact of this development on the theory and practice of realism remains to be seen.

# CHAPTER FOUR

# The Mirror Crack'd

## British Expressionism

Film historians often distinguish between a realist tradition, descending from the brief *actualités* of the Lumière brothers, and another tradition, often loosely described as "expressionist," traced back to the magical fantasies of Georges Méliès. This distinction is in many ways a problematic one, not least because it tends to encourage the idea that realism is the norm, but these broad categories can be useful as long as it is recognized that they refer to tendencies rather than mutually exclusive stylistic options. They inevitably coexist in all films, and the allegiance to one or other approach is a matter of emphasis, with the result that many films seem to belong equally to both traditions. *Citizen Kane* (Orson Welles, 1941) is one celebrated example of a film whose realism, stressed by critics like André Bazin, exists in a complex relationship with expressionist techniques. As discussed in the previous chapter, *Brief Encounter* is another.

Most realist filmmakers would accept Bazin's definition of realism as an aesthetic in which "the image is evaluated not according to what it adds to reality but what it reveals of it."[1] From this perspective, the expressionist tendency involves the creation of images that add to reality by using cinematic techniques such as lighting, camera angle, and montage to express a distinctive view of reality. Bazin assumes that the image can reveal reality by making us aware of things that are visible but may have escaped our attention. The expressionist tradition seeks to go beyond what is visible and stresses the power of the imagination.

In its more narrow sense, "expressionism" in film studies usually refers to a number of German silent films produced in the aftermath of World War I. Films like *The Cabinet of Dr. Caligari* (Robert Wiene, 1919) and *Nosferatu* (F. W. Murnau, 1922) created dark, distorted visions that expressed the psychological anxieties of the characters and the cultural dislocation of the nation. German expressionism was a major influence on the later development of the horror film and the film noir, in Hollywood, but also in British and other national cinemas. There were many contacts between the German and British film industries in the 1920s (Hitchcock made his first film in Germany), and German émigrés had a significant impact in the 1930s, but I am using the term "expressionism" here loosely to refer to tendencies in British cinema that often alienated critics who valued realism and restraint.

The influence of the realist tradition extended into films whose genre and style point in quite different directions, but it was frequently challenged by what Christine Gledhill calls "excessive strategies."[2] Gledhill applies this term to film melodramas in which expressionist techniques are used to heighten the emotional impact, but it is also pertinent to certain kinds of "art cinema." These films use such strategies to very different effects, but their emphasis on the expressive power of film form links them to the traditions of theatricality and showmanship developed by Alexander Korda in the 1930s.

## STORYTELLERS AND FANTASISTS: GAINSBOROUGH AND THE ARCHERS

During the 1940s, Korda's influence was apparent in two otherwise quite different groups of films that provided critics with examples of what they did *not* mean by "quality" cinema: the melodramas produced at Gainsborough Studios and the "art films" of Michael Powell and Emeric Pressburger. Most critics dismissed the Gainsborough films – with their far-fetched plots and exotic settings – as trivial and formulaic, but they were also suspicious of the artistic ambitions of Powell and Pressburger, whose films they often found self-indulgent and pretentious. Despite the apparent opposition between popular genre films and challenging art films, both coupled a stylistic rejection of the realist tradition with a focus on questions of sexuality and desire that ran counter to conventional standards of moral decency.

Beginning with *The Man in Grey* (Leslie Arliss, 1943), Gainsborough melodramas appealed especially to women, offering an alternative to the largely masculine action of war films as well as to the emotional restraint of films like *Brief Encounter* (which was, as we have seen, not as "realistic" as it was often taken to be). Their plots were typically melodramatic contests between good and evil, in which sexual desire becomes entangled in the politics of class. Yet, while the villains were inevitably punished, it was the actors who portrayed them, notably James Mason and Margaret Lockwood, who were most popular with the fans. Mason and Lockwood both appeared in *The Man in Grey,* but their defining performances came shortly after: Mason as a sadistic aristocrat in *Fanny By Gaslight* (Anthony Asquith, 1944) and Lockwood as the title character in *The Wicked Lady* (Arliss, 1945) who becomes the sexual and criminal partner of Mason's highwayman.

The appeal of these characters and stars skews the apparent moral logic of the film in which they appear. Jeffrey Richards argues that these films reveal a breakdown in traditional moral values as a result of wartime dislocation, encouraging "a greater degree of audience identification with the desire for immediate sexual gratification, however obtained."[3] Although the period settings distance the transgressions, at least in theory, the films pay little attention to historical detail, emphasizing psychological and sexual conflicts and encouraging the spectator, as Marcia Landy puts it, to "appropriate events as contemporary."[4] In any case, the period costumes add to the visual pleasure, especially compared to wartime uniforms and austerity clothing, and allow for the display of parts of the body that they do not always cover.

The films of Powell and Pressburger did not have the same popular appeal, but they offered a similar challenge to the realist tradition. Powell insisted that he and his partner were "storytellers, fantasists," which was why they "could never get on with the documentary film movement."[5] Although the credits on their films insist that they jointly produced, wrote, and directed them, Pressburger was the writer and Powell the director. Powell was British and had gained experience as a director of many "quota quickies," but Pressburger, like Korda, was Hungarian, and many critics found their work quite alien. Richard Winnington, one of the "quality" critics, insisted that their films were not in accord with "the essential realism and the true business of the British movie."[6]

They started working together in 1939 – on *The Spy in Black,* produced by Korda – and formed their own production company, The Archers, in 1942. Their most personal and controversial contribution to the war effort was *The Life and Death of Colonel Blimp* (1943), whose title refers to a cartoon figure created by David Low to satirize the prewar, class-bound military establishment. The film, however, skews the apparent moral by combining the satire with a feeling of nostalgia for the chivalric values of the past, however absurd and wasteful they may have been.[7]

The colorful and rambling narrative has none of the austerity and urgency of contemporary war films, and it anticipates the filmmakers' later work through the uncertainty about how to respond to the Blimp figure, Clive Candy (Roger Livesey). The historical examination of his military career is complicated by his romantic attachments to three women from different generations, all of them played by Deborah Kerr. This device unsettles the distinction between fantasy and reality (Do all the women really look alike or are we seeing Candy's subjective view of them?) in a way that hardly clarifies the politics of the film but nevertheless provides a vision of "an England 'made strange' in Brechtian fashion by the witty, self-conscious manner of its presentation."[8]

Two films released in the last year of the war, to the outrage of the critical establishment, illustrate the provocation that Gainsborough and the Archers posed to prevailing ideas about national identity, cinematic achievement and the war effort. Gainsborough's *Madonna of the Seven Moons* (Arthur Crabtree, 1944) is a melodrama about a woman who, after being raped as an adolescent, lives a schizophrenic existence: as Maddalena, she is an old-

**Figure 20.** Maddalena (Phyllis Calvert) is shocked by the arrival of her thoroughly modern daughter (Patricia Roc) in *Madonna of the Seven Moons*.

fashioned and nervous mother (like Laura in *Brief Encounter*) but, as Rosanna, she becomes an uninhibited gypsy figure, the passionate mistress of a bandit. The Archers' *A Canterbury Tale* is an apparently more "serious" film that seeks to bridge the gap between Geoffrey Chaucer's England and the People's War, but the main defender of traditional values in the film is eventually exposed as an unstable misogynist.

Most of the characters in *Madonna of the Seven Moons* are Italian, but all the actors are distinctly English. The resulting collision between national stereotypes creates a distancing effect that complicates the emotional impact of the melodrama. Despite the evident artifice, the film opens with a caption brazenly insisting on its realism: The story is "taken from life" and "the medical world has verified" Maddalena's case and others like it. After this gesture of defiance at the critics, the first shots confront us with the traumatic event that triggers Maddalena's schizophrenic condition: A schoolgirl walking alone in a wood meets a man and desperately runs away as he starts to chase her.

While she is still running, there is a fade, and we then see her enter a convent school looking distraught. In the next sequence, the Mother Superior informs her of the marriage her father has arranged for her. The question of the psychological effect of the apparent rape is deferred because the plot now jumps forward to the point at which Maddalena (Phyllis Calvert) and her husband await the return to Rome of their adolescent daughter from a school in England. The arrival of Angela (Patricia Roc) causes a disturbance when her mother is shocked by her casual friendships with men and by her daring outfits (Figure 20). When the family doctor tells Maddalena that her daughter is the product of "an unconventional age" and suggests that she should "develop the other side of your nature" to get on with Angela, Maddelena angrily insists that she does not have another side.

Shortly afterward, she disappears, and we discover that she not only has another side but leads a second life in which she has no memory of her other self and in which she lives with a bandit (Stewart Granger). This deferred revelation draws attention to the gaps and lapses of memory on which the plot depends, already foreshadowed by the ellipsis that conceals the rape. Her husband has remained silent about Maddalena's earlier absences, and the final resolution of the mystery depends on a pattern of forgetting and remembering that stresses the power of the unconscious mind. There is also no sign of the war or of the political tensions that preceded it, which is odd since Angela was born in 1920 and thus her journey from Britain to Italy must take place in the late 1930s.[9]

The melodrama is acted out in a hybrid location of mixed cultural codes: The signs of modern life often seem intrusive in a film that works like a costume melodrama, and it comes as a surprise to be reminded that Maddalena's decent and undemonstrative husband is called Giuseppe. Although the ersatz "Italian" culture encompasses both Catholic piety and carnival license, these extremes are integral parts of a single way of life; in Maddalena's case, however, they become symptoms of a psychological trauma. The conflict can be resolved only by her death, but the appeal of the film stems from its refusal to resolve the tensions between security and passion and between tradition and modernity.

*A Canterbury Tale* seems to be a more socially responsible film insofar as it deals with wartime experience in a recognizably English location, but it also involves tensions between tradition and modernity that become entangled with questions of sexuality. Filmed in black and white and with many nonactors in its cast, the film has clear links to the realist tradition, but Graham Fuller has aptly described it as "a film on the edge of noir that never quite takes the plunge," adding that, "stylistically, it is a long flirtation with Expressionism."[10]

It begins with a flourish that places the present emergency in the context of the national heritage. A commentator recites the opening of the Prologue to Chaucer's *The Canterbury Tales,* and we see pilgrims riding through the countryside. When the Knight releases his falcon and looks up to see it fly, there is a cut to a plane streaking across the sky and then to a modern soldier looking up. This effect, anticipating the cut from bone to spaceship in Stanley Kubrick's *2001: A Space Odyssey* (1968), sets up the relationship between past and present as one of continuity and difference. The shift is not just a matter of time but also of style, as the "poetic" voice gives way to a commentary in the documentary tradition.

The film immediately shifts ground again: The voice-of-God commentary comes to an end, and there is a cut to a train arriving at a station so dark that it is difficult to make out what is going on. As a familiar aspect of everyday life during the war, the blackout is a further demonstration of the film's ties to reality but, as Antonia Lant suggests, the extreme darkness introduces a disturbing sense of "instability and uncertainty."[11] Bob, an American soldier (played by John Sweet, a sergeant in the U.S. Army) gets off the train thinking he has arrived in Canterbury but finds that he is in Sittingbourne, one station too early. After he meets up with Peter (Dennis Price), a British soldier, and Alison (Sheila Sim), a member of the women's land army, they walk into town together, and Alison becomes the latest victim of a man who terrorizes the local women by pouring glue on their hair.

They decide to investigate and soon become suspicious of the local justice of the peace, Thomas Colpeper (Eric Portman). It appears that his desire to preserve traditional values has become an obsession that leads him to attack women who become friendly with soldiers billeted in the area. However, the younger characters gradually become fascinated with his vision because, despite their commitment to the war effort, they all feel that something is missing in their personal lives: Alison was engaged to an RAF pilot reported killed in action; Bob's girlfriend in the United States has stopped writing to him; and Peter thinks that he has wasted his musical training by working as a cinema organist.

Peter's attitude is crucial because it accords with Colpeper's view of the cinema as a product of the modern age. He assumes that Bob, as an American, must have been shaped by the movies and asks him what will happen if people get used to sitting back to watch the world as if they were in a cinema. After he finally gets to Canterbury, Bob is reminded of Colpeper's remark when he goes to a café with another U.S. soldier who invites him to sit at the window to watch the world go by. By this time, however, Bob is no longer satisfied with this kind of voyeurism, thanks to the vision of a man whose dark secret seems to reflect a disturbance in his own sexual life. If the ending pulls back from the "edge of noir," it does so not by a return to documentary realism but through a series of "miracles": Alison discovers that her fiancé is alive (Figure 21); Bob receives a package of delayed letters; and Peter plays the organ in Canterbury Cathedral.

Like *Madonna of the Seven Moons, A Canterbury Tale* refuses to resolve its contradictions. The miraculous ending seems to emanate from Colpeper's vision, but it does not exonerate him for his perverse sexual assaults. His antimodern (and anticinematic) stand is discredited by the film itself, but the film is an implicit call for a new kind of cinema that will reconcile past and present, public and private, conscious and unconscious, realism and expressionism.

## AN EXCESS OF PERCEPTION: RUSSELL, ROEG, AND BOORMAN

In 1960 the trial and acquittal of Penguin Books, for publishing a paperback edition of D. H. Lawrence's novel *Lady Chatterley's Lover,* dismayed the guardians of public morality, who anticipated a flood of obscenity and pornography. Another major sign of the times in the same year was the release of a film directed by Powell, now working without Pressburger. *Peeping Tom* was one of a series of films produced by Anglo-Amalgamated Productions to compete with the Hammer horror films that had, in the mid-1950s, succeeded the Gainsborough melodramas as British cinema's most popular, but critically derided, genre (see Chapter 9). The torrent of abuse that greeted Powell's film – in which a serial killer films the terror of his female victims, who see their reflections as they are about to die – was oddly excessive for writers who saw themselves as defenders of restraint and good taste.

Although Powell and Lawrence seem to represent quite different aspects of British culture, they both came under attack for their aesthetic and moral audacity. In 1960 they could both be seen as precursors to new cultural developments that challenged the traditional idea of a national character based on restraint and inhibition. Unlike Powell, Lawrence could be harnessed to the realist cause, and he was a major influence on the writers of the northern working-class novels that inspired the British New Wave (see Chapter 3). It is not surprising that an adaptation of *Sons and Lovers* (Jack Cardiff, 1960) appeared at the height of the New Wave and that it would stress the "realist" side of Lawrence, although its credentials were compromised by the casting of a Hollywood actor (Dean Stockwell) as Paul Morel, with no attempt at an appropriate regional accent, and by a lush orchestral score (by Mario Nascimbene) that seems more appropriate to a 1940s melodrama.

It is in the handling of Paul's sexual encounters with Miriam (Heather Sears, *Room at the Top*'s Susan Brown) and Clara (Mary Ure, who was Jimmy Porter's wife, Alison, in *Look Back in Anger*) that the film seems most inadequate to Lawrence's vision. In typical Hollywood fashion, the lovemaking is expressed through ellipses and symbolic imagery, with the "realism" found mainly in the unhappy outcome of both affairs. The film stayed within the limits set by a censorship system that would soon be tested by glimpses of bare female breasts in Ingmar Bergman's *The Silence* (1963) and Sidney Lumet's *The Pawnbroker* (1965). By the end of the decade, the situation had changed to such a degree that it was possible for a number of "rogue talents" to make films that included full frontal nudity and explicit sexual imagery. Foremost among these were Ken Russell, Nicolas Roeg, and John Boorman.[12]

Like Lawrence and Powell in their times, these filmmakers were often accused of technical incompetence. Pauline Kael argued that Russell's weak grasp of "film technique" was apparent in the way he "starts by lunging into

**Figure 21.** Just before she learns that her fiancé is alive in *A Canterbury Tale,* Alison (Sheila Sim) walks through the bomb-damaged streets of Canterbury, which now afford a good view of the cathedral.

the middle of a situation and then just keeps throwing things at you," and Roeg was similarly taken to task for bombarding the audience with fragmented images that become "just too much for us to absorb."[13] These complaints point to the refusal of these filmmakers to accept the constraints of conventional film form. From a more sympathetic standpoint, Michel Ciment refers to Boorman's "taste for baroque flamboyance and sensuality" and suggests that his films involve "an 'overfiguration,' an excess of perception, though one which is never exaggerated."[14]

The work of these filmmakers was fundamentally opposed to the virtues of "realism" and "unity" endorsed by the supporters of "quality" films in the 1940s and still espoused by many critics thirty years later. Derek Jarman, who worked as a set designer on Russell's *The Devils* (1971) and *Savage Messiah* (1972), said that his own later work as a filmmaker was inspired by the way in which Russell "would take the adventurous path even when that interfered with the coherence of the film."[15] For many critics, however, this approach seemed self-indulgent and, while Roeg and Boorman were rather less flamboyant personalities, their films also came under attack for their extravagance and pretension.

Joseph Gomez points out that Lawrence had also been denounced as "self-indulgent, extravagant, and excessive," especially after he "eschewed realism . . . and embraced metaphorical and symbolic techniques."[16] According to Gomez, Russell followed a similar path by abandoning realism after his work for the BBC television series *Monitor* in the 1960s. Yet the dramatized documentaries on the lives of famous artists (usually composers) that Russell contributed to this series often caused controversy, partly because of their irreverent treatment of their subjects and the art world but also because of their rejection of the traditional documentary virtues of sobriety and objectivity.

The use of metaphor and symbol is already apparent in these television films, but Russell's affinity with Lawrence became fully apparent in his adaptation of *Women in Love* (1969). Russell later directed *The Rainbow* (1989) and *Lady Chatterley* (a television miniseries, 1992), and although Roeg and Boorman did not use Lawrence's work directly, their films also exhibit a Lawrentian concern with the social repression of bodily desire and the apparently contradictory desire to transcend the body. Indeed Roeg has been called the "most Lawrentian of modern directors."[17] Commercial considerations were certainly a major factor in persuading producers to invest in films that exploited the relaxation of censorship, but the naked bodies and sexual activity depicted in the films were, as in Lawrence, part of a provocative insistence on the importance of the imagination and the power of myth.

Russell called himself "a myth-maker," and Boorman stressed the need to "listen carefully to the echoes of myth."[18] The problem for the critics, however, would seem to be that the films simultaneously presented themselves as myth and as skeptical deconstructions of myth, apparently drawing on familiar mythic structures but resisting symbolic interpretations. Despite her animosity, Kael does effectively capture the spirit of Russell's films by calling them "unstable satires on romanticism," and it was this instability that alienated the critical establishment as well as left-wing critics concerned with the ideological implications of film form.[19]

The Marxist theorist Fredric Jameson expressed interest in the "open form" of Boorman's *Zardoz* (1974) but ultimately concluded that it could not "ensure that the ideologically correct conclusions will really be drawn in the long run."[20] In a more sympathetic discussion of Roeg's work, Robert Kolker also referred to "open texts" but argued that it was less important to provide conclusions than to encourage spectators to "ask questions."[21] As Kolker suggests, all three filmmakers would probably agree with Russell's assertion that "anyone who thinks he has an answer is dangerous."[22] It is in the way in which their films challenge conventional social, political, and psychological explanations of human behavior that these directors come closest to Lawrence.

Russell defiantly rejected the "understatement" traditionally associated with British cinema and justified his approach by claiming that he wanted to "arouse people who have become desensitized."[23] As a former dancer, he stressed the importance of choreography in his films: "if the actors aren't making patterns the camera is usually doing it for them."[24] His style is thus resolutely opposed to the emphasis on dialogue supposed to characterize British cinema and not obviously suited to the highly articulate characters in Law-

**Figure 22:** "It's never quite the same in England": Gudrun (Glenda Jackson), Gerald (Oliver Reed), Ursula (Jennie Linden), and Birkin (Alan Bates) let themselves go on their arrival in Switzerland toward the end of *Women in Love*.

rence's novels. However, while the stress on movement and gesture does give his films a "theatrical" quality, the effect is appropriate to characters who tend to dramatize themselves and to films that deal with the impact of social conventions on both the imagination and the body.

The physical body is central to the imagery of *Women in Love,* most notoriously in the nude wrestling bout, invented for the film, between Rupert Birkin (Alan Bates) and Gerald Crich (Oliver Reed) that graphically evokes Lawrence's theme of the need for close male relationships. Birkin wants to overcome the separation of the body and the spirit, and the film presents his failure to achieve his goal as simultaneously tragic and absurd, a dual response most vividly captured when he and Ursula Brangwen (Jennie Linden) make love outdoors and Russell turns the camera on its side, giving their naked bodies a sense of weightlessness. This effect contrasts with their earlier coupling beside the lake, edited together with the discovery of the interlaced naked bodies of a drowned couple, and with the later lovemaking of Gerald and Gudrun Brangwen (Glenda Jackson), after which she finds herself pinned down by his body.

Robin Wood complains that "Russell hates the human body" and that his films are "a sort of cultural pornography."[25] It is true that in Russell, as in Lawrence, characters often find it difficult to come to terms with their own sexuality, which becomes linked to their fear of death. Yet the films' playful refusal to take themselves too seriously gives their choreographic images of bodies in motion an exuberance that counterpoints their darker implications (Figure 22). In *Women in Love,* as Gomez suggests, Russell "sensed the dancelike variations which served as the backbone of Lawrence's novel, and he created a film patterned after the structure of dance rhythms."[26]

Ana Laura Zambrano uses the idea of counterpoint to discuss the structural relations between "the lyrical, often humorous love affair between Ursula and Birkin" and "the morbid tragedy of Gerald and Gudrun" as well as the way in which "Russell expands the novel into rhythmic counterpoint with its author."[27] When the film was released, a reviewer in *Sight and Sound* perceptively described it as "a kind of critical re-creation" of the novel, "a film *about* the novel, rather than *of* it."[28] In a sense, this is what all adaptations are, but Russell foregrounds the sympathetic, but not uncritical, dialogue between his own vision and that of Lawrence. During the opening credits, an orchestral version of "I'm Forever Blowing Bubbles" accompanies images of Ursula and Gudrun in a tram full of miners, and this music-hall tune becomes a leitmotif in the film, simultaneously establishing and undercutting the complex interplay of social reality, sexual exploration, and painful idealism in the characters' relationships.

The "counterpoint" discourages us from accepting too readily the meanings on which Russell's films, or their characters, seem to insist. A similar instability emerges from the nonlinear structures through which Roeg creates a "montage of the mind" or "metaphoric montage" to capture the way in which "different times, different places intersect in human thought."[29] The resulting flow of fragmented images simultaneously demands and resists interpretation. Thus Tom Milne is right to insist that "Roeg does not deal in symbols" and that "everything that comes under his camera's scrutiny has its own existence," with the result that the spectator cannot rely on "built-in meanings or casual assumptions of significance."[30] On the other hand, as Kolker puts it, this "anti-discursive quality . . . is countered . . . by a strong literary and cinematic allusiveness."[31]

In *Don't Look Now* (1973), Roeg uses this technique to present the different responses of a couple to the death of their daughter. In the opening sequence, John (Donald Sutherland) senses that his daughter is in danger and rushes from the house to find that she has drowned. The rest of the film is set in Venice where he works as an architect restoring a church. When he and his wife, Laura (Julie Christie), meet a blind woman who claims to be a psychic with a message from their daughter, Laura is intrigued, but John tries to persuade her to listen to reason and denies his own apparent telepathic powers. Their marital crisis occurs while a serial killer commits several murders beside the canals, and John is finally stabbed to death when he follows a mysterious figure in a red cloak, like the one worn by his daughter when she drowned.

The power of the film comes not from its plot but from the patterns of association that develop across space and time. As James Palmer and Michael Riley suggest, the film "repeatedly 'makes strange' its own codes of association, undermining one's confidence in interpretation."[32] The most obvious

**Figure 23.** *Don't Look Now:* John sees Laura (Julie Christie) glide past on a boat on a canal in Venice, a shot that turns out to be his premonition of his own funeral.

pattern involves the red cloak and the many red objects that remind us of it. Although the associations to which the film constantly draws our attention may be coincidental, they may have a concealed meaning that indicates some spiritual force at work within the world of the film. The spectator must deal with a kind of "sensory overload" caused by Roeg's omission of the "narrative markers" that conventionally distinguish between subjective and objective images, with the result that "inner and outer worlds are mixed up in a terrifying and tragic way."[33]

The murders almost seem to be a projection of the inner states of the characters, just as the decaying beauty of Venice and its churches may link the action to a more general cultural condition. All this is perhaps not unusual in the thriller genre, but it is complicated by the temporal fragmentation caused by the use of brief flashbacks, that seem to represent the characters' memories, and occasional flashforwards, which, if subjective, may have a psychic origin. In the film's most controversial sequence, John and Laura make love (for the last time, as it turns out), and the camera and editing provide erotic images of their naked bodies. However, this moment at which the couple are most together and apparently feeling whole and complete is fragmented by intercut shots of them dressing for dinner afterward.

The spectator is left to wonder whether the temporal dislocation represents the filmmaker shaping his material (but for what ends?) or the subjective experience of the characters (but, then, does it imply anticipation of the future as they are apparently engrossed in their lovemaking or memory of their union turning the banal act of dressing afterward into a sensuous ritual?). Shortly thereafter, John sees Laura standing, dressed in black, on a launch when she is supposed to be in England visiting their sick son (Figure 23). He assumes she has been kidnapped and goes to the police, only to become involved in the murder investigation; but we later discover that what he saw was a flashforward to his own funeral.

A similar temporal fragmentation, coupled with uncertainty about the objective or subjective status of the images, appears, to very different effect, in Boorman's American-made thriller *Point Blank* (1967). In his British films, Boorman, who like Russell began his career in television, tended to be more adventurous than in the Hollywood genre films, like *Point Blank* and *Deliverance* (1972), for which he is best known. In both groups of films, however, Boorman's representation of the body is more likely to involve violence than in the films of Russell and Roeg. In *Zardoz,* for example, Boorman uses Sean Connery's muscular body to evoke "the James Bond myth figure" in contrast to the sexless and androgynous figures in the supposedly utopian world of the Vortex which he enters on a mysterious mission.[34]

Like Russell and Roeg, Boorman creates images that have an erotic force but places them within narrative structures that are dreamlike and mythic. In *Excalibur* (1981), he deals with one of the founding myths of British culture, the legend of King Arthur and the Knights of the Round Table. He presents the myth with a deliberate naiveté that simultaneously affirms its timeless quality and allows for a skeptical demystifying perspective. The key to this duality is the character of Merlin (Nicol Williamson), who, as described by Boorman, is "prescient and clever" but with "a certain phoniness . . . as well as a slightly crazed sense of humor." Significantly, Boorman suggests that he himself possesses these qualities as a filmmaker who "functions as a Merlin in the sense that he tries to organize the world" and seeks to explore "the relationship between film, dreams and the unconscious."[35]

According to Boorman, the film depicts "man taking over the world on his own terms for the first time," and he thus set out to create "a contingent world . . . *like* ours but different" with "a primal clarity, a sense that things are happening for the first time."[36] He recommended that the spectator, who would probably "feel, on occasion, the absence of many of the usual spatio-temporal guidelines," should "allow himself to be carried along, even if, sometimes, he may lose his footing."[37] Some critics felt that the film often tips over into "absurdity," and Boorman agreed that "if you stand outside the film it looks ridiculous."[38] Philip Kemp complains that it often "sounds ridiculous" because of the lack of "dialogue of weight and resonance," but Boorman has deliberately subverted the traditions of British historical cinema by avoiding "standard English as far as possible" and distinguishing each character with a "regional accent."[39]

The use of music by Richard Wagner adds to the tension between familiarity and mystery, linking the Arthurian legend to other mythic systems, thereby suggesting its universality, but also creating tensions through its associa-

**Figure 24.** Arthur (Nigel Terry), encased in armor, finds Lancelot (Nicholas Clay) and Guinevere (Cherie Lunghi) sleeping naked in the forest in *Excalibur.*

tions with high culture and German fascism. It is, however, in the treatment of sexuality and the body that the film sets up its basic tension between physical existence (stressed by the "primitive" living conditions) and the romantic desire for transcendence. As in all of Boorman's films, the elemental imagery of earth, water, fire, and air works to link the mythic patterns to natural processes, and images of flesh and blood contrast with the clothes, masks, and armor with which the characters express and conceal themselves (Figure 24).

As Ciment suggests, "in a universe governed by betrayal, the power of sexuality can only be destructive." Arthur (Nigel Terry) attempts to restore order by creating Camelot, a utopian community that, however, fails "to account for either nature or spirituality."[40] He is plunged into despair when he discovers Lancelot (Nicholas Clay) and Guinevere (Cherie Lunghi) making love and revives only with the discovery of the Grail. After a battle in which he destroys the evil magic of Morgana (Helen Mirren), the dying Arthur speaks of himself as the subject of "future memories," and his body is carried off into the mists of time. His legacy is a utopian vision from which Christianity and modern Britain will emerge, but the film suggests a deep ambivalence about the possibility of reconciling the sexual and spiritual dimensions of the myth.

## NIGHTMARE VISIONS: DEREK JARMAN AND PETER GREENAWAY

The films of Russell, Roeg, and Boorman belong to what Peter Wollen identifies as a tradition of "English romanticism" opposed not only to the realist tradition but also to the modernist outlook that sustained avant-garde filmmaking in many countries. In Britain, according to Wollen, "modernism never took root in any lasting way," and the modernist impulse found in a number of experimental silent films in the 1920s was eventually "channeled into the

. . . British documentary film movement."[41] Whereas modernist movements usually defined themselves against realism, John Grierson and his colleagues were the British filmmakers who most visibly took up the "modernist" montage practices of Soviet filmmakers like Sergei Eisenstein, Vsevolod Pudovkin, and Dziga Vertov.

By the 1980s, "postmodern" cultural practices were breaking down the distinction between high and mass culture on which modernist aesthetics depended. The distinction between popular and "art" cinema also became less clearly defined, and techniques that would once have been avant-garde began to appear in commercial films. At the same time, new sources of funding from bodies like the British Film Institute and Channel 4 television created the possibility for avant-garde filmmakers to make longer films with somewhat higher production values that might cross over into the mainstream. The most successful were Peter Greenaway and Derek Jarman, whose films combine formal innovation with a critical reappraisal of cinematic and national traditions.

Like many other avant-garde filmmakers, Greenaway and Jarman came to film from the visual arts, and their films are full of allusions to paintings (as well as to many other cultural texts). Jarman was more prepared than Greenaway to place himself within the traditions of British cinema, but he identified with filmmakers opposed to the realist paradigm. He worked for Russell as set designer on *The Devils* and *Savage Messiah,* and he admired Roeg and acknowledged his support.[42] Greenaway started to make films while working for the Central Office of Information, and his archival work there inspired his later use of lists and catalogs as ordering devices in his films. Although he objected to the treatment of Russell and Roeg by British film critics, he more frequently cited European filmmakers like Ingmar Bergman and Alain Resnais as influences on his work.[43]

Their shared interest in the past marks their work as postmodern rather than modernist, although Wollen finds modernist and "neoromantic" tendencies in their films.[44] They had little interest in each other's work, but both created films that oppose traditional ways of seeing, incorporating elements of realism and narrative but introducing other aesthetic principles that disrupt the usual expectations of mainstream cinema. In very different ways, their films attempt to rescue the idea of "heritage" from the connotations it had gained under Margaret Thatcher (see Chapter 11).

Jarman saw himself as working within English traditions that were rapidly vanishing. When he turned to European art for inspiration, as he did in *Caravaggio* (1986), he used anachronisms, as well as the visibility of the warehouse that functioned as a studio, to remind the spectator of the relevance of the film's treatment of power, sexuality, and art to Thatcher's Britain. Greenaway's cultural references are more cosmopolitan, mainly European but extending to Eastern traditions in *The Pillow Book* (1995). Whereas Jarman set his adaptation of Shakespeare's *The Tempest* (1979) in an English country

**Figure 25.** Past meets future in the postmodern present: Street gangs roam the streets of the London to which Queen Elizabeth I is transported in Derek Jarman's *Jubilee.*

house, Greenaway's *Prospero's Books* (1991) stresses the same play's indebtedness to a wide range of European traditions and texts.

Many of Jarman's films work by yoking together heterogeneous elements to create a rather more extreme "montage of the mind" than Roeg's temporal mosaics. In *Jubilee* (1977), the past and future are brought together when Elizabeth I is transported from the quiet gardens of her own times to a violent and polluted wasteland that represents Britain's near future, even though its references to punk culture and the Labour government are very much of the present (Figure 25). *The Last of England* (1987) makes the most complex use of these techniques, layering fragmented and often superimposed images and sounds from many sources, and *Edward II* (1991) works much like *Caravaggio* in its use of anachronisms to demonstrate the relevance of Christopher Marlowe's sixteenth-century play to contemporary Britain.

Jarman insisted that he made his films in support of "the tradition of hedgerows and fields with flowers – in opposition to the commercialization or the destruction and rape of the countryside and cities."[45] He felt that this tradition was being undermined by some of those who most claimed to support it. According to Lawrence Driscoll, Jarman fought for "Blake's 'Jerusalem' (as opposed to the public school/*Chariots of Fire* version appropriated by the Right)."[46] Jarman's sense of tradition encompassed the punk aesthetic, with its anarchic assault on national institutions, as in the Sex Pistols' version of "God Save the Queen," and Michael O'Pray thus describes Jarman's "home movie-making" as a cinematic equivalent to "punk's demystifying of pop music professionalism and do-it-yourself aesthetic."[47]

This vision is fully developed in *The Last of England,* Jarman's alternative to heritage films in which, according to Andrew Higson, "the splendor of the society in place always undercuts images of the last of England."[48] As in most of his films, Jarman rejects "the stories and the equipment of traditional British cinema" in an attempt to "destabilise" the situation.[49] Shot on Super-8 film, using video in the editing process, *The Last of England* has a rudimentary narrative in which soldiers patrol a derelict urban landscape, executing and deporting apparent dissidents. The film also includes home-movie footage of Jarman and his family when he was a child, a seemingly idyllic past but whose allusions to the nation's imperial history and to World War II suggest the causes of the present nightmare.

The soundtrack consists of the words of a poet, seen at the beginning (Jarman himself, although the text is spoken by Nigel Terry), who experiences a "dream allegory" set in "a visionary landscape where he encounters personifications of psychic states."[50] As Jarman describes it, "the sound track is a palimpsest," in which this poetic narration clashes with recorded fragments that bind past (one of Hitler's speeches) and present (an American home-shopping broadcast).[51] The film constantly threatens to fly apart under the stress of its "fragmented imagery and incoherent storyline," which, as Robert Hewison puts it, resist "the symbolic order of rationality so as to render the extremity of the dislocation that Jarman perceives."[52] It is through the appeal to memory that the film – barely – holds together, offering what Annette Kuhn calls "a repertory of images of and from particular moments of the nation's past, with all the (sometimes contradictory or contested) meanings attached to them in the present."[53]

The sense of a culture in fragments is one that Jarman shares with Greenaway, but Greenaway is a much more impersonal filmmaker who draws on the cultural image bank rather than his own memories. Although he once suggested that he and Jarman were the "only two true *auteurs* in Britain," most critics have stressed the differences between their visions.[54] The raw energy of Jarman's work testifies to his personal investment in films that often scandalized critics by their graphic representations of gay sexuality. After he was diagnosed with AIDS in 1986, an awareness of his condition shaped public response to the films he made between then and his death in 1993. Greenaway also created scandal through the emphasis on the body and (hetero)-sexuality in his films, but he also often came under attack for the detachment and apparent coldness of his treatment of his characters. Boorman, for example, attacked Greenaway's "cruelty, coldness, and awesome sterile certainty."[55]

Whereas Jarman's films often appear about to explode, Greenaway's seem to be under excessive control, as he imposes arbitrary patterns on the materials: the twelve drawings of a country house in *The Draughtsman's Contract* (1982), the numbers one to a hundred that appear in order in *Drowning by Numbers* (1988), and the daily menus in *The Cook, the Thief, His Wife & Her Lover* (1989). Yet the apparent rigidity of these numerical grids is contradicted by their ultimate failure to create meaning. Greenaway suggests that these devices push to an extreme the human desire for "some sense of coherence, of order in the world" that is, however, "always defeated."[56] His films thus depend on the "contradiction between the romantic and the classical; violent, absurd, bizarre subject matter treated with a severe sense of control."[57]

James Park points out that "Greenaway's films are a complete denial of realism," and he sees the frequently hostile critical response as "testimony to the stranglehold that realist attitudes continue to exercise on British cinema aesthetics."[58] Other critics have stressed the allegorical dimensions of the films. Michael Walsh thus describes Greenaway as "an allegorist whose features comment indirectly but decisively on the crisis of postimperial Britain to which Thatcherism also responds," but Vernon Gras emphasizes that the allegorical effect incorporates an awareness of the "inevitable failure of whatever ordering principles his protagonists engage in."[59]

The resistance to meaning is bound up with Greenaway's representations of sexuality, which draw on Western traditions of nude painting. Nude bodies (male and female) abound in his films, but they (and the sexual desires that they express and provoke) constantly overflow the visual and verbal frames that seek to contain them. Many critics have associated Greenaway with the baroque style in art, which is "based on an absolute and compelling refusal to separate mind and body, thought and flesh."[60] David Pascoe argues that the films explore "the choice between print and flesh, the book and the body," but they also explore the ways in which the body is a text as well as the ways in which it refuses to be a text.[61] This theme is most explicitly developed in *Prospero's Books,* in which Prospero's magic conjures up very physical spirits and uses them to script his drama, and in *The Pillow Book,* which celebrates Japanese calligraphic traditions of writing on bodies.

Greenaway's shocking images and bizarre narratives are "excessive strategies" that disrupt conventional responses to fiction films. *The Cook, the Thief, His Wife & Her Lover,* for example, came under attack for failing to provide "the necessary depth of characterization," with the result that "the audience is largely an observer, shocked rather than moved by what it sees."[62] Yet this is really only to say that the film does not ask the spectator to identify with its characters but rather to engage with its formal system. As William Van Wert suggests, "to understand fully *The Cook* as film is to understand how [Michael] Nyman's score and [Sacha] Vierny's camera play off each other, not what happens to Georgina and Michael and Albert."[63]

Albert (Michael Gambon) is the thief of the title, who owns a French restaurant, where he and his gang abuse the cook and his staff, the gourmet food, and the other customers. Georgina (Helen Mirren) is his wife, who conducts an affair with Michael (Alan Howard), a quiet, book-loving customer, in various parts of the restaurant. When her husband learns the truth, he kills the lover by forcing him to eat his own books, and Georgina takes her revenge by inviting Albert to a meal at which she presents him with Michael's body prepared by the cook, forces him at gunpoint to eat, and then executes him (Figure 26). This lurid plot has much in common with the Jacobean revenge tragedies popular on the English stage in the seventeenth century, and Greenaway draws attention to its theatrical ancestry by using a curtain to open and close the film. There are also many allusions to the visual arts, including a huge reproduction of a Frans Hals painting of Dutch burghers of the seventeenth century, offering both a parallel and a contrast to their modern British counterparts.

A more contemporary allusion is to the British crime film. Albert is an extreme version of the gangster figure played by Bob Hoskins in *The Long Good Friday* (John Mackenzie, 1979), who is very much a Thatcherist entrepreneur (see Chapter 9). His wife may be called Georgina, but since he is Albert, she might well have been Victoria, the name of the gangster's wife played by Mirren in *The Long Good Friday*. Greenaway "purposely avoided the cliché of the lovable cockney gangster" and depicts Albert as an egotistical and belligerent monster, representing both the brutal and philistine attitudes that the director identified in Thatcher's Britain and the traditions in bourgeois culture to which Thatcher appealed when she called for a return to "Victorian" values.[64]

While many critics recognized the political allegory, they often accused Greenaway of elitism because he uses a vulgar and barbarous working-class man to represent the decline of British culture. However, despite his monstrosity, Albert's diatribes do expose a reality concealed behind the sophistication of French cooking and the learned books stored in Michael's book depository. As Greenaway puts it, the film examines "the link between sex, food, greed and violence," and its does so by creating a nightmare vision of "a consumer-oriented exploitative society."[65]

Like Jarman, Greenaway deplores the state of contemporary British culture, but both filmmakers also recognize the pleasure that can be found in reorganizing and scrambling the fragmentary relics of older systems. In so doing, they challenge the myths of heritage that stress continuity and the appeal of supposedly simpler values from the past. The idea that avant-garde films might move closer to the mainstream has not been sustained since Jarman's death and the failure of Greenaway's more recent films to find critical favor or broad distribution. There have been a few other attempts, notably in the films of Sally Potter (see Chapter 7), but visual artists who are interested in the moving image are now more likely to work in video than in film. The development of digital media, in which Greenaway has played an important role, has also blurred the distinction between film and video and encouraged a more adventurous approach to image making in general. In these condi-

**Figure 26.** Georgina (Helen Mirren) takes her revenge on Albert (Michael Gambon) at the end of Peter Greenaway's *The Cook, The Thief, His Wife & Her Lover.*

tions, many films now incorporate elements of both the realist and expressionist traditions, but although new audiovisual patterns are clearly emerging, British cinema has always depended on an intricate interaction between these traditions.

# CHAPTER FIVE

# Millions like Us

## National Cinema as Popular Cinema

At the end of his essay on "The Concept of National Cinema," Andrew Higson asks: "What is a national cinema if it doesn't have a national audience?"[1] Throughout most of the world, Hollywood *is* popular cinema and, in countries with large film industries, the national cinema usually seeks to become popular by complex strategies that involve both differentiating its films from, and competing with, those of Hollywood. As to British cinema, box-office figures show that the national audience prefers Hollywood films, although the extent of this preference has often been exaggerated.

As Thomas Elsaesser has insisted, "Hollywood can hardly be conceived, in the context of a 'national' cinema, as totally Other, since so much of any nation's film culture is implicitly 'Hollywood.'"[2] The cultural dynamics at work are described by Tom Ryall when he points out that "British film genres, although developed in the context of the national culture, were addressed to audiences steeped in the 'foreign culture' of Hollywood cinema."[3] Even when British films are not partially or completely funded by Hollywood studios, British filmmakers are aware that they must attract audiences whose expectations have been shaped by their experience of Hollywood films. In these circumstances, the drive for commercial success is often seen as a denial of the distinctive characteristics of the national culture.

These considerations complicate the traditional approach to national cinema discussed in the Introduction. If we study a national cinema to discover what Siegfried Kracauer called "the psychological pattern of a people," what does it mean if the people spend most of their time watching films from another national cinema?[4] The problem is that "people" and "nation" are not synonymous. In discourses of nationalism, and most accounts of national cinemas, the "people" are the citizens of that nation; in other contexts, however, the term refers only to those citizens who consume popular culture. These "people" do not constitute a clearly defined social class, although they are usually equated with the lower classes or "masses," as opposed to elite groups who set cultural standards and hold political power.

Just as it is often difficult to tell who the "people" are, the meaning of the word "popular" remains slippery and elusive. Indeed, according to Raymond

Williams, "the key to an understanding of the cultural history of the last two hundred years is the contested significance of that word."[5] One important thread in this history is the different ways in which the shifting meanings of the "popular" have been associated with (or dissociated from) the idea of the "nation," a political institution that also emerged in its modern form during the same period.

There is little doubt that the most influential account of the relations between national and popular culture is that provided by Antonio Gramsci, the Italian political and cultural theorist, who spent the last years of his life (1926–37) as a prisoner under Benito Mussolini's fascist regime. Gramsci attributed the rise of fascism in Italy to the lack of a genuine "national-popular" culture, arguing that Italian authors belonged to "a caste tradition that has never been broken by a strong popular or national political movement from below."[6] The official national culture was thus cut off from the popular culture through which the people lived out their everyday lives.

Although Britain has a long tradition of popular-cultural forms, Higson argues that "the terms 'national' and 'popular' are . . . not generally equivalent within British film culture, with 'national' tending to indicate bourgeois interests, values, and tastes."[7] Popular traditions exist in the shadow of the masterpieces of high culture that constitute the national heritage and, for many critics, especially in the first half of the twentieth century, Hollywood films – and American popular culture in general – posed a threat to all that was best in the national character. Thus Q. D. Leavis, in her influential survey of *Fiction and the Reading Public,* first published in 1932, looked back approvingly to the Elizabethan age, when "the masses were receiving their amusement from above instead of being specially catered for by journalists, film-directors, and popular novelists, as they are now."[8]

Leavis wrote from a position within "high" culture, but even journalists in popular newspapers warned that Hollywood films worked against the national interest. In 1927 a writer in the *Daily Express* lamented that "the bulk of our picture-goers are Americanised" and claimed that Britain now had "several million people . . . who, to all intent and purpose, are temporary American citizens."[9] The apparent disjunction between popular pleasure and national allegiance continued to worry critics, who emphasized the hypnotic effects of film viewing on spectators seduced by illusion and spectacle.

There is no doubt that American popular culture did have an impact that altered many of the traditional patterns of British life. However, more recent studies of popular culture have shown that its effects are far more complex and contradictory than earlier accounts assumed. As Stuart Hall has pointed out, popular cultural forms "don't function on us as if we are blank screens." Hall conceives of "the terrain of national-popular culture and tradition as a battlefield" on which different social groups struggle to impose their sense of the "people."[10]

As Gramsci well knew, it is difficult to distinguish his concept of the "national-popular" as a progressive force from the use made of similar ideas by groups with quite different political agendas, such as the Italian and German fascist movements. In the British context, the relations between popular culture and national traditions are highly volatile and constantly shifting according to social and political circumstances. For example, Jeffrey Richards reads the career of music-hall/film star Gracie Fields in the 1930s as a gradual process in which her status as "a symbol of the working classes" was appropriated by "the Establishment" as a means of promoting "national consensus."[11] Phenomena such as the People's War, the rise to power of Margaret Thatcher, and the events surrounding the death of Princess Diana have all led to debates over the extent to which they were the outcome of bottom–up movements among the "people" or imposed from above by government or media manipulation.

Similar questions arise about why certain films become popular and why British audiences prefer Hollywood films to their own national cinema (and perhaps why so many people exaggerate this preference). It is clear that spectatorship and citizenship are intricately related but also that this relationship is highly complicated.

## TRANSFORMING INHERITED FORMULAS: *THE THIRD MAN*

In his film reviews of the 1930s, Graham Greene produced a running commentary on the failure of the British film industry to produce either a convincing national cinema or a popular cinema, let alone a national-popular cinema. His main explanation for the failure to create a viable national cinema was the "alien control" exerted by Alexander Korda and other European émigrés that encouraged the production of "cheap silly international pictures" (see Chapter 2).[12] Ironically, it was Korda who later gave Greene his opportunity to put his ideas into practice, first by hiring him to write the screenplays for two films that Greene preferred to forget, and then by producing two films that quickly became classics of the national cinema, *The Fallen Idol* (1948) and *The Third Man* (1949), both directed by Carol Reed from Greene's screenplays.[13]

Korda produced *The Third Man* in association with David Selznick, the American producer who had lured Hitchcock to Hollywood, and it became very much an international production. Although Greene and Reed apparently resisted Selznick's requests for changes to make the film more suitable for U.S. audiences, the film was not only set entirely outside Britain but British

**Figure 27.** *The Third Man:* Harry Lime (Orson Welles) takes Holly (Joseph Cotten) for a ride on a Ferris wheel and tries to convince him that "the world doesn't make heroes."

characters (and actors) were marginal to its action. The decision to cast Joseph Cotten as Holly Martins, a writer of popular fiction who comes to postwar Vienna to meet a childhood friend, altered the complex mix of national identities. In the screenplay, the character was English but, once he became an American, his friend also had to be American, leading to the powerful presence of Orson Welles as Harry Lime (Figure 27).[14]

Most of the other characters are European expatriates, and the only significant British character is Major Calloway (Trevor Howard), the head of Military Police in the British zone of the occupied city. He acts as Holly's (and our) guide to the city and tries to protect the writer when he discovers that his friend has died in suspicious circumstances. As Robert F. Moss suggests, Calloway is "an exemplar of sturdy Anglo-Saxon values," but he remains marginal to the story of Holly's investigation and his growing feelings for Harry's former mistress, Anna, a Czech refugee played by an Italian actress (Alida Valli).[15] On the other hand, Calloway's "realism" is a stabilizing force in a cruel and absurd situation, suggesting that Britain may have a useful, if peripheral, role in the postwar world order.

The international flavor of *The Third Man* suggests that Greene had modified his view of the national cinema since his prewar denunciation of foreign influences, but his attitude was, in any case, complicated by his interest in popular cinema. During the 1930s, he complained that British films too often dealt with "the leisured class" and thus rarely became popular in the manner of Hollywood films that "convey the sense the picture has been made by its spectators and not merely shown to them."[16] As we have seen, he was not even convinced by the thrillers of Hitchcock, a filmmaker with whom he would otherwise seem to have much in common, and it is instructive to compare their different approaches to the thriller genre.

As David Thomson has pointed out, Greene and Hitchcock were born "just five years and 25 miles apart," and both were Catholics whose religious background emerged in their work as a fascination with evil, especially in their treatment of violence and sexuality.[17] Both turned to the thriller in the 1930s, exploiting the unsettled political conditions of the time, and their use of popular forms was a challenge to established cultural values. Brian Diemert refers to Greene's decision to write thrillers as a gesture of resistance against "an élite that was identified with both modernist experimentation and political conservatism," while Thomas Elsaesser argues that Hitchcock's "cultivated unseriousness" had a similar purpose.[18]

Greene was less willing than Hitchcock to deny the "serious" intentions of his work. He called his thrillers "entertainments," thereby challenging the pejorative connotations of the term in 1930s culture but also uneasily reaffirming the distinction between high and popular culture. A similar ambivalence comes through in his argument that in cinema "popularity . . . is a *value,* as it isn't in a book" because "films have got to appeal to a large undiscriminating public."[19] Yet Greene's aim in his film work in the 1940s was clearly the same as in his popular fiction, in which he tried, according to Diemert, "to revitalize and transform the inherited formulas of popular writing . . . so as to make these formulas the vehicles of both entertainment and 'serious' purpose."[20]

Greene's literary thrillers were influenced by earlier British adventure stories, such as those of John Buchan (whence Hitchcock's *The 39 Steps*), and by contemporary American "hard-boiled" writers, but they also owed much to popular cinema. There has even been a suggestion that he adapted "the devices of the Hitchcock movie camera."[21] Since literary censorship was much less restrictive, however, Greene could include political and sexual material that would have been unacceptable in British films, and he thus felt that even his entertainments were more "realistic" than "the polished fairy-tales of Mr. Hitchcock."[22] For this admirer of Grierson and the documentary movement, "realistic" was almost a synonym for "serious," and it is significant that the one Hitchcock film that Greene did enjoy was *Sabotage* (1936) because, for once, he found "this melodrama convincingly realistic."[23]

The striking opening sequence of *The Third Man* seems designed to drive home the distance separating this film from Hitchcock's thrillers. Whereas *The Lady Vanishes* opens with obvious model shots that proclaim the "fairy tale" alibi it uses to avoid censorship (see Chapter 2), the opening sequence of *The Third Man* consists of location shots of the ruined city accompanied by a voice-over narrator describing the political situation and the risks of living there. In the film that follows, "the ubiquitous debris of war-ravaged Vienna has as much 'presence' . . . as any of the protagonists" and provides a constant reminder of "an evil far greater than Harry Lime's little racket."[24]

While the location shooting creates a strong sense of "realism," the narrator is not a documentary voice-of-God commentator. The voice is Carol Reed's, but he speaks in the first person and casually refers to himself as a black-market operator. He announces that he will tell the story of Holly Martins, but he never becomes a character in the film, and his narration disappears after the opening sequence. Apparently it was added at Korda's insistence to explain the political situation in the divided city, but the effect (rather like in some of the novels of Joseph Conrad) is to call attention to the act of storytelling. In the U.S. release prints, the opening narration was spoken by Cotten/Holly, creating a rather more conventional effect and shifting the balance toward subjective rather than objective realism.

If the opening was partly designed to distance the film from Hitchcock, it was not always successful. An enthusiastic American reviewer described *The Third Man* as "crammed with cinematic plums that would do the early Hitchcock proud," and many other references to Hitchcock appeared in critical accounts of the film.[25] These comments would have made Greene uncomfortable, no doubt, but they are an appropriate response to the "entertainment" aspect of the film, which is held in constant tension with its "serious" purposes. In this respect, the effect of the film may not be that different from *The Lady Vanishes,* although the "fairy tale" has become a nightmare (as it also does in Hitchcock's later films).

This tension shows through in the widely different critical responses. Roy Armes, for example, argues that "though there are elements of a serious nature . . . the tone remains that of one of Graham Greene's typical entertainments."[26] In contrast, other critics insist on the film's "complete seriousness" or stress the ways in which it transcends its "nominal classification as a thriller."[27] The film incorporates this tension in many ways and constantly unbalances the spectator, not just through its off-center visual compositions but also through its tonal shiftiness.

One of the most obvious examples of this effect occurs when Holly is apparently kidnapped from his hotel and driven through the city streets at high speed. He thinks he has been picked up by Harry's killers but finds himself welcomed to a literary gathering at the British Cultural Institute, at which he had earlier agreed to speak but which he has forgotten because of his investigation. Although Holly writes pulp westerns, the audience expect a "serious" author and ask questions about such topics as "stream of consciousness" in the modern novel. The comic effect recalls a similar episode in Hitchcock's *The 39 Steps* (1935) when the hero, on the run from police and spies, stumbles into a political meeting and is mistaken for an election candidate.[28]

There was almost another link to Hitchcock in that the filmmakers had considered casting Basil Radford and Naunton Wayne as the joint heads of the Cultural Institute. These actors were well known for their performances as Caldicott and Charters, the upper-class odd couple first introduced in *The Lady Vanishes.* They proved so popular that Launder and Gilliat used them in other screenplays, including that for Carol Reed's *Night Train to Munich* (1940), in which they were again passengers on a train in Europe who assist a romantic couple to escape from the enemy. With the outbreak of war, it was now possible to identify the enemy as German Nazis, but the overall tone is only slightly darker than Hitchcock's film.

Greene and Reed probably felt that the familiarity of this pair, whose appeal was poised ambiguously between satire and affection, would lighten the tone of *The Third Man* a little too much, and they eventually went back to the original idea of using a single character.[29] On the other hand, this character, a cheery, upper-class old man named Crabbin (Wilfrid Hyde-White), still provides comic relief. He is constantly accompanied by a young woman, to whom he is first heard saying he can't introduce her to everyone, and he seems completely out of touch with postwar reality. He thus not only provides a more old-fashioned version of the British national character than that represented by Calloway but also acts as a parallel and contrast to the young American who becomes involved in political and sexual affairs that he does not understand.

As the author of pulp fiction in which moral issues are clearly defined, Holly must be convinced of the extent of the corruption in the postwar city and of Harry's involvement in it. When he sets out to find the "third man" who apparently witnessed Harry's death, he acts like a character in one of his own novels in pursuit of justice. His naiveté is both refreshing and dangerous and seems to represent Greene's ambivalent attitude to his own entertainments (of which this film is certainly one). Instead of revenging his friend, he uncovers a corrupt and confusing reality that forces him to abandon his romantic illusions. He discovers that the "third man" was Harry himself, who faked his own death and is now living in the Russian sector. Holly must then choose between loyalty to his friend and betraying him to the authorities.

Holly's moral choice involves tensions that parallel the formal tensions between melodrama and realism, entertaining and serious fictions, objective and subjective reality. After Harry takes Holly for a ride on a Ferris wheel and asks whether he can really feel concern for the deaths of people seen far below, Calloway takes the writer to a hospital to see the effects of the diluted penicillin in which Harry has been dealing. He confronts Holly with sick and

**Figure 28.** The disputed ending of *The Third Man:* After Harry's funeral, Holly watches passively as Anna (Alida Valli) walks past him.

dying children, but the horror is left to our imaginations, since the patients remain offscreen and we see only the shock on Holly's face.

Despite this visual restraint, Pauline Kael objected that "we've been en-joying all this decadence and stylish acting and these people living on their nerves, and then we're forced to take evil seriously." Greene insisted that the filmmakers only wanted to "entertain" the audience, but the "serious" issues at stake ensured that the plot cannot center on a trivial "MacGuffin," again un-derlining the difference from Hitchcock.[30] Yet, when it came to the ending, it was Greene who took the side of entertainment in a dispute with Reed.[31]

After visiting the hospital, Holly betrays his friend and helps the police in a thrilling chase through the sewers of Vienna. With Harry wounded and trapped at a grating, through which his fingers reach out to the open air, Holly shoots him to put him out of his misery. In the screenplay, Holly then walks away from Harry's funeral with Anna, but Reed insisted on a darker ending, in which Holly waits for Anna after the funeral but she walks right past him (Figure 28). The long take in which this occurs is highly unusual and verges on absurdity – Holly leans against a cart standing at the side of the road and does not move toward her, says nothing as she passes, and then lights a cig-arette – but it is a powerful and striking final image.[32]

Greene came to accept that Reed was right, but his first impulse was to argue that *The Third Man* "was too light of an affair to carry an unhappy end-ing."[33] Since most of his literary entertainments have dark or uncertain end-ings, Greene was apparently assuming that popular cinema's "large undiscrim-inating public" demanded a happy ending. Reed's ending is more in accord with the spirit of Greene's writing and with the tone of a film in which, as James Naremore suggests, "the seductions of melodrama are never offered without countervailing irony or deflation."[34]

## BRITISH CINEMA WILL NEVER BE THE SAME AGAIN: THE BOND PHENOMENON

Greene would certainly have agreed with the critic who wrote that "even in his entertainments Greene has never been able to bring himself to create handsome heroes of the James Bond variety or to tell a story that offers escapist adventure for its own sake."[35] Ian Fleming's novels about secret agent James Bond, published between 1953 and 1965, are usually described in these terms, as escapist fictions lacking any claims to literary merit or serious purpose. Yet, although Fleming, like Hitchcock, often insisted that his work was not intended to be taken seriously, he claimed at other times that his novels were "thrillers designed to be read as literature," in the tradition of American hard-boiled crime novels and Greene's entertainments.[36]

Unlike Greene, Fleming was an admirer of Hitchcock and thought that he would be "the best director for a James Bond film," but it was Korda who first expressed interest in bringing Bond to the screen in the 1950s.[37] The filmmakers who eventually bought the rights to the Bond novels acknowledged Hitchcock's influence, but they set out to intensify the entertainment factor by increasing the number of shocks and thrills in order to create a "larger-than-life approach to action-adventure pictures."[38] The roller-coaster effect led Robin Wood to argue that, whereas Hitchcock's *North by Northwest* (1959) is "a light entertainment" that nevertheless expresses "mature moral values," a Bond film like *Goldfinger* (Guy Hamilton, 1964) is "a collection of bits, carefully calculated with both eyes on the box office."[39]

However, just as Wood enjoined us in 1965 to "take Hitchcock seriously," James Chapman's recent cultural history of the Bond films begins with a chapter entitled "taking James Bond seriously."[40] Whereas Wood argues the case for seeing a popular filmmaker as a great artist, Chapman's claim is, in keeping with critical changes in the intervening years, not that the Bond films are major works of art but that their popularity draws on and illuminates the cultural contexts in which they were made.

The Bond films became key texts in the argument about popular cinema and national traditions, with many critics arguing that they are not really British films. The critics immediately recognized that *Dr. No* (Terence Young, 1962) introduced something new to British cinema, but many deplored what it represented (Figure 29). In a short review in *Sight and Sound,* Penelope Houston anticipated Wood's objection by suggesting that this "reprehensible (but admittedly watchable) film" was made with "a watchful eye on the Amer-

**Figure 29.** "My intentions are strictly honorable": James Bond (Sean Connery) gets to know Honey Ryder (Ursula Andress) after her surprise arrival on Dr. No's island in the first Bond film.

ican market."[41] Richard Whitehall in *Films and Filming* called it "the headiest box-office concoction of sex and sadism ever brewed in a British studio" and feared that it would lead to "a fascist cinema uncorrupted by moral scruples." Noting that "at one point Bond nonchalantly fires half a dozen shots into the *back* of a helpless opponent," he forecast that "the British cinema will never be the same again."[42]

Bond would use his "license to kill" rather more responsibly in the subsequent films, but critics continued to complain that he was a hero "in a grand fascistic tradition" and to find it "quite terrifying . . . that an audience could be so easily predicted."[43] On the other hand, by the time of the release of *Goldfinger,* Houston had warmed to "the charm of the Bond films," which she attributed to their playful use of conventions. She argued that, "where Hitchcock manipulates a response," the Bond films assume "a mood of good-humoured complicity with the audience." On the basis of her observations, she noted that "the reactions of the audience make it clear that they know precisely what they are watching," and she insisted that "these are not the kind of fantasies likely to seduce the unwary."[44]

Both detractors and admirers agreed that the pleasures offered by the Bond series were essentially formulaic. *Dr. No* was, of course, the only Bond film that could not draw on its audience's memories of previous Bond films. Yet Bond was already well known from Fleming's novels, as well as from the comic strip based on his adventures that first appeared in the *Daily Express* in 1957. As the series developed, it encompassed all the novels, sometimes faithfully adapted, sometimes loosely, and sometimes using only the title and a few names. After the novels were exhausted, the films were based on new stories using and adapting the old formula.[45]

*Dr. No* included a remarkable number of features that would become part of the cinematic formula. Some of these derive from the novels, as is the case with the obligatory sequence in which Bond reports to the office of M, the head of the Secret Service, and exchanges suggestive remarks with his secretary, Miss Moneypenny. Others became virtual trademarks of the film series, including most of the elements found at the beginning of all subsequent Bond films: the opening shot in which Bond is seen through a circular aperture that could be the barrel of a gun, a camera lens, or an eye, before he turns and shoots directly at it (and the spectator); the James Bond musical theme (composed by Monty Norman); and a colorful credits sequence (designed by Maurice Binder, as in all but one of the films until 1989). In *Dr. No,* the credits are more abstract than in later films when they usually consist of artfully photographed naked women in conjunction with guns. There is no specially composed title song by a star performer and there is no spectacular precredits sequence, but these duly made their appearance in the second film, *From Russia with Love* (Terence Young, 1963).

The "complicity" to which Houston refers depends heavily on the knowing use of a formula in which some elements remain the same and others constantly change. Five different actors have so far appeared as Bond and, with each change, the star persona of the new actor enters into a kind of dialogue with the Bond character already established in the novels and the earlier films. The formula thus enables patterns of continuity and variation that provide much of the pleasure for spectators familiar with earlier films, with Fleming's novels, and with the other popular films with which the Bond films have interacted over the years.

Certain recurring characters, such as Felix Leiter, Bond's friend in the CIA, and the villainous Blofeld, were always played by different actors, but Bond's associates in the Secret Service were embodied by the same actors for many years. The regular actors, of course, aged as the series progressed, while Bond's age varied with the actor who played him but generally remained apparently about the same. Bernard Lee (the original M) died in 1981, and Lois Maxwell (Miss Moneypenny) retired in 1985; but Desmond Llewellyn, who first appeared as Q, the officer who equips Bond for his adventures, in *From Russia with Love,* played the role, with frequent jokes about his age, through *The World Is Not Enough* (Michael Apted, 1999). In that film he introduced his successor, R, played by comedian John Cleese, best known for his work in television and film with the Monty Python troupe (see Chapter 8).

As in Hitchcock's 1930s thrillers, humor has always been part of the formula in the Bond films. Houston argued that the effect depends on "playing off one set of associations against another, allowing a geniality in the acting to undercut the brutality, using humour as a disinfectant and exaggeration as a calculated effrontery."[46] Other critics objected to the way in which sequences of violent action in which Bond finally defeats his opponent end with a one-line joke, often delivered directly to the camera, very much in the tradition of the excruciating gags in Britain's other long-lived cinematic series, the farcical *Carry On* films (see Chapter 8).

These comic asides seemed to confirm concerns about the films' "fascism," through their disregard for victims of violence, but critics also saw them as a sign of changing patterns of film spectatorship in the age of television. Tony Bennett and Janet Woollacott thus argue that "the organisation of the later Bond films, described by the film-makers as 'a series of circus acts,' encourages the more 'distant,' less involved viewing which is typical of television rather than films."[47] As early as *Dr. No,* several critics pointed to the use of the techniques of television commercials, with the result that "non-stop action and fast cutting kept the eye dazzled and the mind reeling so that one didn't have time to think about it all."[48]

Younger viewers, seeing *Dr. No* in the light of later Bond films and many Hollywood blockbusters, are likely to find the pacing painfully slow. Speed is of the essence in the contemporary media environment, but Kristin Thompson traces the "constant ratcheting-up of the stakes" in Hollywood action films back to the first Bond films.[49] These can thus be seen as an early sign of the emergence of a new "cinema of attractions," like that of early cinema, in which action and spectacle are more important than plot and character.[50]

There can be no doubt, however, that the figure of James Bond is the main reason for the longevity of the series. According to Bennett and Woollacott, Bond is "arguably the most popular – in the sense of widely known – figure of the post-war period, if not of this century."[51] While he is certainly a "popular hero," many critics have been reluctant to see him as a national hero. The producers of *Dr. No* were Harry Saltzman, a Canadian, and Albert "Cubby" Broccoli, an American, who had both been working in Britain for some time, and United Artists provided the relatively modest budget. Much of the film was shot on location in Jamaica, and exotic foreign locations are a major factor in the Bond formula.

In casting the leading role, the producers faced a dilemma because they wanted an actor with international appeal who would be convincing as Fleming's British hero. They sought to avoid too-obvious class or regional connotations and eventually chose Sean Connery, whose screen persona retained traces of his Scottish origins. As Alexander Walker noted of his accent, "being 'non-English,' it avoided pigeon-holing Bond anywhere in the Anglo-Saxon class system, yet it was authentically 'British' enough to avoid any accusation that he had been located in some mid-Atlantic limbo."[52] Of the four other actors who have played Bond to date, only Roger Moore is "English," both literally and in terms of his screen persona.[53] The current Bond, Pierce Brosnan, is of Irish descent, Timothy Dalton (two films in the 1980s) has a Welsh background, and George Lazenby (who temporarily replaced Connery in *On Her Majesty's Secret Service* [Peter Hunt, 1969]), is Australian.

As a British secret agent fighting international conspiracies, Bond caters to what Chapman calls "a nationalist fantasy in which Britain's decline as a world power did not really take place."[54] Kingsley Amis remarks that Fleming's Bond functions according to "an elementary moral system" held together by "a series of ideas about England," thereby illustrating Chapman's point that the novels depict Bond as "a defender of the realm, committed to preserving the institutions of his country, which typically is referred to a 'England' rather than 'Britain.'"[55] Yet he does not fit comfortably into "the tradition of English ruling class heroes," who tended to be upper-class amateurs.[56]

In the films, too, Bond is usually regarded as an Englishman, despite the backgrounds of most of the actors playing the role. As with the heritage films discussed in Chapter 11, the Bond films developed an image of the national character that had international appeal, but this image was an unstable mixture of traditional and modern elements. In keeping with the cultural changes in British culture in the 1960s, the Bond films tended to undercut traditional stereotypes by shifting the idea of "class" away from the social hierarchy onto matters of style and infusing it with a new sexual "permissiveness."

During the 1960s, the films participated in a new sense of British-ness associated with an emerging youth-oriented consumer culture that made the British film industry attractive to Hollywood (see Chapter 7). Though the films starring Moore moved closer to the image of the gentleman hero, the plots still drew on the modern connotations of the Bond image, most notably in *Moonraker* (Lewis Gilbert, 1979), in which Bond pursues the villain to a space station from which he plans to destroy the human race. Throughout the series, Bond moves rapidly around the globe thanks to the speed of modern transportation and typically works against villains who exploit technology to threaten the entire world.

The films draw on widespread anxieties about the threat of nuclear war and terrorism, usually setting their plots against the background of international political tensions but with villains who exploit these tensions for their own private purposes (Figure 30). Bond often rescues the world despite the tendency of the major powers to react too quickly to threats designed to destabilize the world situation. Thus the political significance of Bond's mission in *You Only Live Twice* (Lewis Gilbert, 1967) emerges in a sequence at the United Nations where a British diplomat sits between the United States and Soviet delegates and reacts calmly as they direct insults at each other. On the other hand, the villain in *Diamonds Are Forever* (Guy Hamilton, 1971) tells Bond that his "pitiful little island hasn't even been threatened."

The political coordinates of the Bond films have shifted frequently in reaction to changes in the world situation. Critics have always been ready to denounce them as politically irresponsible, if not reactionary, but the films tend to disarm such criticism by their refusal to take themselves seriously. There is once again a "fairy tale" alibi because, despite the contemporary allusions that

**Figure 30.** "The aim is world-wide domination": Elliot Carver (Jonathan Pryce), a rare British villain in a Bond film, plans to use his media empire to provoke a third world war in *Tomorrow Never Dies*.

provide a semblance of realism, Bond fights not against a political opponent but against a villain who is pure evil, and often insane. He can be seen as a national-popular hero who functions as "a latter day St. George fighting against evil incarnate . . . but with the hero and villain adapted to our technological age."[57] The Bond films are national-popular films, in which the relations between the national and the popular remain powerful because highly unstable.

## ENTERTAINMENT AND UTOPIA: THE WORKING-CLASS FEEL-GOOD MOVIE

In an influential essay that deals with Hollywood musicals but is relevant to a broad range of popular culture, Richard Dyer argues that "entertainment" appeals to audiences because of its "utopian" nature. Dyer suggests that popular texts do not normally offer fully realized visions of utopia but rather create utopian "feelings" as an imaginary compensation for the shortcomings of everyday life. The pleasures of popular entertainment thus serve an ideological function, but the "utopian sensibility" must "take off from the real experience of the audience." He concludes that "to draw attention to the gap between what is and what could be, is, ideologically speaking, playing with fire."[58]

Among the most popular British films of the 1990s was a group that drew on the tradition of northern working-class realism but depicted characters who sought to escape the harshness of their everyday lives by performing as entertainers. These films – which include *Brassed Off* (Mark Herman, 1996), *The Full Monty* (Peter Cattaneo, 1997), and *Billy Elliot* (Stephen Daldry, 2000) – represent a "soft" realism as opposed to the "hard" realism of films, like *Nil by Mouth* (Gary Oldman, 1997) and *The War Zone* (Tim Roth, 1998), that intensify the claims of the realist tradition to represent "what is" (see Chapter 3). According to John Hill, these films "offer a certain utopianism about the possibility for collective action," and they belong to a loosely defined international phenomenon that became known as the feel-good movie.[59]

**Figure 31.** "It's the Arsenal off-side trap": Soccer tactics make choreography easier to follow as the men rehearse for their big performance in *The Full Monty*.

As Julia Hallam has argued, they "occupy an ambiguous cultural terrain." Drawing on the familiar iconography of the industrial north, "they celebrate locality, yet at the same time they commodify the cultural identities of economically marginalised communities, re-packaging their experiences for sale in the global marketplace."[60] Critical concern about the U.S. funding and distribution deals for most of these films is now less likely to stress Hollywood's influence on British culture than to express fears that the national interest will become lost in an increasingly globalized entertainment industry.

The biggest success story among this group of films was *The Full Monty.* It takes off from the plight of unemployed men in Sheffield, a northern city whose once thriving steel industry disappeared as a result of the free-market policies of the Thatcher government in the 1980s. While each of the characters faces a desperate situation, the film not only draws on northern traditions of humor in the face of adversity but also gradually shifts its focus from their grim prospects to their successful performance as male strippers.

It opens with a brief public-relations newsreel called "Sheffield: City on the Move." Projected on a small screen within the screen, this film clearly comes from the past, as it depicts a thriving industrial city. As well as showing men at work, it also celebrates the provision of leisure activities, night life, and modern housing. When it ends, a caption sets the story "25 Years Later," and the screen fills with empty and derelict factories. The film thus begins with utopian images of a past in which the people enjoyed full employment and a satisfying cultural life, although we may well suspect, as one critic puts it, that "such a Utopia only existed as a construct of the carefully written and filmed 'documentary.'"[61]

The utopian sensibility reappears when the men get the idea for the strip show and, after initially discouraging rehearsals, begin to gain confidence as performers (Figure 31). Their final triumph occurs when an audience of wom-

**Figure 32.** The band, led by Danny (Pete Postlethwaite), is in good form at the beginning of a competition in *Brassed Off*, but the temptations of the local pubs prove too strong as the day wears on.

en applaud enthusiastically as the men do the "full monty," stripping completely naked, unlike the professional dancers who inspired them. To some extent, the film does provide the expected feel-good ending, but its impact is somewhat modified by its abruptness. At the climax of the performance, a freeze-frame shows the men from behind as they reveal all to the cheering audience, an effect that confirms their success – but simultaneously reminds us that we cannot see what the onscreen audience sees.

According to Greg Howard, this ending is designed to avoid "admitting that the laughter disappears two minutes after the performance finishes," but there seems rather to be a conflict between the pleasure of the moment and an awareness that this is only a temporary solution to long-term problems.[62] The men insist that this is a "one time only" performance, but it is possible to imagine they will change their minds, and to wonder about a society that allows them this possibility but not that of more traditionally productive work.

Similar issues structure the plot in *Brassed Off,* set during the time of large-scale pit closures by the Thatcher government that destroyed the British coal industry. According to a caption at the end of the film, 140 mines were closed at the cost of nearly a quarter of a million jobs.[63] The film deals with the process by which workers are persuaded to accept the closing of a mine in a Yorkshire town, even though the government's own figures show that it is a profitable operation. Its utopianism is apparent primarily in the determination of the members of the colliery's brass band to win a national competition even after the mine has closed, but also in a romantic subplot that eventually unites Gloria, a government geologist (Tara Fitzgerald), and Andy (Ewan McGregor), one of the miners.

When one of the musicians tells Danny, the band's conductor (Pete Postlethwaite), that "if the pit goes, the band goes," he insists that the band symbolizes the town's "pride" (Figure 32). The band travels to London, where it wins first prize in the contest at the Albert Hall, yet Danny refuses to accept the cup because of the way the miners have been treated. Another band member takes the cup anyway and, in the final sequence, the band celebrates on the open top of a double-decker bus. As they pass the Houses of Parliament, Danny leads the band in a performance of Edward Elgar's *Pomp and Circumstance March No. 1.* They have regained the pride lost by the miners, and the shame has been shifted to Margaret Thatcher and her government.

The band is both a symbol of working-class "heritage" (contesting the definition of this term in the heritage films that dominated British cinema in the 1980s) and a utopian force opposed to the reality of the pit closures (as suggested by the ease with which the band performs new numbers without rehearsal and the unexplained augmentation of the band for the final competition). As in the film musical, the spontaneity of performance is set against the calculation that lies behind the travesty of democracy that Thatcherism represents.

The final shot is a close-up of Danny's face that fades to black, acting as a reminder that the band's triumph has not cured the illness (caused by working in the mines) that almost prevented him from coming to London, nor solved the unemployment problem. Yet the fictional band might decide to follow the example of the actual colliery band that provided the music for the film and that continued to perform professionally after the closure of the mine in which its members worked, in keeping with the shift from a production-based economy to one that depends on performance. Since the band's repertoire consists of classical music (like Elgar's) and folk music, it is also clear that the working-class tradition of brass bands is already an ambiguous one, even before it takes its place in the global marketplace.

Like the films of the British New Wave, these films explore the effects of social change on gender relations and, like the New Wave films, they have been accused of misogyny. According to Paul Marris, *Brassed Off* and *The Full Monty,* as well as *Billy Elliot,* "effectively cast the crisis of postindustrialism as the crisis of masculinity," and Claire Monk suggests that they reflect the emergence of "New Labour" under Tony Blair, offering "narratives where post-industrial despair and masculine crisis are resolved through an engagement with the entertainment or cultural industries."[64] The onscreen audiences at the end of *Brassed Off* and *The Full Monty* include the women who have earlier caused problems for the men (but the films also make clear that the men are not easy to live with). There is little to prepare for their change of heart, but its improbability also stresses how difficult it is to resolve "realistically" the issues that the films have raised.

Monk argues that *Billy Elliot*'s focus on a working-class boy who wants to become a ballet dancer leads to "a more equivocal relationship to dominant masculinity," but she also feels that the effect of the film is to "reduce the bitter politics of the 1984 Miners' Strike to little more than an expression of working-class machismo."[65] This is true in that the film presents the strike from the point of view of a young boy whose father and brother are striking workers who are ashamed that he prefers ballet to boxing. One of the film's most striking images (based on a contemporary news photograph) shows Billy and a young girl walking unconcernedly past a line of policemen with riot shields. Their indifference suggests that such sights have become part of everyday life and that this social division is what adult society has to offer them.

The film goes out of its way to make clear that Billy is not gay, unlike his best friend. Yet, as in *The Full Monty,* its feel-good ending is rather abrupt and is not as closed as it might first appear. After Billy leaves for ballet school in London, there is a cut to a performance of an all-male version of *Swan Lake* in which he is the star, watched by an audience that includes his father and brother. His triumph, and their acceptance of his new identity, has a utopian quality, and Billy's "escape" provides a more permanent solution (at least for him) than that achieved by the band in *Brassed Off* and the strippers in *The Full Monty.* Yet we see him only as a performer at the end and learn nothing of his offstage situation, with the result that the ending not only leaves intact the north–south divide in British culture but also suggests that what we have seen is a "fairy story," in the fullest sense of the term.

Just as the band in *Brassed Off* makes its protest and takes the cup too, these films seek to have it both ways, as both national films and global entertainment, and as utopian visions that raise at least some questions about their ideological contexts. Iconographically, they retain their roots in northern realism, but the performative aspects make their structures very like the musicals discussed by Dyer. The energetic "numbers" provide a relief from the narrative that otherwise involves all those qualities that Dyer sees as characteristic of the reality that utopia seeks to displace: scarcity, exhaustion, dreariness, manipulation, fragmentation.[66] While this alternation structures the narrative, however, the films depend less on the opposition between realism and escapism than on a sense that the two are inextricably entwined. They suggest not only that the national-popular must now be defined in the context of the global-popular but also that the one has not completely eliminated the other.

# CHAPTER SIX

# The Stars Look Down

## Acting British

Critics often refer to the close relations between the theater and the British film industry as a negative factor that has discouraged film-makers from developing the full possibilities of their medium. When the major film studios developed in the 1920s, they were located in and around London, within easy reach of the West End, as opposed to the large distance that separated Hollywood from the New York theaters. It is true that this circumstance made it easy for British film producers to recruit stage actors who could return for evening performances after a day of filming. It is also true that some productions seemed artificial and stagebound, especially in the years immediately following the introduction of sound. Yet many actors, playwrights, and directors have moved back and forth between stage and screen with uneven, but often effective, results. In any case, the theatrical influence came not just from the "legitimate" stage but from more "popular" forms, especially music hall and variety.

Although the influence of the realist tradition encouraged the idea that film acting should be more restrained, and thus more "natural," than theatrical performance, acting in the form of role-playing is very much part of everyday life and is often associated with national stereotypes. Similarly, although dramatic conventions and structures may seem ill suited to the more fluid sense of space and time of the film medium, they can be used to convey a sense of the social conventions and scenarios that frame our lives. It is thus possible to see the close links between theater and film less as an obstacle to achieving some kind of cinematic purity than as an opportunity to explore the interplay between the photographic realism of the film image and the conventions that shape our sense of cultural and national identities.

During the silent era, despite the emergence of several British film stars, producers often hired European or Hollywood actors to give their films international appeal. This practice continued after the coming of sound, but now the actors' accents had to be explained in narrative terms. The theater provided an alternative source of actors with some publicity value but whose accents often seemed equally inappropriate in the cinematic context (as we have seen in the case of the dubbing of Annie Ondra's voice in *Blackmail;*

see Chapter 1). According to Jeffrey Richards, British film stars in the 1930s "came to the cinema ready-made from the West End stage, from the music-hall, from musical comedy," and "only a handful of stars, notably Anna Neagle and Robert Donat, were actually *created* by the cinema."[1] This situation ensured that there would be a constant interaction between established theatrical traditions and the emergent practices of British cinema.

Douglas McVay argues that, in their best performances, British actors developed a style in which "theatrical and filmic elements are so carefully interwoven as to become virtually indistinguishable."[2] The assumption is that this kind of acting is the product of national cultural traditions that also encourage a formal and ceremonial approach to social and personal relations. However, the attempt to relate actors and acting styles to myths of national identity is complicated by the long history of the international exchange of actors among national cinemas.

Despite the international success of many British actors, it is also often assumed that the theatrical basis of British acting produced "character" actors rather than stars. If star acting means projecting a compelling screen personality (often wrongly assumed not to require acting skills), British actors were more often praised for subordinating their own personalities to allow them to create distinctive and varied characters. They did not draw on their own experience to ensure the authenticity of their performances, as the later "Method" actors would do, but instead emphasized the importance of technique in the creation of a character. In a discussion of acting "in the heritage film (and much British cinema more generally)," John Hill suggests that it "involves neither an immersion of the actor into a part nor a subordination of a role to their star image so much as a 'performance' of the role, involving a clear display of 'actorliness.'"[3]

Although by no means all British actors work in this way, "acting" emerges from such accounts as a powerful if unstable metaphor for the performance of national identity. The British film industry did produce stars, some with an international appeal, but it could not rival the "glamour" with which Hollywood invested its stars. When it tried to do so, the effect was complicated by the entanglement of glamour with status and class in British culture. As Bruce Babington points out, the British equivalent to "the razzle-dazzle of Hollywood premières" was the Royal Command Performance.[4]

However, the linkage between cinema and royalty was to some extent a rearguard action designed to offset the impact of mass culture on the class system. As Geoffrey Macnab suggests, the growth of modern advertising in the 1920s and 1930s "implied that the kind of glittering lifestyle which had once seemed to be the exclusive preserve of high society . . . was now accessible to everyone."[5] Whereas the "rags to riches" story is a basic myth of stardom, both as a plot mechanism in the films and in the lives of the stars them-

**Figure 33.** Jessie Matthews displays her "long tubular form" in a solo dance number from *Evergreen.*

selves, its British variant usually required the acquisition of the social manners and vocal qualities of the upper classes. Yet the star system also produced a publicity apparatus that ensured that audiences were aware of the stars' actual social origins, even though biographical information was often romanticized and manipulated.

Everybody knew, for example, that Jessie Matthews was the daughter of a London greengrocer, despite her "absurdly over-elocuted Mayfair accent."[6] Her accent was rarely suited to the social status of the characters she played, but her best musical comedies, like *Evergreen* (Victor Saville, 1934), exploit the tensions among her genteel voice, an underlying awareness of her class origins, and the erotic appeal of her slim and lithe body (her "long tubular form," as Graham Greene put it) exhibited in athletic dance numbers (Figure 33).[7] Her films often involve disguise and mistaken identities, as when she impersonates a female impersonator in *First a Girl* (Saville, 1935), and her star persona depended on her ability to demonstrate that class distinctions are as artificial as theatrical conventions.

The male equivalents were such "romantic leading men" as Robert Donat and Leslie Howard, who displayed what Jeffrey Richards calls "the effortless superiority of the gentleman amateur."[8] This image had wide appeal because it seemed to rescue the idea of "class" from the affected accents and effete mannerisms that audiences often found tiresome in British films. *The Scarlet Pimpernel* (Harold Young, 1935) foregrounds this distinction, depicting

**Figure 34.** In the final sequence of *The Scarlet Pimpernel,* Sir Percy (Leslie Howard) throws off his disguise, but he is still able to outwit the French with the help of his gallant band of Englishmen.

Sir Percy Blakeney (Howard) as a dashing, quick-witted British lord who rescues many victims from the guillotine during the French Revolution but hides behind the disguise of foppish aristocrat of the old school (Figure 34). The effect is to stress Howard/Percy's acting ability as an emblem of English flexibility opposed to the intolerance and rigid class divisions in France. In the context of the highly visible social inequality in Britain in the 1930s, French history acts as a warning, while Percy represents a utopian national spirit that transcends class differences.

These British actors often convey a sense of performing a role that critics often found more suited to stage than screen but that may now seem more resonant in a "postmodern" culture that stresses the performance of identity. Of course, this is far from a new phenomenon, and the pleasures of role-playing and masquerade are celebrated in many theatrical and cinematic genres. The stress on flexibility in the screen personas of British stars like Howard and the multiple identities taken on by character actors were attractive because of the contrast with the fixity of the class system and the stereotypes associated with it. Such stereotypes certainly persist today, but they do so in a global media marketplace that offers an often bewildering array of possible identities. Star personas and acting styles may reinforce or contest the stereotypes of national character, but the patterns of identification that they make possible are increasingly difficult to pin down.

## GREAT ACTOR–BLONDE BOMBSHELL:
## LAURENCE OLIVIER AND DIANA DORS

The events surrounding the death and funeral of Princess Diana in 1997 provoked many commentators to claim that there had been a major change in the national culture. Public emotions ran high, and the Queen and the Royal Family came under attack for their apparent indifference. French author Régis Debray argues that there was a conflict between the symbolic, ceremonial approach to public life associated with the traditions of the monarchy and the more intimate, informal behavior with which Diana had captured the popular imagination. In concluding that the Royal Family had nevertheless regained control of the situation, he used a theatrical metaphor: "Laurence Olivier had upstaged the Actors Studio."[9]

As this analogy suggests, Olivier (who died in 1989) remained the classic representative of a style of acting associated with a version of the national character that still endured, despite many pressures and contrary influences. In the context of British cinema, however, Olivier was a more complex figure than this view of him allows. His career exposed many of the tensions involved in the discourses on acting in British cinema. In the mid-1950s, for example, he took on an apparently atypical project, *The Prince and the Showgirl* (1957), which he directed himself and in which he costarred with Marilyn Monroe. His performance in this film, and its reception, can be compared with another surprising project of about the same time in which Diana Dors, previously regarded as a sex symbol rather than actress, was cast in a dramatic role in *Yield to the Night* (J. Lee Thompson, 1956).

Olivier appeared in his first film in 1931, but his reputation rested mainly on his stage performances. By the late 1970s, he had achieved such stature that an interviewer could introduce him as "the greatest actor in the world" with no apparent fear of contradiction.[10] It was often forgotten that during the 1930s both Alexander Korda and Hollywood sought to turn him into a star in the romantic-hero mold. Korda came closest to achieving this in *Fire over England* (William K. Howard, 1937), in which Olivier plays a dashing young courtier for whom the aging Elizabeth I (Flora Robson) develops an infatuation, and his most successful Hollywood role was as Heathcliff in *Wuthering Heights* (William Wyler, 1939). His status as a star was enhanced by the publicity surrounding his relationship with Vivien Leigh when they were both married to other partners.

Yet Olivier did not fit comfortably into the established formulas of stardom. During the 1930s, Graham Greene compared him to Robert Donat, whom he thought "the best film actor – at any rate in star parts – we possess." He regarded Olivier as Donat's nearest rival but felt that "Mr. Olivier's acting is of the nerves: it demands an audience and a partner."[11] This comment appeared in a review of a Korda production, *Knight without Armour* (Jacques

Feyder, 1937), in which Donat starred with Marlene Dietrich and was thus, according to Greene, acting without a partner. Two decades later Olivier found himself in a similar situation, with the added complication that he was a highly regarded stage actor who stood for "craftsmanship, professionalism, practical intelligence and the highest seriousness," whereas his costar was a Hollywood sex symbol who epitomized the "dumb blonde" stereotype.[12]

*The Prince and the Showgirl* was adapted by Terence Rattigan from his own stage play *The Sleeping Prince*. The title was changed to give equal weight to Monroe's role as Elsie Marina, the showgirl who captures the interest of the prince regent of a mythical European nation at the time of George V's coronation. Apparently Olivier would have preferred to work with Leigh, by then his wife, with whom he had appeared in the 1953 stage production. According to Donald Spoto, Olivier at first regarded Monroe as "merely a Hollywood product," and the critics did not understand why he was demeaning himself by becoming involved "in so obviously a commercial enterprise."[13]

The situation was complicated by Monroe's desire to be recognized as a "serious" actress. With this in mind, she was taking lessons in Method acting from Lee Strasberg, but Olivier was the least likely director to have sympathy for this approach. He insisted that he worked "mostly from the outside in" and ridiculed the efforts of Method actors to find the inner motivations of their characters.[14] Yet even this apparent opposition between the two performers was not as simple as it seemed. Olivier stressed the childlike aspect of Monroe's star persona, observing that she was "happy as a child when being photographed," but he was also wont to describe acting as "a masochistic form of exhibitionism" with "an immaturity about it."[15] This underlying sense that acting may be a childish pursuit helps to account for the nervous energy that Greene found in Olivier's persona, and it is certainly evident in his portrayal of the regent, whose masculine pomposity seems designed to conceal an insecurity as great as that for which his costar was already legendary.

The expectations aroused by the pairing of this odd couple affected critical responses to the film. Some critics felt it lived up to its dubious billing: Pauline Kael refers to "Miss Monroe's polymorphous perverse non-acting," while David Thomson suggests that Olivier was so "elementally opposed to his blancmange partner" that he built his part "around the clenched tics of a monocle and an accent like a mouth-sore."[16] On the other hand, Richard Schickel refers to Olivier's "marvelously sly and fully realized comic performance."[17] Other critics thought that Monroe's performance showed up the theatrical backgrounds of the film's British actors. Spoto refers to a sequence in which the regent brings Elsie to the embassy to seduce her but then ignores her to conduct state business on the telephone. As Elsie eats the meal he has provided and slowly gets drunk, Spoto suggests that Monroe steals the scene "right under Olivier's patrician nose."[18] Graham McCann also praises the "suggestiveness and subtlety" of her performance.[19]

**Figure 35.** The actor and the sex symbol: His Royal Ducal Highness (Laurence Olivier) is formally introduced to Elsie Marina (Marilyn Monroe) in *The Prince and the Showgirl.*

After her death, Olivier expressed a greater appreciation of Monroe's talents, acknowledging that "no one had such a look of unconscious wisdom, and her personality was strong on the screen." He now thought that "she gave a star performance" in *The Prince and the Showgirl.*[20] Like all star performances, it is reflexive, drawing on the star's onscreen and offscreen past, as in the sequence in which the regent is introduced to Elsie in the theater and her shoulder strap breaks, just as it had done when Monroe first met Olivier in New York a few months earlier (Figure 35). It is also a star performance because, as McCann suggests, "Monroe seems to hide behind nothing, revealing herself both physically and emotionally: she . . . speaks the way she always speaks."[21] As the regent, Olivier hides behind a uniform, makeup, and a Hungarian accent. He is part of the world of deceit and disguise that threatens to cause a world war, and it is Elsie who exposes the young king's plot to create an alliance with Germany and restores harmony to the royal party.

The British equivalent to Monroe in the 1950s was Diana Dors. Yet the "blonde bombshell" persona meant something rather different in the British context. She was unlike other British female stars of the time not only because of her ample physical proportions but also because she played working-class roles. Her sexual allure was coded as "excessive" and often had criminal connotations. In *Good Time Girl* (David MacDonald, 1948) and *The Weak and the Wicked* (J. Lee Thompson, 1953), for example, she plays juvenile delinquents whose pursuit of pleasure puts them on the wrong side of the law but who eventually reform, thanks to the efforts of a new enlightened justice system. Offscreen, Dors seemed to enjoy the glamour of stardom, and she caused

**Figure 36.** The sex symbol as actor: Mary Hilton (Diana Dors) shoots her rival in the delirious precredit sequence of *Yield to the Night,* before she is stripped of her glamour as she awaits her execution in a prison cell.

a minor sensation when she posed for a pinup photo in a fur bikini. Whereas Monroe's early death only enhanced her status as a cultural icon, however, Dors lived until 1984 struggling to cope with a failing career and ill health.

*Yield to the Night* offered Dors "the chance to transcend her public persona and demonstrate her dramatic prowess," and the preproduction publicity stressed that she welcomed the chance to play "a really strong dramatic role."[22] The film centers on a prison cell where Mary Hilton is confined after being sentenced to death for a murder that we see her commit in the opening sequence. Flashbacks show the events leading up to the murder, but the suspense is built around Mary's anxious wait to hear if she will get a reprieve. The reprieve does not come, and the film ends with Mary being taken to her execution. Dors's involvement certainly helped in finding an audience for such a downbeat story but, as Pam Cook notes, the critics found it difficult to take her performance "seriously" because "the blonde bombshell image was so firmly established."[23]

A powerful indictment of capital punishment, the film was highly topical in that its production coincided with the execution of Ruth Ellis, the last woman to be hanged in Britain.[24] As Christine Geraghty suggests, it uses its star's persona to set Mary's "lack of pretensions . . . against the upper-class arrogance of the woman she kills."[25] In this way, the film plays with the tensions between the social and erotic connotations of her star image. The precredit sequence begins with a close-up of a woman's legs, evoking the familiar tendency to objectify and fragment the female body (Figure 36). As we may have already realized, these are the legs of Dors/Mary, but the sudden transition from the killing to a prison cell (omitting the trial) confronts us with the star stripped of her glamour. Mary's feet hurt in her prison shoes, and one of the flashbacks is introduced by her memory of the other woman's legs.

The ordered progression of the flashbacks, which Mary narrates in a self-possessed tone, contrasts with the visual style of the opening, whose fragmentation and canted shots express the obsessive feelings that entrap her as much as the actual prison. This tension blurs the boundaries between dream and reality, inside and outside, light and dark, so that the murder and the execution are seen simultaneously as the outcome of a nightmare logic and everyday social conditions. The star's performance is a major element in the film's impact but, while her persona contributes to the unsettling effect of the narrative, the idea that she could "act" proved as distracting to the critics as Olivier's involvement in a farce like *The Prince and the Showgirl.*

## THE THEATRICAL–TELEVISION–FILM NEXUS: PINTER, HARE, AND POLIAKOFF

As in all national cinemas, the adaptation of plays and novels (and not just by British writers) has been a constant feature of the British cinema. However, the close relations between theatrical and film culture in Britain also encouraged many playwrights to take a direct interest in film production. The "quality" films of the 1940s owed as much to the screenplays of Nöel Coward and Terence Rattigan as they did to the documentary movement. John Osborne was a key figure in the British New Wave, not only as the author of *Look Back in Anger* and *The Entertainer* (although not of their screenplays) but also as one of the founders of Woodfall Films (see Chapter 3).

By the 1960s, television had emerged as a medium that could provide dramatists with new outlets. Both the BBC and the commercial ITV network produced drama series that emphasized the realist techniques thought to be most suitable to the medium, but they also allowed room for more experimental approaches. The result was the development of what Babington has called "the theatrical–television–film nexus of British film."[26] One of the earliest, and most innovative, dramatists to take advantage of this new situation was Harold Pinter.

During the 1960s, Pinter produced a succession of disturbing and often controversial plays for stage, radio, and television. Often seen as contributions to the Theater of the Absurd, a term coined to describe the work of playwrights like Samuel Beckett and Eugène Ionesco, Pinter's stage plays used spare and cryptic dialogue, punctuated by carefully planned silences, to create a sense of menace in what would otherwise be rather banal situations. It is arguable, however, that his major achievement was his work for film, especially the three screenplays that he wrote for the American director Joseph

Losey, who had been working in Britain since being blacklisted by Hollywood in the 1950s. Pinter went on to write imaginative screenplays for numerous directors, but it was his collaboration with Losey on *The Servant* (1963), *Accident* (1967), and *The Go-Between* (1971) that proved most influential.

Pinter's screenplays are mostly adaptations of novels by other writers, but he usually manages to assimilate the novelist's vision into his own distinctive style and vision. What is not said is often more important than what is said in his work in all media – a quality often associated with the national character. In particular, critics praised the films with Losey for their subtle depiction of the British class system and the tensions that lie beneath the surface of social decorum. Since Losey was American and Pinter the son of a Portuguese-Jewish immigrant, their films offered the perspective of outsiders who noticed details that might escape the attention of native observers.

The central tension in their films is between the theatrical quality of daily life and the reality that lies behind the mask. As Margot S. Kernan remarked in a suggestive review of *Accident,* "the ultimate persuasiveness of the film stems from its lyrical evocation of physical reality – fields and trees, arms, hands, sun-dappled skin – while involving us with people who are trying as hard as they can to deny this reality."[27] The films hinges on a traumatic encounter with reality that Stephen (Dirk Bogarde) undergoes in the opening sequence when a car crashes outside his house. He rescues a young woman (Jacqueline Sassard) from the overturned car but finds that her male companion (Michael York) is dead. The crash occurs offscreen during a long-held opening shot of the house at night, as if what is real cannot be shown, and this will prove to be one of the basic principles of the film's style.

Stephen evidently knows the young people, but we do not know why he conceals the woman's presence from the police. As she lies on a bed in his house, he watches her leg move spasmodically, and there is a sudden flashback to her foot stepping on the face of the dead youth as she climbed from the car, quickly followed by another cut to the smiling face of the same young man, very much alive.[28] We discover that he is William, an aristocratic student at Oxford University, where Stephen is his tutor. Their conversation is interrupted by the arrival of Anna, the woman from the car, who is reputedly an Austrian princess and also Stephen's student. The abrupt cuts define the flashbacks, which make up most of the film, as Stephen's involuntary memory of recent events. Losey described the accident itself as a "catalyst" that forces suppressed feelings to the surface, and Anna is also a catalyst whose presence disrupts the lives of the people she encounters.[29]

The narration proceeds more or less chronologically until it reaches the point at which the flashbacks began. However, even though there is now plenty of dialogue, the film conveys the sense that the words do not express what the characters are really thinking. Beverle Houston and Marsha Kinder describe the effect: "just as the characters don't understand each other's behavior, we don't know anyone's full motivation," and we are forced "to play the same game as the characters – trying to make things out within a limited field of observation."[30] Although Stephen teaches philosophy and his colleague Charley (Stanley Baker), who becomes Anna's lover, is an archaeologist who often appears on television, Pinter and Losey show that these educated and articulate people "still don't have many answers" (Figure 37).[31]

The narrative structure stresses Stephen's inability to escape his past and leaves us wondering how much what we see has been affected by his subjective perception of events. There is no voice-over commentary (as in *Yield to the Night*) to remind us that the narration represents his memory, but he is present in almost every sequence. While he seems to resist his own evident attraction to Anna, he is disturbed to find that she is having an affair with Charley and then that she has agreed to marry William. The rivalry among the men remains largely unspoken but is acted out in a series of verbal and physical games, while Anna's largely silent presence gives few clues as to her feelings and turns her into a blank screen on which the men project their desires and anxieties. When the narration returns to the present, Stephen takes advantage of Anna's shocked state to rape her, although (inevitably) this occurs offscreen. He then returns her to her residence and prepares to resume his "normal" family life.

The final shot repeats the opening shot of the house, except that it is now daytime and Stephen is playing with his children. On the soundtrack, we hear the sound of a car approaching just like at the beginning and, as Stephen and the children go inside, there is a crash. James Palmer and Michael Riley argue that "the repeated sound of the car accident . . . is best understood as both the third-person narration's metaphor for Stephen's ongoing moral tragedy – an assertion of the inescapable presentness of the past – and also as subjective sound, what Stephen's mind figuratively hears and cannot evade."[32] Since the family dog runs away during this shot, there is also an odd sense that this may be *another* accident, underlining the futility of the attempt to shut out the real. The dog's behavior was apparently the result of an "accident" in the shooting but, coupled with several other animal images in the film, it becomes a fortuitous metaphor for the resistance of nature to human control.[33]

Although Stephen initially appears to be a more sympathetic character than the aggressive and boorish Charley, the film often hints at an affinity between the two men that Stephen is reluctant to acknowledge. One critic has suggested that they are "absolute monsters, and they know it," and there were many complaints that it was difficult to identify with any of the characters.[34] Losey responded that he wanted us "to feel sympathy with everybody in one way or another, and not with any particular person," but the problem of identification is one that arises when critics judge Pinter's work by the standards

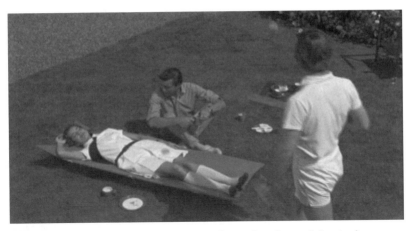

**Figure 37.** "I'm so comfortable": Anna (Jacqueline Sassard) lies in the sun as Steven (Dirk Bogarde) and William (Michael York) compete for her attention in *Accident.*

of the well-made play or classical narrative cinema.[35] *Accident* involves the spectator in deciphering the relations between inner and outer experience, a tension that also involves the relations between Pinter's elliptical dialogue (which constantly makes us imagine what is unsaid) and the vividness of the images.

A similar tension between the theatricality of public life and the pressures of repressed reality informs the work of David Hare and Stephen Poliakoff. They both emerged from the so-called fringe theater movement of the late 1960s and early 1970s, which sought to develop new forms of political drama. Hare was an active participant in the Portable and Joint Stock companies, and Poliakoff, who was younger, also made his debut in similar circumstances. Both moved into the "theatrical–television–film nexus" at a time when the boundaries between television and film were becoming blurred, partly because of an increased use of film in television "plays" and partly because of the growing involvement of television companies in film production.

While their stage plays were already "filmic in scope and scale," critics have often found the films of Hare and Poliakoff too "theatrical."[36] They have both directed several of their own screenplays, but their films have been relegated to the "fringe" in most accounts of recent British cinema. In these films, as in their later plays, both dramatists move away from the "agit-prop" methods of their earlier work, but the result is a "kind of hybrid 'social art' cinema" that critics find hard to classify.[37] Their films illustrate a development that C. W. E. Bigsby noted in the work of many British dramatists at this time who began "to explore not just the lines of force which connect private and public experience, but the uncertain language which is the imperfect tool of that exploration," thereby questioning "the nature of the real, which these playwrights had once assumed so self-evident."[38]

As Karen DeVinney suggests in a discussion of two of Hare's television films, his work depends on "linking political and ethical decline to his characters' personal lives," and it does so by creating "a charged viewpoint" in which the subjective camera comes up against what Hare calls the 'thingyness' of the film medium."[39] In this respect, the films of both Hare and Poliakoff owe much to the techniques developed in Pinter's screenplays. Although Julian Petley thought that Hare would be embarrassed if "the dreaded epithet 'Pinteresque'" were applied to his work, the parallels are very apparent in the first feature films directed by the two playwrights, Hare's *Wetherby* (1985) and Poliakoff's *Hidden City* (1987).[40]

Petley insists that Hare differs from Pinter because of "the care he takes to place his characters' inner turmoils at a very specific political, ideological and national conjuncture." In *Wetherby,* the specific conjuncture is the condition of Britain under Margaret Thatcher, and the film is certainly more politically explicit than *Accident;* but its flashbacks work in a very similar way. Instead of an accident, the catalyst in *Wetherby* is the suicide of a young man, John (Tim McInnerny) who infiltrates a dinner party given by Jean (Vanessa Redgrave) and then returns the next day to shoot himself in front of her. Jean is a schoolteacher, and her friend Marcia (Judi Dench) a librarian but, like the professors in *Accident,* their knowledge does not provide answers to the problems in their own lives. They dislike Nixon and Thatcher, but the flashbacks reveal that Jean's personal life is as compromised as their politics.

The flashbacks go much further back than those in *Accident,* but when the bloody suicide triggers Jean's memories of her adolescence in the 1950s, the link between present and past is made in a series of shots not unlike those in the earlier film. There is a sudden cut from Jean's horrified reaction to an exterior shot of her cottage, over which we hear her cry out, "No! No!" and then there is another cut to a young woman who cries out, "Yes! Yes!" in the throes of lovemaking. We soon discover that this is Jean's younger self (played by Redgrave's daughter Joely Richardson), and the film sets up a parallel between her shock and confusion in the present and the events leading up to the death of her airman fiancé in Malaya, for which she blames herself because she suppressed her own feelings and did not ask him to stay with her.

There are also flashbacks to the more recent past as the police and the other guests try to find an explanation for John's behavior. At the dinner party, everyone assumes that someone else invited him, but there is much discussion of a brief period when he left the room with Jean to repair a leak in the roof. Jean insists that nothing happened between them, but a belated flashback depicts a passionate sexual encounter. Like the flashbacks to the 1950s, these images seem like an involuntary memory, but they could be her imagination, and they hardly explain his later actions. John exhibits a strange "blankness" that Marcia also attributes to a young woman working at the library and that is even more apparent in the young woman who shows up for his funeral and moves in with Jean. Like Anna in *Accident,* these blank people function as catalysts who bring out the underlying tensions in the community.

Hare is more interested in the causes of their apathy, but the film makes it difficult to distinguish cause from effect in the relations of past and present, personal and public life. The effacement of individuality may have social and cultural explanations, but it goes so deep that the encounter with these characters has the traumatic impact of a confrontation with the real. Hare explains that he writes "love stories" because sexual passion causes "dislocation" and "offers . . . the most intense experience that many people know on earth." This intensity often pushes his work to the verge of the ridiculous, but it becomes a means of exposing "the difference between what a man says and what he does."[41] Hare's films thus fuse the cinematic and the theatrical and refuse to loosen their hold on the historical and political contexts of narratives that are often structured like dreams.

Paul Giles argues that the flashback structure in *Wetherby* implies that Thatcherism was "a cumulative product of postwar British history rather than just a grotesque aberration."[42] It represents a deep-rooted failure of the nation to embrace the possibilities for social change that emerged at the end of World War II and again in the 1960s. This sense of lost opportunity, on the personal and political levels, is also central to Poliakoff's work for theater, film, and television.

*Hidden City* also refers back to World War II, but not through subjective flashbacks. Instead, a kind of collective memory is evoked by the discovery of a film that apparently exposes the disastrous effects of a wartime experiment using radiation. James (Charles Dance), a middle-aged writer and educator, is working on the effects of the mass media on children, but his sterile personal life is disturbed when he meets Sharon (Cassie Stuart), a young single mother who shows him some disturbing images that have been spliced into an innocuous documentary on rural life. In their efforts to find the films in which more footage has been spliced, they discover a vast bureaucratic empire of low-grade secrets, including a network of tunnels beneath London. Sharon comments that "they're so drowning in secrets that they don't know where the important ones are anymore."

When Sharon claims that her apartment has been ransacked by men apparently looking for the film, James tells her that she is suffering from "paranoia," and a friend later accuses him of being "paranoid" after he is attacked in the street. It turns out that they *are* being followed, not because of the film but because James has picked up from a garbage dump the medical records of an unnamed public figure who is suffering from "schizophrenia." As the couple wander through contemporary London, dominated by modern buildings and construction sites, the film stresses the visual continuity between the city in the old film and the places they visit. The past haunts the present but, because it is hidden and repressed, there is a kind of cultural amnesia that manifests itself in mental disorder.

The hidden film is supposedly a documentary, but it is edited like a fiction film. Its black-and-white images, evoking postwar film noir, have a nightmare quality that infiltrates the drab color images in the present. James's interest in children with learning disabilities also suggests that modern technology is merely amplifying the effects of the repressed past. He visits a friend who has found a way to videotape his dreams and, when James begins to describe one of his dreams about his childhood, the friend says that he has it on video and begins to show it. James then wakes up in bed in Sharon's apartment, apparently redefining this sequence as a dream within a dream, but the possibility of recording dreams simply intensifies the blurring of the boundaries between personal and public experience, and between documentary and fantasy, that the film sees as a symptom of the decline of the national culture.

## WE MEAN BY SHAKESPEARE: *HENRY V* AND *SHAKESPEARE IN LOVE*

In *Wetherby* Jean asks her class, "Is Shakespeare worth reading even though it's only about kings?" That she even raises this question defines her as a progressive teacher who does not stick unquestioningly to the prescribed curriculum. Most Britons have their first encounter with Shakespeare in school and are taught to regard his plays as the crowning achievement of the national culture. Three years after Hare's film, the Thatcher government enacted the Great Education Reform Bill that reaffirmed Shakespeare's importance to the National Curriculum. In the following year, the commercial success of Kenneth Branagh's film of *Henry V* initiated a new wave of Shakespeare adaptations and provoked widely different responses to its cultural significance.

Shakespeare wrote his plays in the late sixteenth and early seventeenth centuries for a theater company in which he was an actor and investor. In the centuries since his death, the plays have been continually read and performed, and their characters and language are familiar components of everyday life. As Jonathan Bate puts it, "the Shakespearian temperament was seen to match the English temperament: empirical, sceptical, unsystematic, ironic" and, while some of these qualities were not always unreservedly admired, he was elevated to the status of the "national poet."[43] However, his "genius" transcended national boundaries, and his plays have been staged and filmed all over the world. American critic Harold Bloom has recently declared that, "if any author has become a mortal god, it must be Shakespeare" and that "he has become the first universal author, replacing the Bible in the secularized consciousness." He even asks, "can we conceive of ourselves without Shakespeare?"[44]

If Shakespeare created the modern sense of what it means to be "human," as Bloom suggests, he also had an enormous impact on what it means to be British. The history plays, in particular, create "a myth of England" that has often been used in support of a chauvinist nationalism but, as Bate points out, "for Shakespeare . . . national identity is ragged around the edges," and he "has survived and been made to matter as a voice of radical culture, not just established culture."[45] His plays have such power because they open up to divergent, often opposed, interpretations, but this is because they resist being confined within the ideological frameworks within which critics and directors often try to place them. Passages quoted out of context can be used to produce meanings that suit a specific argument, but we need to recognize that "Shakespeare doesn't mean: *we* mean *by* Shakespeare."[46]

Many literary critics view Shakespeare as a poet rather than a playwright, but the plays continue to attract large and diverse audiences in the theater. Film adaptations have broadened this audience still further, although both literary and dramatic critics often lament the changes made to adapt the plays to a new medium. Branagh's film versions have proved especially controversial. Since *Henry V*, he has directed and starred in a spirited *Much Ado about Nothing* (1993), a full-text adaptation of *Hamlet* (1996), and a musical version of *Love's Labours Lost* (2000), as well as several non-Shakespeare films.

These films grow out of Branagh's earlier work as a stage actor for the Royal Shakespeare Company and for his own Renaissance Theatre Company, founded in 1984. The RSC productions since the 1960s had established a modern approach to Shakespeare based on the innovative and challenging concepts of a number of major directors. In creating his own company, Branagh wanted "to get Shakespeare away from the big companies and into the actors' power again."[47] In some ways, this seems like an old-fashioned approach unlikely to suit the new medium, leading one critic to suggest that, "as a movie director, he has so far proved more actor-manager than auteur."[48] On the other hand, Branagh himself regards his approach, on stage and screen, as an attempt to reaffirm the plays' popular appeal and contemporary relevance. His films evidently have their roots in theatrical traditions, but they can be seen as a "welcome reminder of how much film and theatre actually have in common."[49]

A good example of Branagh's approach is the use of flashbacks in *Henry V*. These depict events from the *Henry IV* plays in which Shakespeare portrays the young Prince Hal as a rebellious youth who prefers to spend his time in taverns rather than at court. Many critics found these interpolations heavy-handed, but they are designed to help audiences unfamiliar with the earlier plays. They are also part of a strategy to adapt the play to a cultural context in which visual information is more accessible than the dense poetic images through which Shakespeare communicated on the bare Elizabethan stage. It is not just a question of information, however, since the flashbacks "help to humanize Henry V's character; by giving him memories to face they create a personal story for him," and they thus contribute to Branagh's stress on the psychological costs of the king's actions.[50]

In tackling *Henry V* as his first Shakespeare film, Branagh could not avoid comparisons, both as actor and director, with the celebrated film directed by Olivier in 1945. Olivier's film was a contribution to the war effort, with Henry leading his outnumbered soldiers to victory over the French in much the same way as the British people overcame the might of the German war machine. The film opens with a performance of the play in an Elizabethan theater, invoking the English heritage for which the war was being fought, and gradually moves into a more cinematic space until it reaches a spectacular climax with the tracking shots of the two armies riding into battle at Agincourt.

As many critics pointed out, Branagh distances himself from the chivalric view of war by depicting the same battle as a bloody struggle in the mud and by placing his own long tracking shot *after* the battle, with Henry wearily carrying the body of a boy through the battlefield strewn with the dead and dying (Figure 38). Critics were deeply divided about the ideological implications of Branagh's interpretation. John Simon argued that Branagh shows "leadership as a hard-won personal achievement, rather than, as with Olivier, the divine right of kings and movie stars."[51] For Jill Forbes, however, "Branagh's production, ostensibly much more democratic" than Olivier's, "ends up as more respectful of Henry's position," and Colin MacCabe denounced "the cultural nostalgia of Branagh's project," which was complicit with "Thatcher's hideous mimicry of Churchill."[52]

The critical differences point to a tension in the film that reaches its height after the battle. While the tracking shot offers visual evidence of the horrors of war, it is accompanied by music (composed by Patrick Doyle) that begins with a single soldier singing an anthem and swells to a rousing chorus. The discord between sight and sound creates an ambiguity that many critics chose to ignore but, as Michael Manheim suggests, it is part of an overall strategy that "radically divides our sympathies."[53] Branagh describes Henry as "a man of doubt who has to suppress his own innate violence" and who becomes part of "a highly complicated and ambiguous discourse on the nature of leadership."[54] Whereas Olivier stressed the play's concern with acting

**Figure 38.** "God fought for us": Henry (Kenneth Branagh) carries the body of a boy killed by the French through the aftermath of the battle in *Henry V.*

as a metaphor for the way in which Henry creates himself as king and eliminated the darker elements that complicate this view, Branagh depicts a man who must convince himself as much as his people.

In the opening of the play, it is uncertain whether the clergy manipulate Henry into war to preserve their own wealth or whether Henry uses them to justify his own policy. Olivier downplays this question, distracting us by having the actors playing the clerics drop and muddle their papers. In Branagh's version, Henry seems quite sincere in asking if his cause is just, but he is encouraged by the assembled noblemen who are eager to fight the French. Because of this refusal to simply celebrate or condemn Henry, the film has been seen as an instance of "a postmodern aesthetic" that makes it impossible to tell "which discourse, the critical or the nostalgic, is pulling which inside out."[55] Alison Light defines this aesthetic when she suggests that "it's as though Branagh has no style of his own, or rather a pick-and-mix repertoire which *is* his style." She argues that "Branagh is no more simply a man of the people than he is a Thatcherite entrepreneur (though there may be something of both in his make-up)" and poses the question of "how far these old polarising habits of thinking – conservatism vs radicalism, high culture vs popular – can take us in understanding and discriminating between new forms of cultural hybridity."[56]

Hybridity is, of course, a quality already present in Shakespeare's plays, even if it has been downplayed in certain nationalist and critical discourses. The plays often mix comedy and tragedy and defy conventional notions of dramatic unity. This is not to suggest that *they* are postmodern but rather that

the new interest in Shakespeare films, in the wake of *Henry V,* may be partially attributed to a cultural situation in which traditional oppositions and hierarchies are called into question. According to John Drakakis, "Shakespeare
now *is* primarily a collage of familiar quotations, fragments whose relation to
any coherent aesthetic principle is both problematical and irremediably iron-
ical," creating a complex situation in which "cultural icons, such as 'Shakespeare' . . . are both fetishized and *at the same time* are deployed in resistance
to fetishization."[57]

*Shakespeare in Love* (John Madden, 1998) might have been made to illustrate this point. Its screenplay was cowritten by Tom Stoppard, best known
for his play *Rosencrantz and Guildenstern Are Dead,* a comedy in which
two minor characters from *Hamlet* ponder their roles as the play takes place
around them, mostly offstage. Stoppard himself directed its film adaptation
in 1990 but, despite strong performances by Gary Oldman and Tim Roth, it
did not capture the public imagination in the same way as the later film.
*Shakespeare in Love* displays the same playful approach to language and conventions and applies it not to one of Shakespeare's plays but to the author
himself.

The film offers a deliberately far-fetched account of the creative process
that produced *Romeo and Juliet* and *Twelfth Night.* It is full of anachronisms,
as when Will (Joseph Fiennes) unburdens himself on the couch of an apothe-
cary who offers mock-Freudian interpretations of his dreams while the ses-
sion is timed with an hourglass. The speculation that Shakespeare was a homosexual is explained by his being seen kissing a boy actor who is, however,
really Viola (Gwyneth Paltrow), a young noblewoman in male disguise (like
her namesake in *Twelfth Night*) in defiance of the Elizabethan ban on female
actors (Figure 39). In typical postmodern fashion, the film simultaneously de-
mystifies the idea of the author, revealing the plays as a network of quotations
picked up by Will from his environment, *and* stresses the "mystery" by which
the author transforms this material into powerful and moving plays.

As Kenneth Rothwell suggests, "behind all the badinage, the movie almost
nostalgically yearns for the transcendent power of words to represent human
emotion."[58] *Shakespeare in Love* stresses the theatricality of life as well as
theater, and its cavalier treatment of history implies that the cultural heritage
represented by Shakespeare is a fiction – but no less important because of
that recognition. The plot hinges on a bet that requires Shakespeare to write
a play depicting the "truth" about love. After witnessing a performance of
*Romeo and Juliet* (starring Will and Viola as the star-crossed lovers), Queen
Elizabeth (Judi Dench) determines that he has succeeded; but even she is unable to go against the law that requires Viola's departure for America with her
husband.

**Figure 39.** Shakespeare (Joseph Fiennes) kisses Viola (Gwyneth Paltrow), in her disguise as a boy actor, during a break in rehearsals in *Shakespeare in Love*.

The theatrical performance thus convinces the queen that it captures the truth of reality, but the film underlines the fictional basis of this truth and its inability to overcome the power of social convention. In so doing, it accentuates the tension that is central to much of the "theatrical" tradition in British cinema.

# CHAPTER SEVEN

# No Sex Please – We're British

## Sex, Gender, and the National Character

The emergence of Diana Dors in the 1950s as Britain's answer to Marilyn Monroe was widely interpreted as a challenge to the restraint that traditionally prevailed in representations of sexuality in the national culture. Dors presented herself as "the first sex symbol this country ever had" but lamented that "British directors . . . are afraid of sex."[1] Sex was certainly far from absent in earlier British films, but it was usually treated discreetly, by implication and innuendo. Much the same could be said of Hollywood cinema after the introduction of the Production Code in the early 1930s, but the star system invested the films with an aura of glamour that had a sensuous and erotic appeal. As we saw in the last chapter, glamour in British films was so bound up with the class system that it often seemed quite remote from popular audiences, and sexuality was represented primarily through the chivalric codes of gentlemanly and ladylike behavior.

Glamour is, of course, partly a matter of production values, and there was, in Britain as in Hollywood, a low-budget sector of production – mainly action genres and working-class comedies – in which a more down-to-earth approach to sexuality prevailed. Yet the trappings of glamour dominated film publicity and excited the fantasies of filmgoers. It constituted the "tinsel" that was anathema to the realist critics and filmmakers who feared its effects on the national culture. John Grierson, for example, felt that the romantic plots of Hollywood films depended on "the face-to-face love-howls of hero and heroine" and wished that there could be "exclusively women's theatres which men may know to avoid."[2] On the other hand, while Alfred Hitchcock agreed that "in Hollywood films are made for women," he told André Bazin in 1954 that "in England films are still made for men, but that is also why so many studios close down."[3]

Hitchcock was probably thinking of the "stiff-upper-lip" heroics of the British war film, but his view of Hollywood cinema – shared by Grierson despite his very different conclusions – apparently contradicts the prevalent account of gendered spectatorship in much feminist film theory. According to a highly influential essay by Laura Mulvey, originally published in *Screen* in 1975, "mainstream film" assumes the male spectator as the norm, organizing narrative and spectacle so that "the determining male gaze projects its phantasy on to the female figure," which thus connotes "*to-be-looked-at-ness.*"[4] While Mulvey's argument does capture the general dynamic found in representations of sexuality and gender in modern popular culture, it needs to be modified – as Mulvey and other later theorists have recognized – to account for different genres and the complex ways in which actual spectators engage with films.

If cinema tends to reinforce traditional gender roles by representing women as the passive objects of the active male gaze, "mass culture" theorists argued that *all* spectators were encouraged to become passive consumers. It is hardly surprising, then, that a powerful critical tradition has engaged in what Andreas Huyssen calls "the gendering of an inferior mass culture as feminine."[5] In the British context, a supposedly feminized mainstream or "middlebrow" culture was set against the active response demanded by modernist high culture as well as the robust masculinity of traditional working-class culture (both of which inspired the documentary movement of the 1930s).[6] This discourse was accompanied by concerns about the impact of American popular culture on social and gender relations in Britain.

The journalist who wrote in the *Daily Express* in 1927 that "the bulk of our picture-goers are Americanised" (quoted in Chapter 5) added that it was "mostly women, who, to all intent and purpose, are temporary American citizens."[7] During the 1930s, as Geoffrey Macnab points out, the Hollywood star system and the rapid growth of the advertising industry implied that glamour was no longer "the exclusive preserve of high society" and "was now accessible to all."[8] Mass culture thus threatened traditional class distinctions as well as gender relations. The arrival of many actual (mainly male) American citizens in Britain during World War II provoked a moral panic, leading a Home Office study to worry about the effect on "girls brought up on the cinema, who copied the dress, hairstyles, and manners of Hollywood stars."[9]

The attraction of Hollywood glamour was all the more powerful in comparison with the drabness of everyday life in wartime, and the discourses of the People's War sought to harness and contain the appeal of American popular culture. It was the unsettling effect of the war itself, the constant danger and the prolonged separation of families, that created the conditions in which traditional values came under pressure. As Cate Haste remarks, "the war entered the fabric of everyone's lives, disrupted the continuity of family life and offered new opportunities, experiences and choices to individuals released from the normal sanctions on sexual behaviour."[10] Many wartime and postwar films register the impact of these changes, but Alexander Korda's *Perfect Strangers* (1945) makes highly reflexive use of the star system and its gender codes to explore the disorienting effects of the war.

The film deals with the transformation of an "ordinary" couple, Robert (Robert Donat) and Cathy (Deborah Kerr), during a three-year separation while they are both serving in the navy. When they finally meet again, each expects to find that the other is still as unprepossessing and inhibited as in their prewar lives. They find it difficult to adjust to their new identities, but they eventually reconcile, emerging as a dynamic and self-confident couple ready to meet the challenges of the postwar years.

The film was made under very difficult conditions, and critics disliked "its cardboard sets and caricatured characters." The *Monthly Film Bulletin* called it "a superficial film which assumes that all that is needed for marital happiness and success in life is physical well-being and glamour" and, more recently, Robert Murphy has agreed that "the transformation is so complete that they do indeed appear perfect strangers and their shared experience of a failed marriage seems a flimsy and unconvincing basis for a happy new relationship."[11] These objections are, however, made from a realist perspective that is quite out of sympathy with the film's self-conscious construction as a modern fable.

In the opening sequences, the stars' identities are hidden, Donat's behind a moustache, Kerr's behind a runny nose (Figure 40), but their familiar features and star personas emerge once they escape from the confinement of their small and dingy apartment. The whole central portion of the film consists of a symmetrical pattern of intercut sequences that depict their parallel experiences during their separation. One of Robert's crewmates deduces from Cathy's picture that she is "quiet" and dependable but not much "fun," while Cathy explains that her husband is "dependable" but admits that he is no Clark Gable. After they meet again, he acknowledges that he was "a little lacking in star quality" and she admits that she was "not exactly a pin-up girl."

Both are tempted to have affairs, but the film makes quite clear that they do not succumb. There is no depiction of sexual activity and no suggestive ellipses of the kind often used in Hollywood melodramas. However, given the audience's knowledge of, on the one hand, the actual pressures on sexual relations under these conditions and, on the other, the conventions of romance, it would be easy to imagine that the issue is sexual infidelity. Cathy assures Robert that she is still "a respectable married woman," but she thinks that it is "downright immoral" to expect her to "behave like a wife" after three years apart. At the end, the stars embrace romantically in a window seat in their apartment that is now much brighter because the wall that blocked the light has been demolished by bombs. The effect draws on the actual experiences of the spectators, but it also depends on the awareness that these are idealized characters – whose glamour is enhanced not contradicted by their uniforms – who embody the fantasies on which popular cinema thrives.

**Figure 40.** Stars in disguise: Robert (Robert Donat) and Cathy (Deborah Kerr) at the start of "the most exciting day in their lives" in *Perfect Strangers*.

## WHAT'S IT ALL ABOUT? *DARLING* AND *ALFIE*

At the end of his survey of "changing values" during World War II, John Costello argues that, despite an "immediate post-war reaction" against the changes, "the trend to permissiveness was firmly established with the commercialization of eroticism in the films, television, and advertising industries which had followed the lead of the wartime pin-ups and girlie magazines."[12] The career of Diana Dors offers support to this argument, although she was very much an exception to the rule in British cinema during the 1950s when, according to producer Joseph Janni, "sex was regarded, if it was regarded at all, as an exclusively Continental pursuit."[13] This is certainly an exaggeration, but it is true that sexual women in British films of this decade were often played by foreign actresses, usually French, Italian, or Swedish, culminating in the casting of Simone Signoret in *Room at the Top* (see Chapter 3).[14]

According to Janni and many others, the turning point came with the British New Wave films that shifted the balance away from the middle-class southern English culture that was so often identified with the British "national character." In British cinema, as in the culture at large, the stifling censorship apparatus quickly crumbled, and sexual themes became a commonplace in mainstream films and in the now more visible pornography industry. As Haste suggests, "sex was politicised in the 1960s," most notably by the tabloid journalism surrounding the Profumo Affair in 1963, which led to the downfall of the Conservative government and "unlocked the outrage about declining moral standards which had built up during the 1950s." Haste comments that, "as the political currency of sex changed, so did its commercial currency," with the result that sex ceased to be "private and secretive" and "became suddenly public, available and accessible."[15]

A much-quoted article published in *Time* magazine in 1966 presented London as "a city steeped in tradition, seized by change, liberated by affluence" and asserted that "Victorianism was only a temporary aberration in the British character, which is basically less inhibited than most."[16] Sexual freedom and changing gender roles were a central feature of the youth culture that focused international attention on "swinging London" in the 1960s, but the changes were hardly uncontested, and the forces of reaction soon set in. Two key films of the mid-1960s, *Darling* (John Schlesinger, 1965) and *Alfie* (Lewis Gilbert, 1966), illustrate the "social division, ambiguities in practices and duplicities in behaviour" that Haste sees as characteristic of the period.[17] With their youthful protagonists, played by rising stars Julie Christie and Michael Caine, these films offered female and male versions of the new sexual attitudes, while raising awkward questions about the point of view from which they observed the characters.[18]

Both films are narrated by their title characters, although the narration is presented in quite different ways. Diana's voice-over, in *Darling,* is introduced by a male interviewer and represents her "story" as she looks back on it for a women's magazine. The images often contradict her words, and the film includes events about which she could not have known at the time. Many critics felt that the film thus distances itself from her and discredits her approach to life. Carrie Tarr stresses the film's use of "a formidable battery of devices to prevent possibilities of identification with the female point of view," but other critics suggest that the narrative, in which Diana becomes a celebrity but fails to achieve happiness, does not cancel out the impact of the images of a free and independent young woman.[19] Christine Geraghty argues that "from a female viewpoint . . . , the presentation of Diana's sexuality may suggest that pleasure on one's own terms is imaginable if not narratively possible," and Moya Luckett includes *Darling* among a number of 1960s British films that "heralded a new feminine perspective marked by the importance of sexual expression to self-identity."[20]

The tone of the film is established during the opening credits, which appear over shots of a workman putting up a large poster on a billboard. The new poster is pasted over an image of starving African children and eventually turns out be an advertisement for Diana's "story" in a magazine called *Ideal Woman* (Figure 41). While the satiric intent is blatantly apparent, this opening also implicates the film in the world of publicity and image making (because the magazine article, after all, provides its narration). On the one hand, the film insists on its allegiance to the working-class realism of the British New Wave, with which both its director and producer (Janni) were as-

**Figure 41.** The poster is finally up on the billboard at the beginning of *Darling*, introducing Diana (Julie Christie), who begins to narrate the story that it advertises.

sociated; on the other, it gains much of its energy from the sophisticated and cynical screenplay (by Fredric Raphael).

The black-and-white cinematography affirms the film's realist credentials, insisting on the difference between the superficiality of the fashion and advertising industries and more serious and authentic cultural traditions. These are represented mainly by Robert (Dirk Bogarde), a television journalist with whom Diana has an affair. Together they visit an outspoken old poet who stands for "a certain flinty integrity," as Robert puts it, that now seems old-fashioned. Robert is caught between his convictions and his attraction to Diana. In one of their happiest moments together, they arrive at a hotel with luggage they have just bought and throw the newspapers with which they have stuffed the cases on the bed, revealing a headline referring to "lost hope" for trapped miners.

What might be called the realist and satiric discourses in the film thus both seem to work against Diana, but the effect is complicated by the impact of Julie Christie's star persona. In Schlesinger's previous film, *Billy Liar* (1963), she appeared as a free-spirited young woman who offers to make the fantasies of the title character come true. She invites him to leave the northern industrial city where they grew up and come to London with her. Billy decides to stay but, for Philip French, the ending of this film epitomized a major shift in British culture: "When Liz caught the midnight train to London at the end, the camera may have remained to follow Billy . . . , but spiritually the film-makers had a one-way ticket to ride south with Miss Christie."[21]

Julie Christie became "the chief symbol of liberated womanhood in Swinging London" and, as we have seen, it is possible to argue that her star image "transcends the pessimism of *Darling*'s narrative closure."[22] There is certainly a tension between the attractiveness of the star and a narrative that uses her as a symbol of the social trends that it denounces. While the satire exposes the superficiality of the images manipulated by the fashion and advertising industries, Christie/Diana embodies what Geraghty calls "a self-confidence based on but not limited to a new approach to fashion and style."[23] Many critics viewed this tension between condemnation and fascination as a sign of incoherence and cynicism.

Alexander Walker objected that the film lacked a "strong moral positive," insisting that "either it should have been a more astringently moral film or she should have been a more defiantly amoral person."[24] These options, however, would simplify the effect of the film which is, any case, characteristic of a culture in which satire became a popular weapon against the "establishment" but lacked the focus and moral certainty usually demanded of the genre.

A similar, although rather simpler, ambiguity around identification and point of view is found in *Alfie*. In this film, the main character is a male representative of the affluent working class, clearly descended from New Wave protagonists like Arthur in *Saturday Night and Sunday Morning* (see Chapter 3). Writer Bill Naughton, who adapted his own stage play, had ties with northern working-class realism, but *Alfie* was filmed on location in London and, as played by Michael Caine, its title character is a cheerful cockney hedonist. The film's style owes little to the New Wave and seems more straightforwardly commercial than *Darling*. It is very much in keeping with Caine's previous film, *The Ipcress File* (Sidney Furie, 1965), in which he established his persona in the character of a secret agent who works in rather less exotic circumstances than those featured in the James Bond films.

The most striking feature of the film is that Alfie is the onscreen narrator of his own story, offering his views on his sexual conquests as they are happening. His controlling perspective is established in the opening sequence when he gets out of a car, in which he has been trying to get comfortable with one of his "birds," introduces himself, and assures us that the credits will not appear as usual at this point (Figure 42). Whereas Diana looks back on events that occurred in the past, the narration in *Alfie* is very much in the present tense, and the images never contradict what Alfie tells us. The difference between the treatment of these male and female narrators seems to confirm the judgment that "the shifts in attitudes to sexuality . . . clearly benefited men more than women."[25]

Yet Alfie's casual attitude to the women in his life – he often uses the pronoun "it" when he discusses them – is so blatant that he seems to be putting on a performance. There are strong hints that he cares more for the women

**Figure 42.** At the beginning of *Alfie,* the eponymous hero (Michael Caine) discusses the "bird" in the car behind him and then assures the audience that the credits will not appear in their usual place.

than he admits. When Gilda (Julia Foster) becomes pregnant, he refuses to marry her, but he supports her and comes to enjoy being with his son. He explains that he does not want to get involved because it will only result in pain. When he becomes seriously involved with Ruby (Shelley Winters), an older American woman, she betrays him with a younger man. He is left on the Embankment making a date with the married woman from the opening sequence, complaining that he has lost his "peace of mind" and asking, "What's it all about?"

The narrative structure thus works very much as it does in *Darling,* although the combination of didacticism and uncertainty is made more explicit. It is clear that "the audience is ultimately requested to disavow the character for his selfishness and shallowness," but the star image once again creates tensions.[26] As Murphy suggests, the device of having the character talk to the camera "disconcertingly prevents us from distancing ourselves from Alfie's blind egocentricity."[27] This device also blurs the distinction between character and actor, and Alexander Walker suggests that "Caine's throwaway, ribaldy [*sic*] ironic voice lent Alfie more humanity than his sexual reflexes warranted."[28] Jeffrey Richards goes even further when he claims that "Michael Caine's ingratiating charm as he addresses the audience directly, taking them into his confidence and engaging their complicity, made him a role model rather than an object of condemnation."[29]

As with Christie/Diana, Caine's star persona invests Alfie with a contemporary quality that is partly a matter of style and fashion. One critic suggested that, "like the new bright clothes on the new bright boys, he suggests a subterranean national character rising to surprise even the locals."[30] Caine and Christie embody the vitality of the new discourses of sexual liberation, but these films suggest that the moral issues were more complex than either the supporters or the opponents of change admitted.

## PRUDERY AND EXCITEMENT:
## THE BRITISH SEX FILM

In his survey of the British sex film, appropriately titled *Keeping the British End Up,* Simon Sheridan insists that "the images of Robin Askwith peeping through a window at a naked woman getting out of a bath, Mary Millington dressed as a nurse in black stockings and suspenders and Joan Collins squeezed into a corset with a chauffeur's cap perched on her head are just as indelible a part of our cinematic heritage as Celia Johnson and Trevor Howard embracing on a railway platform in *Brief Encounter* or Michael Caine walking menacingly along a beach in *Get Carter.*"[31] The films in question – *Confessions of a Window Cleaner* (Val Guest, 1974), *Come Play with Me* (George Harrison Marks, 1977), and *The Bitch* (Gerry O'Hara, 1979) – are hardly likely to figure prominently in lists of the best of British cinema. Nonetheless, low-budget sex films became a mainstay of the struggling film industry in the 1970s, and they cannot be ignored in discussions of the national cinema.

During the 1960s, the implications of sexual "liberation" became a major issue in many "swinging London" films, including *Darling* and *Alfie,* but the sexual activities were presented quite discreetly. Sex films began to appear, mainly pseudodocumentaries about nudism, but it was the 1970s that saw what Leon Hunt calls "the trickle-down of permissiveness into commodity culture."[32] Filmmakers, anxious to compete with television, exploited the more liberal censorship rules and, while hard-core pornography was still confined to illicit operations, usually located in clearly defined areas of the major cities, full frontal nudity and graphic depictions of (simulated) sex became more common, even in mainstream films. "Sexploitation" films were among the most popular British films of the decade.

Critics often attacked these films for their aesthetic deficiencies, but it was the defenders of public morality who were most outraged. Mary Whitehouse's persistent campaign for the restoration of traditional values began at this time, and she was one of the organizers of a much-publicized demonstration in Trafalgar Square in the summer of 1971. However, the backlash often backfired, and the producers of the sex films relished – and provoked – the publicity generated by these attacks. The result was a proliferation of discourses about sex that bore a remarkable resemblance to Graham Greene's description, at the beginning of World War II, of the "national mixture of prudery and excitement" that characterized "British sexuality."[33]

The new openness about sexuality that emerged in the 1960s should have rendered Greene's definition superfluous, but the British sex film thrived on just this mixture. *No Sex Please – We're British* (Cliff Owen, 1973) was not a sex film but rather an adaptation of a long-running West End farce that invoked the traditional view of the "national character" even as it exploited the new developments. Its frantic plot involves a bank manager's campaign against a new pornographic bookstore in the neighborhood. When packages of pornographic postcards, books, and movies are delivered to the bank in error, the staff try desperately to dispose of them in case they are suspected of having ordered them. Despite the allegedly explicit nature of the pornographic materials, they remain unseen and function mainly to provoke a series of gags based on sexual innuendo.

This updating of the traditional bedroom farce plays on the so-called sexual revolution, but the humor depends on a sense that restraint and inhibition are deeply ingrained in the national character. Much the same could be said of *Carry On Emmannuelle* (Gerald Thomas, 1978), a parody of the French erotic film *Emmanuelle* (Just Jaeckin, 1974) and its sequels – the main rivals of the British sex films.[34] It sets up a collision between the lush eroticism of the French films, in which the glamorous and sophisticated heroine has sexual adventures in exotic places, and the comedy of sexual frustration and ineptitude for which the *Carry On* series was known (see Chapter 8). Suzanne Danielle, the film's substitute for Sylvia Kristel, was, in fact, English, but many of the sex films also featured British actresses with foreign accents.

The "foreign" woman is a key iconographic feature in the British sex film, as she had been in many earlier mainstream films. In the sex films, this woman is often an "au pair girl," an increasingly common figure in affluent households at the time, whose function in the films is primarily erotic rather than domestic. In *Monique* (John Bown, 1969), for example, the eponymous French au pair (Sibylla Kay) initiates a suburban English couple into the joys of sex, seducing first the husband and then the wife. At the beginning of *Au Pair Girls* (Val Guest, 1972), four young women arrive at London airport – from Sweden, Denmark, Germany, and China – and immediately become involved in a series of erotic situations. In a twist on the usual convention, it is the British daughter of a suburban couple who arranges for the Swedish au pair to lose her virginity with a pop star. Their experiences with British men are evidently less than satisfactory, and they all fly off at the end to join the harem of an Arab oil tycoon.

The foreign – or pseudoforeign – women in sex films may suggest a desire to compete with the European "art" films that were often released in Britain on the sex-film circuit. However, as Ian Conrich points out, the British films were remarkable for their lack of "glamour and sophistication" and for the "ordinary" appearance of the naked bodies on display. He argues that, "where the European and American sex films glorify, exaggerate and make explicit their pornographic content, British sex is presented as eccentric, peculiar and ambiguous."[35] Sex-film producer and director Stanley Long referred to the "national trait that we aren't very good at being erotic" but, while he clearly meant to suggest that the sex films contested this limitation, the kind of eroticism that they purveyed was often – explicitly or implicitly – built around the failure to be "erotic" in the usual sense of the term.[36]

Perhaps the best known and most successful British sex film was *Confessions of a Window Cleaner,* which was the highest-grossing British film of 1974. Its success led to a several sequels and a rival series produced and directed by Long, beginning with *Adventures of a Taxi Driver* (1975). There were also many other sex comedies with titles like *Ups and Downs of a Handyman* (John Sealey, 1975). The picaresque narratives of these films allow the male heroes to become involved with a succession of women, moving from one compromising situation to the next. It is not their looks or potency that attracts the women but simply chance that places temptation in their way. The fantasy that the films offer is thus one of a "sexual utopia" that does not stray too far from the possible and, as Hunt suggests, is very much aware of its limits.[37]

The *Confessions* series made a star of Robin Askwith, whose persona is that of "a blond mop-topped cheeky monkey."[38] He had already appeared in several films, including *Carry On Girls* (Gerald Thomas, 1973), and starred in *Cool It Carol!* (Pete Walker, 1970), a relatively early sex film that explicitly addressed the limits of the "sexual utopia." Like Walker's later horror film *House of Whipcord* (see Chapter 9), this film develops an ambiguous and unsettling moral vision. Aptly described by David McGillivray as "a glossy and entertaining morality tale" and a "stylish and attractively witty film of our times," the film simultaneously exploits and exposes the commodification of sexuality.[39]

It begins as if it will be a conventional sex comedy in which a naive young couple from the country set out to make their fortunes in London (Figure 43). Joe (Askwith) boasts that he already has a job there as a car salesman, while Carol (Janet Lynn) dreams of becoming a model after winning a local beauty contest. In the painfully comic opening sequence, the son of the butcher for whom Joe works accidentally chops off his finger and hardly seems to notice. As Hunt suggests, it is appropriate that the film should begin with "a gag about male impairment," but it also introduces the idea of the body as meat that the film will develop later.[40] Not surprisingly, Carol's father is an undertaker who looks forward to the coming of winter when he hopes his business will improve.

On the train to London, Carol undresses in front of Joe and distracts him from the sex magazine he is reading. She tells him that she quite enjoys being looked at, and they make love in the compartment, much to the surprise of a railway worker who catches a glimpse from his signal box. Once they are in London, the tone changes when Joe soon loses their money. In order to get the photographs she needs to become a fashion model, Carol poses nude, and Joe then persuades her to sell her body. When she is with her first client, the

**Figure 43.** "Hey, Joe. Do you see all the black men?" Joe (Robin Askwith) and Carol (Janet Lynn) are amazed by their first sight of the big city in *Cool It Carol!*

camera stays with Joe outside the bedroom, and shots of him uneasily listening are intercut with close-ups of a kettle boiling. The refusal to show the sex and the blatant montage effect draw attention to the film's – and our – complicity in what is happening to Carol, and the point is made more explicitly when both Joe and Carol are hired to perform in a seedy hard-core pornographic film.

The sex comedy seems to have given way to the social-problem film exposing the evils of the sex industry. However, the tone changes once again when the couple start making money. They throw a party that is attended not only by all the characters from earlier in the film but by members of the establishment who have employed Carol's services. The allusion here is to the Profumo Affair of a few years earlier, and the film's publicity traded on this association by using an image of "a naked Lynn straddling a chair in the classic Christine Keeler pose."[41] After the party, Joe and Carol discuss the money they have been promised, but they decide they are not happy and return to their hometown. The final sequence repeats images from the beginning, but Joe and Carol now seem content with their situations.

In the actual case on which the plot was based, the couple were punished, but Walker shows them apparently none the worse for their experience. The "happy ending" defies moral and generic conventions but is quite in keeping with a film that consistently depicts the perversity of traditional moral values. When Carol asks if she can go to London, her father asks her if her "maidenhead is intact" and gives his permission – and some money for expenses – only when she assures him that it is not. As Steve Chibnall suggests, *Cool It Carol!* is "a parable of the resilient spirit and, in its rejection of orthodox morality, remains one of Walker's most dissident films."[42] In some ways, it paves the way for the sex comedies in which sexual pleasure does not usually entail punishment, but it also concludes that "fun" and "happiness" are not the same. The film thus expresses concerns about the state of British society that were shared by Mary Whitehouse and Margaret Thatcher, but it rejects their moralistic stance and their confidence that a return to traditional values would solve the problem.

## THE WATCHER AND THE WATCHED: WOMEN DIRECTORS IN THE 1990S

As in most national cinemas, the number of women occupying positions of power in the British film industry has been very small until quite recently, and women directors still represent a small minority. Muriel Box and Wendy Toye made several feature films in the 1950s. In an essay on both filmmakers, Caroline Merz argues that while they worked for "large male-dominated organisations . . . , their films do emerge as expressing and anticipating legitimate feminist concerns," but neither was able to make a major impact (although Box was influential as a producer).[43] In the 1960s and 1970s, the films dealing with changing sexual attitudes were all directed by men, and the sex films were addressed primarily to a (heterosexual) male audience. It was only in the 1990s that a number of female directors were able to make feature films that engaged with issues of sexuality and gender that had long been debated in feminist theory.

In her essay on "visual pleasure," Mulvey argued that mainstream films perpetuated the dominant patriarchal ideology, and her own films (made with fellow film theorist Peter Wollen) encouraged the idea that women filmmakers should reject traditional narrative structures and realist techniques. Their most influential film was *Riddles of the Sphinx* (1977), which addressed the topical issue of day care within a framework of psychoanalytic theory and formal experiment. The film does provide a good deal of visual pleasure, but its highly fragmented structure could only alienate audiences unfamiliar with its intellectual premises. It was thus partly by choice, as well as by necessity, that feminist filmmakers worked primarily in the fields of documentary and avant-garde cinema.

By the 1990s, the situation in the industry had changed to the extent that it became more possible for women to direct feature films, although by this time most filmmakers had to cobble together funds from a variety of different sources to get their projects made. Sally Potter turned to Russian, French, Italian, and Dutch production companies, as well as the European Co-Production Fund, to make *Orlando* (1992), an adaptation of Virgina Woolf's novel in which she incorporated many of her earlier concerns as an avant-garde film-maker into a film that gained wide commercial release. It updates Woolf's story of an Elizabethan man who is granted eternal youth and eventually turns into a woman, addressing changing attitudes to gender roles in different historical periods.

Potter's next film, *The Tango Lesson* (1997), was less well-received than *Orlando,* but it offers a witty fable about the cultural constraints that affect women's sexuality and creativity. Potter appears in her own film as a film-maker called "Sally Potter," who is working on the screenplay for a thriller but becomes distracted by her interest in the tango and, in particular, a tango dancer called Pablo Veron (who also plays himself). He teaches her to dance and, after she loses interest in the thriller when the Hollywood producers demand changes, she asks him to take part in her new film project about the tango. While Potter claims that the film is about "the attraction of opposites: between Anglo-Saxon and Latin-American cultures; between male and female; between the watcher and the watched," Claire Monk adds that it is also about "the *imbalance* of power between man and woman – a theme for which the tango itself stands as a potent metaphor."[44]

The film opens with a hand cleaning a white surface, which turns out to be a round table, viewed from above, on which a woman places a blank writing pad. When she writes the first word, "Rage," there is a cut to a color image of a woman in a red dress who is shot down as she runs away. Sally is trying to write a film treatment to sell to a Hollywood studio (based on an actual project of Potter's), but she is clearly suffering from writer's block. When she finds a crack in the wooden floor of her apartment and is informed that it should be replaced, she quickly decides to go to Paris, where she sees Pablo perform and becomes his pupil. She also goes to Argentina to explore the roots of the dance form.

By putting herself in her own film, Potter sets up a situation like that confronted by women performance artists who, she suggests in an earlier essay, "use their own bodies as the instrument of their work" and "constantly hover on the knife edge of the possibility of joining this spectacle of woman."[45] The dilemma is intensified by Sally's passionate interest in the tango, a dance form in which, at least as practiced by Pablo, the woman must follow the lead of the man and leave him room to express himself. After she dances with him in a public performance, she is stunned that Pablo accuses her of trying to dominate him, and their personal and professional relationship almost breaks down. However, she persuades him to accept the part in her film and to follow her directions.

When Sally describes a sequence in the planned film in which a couple reveal their Jewish backgrounds to each other and weep, Pablo says that he is unwilling to do it. She accuses him of not wanting to follow her lead, but we have already seen this sequence earlier in the film in which Sally and Pablo are finally brought together most obviously by their fascination with the tango but also by the Jewish cultural heritage whose significance they only gradually acknowledge. The film that we have been watching is, in effect, the film that Sally conceived and began to plan during the film. At the end, she tells Pablo that she still does not have the money to make it, but the final sequence is a utopian musical number in which the couple sing and dance, celebrating their relationship and the completion of their film.

Jewish cultural traditions also serve as a key motif in *The Governess* (Sandra Goldbacher, 1997) in which the central metaphor is photography. Set in the nineteenth century, the film tells the story of Rosina (Minnie Driver) who leaves the patriarchal confines of her Jewish family in London to become a governess in a Christian family on the island of Skye. The patriarch in this family is Charles (Tom Wilkinson), a scientist who spends most of his time in a laboratory where he is experimenting with photography. Rosina becomes his assistant and accidentally discovers the process he is seeking that will allow him to "fix" the ephemeral images produced by his camera.

As established in the opening sequences, the Jewish community is warm and supportive but stifling for women like Rosina. The film begins with male voices chanting while the women watch the ceremony from a balcony and, after her father's death, Rosina bursts in on a group of men conducting a ceremony over his body. It becomes clear that the father died while visiting prostitutes, like the ones who taunt Rosina in the street after she leaves the synagogue, and her desire to become an actress is associated with a scandalous refusal to conform to traditional gender roles. After her sister reads a maxim that insists that a true gentlewoman should never raise her eyes to meet a male gaze, Rosina announces that she would rather become a prostitute than accept the marriage that her family has arranged for her.

Instead she becomes a governess, as in the tradition of Gothic fiction, to which she alludes in one of the letters to her sister that provide the voice-over narration, but her effect on the Christian family is more like that of the au pair girls in the sex comedies discussed earlier. She conceals her Jewish identity and masquerades as "Mary Blackchurch," but the tension between her Jewish roots and her assumed Christian persona gradually gives way to that between her passionate nature and Charles's scientific detachment. His attempt to discover a way to "fix the moment" is carried out in the name of science, but Rosina sees its artistic possibilities and contests his control of the gaze. Their collaboration develops into a sexual relationship that is defined in terms of image making.

She tells him that "the ancient Hebrews expressed love for each other entirely covered," but she helps him in his research into making things visible. After they make love, she speaks of wanting to "fix this moment forever" and,

**Figure 44.** Rosina/Mary (Minnie Driver) usurps the power of the gaze as she prepares to photograph her lover's naked body in *The Governess*.

later, she photographs his naked body while he is asleep (Figure 44). He feels violated, ending their affair and going back on his promise to give her joint credit for their discovery. She takes revenge for his betrayal by giving the photograph to his wife in the middle of a family dinner. The taboo against looking at the naked male body echoes Rosina's exclusion from the ceremony over her father's dead body (she dreams that he tells her he was only sleeping). Photography is thus linked both to cultural codes in which looking involves a power relation and to a more primal association of sexuality and death.

As Lynette Felber suggests, "the film partially confirms and partially contests" Mulvey's ideas on gendered spectatorship.[46] At the beginning, Rosina's desire to be an actress is frustrated because respectable women should not make a public display of themselves, but her performance as the governess deceives those who think they have power over her. After she returns to London, she becomes a successful portrait photographer, and the ending celebrates her new independence and her control over the camera. Charles visits to sit for his portrait, but she does not ask him to stay. Her final voice-over claims that she "hardly ever thinks of those days at all," as the camera pans over her photographs and comes to rest on the portrait of Charles.

As at the end of *The Tango Lesson,* the woman artist manages to express herself despite the obstacles against which she has struggled in the rest of the film. Similar endings are also found in two low-budget features by women filmmakers, released at about the same time, that take even greater risks with their representations of female sexuality. Writing of *Stella Does Tricks* (Coky Giedroyc, 1996) and *Under the Skin* (Carine Adler, 1997), Charlotte Brunsdon suggests that they are "unimaginable without second wave feminism, but they are also post-feminist in a number of ways."[47] In other words, they are less concerned with providing positive images of women to counter the demeaning images in mainstream media than with depicting "sexual experiences from a female point of view."[48]

Both films could easily have been conventional social-problem films, depicting young women as victims of male abuse, and their plots could have provided the basis for a 1970s sex film. However, the intense focus on the body and sexuality is only one aspect of films that deal with the inner dimensions of physical experience (and abuse) in ways that are similar but subtly different. Brunsdon stresses the "Loach-like" naturalism with which Barry Ackroyd's camera captures the London settings in *Stella Does Tricks,* as opposed to the more "expressionist" work of the same cinematographer in *Under the Skin,* but both films use location shooting to set up a tension with the imaginary worlds inhabited by their female protagonists.[49]

Stella (Kelly Macdonald) is a teenage prostitute, originally from Glasgow but living in London to escape from her abusive father and stepmother. Her background is revealed only gradually through flashbacks that, however, become increasingly difficult to distinguish from fantasy sequences illustrating the stories she tells to her friends and to herself. The sequence in which Stella and her boyfriend travel to Glasgow to take revenge on her stepmother (by floating inflated condoms into her garden) and her father (by setting fire to his crotch) is apparently real but seems little different from her fantasy (or memory?) of taking her revenge as a child by setting fire to his pigeon loft.

Stella imagines (or remembers) the burning of the loft while she is apparently dying from an overdose of pills. The next shot shows her drug-addicted boyfriend asleep on his bed, and the camera pans across to Stella unconscious in an armchair. There is a cut to her sitting onstage in what appears to be a nightclub, where she is performing as a storyteller. She tells what appears to be a joke (although nobody laughs) about a visit to a psychiatrist to whom she describes her inability to dream. He tells her that this is not a problem because she has told him about her sex life and "nightmares count." The film ends as she uses the phrase with which she liked to introduce her stories, "Picture this scene."

This ending is highly ambiguous. Although the context implies that Stella is dead or dying, she may have recovered and pulled her life together. Her invitation to "picture" her story also suggests the way in which the film presents its story, relegating the sexual abuse to offscreen space where we are forced to imagine what is happening to her. Melanie McGrath aptly argues that the film makes "the point that sexual violence happens in the head as well as the bed."[50] Stella is brutalized by her pimp (James Bolam) but, when he punishes her for leaving by offering her to a group of men who rape her, the camera follows her hand as she reaches out to his. Later she sees another girl with him and denounces him to the police, but it is not clear whether she is tak-

**Figure 45.** *Under the Skin:* Iris (Samantha Morton) attracts attention as she wanders through the city at night wearing a wig that belonged to her dead mother.

ing revenge, trying to save the girl or jealous of her replacement. The ambiguity is characteristic of a film that sets up a tension between Stella's apparent resilience and our awareness of the psychological damage caused by the abuse.

The title of *Stella Does Tricks* refers to her situation as a prostitute but also to the tricks she plays as an enjoyable, but ultimately futile, means of asserting herself. She is, in many ways, still a child, one who tries to turn her reality into a game. Similarly, Adler suggests that for Iris (Samantha Morton) in *Under the Skin* "sex is like a game," but she adds that it is "an extremely dangerous game to play" because her "grip on what's real is very fragile."[51] After the death of her mother (Rita Tushingham), Iris leaves her boyfriend and has a series of casual sexual encounters with men (Figure 45). In her review of the film, Pam Cook suggests that "Iris' masquerade, and her sexual fantasies, have the quality of a children's dressing-up game in which adult sexuality is tried on but doesn't quite fit" and that "her grief provokes an exaggerated performance of sexuality that masks a longing for something else."[52]

These comments could also be applied to Stella but, in a sense, Iris's sexual behavior is more problematic because she chooses to undergo abuse. The first image is a close-up of a naked body, revealing the pores of the skin, accompanied by Iris's voice describing how she always wanted to be like her mother. She draws a stick figure on her stomach, and there is a cut to a long shot of her lying naked on a couch in a shadowy room. After a fade, another close-up shows the (clothed) stomach of Iris's pregnant sister being caressed by her mother's hand. The opening thus establishes the physical presence of the body and the concern with what is under the skin, Iris's need for attention from her mother and her ambivalence about her own possible motherhood.

The opening shots are a challenge to the feminist argument that such representations must objectify the female body (only male nudity is shown in *Stella Does Tricks*). Adler points out that the nudity occurs "only when she is alone, as if she can only reveal herself to herself" and that, in any case, "the sex is in her mind" and really happens not when she is with a man but "afterwards, when she repeats the scene in her mind like a loop."[53] Iris's first sexual encounter with a stranger is intercut with the cremation of her mother and ends with an abrupt cut to her leaving her boyfriend's bed (was she dreaming?), saying that she needs some space. The sex becomes an attempt to make contact with the real but, at the same time, it is an escape from her own reality.

As in *Stella Does Tricks*, the sexuality is far from erotic, and both films expose the power relations that sex involves. Like *The Tango Lesson* and *The Governess*, however, they also stress the ambiguity of these relations and the complex relations of the physical and the imaginary. *Under the Skin* ends with Iris, having apparently pulled her life together, singing in a nightclub. She has earlier spoken of her desire to become a singer and auditioned for a church choir, but her recovery still comes as a surprise. Yet the song she is singing, Gilbert O'Sullivan's "Alone Again (Naturally)," and the fact that her performance hardly catches the attention of the audience, suggests that her struggle is not over. All these films end with an assertion of female independence through creative performance, but they also make us aware of the constraints that are still in play.

# CHAPTER EIGHT

# Carry On Regardless

## The British Sense of Humor

n *Pimpernel Smith* (Leslie Howard, 1941), a German minister investigates the claim that the British "secret weapon" in World War II is their "sense of humor." He reads excerpts from several British writers and then dismisses the idea as a myth. The film plays on the contrast between Teutonic pomposity and the intellectual agility that enables its hero (Howard), an apparently inoffensive English professor who is actually a master of irony and disguise, to outwit the Nazi security forces on their own soil. It effectively illustrates Jeffrey Richards's claim that "the war had brought into sharp focus the meaning of England and Englishness" around such ideas as "a love of tradition, of balance and order; a belief in tolerance and humanity; and above all, perhaps, a sense of humour, that redoubtable bulwark against tyranny."[1]

The idea that a nation can have a sense of humor is in itself quite funny, but it is a persistent factor in most accounts of British culture. As one writer on the national character put it, "the surest way to affront any Englishman is to suggest to him that he has no sense of humour."[2] Presumably the same could be said for the Scots, Welsh, and Irish, as well as women from all parts of the nation, but (as in many other cases) the British sense of humor often appears to be predominantly English.

Of course, not all Britons have a sense of humor, and there is probably no one who finds all British comedies funny. Since films must appeal to large audiences, there is a commercial advantage to avoid giving offense, but there is no doubt that certain social groups are more likely to be the butt of jokes than others. As a myth, the idea of a national sense of humor tends to exclude those who laugh at different things, but the sheer variety of comic production ensures that the myth can never become completely stable.

It should be remembered that humor is found not only but also in "serious" films. The ability to make jokes under pressure is an aspect of the "stiff upper lip" posture, and humor is a major factor in war films, for example, although the sangfroid of the officers is quite different from the comic relief provided by the "other ranks." Through the powerful example of Shakespeare's plays, the mixing of comic and serious modes is a generally accepted feature of British cultural forms, as opposed to the demands for generic purity associated with French culture.

On this account, the British not only have a sense of humor but, because they refuse to take themselves seriously, the nation has not succumbed to political excesses, such as fascism. This idea is, to say the least, open to question but, even if it is a national myth, it is one that has often worked in favor of the national cinema. During the 1930s, as we have seen, British cinema lacked a language barrier to protect it from the competition of the Hollywood "talkies," but there was apparently a humor barrier: British audiences showed a clear preference for British comedies.[3]

While this suggests that there may be distinctive national forms of comedy, and most national cinemas produce home-grown comedies that work only in the domestic market, some comic films have succeeded in crossing national boundaries, and it is difficult to pin down what distinguishes one national tradition from another. In the case of British cinema, for example, Alfred Hitchcock associated the comic elements in his films with a tradition of "English humor based on carrying understatement to an absurd extreme," but a writer in the *New York Times* complained in 1935 about the "lack of understatement" in British comedy.[4]

As in so much of British culture, the differences in humor and comic forms often carry class connotations. In an essay published in 1963 and provocatively entitled "Have the British a Sense of Humour?" Ian Johnson distinguishes between "the music-hall tradition" and "the staider middle-class theatre or revue" tradition. He argues that the history of British film comedy consists of "the gradual drawing together" of these traditions.[5]

Jeff Nuttall and Rodick Carmichael make a sharper distinction between traditions of wit and humor, according to which the former is "aristocratic" and elitist, because "a witty man is always in some way demonstrating his superiority," while the latter is working-class and inclusive, producing "survival laughter" and "the perpetual celebration of common factors."[6] According to Nuttall and Carmichael, the comedies of wit are by definition southern in origin and conservative in orientation, as are the middle-class forms, best represented by the Ealing comedies, that fall between the two extremes. They see humor as a characteristic of working-class comedy, not confined to the north but exhibiting its strongest and most subversive forms there.

Many theories of comedy argue that it always includes a critical or subversive element that exposes the conventions on which the social order depends, and several critics have linked this subversive effect to the overturning of social norms and ideals in the tradition of "carnival" that dates back to the Middle Ages. According to the Russian theorist Mikhail Bakhtin, carnival celebrations involved a temporary suspension of social hierarchies and taboos in which the conventions of the everyday world were turned upside down.

Although Bakhtin insisted that he was dealing with a specific historical period, he argued that the medieval carnival had a lasting effect that contributed to a gradual process of social change at the end of the Middle Ages.

In opposition to Bakhtin, some critics and historians point out that carnival was simply a way of allowing people to "let off steam," thereby forestalling more serious threats to the social order, and it thus served an essentially conservative function. In a similar vein, Ian Green writes of "the double function of the comic framework" that acts as a release from censorship but then reimposes it through the "happy ending" in which the social order is restored.[7] On the other hand, Tom Sobchack cites Bakhtin to support his argument that comedies always "show traces of the utopian ideal of a democratic society that lies at the heart of the urge to ridicule authority, even when literally no chance of unseating such authority exists."[8] Film comedies thus engage with national traditions in ways that both support and subvert them and whose final effect depends on the disposition of the spectator.

## SUBVERSION AND CAMOUFLAGE:
### *THE MAN IN THE WHITE SUIT*

Both Green and Sobchack develop their arguments in discussions of the Ealing comedies, not the most obvious candidates for comparison with the boisterous and uninhibited pleasures of carnival. The different conclusions of these critics do, however, parallel the opposing views of director Alexander Mackendrick and producer Michael Balcon on the political implications of their work at Ealing. According to Mackendrick, comedy has a subversive potential because it "lets you do things that are too dangerous or that a certain audience can't accept," but Balcon insisted that the Ealing comedies were "a mild protest, but not protests at anything more sinister than the regimentation of the times."[9]

Although a number of earlier films anticipated aspects of the classic Ealing comedies, the real breakthrough came in 1949 with the release, in quick succession of, *Passport to Pimlico* (Henry Cornelius), *Whisky Galore!* (Mackendrick), and *Kind Hearts and Coronets* (Robert Hamer).[10] According to Charles Barr, *Passport to Pimlico* established a "cozy" image of British life that became a hallmark of later Ealing comedies, like *The Lavender Hill Mob* (Charles Crichton, 1951) and *The Titfield Thunderbolt* (Crichton, 1953), unlike the more acerbic films of Mackendrick and Hamer.[11] Yet *Passport to Pimlico,* despite its genial tone, does set up a tension, between identity as an inheritance from the past and as a cultural fiction, that pervades the Ealing comedies and that we have already seen in the postwar Ealing war film *The Captive Heart* (see Chapter 1).

When a group of Londoners discover a document proving that they are really citizens of the now obsolete dukedom of Burgundy, they declare independence to rid themselves of the restrictions and rationing of postwar Britain, insisting that "it's just because we are English that we're sticking up for our right to be Burgundians." They become disillusioned with their new freedom when black-market operators invade the area, and they decide to rejoin Britain. Their decision coincides with a break in the unusually hot summer weather and a return to normal British rain. While the ending stresses the need for public institutions to restrain the operations of the free market, the comedy exposes the fragile basis of national identity and the so-called postwar consensus.

Barr argues that *Passport to Pimlico* belongs to "the mainstream of Ealing production," which "distils all the nice but weakly romantic elements in the national character," whereas the films of Mackendrick and Hamer are "consciously *about* this character."[12] These directors were thus not comfortable with the atmosphere of "team spirit" that Balcon promoted at Ealing and thus unwilling to accept the reticent approach to politics and sexuality on which Balcon insisted.

Hamer directed only one of the Ealing comedies, *Kind Hearts and Coronets,* a black comedy in which Louis Mazzini (Dennis Price) takes revenge on the aristocratic family that disowned his mother because she married an Italian singer. He invents ingenious schemes for murdering all the members of the family who stand between him and the title. The film invites the spectator to enjoy its puncturing of the hypocrisy and pretensions of upper-class society, while making its murders more palatable by setting the action in the past and by casting Alec Guinness as all the unfortunate victims.

This revenge comedy includes many satirical barbs directed at conventional myths of the national character, but there is room for enjoyment of the elegance of the English language and of the luxurious settings, and the comedy depends on an ambivalent interplay of identification with and detachment from its half-English hero. The wit in *Kind Hearts and Coronets* ensures that the "excesses," of violence and sexuality, never completely disrupt the comic tone, but there is a constant unsettling "tension between the cool surface and what we are conscious of underneath."[13] Balcon was apparently disturbed by the film, but his concern was less with the social satire than with the sexual rivalry that develops around Louis, between Edith (Valerie Hobson), the genteel widow of one of his victims, and Sibella (Joan Greenwood), the seductive wife of one of his friends.

As in most other Ealing comedies, the cultural context within which the comedy operates is that of southern England, although this is the only one to focus mainly on the upper classes. The Ealing studios were located in the London borough from which they took their name, and all the major Ealing comedies were set in or near London, with the exception of three of the four directed by Mackendrick. *Whisky Galore!* and *The Maggie* (1954) were set in Scotland, whereas *The Man in the White Suit* (1951) takes place in the industrial north, as does part of the action in Mackendrick's one noncomic Ealing film, *Mandy* (1952). Only *The Ladykillers* (1955), Mackendrick's last film at Ealing, corresponds to the anglocentric sense of national identity in most other Ealing comedies.

Mackendrick was born in the United States, but his parents were Scottish and he was brought up in Scotland. After joining Ealing as a writer in 1946, his career as a director got under way when the government imposed a heavy import tax on foreign films and the Hollywood studios responded by refusing to release their films in Britain. Like the other British production companies, Ealing stretched itself to the limit to fill the gap, and Mackendrick was allowed to direct *Whisky Galore!* on location in a remote Scottish community. This modest experiment turned out to be "the most profitable film, in relation to its costs, in the history of Ealing Studios."[14]

Although *Whisky Galore!* and *The Maggie* were very popular with Scottish audiences, they came under attack for perpetuating stereotypes that ignored the realities of modern Scottish society. In both films, the modern world intrudes from outside – in the form of an English bureaucrat in the first film and an American businessman in the second – and, in both cases, the apparently simple and disempowered Scots emerge triumphant. In this way, the films work much like other Ealing comedies in which small groups of people fight against big government and big business, and their popularity may be attributed to what Richards calls "the widespread and deep-rooted hatred of modernity – the dehumanization, the exploitation and pollution that it has entailed."[15]

The Ealing comedies thus depend on a resistance to modernity identified by many commentators as an aspect of the national character that contributed to the decline of the nation in the twentieth century (see Chapter 11). Mackendrick draws on this argument in *The Man in the White Suit* in ways that complicate its application to Ealing, or at least to his own films. It is the only Ealing comedy set in the north of England, and its opening sequence establishes the familiar iconography of the northern city dominated by heavy industry. A few shots of drab streets of terraced houses later in the film almost look as if they might have been taken from *Industrial Britain* (see Chapter 2). Of course, this was not the first commercial fiction film set in the north, and the images of the textile mill recall *Hindle Wakes* (Victor Saville, 1931), produced by Balcon, and *Sing as We Go!* (Basil Dean, 1934), a Gracie Fields comedy produced at Ealing before Balcon's arrival.

Both of these earlier films use the textile industry as a background for narratives that intertwine class and gender relations, but both imply that the industrial issues have no connection with the social and cultural values associated with London and the south. *The Man in the White Suit* exposes the real source of power when a crisis in the industry provokes a telephone call to Sir John Kierlaw, an asthmatic old man, who arrives from London like Dracula descending on his unsuspecting victims. As his car speeds through the night, Mackendrick inserts a shot of a road sign that reads simply, "To the North."

The northern setting is reinforced by the accents of some of the factory workers, but the film's realism does not extend to casting northern actors in the main roles. Alec Guinness plays Sidney Stratton, the scientist who sets off the crisis by inventing a material that will last forever, while Joan Greenwood plays Daphne Birnley, the daughter of a mill owner whose attraction to Sidney leads her to break off her engagement to another owner. Both of these actors were born in London. Guinness starred in many Ealing comedies, including *Kind Hearts and Coronets, The Lavender Hill Mob,* and *The Ladykillers,* and was a character actor whose ability to adapt to the style of the film and to blend in with the other actors suited the Ealing emphasis on "team spirit." Greenwood was a more unusual choice for Ealing, since her distinctive throaty voice combined suggestions of upper-class refinement with an unmistakable sexual suggestiveness.

As we shall see, Mackendrick uses these actors to unsettle the spectator, but before we examine how he does this, we need to establish the political and cultural context in which the film was made. On the surface, the narrative seems to conform to the typical Ealing pattern of whimsically following an absurd premise through to its logical conclusion and then opting for a return to normality. Many critics interpreted the film in this way, but its treatment of science and industrial relations cannot be completely contained within this pattern.

In 1951 the Festival of Britain was intended as a celebration of a new postwar national identity, but the Conservative election victory in the same year confirmed the failure of the Labour government to deliver the promised social change. *The Man in the White Suit* is a dark comedy that grows out of this sense of lost opportunity. As Philip Kemp suggests, it depicts "a stagnant, post-Imperial Britain, terrified of change and clinging to a crumbling and threadbare past."[16] From this perspective, the owners and workers who unite to suppress Sidney's invention, because they fear it will destroy the industry, are standing in the way of progress, and the film refers to several other inventions that have not been developed for similar reasons.

Although the final disintegration of the suit eliminates the threat and restores the status quo, Mackendrick felt that the film conveyed a dark and disturbing vision of postwar British society. However, Vincent Porter argues that "Balcon outwitted Mackendrick" because the comedy defuses the social criticism, and even Kemp, who stresses the "streak of blackness" in the film, wonders "how far Mackendrick's subversive purpose got through to audiences, either then or since."[17] On the other hand, a French critic, writing in *Cahiers du cinéma* at the time of the film's release, saw it as an example of "English comedy" in which the comic effect is not at the expense of a protagonist who is "funny because he doesn't conform to social norms"; instead, "it's society that's funny, because it's at odds with itself." The film thus works to unsettle the audience because the humor "lies in seeming to agree with those who are wrong, thus making their error all the more obvious."[18]

Mackendrick insisted that Sidney is "just as selfish and self-interested as the rest of them," but his narrative function as the little man battling against authority suggests that we should identify with him.[19] Daphne jokes that he looks like a "knight in shining armor" when she first sees him in the white suit. In the final sequences, he becomes the object of a nightmare pursuit by owners and workers who want to prevent him from revealing his secret and, at one point, he ends up holding a round tabletop and a stair rail that represent the shield and sword conjured up by Daphne's romantic image.

Yet the invitation to identify with the heroic individual battling against a society opposed to progress is only part of the picture. Sidney is also a scientist who pursues his research regardless of the social consequences, a figure associated with the nuclear threat at a time when the cold war was at its height. Mackendrick originally planned to make a comic film on "the moral issue of the invention of nuclear weapons," and Sidney mentions "radioactive thurium" as an ingredient in his highly volatile formula.[20] The film thus develops a comic dialectic that pits encrusted social traditions against the fear of irresponsible scientific research.

As portrayed by Guinness, Sidney has an intelligence and charm that make him stand out from the social inertia that surrounds him, and Philip Kemp suggests that "the camouflage was a little too effective."[21] The tensions involved emerge most fully in a sequence that Kemp finds miscalculated. It occurs when the owners ask Daphne to seduce Sidney into agreeing to suppress his invention. She first negotiates a price for her services, forcing them to make explicit that they are resorting to prostitution. The effect pushes against Balcon's insistence on sexual restraint in Ealing comedies, and Greenwood plays the role with knowing enthusiasm. When she finally appears before Sidney in a seductive gown, the couple play out a romantic encounter that looks like a Gainsborough or Hollywood melodrama but that is actually a very unstable comedy of role-playing.

According to Kemp, the situation is set up so that "Sidney would supposedly like to make love to Daphne, but restrains himself because there are strings attached," while "Daphne is pretending she wants him to respond, but hopes he won't." Kemp finds that, when they embrace, "Guinness's bemused reaction conveys no sense of desire, suppressed or otherwise; while the sensuality of Greenwood's performance suggests disappointment at his lack of

**Figure 46.** "I want to see something of the world beyond this dirty town": Daphne (Joan Greenwood) tests the resolve of Sidney (Alec Guinness) in *The Man in the White Suit.*

response."[22] Indeed Sidney's single-mindedness makes him immune to Daphne's proposal that they go away together, and she mistakenly believes that he is sacrificing his own desire in the public interest. Yet, when she tells him that she wants to escape to "where people know how to live, like Italy or France," she is expressing something that lurks behind her character and thus behind the film itself (Figure 46).

The ambiguity in this sequence is typical of the film's understated style that allows us to glimpse the distinction between social role and individual character but never spells out what may or may not be going on beneath the surface. Another layer involves the role of Daphne's father, Alan Birnley (Cecil Parker), as the film's narrator, ensuring that we cannot become too closely involved with Sidney's point of view. Birnley opens the film by inviting us to share his relief that the crisis is over and thus to view the events shown in flashback from the owners' point of view. When we return to the present at the end of the film, we recognize that the film does not endorse Birnley's perspective, and the effect is to complicate the expected return to order at the end of a comedy.

Although Neil Sinyard describes Mackendrick's comedies as "films of cruelty and cunning as well as charm that end ambivalently and which deny any kind of comfortable audience identification," many critics feel that the ending of *The Man in the White Suit* supports Porter's view that the comedy undermines the film's political criticism.[23] The old order is restored after Sidney is humiliated when the suit made of the new fabric falls apart, leaving him facing an angry mob in his underwear (Figure 47). Nevertheless, despite the failure

**Figure 47.** "The crisis is over now": Sidney stands unsuited and humiliated before a crowd of relieved workers and bosses at the end of *The Man in the White Suit.*

of the new material, its effect has at least demonstrated the fragility of normal social arrangements, and the final sequence suggests that Sidney will go on working.

Although the disintegration of the suit may seem to evade the issues that the film has raised, Mackendrick refuses to allow the comic ending to become complacent or sentimental. Birnley has the final word as narrator, expressing the industry's relief at Sidney's failure, but he looks down to see Sidney leaving the mill and walking off jauntily after a new idea occurs to him. On the soundtrack, we hear the electronic noise that Mackendrick devised to represent the workings of Sidney's apparatus and that comes to signify "the literally bubbling energy of creative work and imagination."[24]

## THE VOICE OF THE BELLY:
## THE *CARRY ON* FILMS

The Ealing comedies were so successful in the United States that the American perspective on British comedy changed radically. The *New York Times* critic who found British comedies of the 1930s lacking in understatement was comparing the smooth ensemble playing of Hollywood screwball comedies with the broad comic styles of British performers like Gracie Fields and George Formby, whose comic routines originated in the northern music-hall tradition. However, by 1960, another U.S. critic was complaining that the early *Carry On* comedies demonstrated "a vivid lack of those qualities of wit and understatement for which British comedy is famous."[25]

With their grotesque characters and constant allusions to bodily functions, the *Carry On* films would seem to be far closer to Bakhtin's carnival spirit than are the Ealing comedies. Yet critics have more frequently turned to George Orwell to explain the success of this comic series. In an essay first published in 1942, Orwell discussed the bawdy postcards associated especially with seaside resorts but on sale throughout Britain. He argued that "whatever is funny is subversive" and that "low" comedy is "the voice of the belly protesting against the soul." The terms here are not unlike Bakhtin's, but Orwell also anticipated Balcon's attitude to the politics of the Ealing comedies when he added that "a dirty joke is not, of course, a serious attack upon morality, but it is a sort of mental rebellion, a momentary wish that things were otherwise."[26]

*Carry On Sergeant,* the first of the series, was released in 1958, a few months before *Room at the Top* (see Chapter 3), and it had a similar impact. It was a modest black-and-white comedy whose unexpected box-office success led to the production of thirty sequels in the next twenty years, all using the same basic formula and all produced by Peter Rogers and directed by Gerald Thomas. Like many British films in the 1950s, *Carry On Sergeant* had its origins in television, the new medium usually perceived as a threat to the film industry. In this case, the film was officially based on a theatrical play but clearly inspired by the popular situation comedy *The Army Game* (1957–61), one of the first major successes of the Independent Television Network (ITV) that brought commercial television to Britain in 1955.

The television series was set in an army barracks and dealt with the attempts of an eccentric and unruly platoon of soldiers to outwit their long-suffering sergeant, played by William Hartnell, who appeared as virtually the same character in the film (Figure 48). Two other members of the cast of *The Army Game* reappeared in the film, including Charles Hawtrey, who became a mainstay of the *Carry On* films. Another star of the television series, Bernard Bresslaw, later joined the team.

Other members of the pool of comedians on which the *Carry On* series drew also first established their reputations on television. These included the two most frequent stars, Sid James and Kenneth Williams, who had both appeared in the radio and television versions of *Hancock's Half Hour.*[27] Because of the gradual relaxation of censorship at this time, films were able to be somewhat more daring than television shows aimed at a family audience; but in taking advantage of this development, the *Carry On* films were drawing on a long tradition of comic genres such as the seaside postcards and music-hall comedy that, according to Orwell, specialized in "very 'low' humour" and had "no artistic pretensions."[28]

Not all the jokes in the *Carry On* films are "dirty," but many are, and the major source of humor in these films is the body and its functions, of which sexuality is the most privileged but by no means the only one. The gags de-

**Figure 48.** "Look at you, standing as if you was pregnant": The long-suffering Sergeant (William Hartnell) impugns the manliness of Private Bailey (Kenneth Williams) during an inspection in *Carry On Sergeant.*

pend heavily on puns, innuendo, and slapstick, traditionally regarded as the lowest forms of humor. Thus the campsite in *Carry On Camping* (1968) provides ample opportunity for voyeurism and physical comedy as well as verbal double meanings. A classic example of *Carry On* humor occurs when Sid (James) and Bernie (Bresslaw) arrive at what they mistakenly believe to be a nudist camp. At the gate, they are confronted with a sign that reads: "ALL ASSES MUST BE SHOWN." When they ask to see the owner, they are told that "he's gone for a P," and he duly returns with the letter, which he places in the appropriate position on the sign.

If, in the Ealing comedies, the jokes are embedded in plot and character development, plot in the *Carry On* films is simply an excuse for a succession of gags that are often familiar or downright bad but that depend for their effect on the way they are told. We laugh (if we do) less at the joke itself than because we respond to the infectious spirit of the performers. The earlier films (written by Norman Hudis) do retain some respect for plot structures that allow them to end with a restoration of order, but the later ones (written by Talbot Bothwell) almost dispense with plot altogether. What holds the films together is their focus on a specific social institution (or film genre) whose workings are disrupted by individuals with no respect for the rules.

The early films center on institutions through which the state seeks to organize people's private lives, as in *Carry On Teacher* and *Carry On Constable* (both 1959). Not surprisingly, given the emphasis on body humor, the hospital proved to be the privileged site: *Carry On Nurse* (1958) was followed by *Carry On Doctor* (1967), *Carry On Again Doctor* (1969), and *Carry On Matron* (1971). Later films branch out into the private sector, dealing with a taxi company (*Carry On Cabby* [1963]), package holidays (*Carry On Abroad* [1972]), and even a toilet factory (*Carry On at Your Convenience*

[1971]). The series also included parodies of popular genres like *Carry On Spying* (1964) (cashing in on the success of the James Bond films) and *Carry On Cleo* (also 1964) (made on the sets of the British-made Hollywood epic *Cleopatra* [Joseph L. Mankiewicz, 1963]).

Whereas the Ealing comedies prided themselves on the avoidance of stereotypes, the *Carry On* films exploit stereotyping to the hilt. Of course, the Ealing films did not completely eliminate stereotypes, but their realist approach gave their characters an impression of psychological complexity. By comparison, the *Carry On* films give us caricatures rather than characters; but, as Andy Medhurst puts it, "attacking a *Carry On* for using stereotypes is like criticizing a musical because it's unrealistic for people to burst into song like that."[29]

In everyday life, stereotypes help us to cope with the complexity of information and stimuli that surround us, but in comedy (and in popular culture in general) they can harden into reductive myths about specific groups, defined in terms of class, gender, region, and so on. On the other hand, stereotypes can be compared to the wearing of masks in carnival, as a means of simultaneously exposing the role-playing inherent in social conventions and allowing for the concealment of identity to escape from these conventional roles. In specific narrative contexts, as well as in the comic personas of specific actors, stereotypical exaggeration can function as a mask that makes it possible to challenge social conventions. Thus Marion Jordan argues that the "grotesque exaggeration and repetition" in the *Carry On* films enable them to expose "the similar, but hidden, stereotyping elsewhere."[30]

The stereotypes are also highly unstable, in keeping with a comic style that resists being pinned down to single meanings. As in the postcards discussed by Orwell, the jokes often depend on innuendo, bawdy allusions that cannot be "proved" since there is another possible "innocent" meaning. Unlike the postcard humor in which, according to Orwell, "there are no references to homosexuality," the innuendo in the *Carry On* films is by no means confined to heterosexual behavior.[31] The characters played by Hawtrey and Williams are clearly coded as gay, through the use of stereotypical gestures and mannerisms, even though the plots often show them in pursuit of women.[32] In what is generally held to be the final film in the series,[33] *Carry on Emmannuelle* (1978), Williams plays French Ambassador Prevert, who is married to the sex-hungry title character: He thus has to masquerade simultaneously as a Frenchman, a diplomat, and a heterosexual.

The ambiguity of these characters also affects the films' depiction of the heterosexual stereotypes with which they are ostensibly most concerned. Like the postcards, the humor often depends on men pursuing shapely, well-endowed young women and trying to escape from nagging and physically unattractive older ones. Although it is hardly surprising that these stereotypes have been attacked as sexist, Frances Gray argues that "bringing the body into comic collision with major social institutions" in the *Carry On* films "led to some of the most positive images of women in British cinema," noting that the films offer "a definition of sexuality" that combines female pleasure and power and insists that sex must be "fun for both parties."[34]

While Orwell defended music-hall comedians because they "express something which is valuable in our civilization," he added that "their genius is entirely masculine." He thought that "a woman cannot be low without being disgusting, whereas a good male comedian can give the impression of something irredeemable and yet innocent, like a sparrow."[35] Orwell's description applies very well to the male comedians in the *Carry On* company, but the films reject his exclusion of women from "low" comedy. There are frequent jokes about Hattie Jacques's size, Joan Sims's unruly body, and Barbara Windsor's large breasts, but (depending on the situation) they join in the laughter, ignore the remark, or answer in kind. As Gray puts it, they "shared equal status with the male members of the *Carry On* team."[36]

The films represent the national character within a fairly restricted range of "English" stereotypes. There was no film called *Carry on Britain* but, as Gray aptly suggests, the title of *Carry On England* (1976) "might have served for the entire series," although this late film with few of the regular cast was not very successful.[37] Despite their varied settings, the films were usually shot in and around Pinewood Studios just outside London, and the entire cast seems to come from this area. There are no northern or Scottish comedians, and certainly no members of the immigrant communities that were changing the fabric of British society at this time.

One of the few references to the politics of race in contemporary Britain comes in *Carry On . . . Up the Khyber* (1968), a parody of British Empire films. An Afghani tribesman called Bunghit Din (Bresslaw) launches an attack on the British troops and comments, "that'll teach them to ban turbans on the buses." In the same film, the British soldiers belong to a Scottish regiment, and the entire plot hinges on the familiar question about whether they wear anything under their kilts. However, none of the soldiers appears to be Scottish. In the inspired final sequence, the British governor (James as Sir Sidney Ruff-Diamond) presides over a genteel dinner, while the embassy comes under bombardment and the dining room crumbles around the guests (Figure 49). After the meal, Sir Sidney lines the soldiers up in the compound, orders them to raise their kilts, and the rebels flee in terror.

Although the film's title indicates (more or less) the location of the action, it also alludes to cockney rhyming slang in which the Khyber Pass stands for "arse." The appearance of English actors in "brownface" parodies similar casting in serious films about the empire but also suggests that the comedy is centrally concerned with tensions within the concept of Englishness. Although the film pokes fun at the myth of the "stiff upper lip" and ends with a missionary, Brother Belcher (Peter Butterworth), commenting that "they're all raving mad, you know," it clearly enjoys the comic possibilities that their madness entails. As in all the films in the series, national traditions and institutions come up against the vulgarity of bodily desires and functions. It could hardly be otherwise in a film in which the Indian ruler (Williams) is the Khasi (toilet) of Kalabar and is named Rhandi Lal, the Afghani leader is Bunghit Din, and the soldier (Hawtrey) who starts the troubles by wearing underpants is Private Widdle.

In the opening sequence, a "documentary" introduction proclaims the glories of British rule in India and introduces a series of gags involving elephant dung, the flatulence of the governor's wife (Sims), and her obvious sexual interest when she learns that the handsome Indian is "Randy." In his essay on bawdy postcards, Orwell suggested that this "brand of humour only has meaning in relation to a fairly strict moral code."[38] The empire in *Carry On . . . Up the Khyber* stands for values that had become old-fashioned but were still very much present in the culture. Like the other films in the series, its humor exploits tensions between tradition and modernity in the face of apparent radical changes in the national character. In this sense, the *Carry On* films are much like the James Bond films, without the sophistication and the gadgets; and, as we have seen, the one-line jokes with which Bond breaks the tension (see Chapter 5) often seem like quotations from a *Carry On* film.

## PRINCIPLED AMBIGUITY: THE WIT OF MONTY PYTHON

As censorship became less strict and the so-called permissive society seemed triumphant, the *Carry On* films became rather more daring, but many critics saw this development as a major factor in bringing the series to an end. According to Medhurst, after Barbara Windsor's bra finally burst in *Carry On Camping*, "where was the humour in teasing about the possibility of such an occurrence?"[39] However, it is far from clear that the "strict moral code" had disappeared by 1978, when the last film in the original series appeared (just before the rise to power of Margaret Thatcher). After thirty films, the formula had simply reached its limits, the original actors were aging, and younger audiences were looking for something different.

The Monty Python troupe gave them "something completely different," or so the catchphrase from their television series claimed. Although the "tastelessness" of Python comedy inevitably invites comparisons with Bakhtin's carnival spirit, it is much closer to wit comedy as defined by Nuttall and Carmichael.[40] In contrast to the gentle whimsy of the Ealing comedies and the crude innuendo of the *Carry On* films, the Monty Python television shows and films seem to provide "clever humour for clever people."[41]

It is true that five of the six writer-performers who made up the company were graduates of Oxford or Cambridge universities and had gained their

**Figure 49.** "We've all got a little plastered": Sir Sidney Ruff-Diamond (Sid James) entertains Brother Belcher (Peter Butterworth) as the rebels attack in *Carry On . . . Up the Khyber.*

first experience as comedians in undergraduate satirical revues. Their comedy is, however, far from simply intellectual or elitist. Although they did not include the *Carry On* films among their influences, their humor drew on popular comic traditions. The practice of men playing women, for example, looked back to music-hall and pantomime conventions, while the assault on standards of good taste and high culture was really an intensification of the *Carry On* style. These traditional elements became part of an eclectic comic style that constantly drew attention to its own forms and led to claims that it represented the "beginning of postmodern self-reflexiveness" on television.[42]

The various members of the group moved into television during the 1960s when, in an effort to compete against the new commercial network, the BBC was looking for ways to exploit the new interest in political satire. The groundbreaking series was *That Was the Week That Was* (1962–3), a mixture of political comment and black humor hosted by David Frost, on which John Cleese worked as a writer. In the years that followed, Cleese, Graham Chapman, Terry Gilliam, Eric Idle, Terry Jones, and Michael Palin worked on a number of television projects, mainly for the BBC, until they came together in 1969 to create *Monty Python's Flying Circus.*

The show attracted a large and enthusiastic following during its four seasons, although its fragmentary structure, grotesque characters, and deliberate bad taste also served to alienate many viewers. A first attempt to translate this humor on to the large screen, *And Now for Something Completely Different* (Ian McNaughton, 1971), was simply an anthology of their television sketches in which the comic timing did not always suit the new medium. The group then decided to take more control of their own films. Chapman, Cleese, Idle, and Palin continued to function as writers and performers, as they had done on the television series. Terry Gilliam provided animated sequences in all

**Figure 50.** The arrival of the police ends King Arthur's quest – and the film – in *Monty Python and the Holy Grail.*

the films, also emerging as a highly imaginative director of fantastic comedy/satires like *Time Bandits* (1981) and *Brazil* (1985). It was Terry Jones who directed the three innovative films that successfully translated the Python humor into cinematic terms: *Monty Python and the Holy Grail* (codirected with Gilliam, 1974), *Monty Python's Life of Brian* (1979), and *Monty Python's The Meaning of Life* (1983).

In the Pythons' irreverent retelling of the story of the Holy Grail, the episodic plot is suddenly interrupted by "A Famous Historian" who expatiates on King Arthur's actions, as if for an educational program on television, until he is bloodily killed by some passing knights. From this point on, the events supposedly taking place in the distant past are intercut with the efforts of modern policemen to arrest the killers. The final epic charge of Arthur's army comes to an end when a police car suddenly arrives to arrest him and the rest of the cast, bringing the film to a decidedly abrupt end (Figure 50). Despite the absurd and grotesque humor, this film established the style of the Python films, which have a visual density and grandeur that would, in other circumstances, enhance serious treatments of their subjects.

*Monty Python's Life of Brian* took the idea of debunking sacred myths even further with a film whose setting and narrative evoke the life of Christ. In the opening sequence, Brian's mother gives birth in a manger, and the three Wise Men arrive with presents for her child, which they quickly take back when they realize they have made a mistake. Brian's life nevertheless uncannily resembles Christ's, and the film ends with a lavish musical production number representing the Crucifixion. As Brian gains a mass following and becomes entangled with various liberation groups, the comedy functions on two levels: as an outrageous parody of the Christian myth (and biblical epics)

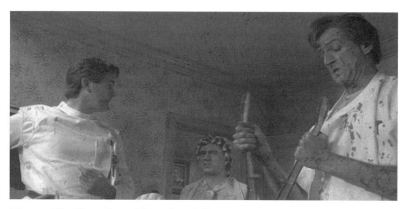

**Figure 51.** "Live Organ Transplants": Two medics (John Cleese, Eric Idle) get to know the wife (Terry Jones) of the man whose liver they are removing (despite his protests) in *Monty Python's The Meaning of Life*.

and as a satire, with contemporary relevance, on social conformism and political splinter groups.

Much of the Python comedy targets mass culture and the unthinking attitudes it supposedly promotes. Yet the depiction of those who seek alternatives is equally derisory. As Michael Palin explained, the infighting among the opposition groups in *Life of Brian* is all "about labels, how political groups become obsessed about what they call themselves, rather than what they represent."[43] While this is essentially absurdist humor, designed to unsettle rather than advance a coherent political argument, Fred Glass suggests that the final Python film is more focused than the first two. He argues that *Monty Python's Meaning of Life* "operates on an overall strategy of subversion: of film and television convention, of its audience's expectations, and of society itself."[44]

The grandiose philosophical question invoked by the film's title immediately collides with the materialistic grossness represented, on an economic level, by the Very Big Corporation of America in the prologue and, on a corporeal level, by the very fat man who explodes at the end of the film. Unlike the earlier films, there is no attempt at even a rudimentary plot but rather a series of sketches linked by the idea of the stages of life. The variety format draws on the zany fragmentation of the television shows, and the numbered captions that introduce each stage evoke "well-mannered BBC documentaries" but also recall similar devices in music-hall and Brechtian traditions.[45]

The only recurring "characters" are the fish who first appear after the prologue (which presents itself as a separate short feature) and notice from their tank that one of their friends is about to be eaten in a restaurant. Throughout, the film exaggerates the "animal" qualities of human existence to highlight the absurdity of the ideologies with which they are surrounded: the Catholic father of a huge family in the "Third World" (Yorkshire), who has to sell his children for "medical experiments" when he loses his job, explains that it is all because the pope will not allow him to use contraceptives; a schoolmaster makes love to his wife in a sex-education class and berates his students for their lack of interest; paramedics arrive at a suburban home to take the liver of a man who has signed an organ donor card, even though he is still alive, and then persuade his wife to give hers too (Figure 51).

The claim to philosophical profundity is also undercut by the banal and anticlimactic moral that the onscreen commentator gives at the end of the film. It would seem, then, that the final joke is on the spectator, although it is doubtful if anyone ever expected the film to provide the ultimate answer. There is certainly an element of cruelty in the humor, and John Walker is not alone in detecting not just cruelty but also "contempt," although he notes that "their audiences laughed heartily."[46] According to Glass, on the other hand, there is a respect for the audience in "the principled ambiguity . . . which refuses to admit that any meaning is settled once and for all," but even he expresses concern that the film's "frantic pace tends to cut back the time necessary to soak in political points."[47]

This concern echoes the debate over whether audiences were likely to recognize the darker undertones of *The Man in the White Suit,* and it raises questions about how to relate comic forms to social and political contexts. Whereas the *Carry On* films effectively came to an end with the development of the "permissive" society, the Monty Python troupe thrived in the new environment. However, George Perry suggests that the Pythons were "commenting on and mocking the very permissiveness for which they were thought to be crusading."[48] As with the Ealing comedies and the *Carry On* films, and despite the major differences among all these forms, the comic spirit proves ambiguous and elusive, preventing us from seeing it as simply reinforcing or subverting national myths.

# CHAPTER NINE

# Sexy Beasts

## British Monsters

Although the revival of British cinema during and after World War II led many critics to celebrate a new "cinema of quality," there were also trends that seemed disturbing to some observers. In 1948 Harold Wilson who, as president of the Board of Trade in the Labour government, was responsible for the film industry, declared, "we are getting tired of some of the gangster, sadistic and psychological films of which we seem to have so many, of diseased minds, schizophrenia, amnesia and diseases which occupy so much of our screen time." He wanted "to see more films which genuinely show our way of life" and refused to believe that "amnesia and schizophrenia are stock parts of our social life."[1]

As a staunch realist, Wilson here conflates two meanings of "normality," as what is common and typical and what is healthy and reasonable. His argument also depends on making clear distinctions between so-called normal states of mind and what Charles Barr calls "the darker forces" at work in the genre films to which Wilson refers.[2] However, the sheer number of these films and the intensity of Wilson's denunciation of them suggest that they did appeal to fairly large audiences, and thus that "our way of life" was not as stable or as homogeneous as Wilson imagined.

The continuing influence of the myth of the People's War and the social policies of the postwar Labour government stressed the need for collective action in the common interest, but according to Robert Murphy, this vision was "more than counter-balanced by the new opportunities for crime that the war opened up."[3] Similarly, while the changing social attitudes produced by the war encouraged a relaxation of censorship and allowed realist filmmakers to tackle issues that would not have been acceptable a few years earlier, these new freedoms also resulted in the production of British films that offered the shocks and thrills previously found mainly in the more sensational Hollywood genres.

Sarah Street has argued that, during the 1930s, "the American films so despised by the majority of British commentators received more lenient treatment by the censors" because they could be seen as the product of a "foreign" culture.[4] The Hollywood gangster films of the early 1930s and the horror films made by Universal Pictures (often based on British literary sources such as Mary Shelley's *Frankenstein* and Bram Stoker's *Dracula*) were shown in Britain, although not without controversy. British filmmakers were discouraged from working in these genres. The popular success of the Hollywood films ensured that some British producers resisted the censor's pressures, but there were few major productions in the 1930s.[5]

The crime film and the horror film were precisely the genres that flourished in postwar Britain. Often cheaply made, these films challenged the critical discourses that celebrated "quality" films and constituted what Julian Petley has called "an other, repressed side of British cinema."[6] They represented a threat to the prevailing myths of the national character as well as to the optimism generated by the winning of the People's War. At the core of both genres is the figure of the "monster," most often associated with the horror film but also with certain kinds of crime film (as well as other films exploring "abnormal" psychology).

According to Stephen Prince's succinct definition, "the monster represents a confusion – a violation – of social categories that specify boundaries between normal and abnormal, human and animal, living and dead."[7] In the context of the national cinema, the monster also violates the boundaries between the domestic and the alien, so that the ambiguous feelings of attraction and repulsion give rise to uncertainty about whether the monster represents a repressed dimension of the national character or an invasive "foreign" influence.

Prince also argues that "the monstrousness of the monster lies in its display of both human and inhuman characteristics."[8] While this may be literally true of many monsters in horror films, it also helps to explain our divided response to many characters who are "inhuman" in a metaphorical rather than a genetic sense. For example, in discussing the psychotic heroes in Michael Powell's *Peeping Tom* and Alfred Hitchcock's *Psycho* (both 1960), Andrew Tudor argues that "we experience discomfort, caught between character traits that attract our sympathy and overt behaviour which undermines it."[9]

As we have seen, this kind of divided response is also a characteristic effect of the British New Wave films that appeared at about the same time as *Psycho* and *Peeping Tom*. Several of the "angry young men" of the New Wave (see Chapter 3) might be classified as monsters in realist clothing, but Adam Lowenstein argues that these films "soothe" the anxieties that films like *Peeping Tom* arouse. Whereas *Peeping Tom* makes "'normal' viewers recognise *themselves* as the 'nuts' they have constructed as their others," Lowenstein finds that the "impeccably 'realistic'" style of *Room at the Top* keeps us at a distance from the working-class character and thus "removes the threat of involvement."[10]

Although the realism of the British New Wave films is certainly less than "impeccable," one of the key issues in monster movies is certainly the extent to which they soothe the anxieties that they arouse. Monsters do not necessarily pose a problem for censors and critics because, in theory at least, their monstrosity reinforces the appeal of normal behavior. Yet monsters are figures of excess whose transgressions often make them more interesting than the law-abiding characters who oppose them. At one level, the monster is an "other" against which "our way of life" is defined, and from which it must be protected; but, as Prince's definition suggests, the monster can also call these boundaries into question.

As Donna Haraway puts it, "monsters have always defined the limits of community in Western imaginations."[11] If the monster is completely alien, evil is represented as an external force against which the community must protect itself (usually by overcoming its divisions and weaknesses); but if the monster is at least partly human, it can be seen as an expression of the human capacity for evil. In both cases, the moral implications of the monster raise the question of why spectators enjoy watching such films. The presence of monsters in British films has been especially disturbing to many critics because monstrosity is excessive and irrational, and therefore alien to versions of the national character that emphasize restraint and common sense.

## AGGRESSIVE INDIVIDUALISM: JUVENILE GANGSTERS IN *BRIGHTON ROCK* AND *THE BLUE LAMP*

The "diseases" to which Wilson referred were the stuff of the popular Gainsborough historical melodramas of the mid- to late-1940s. Schizophrenia is a central theme and plot device in *Madonna of the Seven Moons* (see Chapter 4), and there is almost always a sadistic monster (often played by James Mason). Within a few years, however, critical disgust at these excessive and antirealist melodramas gave way to denunciations of what Tom Ryall calls "the medley of crime pictures – 'spiv' movies, *film noir* and psychological melodramas – that formed a distinct trend toward the end of the 40s."[12]

As Steve Chibnall and Robert Murphy argue, the fascination with crime, both for the characters in the films and for the audiences that watched them, involved a challenge to wartime constructions of the national character: "crime represents a hedonistic and aggressive individualism which stands in opposition to the nation's dominant values of duty, service, thrift, restraint, gentleness and concern for others."[13] It is hardly surprising that these films, vividly depicting a criminal underworld thriving on social corruption, populated by psychologically disturbed characters, should have been seen as a symptom of "post-war depression and spiritual confusion."[14]

Two of the most popular films in the postwar crime cycle were *Brighton Rock* (John Boulting, 1947) and *The Blue Lamp* (Basil Dearden, 1949). They were more respectable, high-profile productions than most crime films:

*Brighton Rock* was based on a novel by Graham Greene, and *The Blue Lamp* was an Ealing Studios production, made with the cooperation of the London police. Despite these credentials, both ran into problems with the censors, and reviewers were often disturbed because they blurred the distinction between "quality" cinema and popular genre films.[15] Their success owed much to powerful performances by relatively new actors as young criminals: Richard Attenborough as Pinkie Brown in *Brighton Rock* and Dirk Bogarde as Tom Riley in *The Blue Lamp*.

At the beginning of *Brighton Rock,* Pinkie first appears when a member of his gang visits his room in the seedy boardinghouse that serves as their headquarters, and we see him from Pinkie's point of view through a "cat's cradle" made of string stretched between his hands, an effect that captures the disturbing combination of menace and childishness that defines his character. He dominates the film, unlike Riley in *The Blue Lamp,* whose presence is, in theory at least, less important than the attention to police procedures. Yet Riley is also a monster who is, as the film's commentator puts it, all the more dangerous because of his "immaturity" (Figure 52).

Both films depend on the intensity of the actors' performances, but they also seek to contain the disturbance that the young criminals represent. With this in mind, they both open with statements that place the filmmakers on the side of the law. In *Brighton Rock,* an opening caption attempts to relegate the criminal activity with which it deals to the past. Greene wrote his novel before the war and based his plot on actual events; in order to gain permission to shoot on location, the filmmakers agreed to preface the film with a caption explaining that, thanks to the police, Brighton is no longer a hotbed of crime but a "large, jolly, friendly seaside town." The film thus presents itself as a flashback to "that other Brighton – now happily no more," even though its location shooting at the height of the season creates a strong sense of immediacy. Andrew Spicer points out that, despite this disclaimer, reviewers wondered whether it was "a genre film or a quasi-documentary about the postwar adolescent delinquent."[16]

The caption, in effect, claims that Brighton is an exception to what the opening commentary in *The Blue Lamp* calls "the post-war increase in crime." The voice-of-God commentator creates a documentary effect, enhanced by location shooting in and around the London borough of Paddington, and delivers the message that crime is an urgent and immediate threat to the "ordinary public."[17] As the commentator forcefully makes this point, we see an exciting police chase that ends with a gunman shooting a bystander who tries to stop him.

Through their location shooting, both films illustrate the tension that, according to Charlotte Brunsdon, is typical of the British crime film, between "the generic space of Hollywood" and "the rather more literal space of the

**Figure 52:** Tom Riley (Dirk Bogarde) threatens Diana (Peggy Evans) as the pressure builds in *The Blue Lamp.*

English location."[18] In *Brighton Rock,* the dark, enclosed world of Pinkie and his gang contrasts with the bright, public spaces associated with Ida (Hermione Baddeley), a performer in a local revue who tracks Pinkie down after he murders a man she has befriended. The criminals get much less screen time in *The Blue Lamp,* but there is a similar contrast between the everyday routines of police life and the disturbed lives of Riley and his friends.

The fusion of British locations and generic action associated with Hollywood became controversial in the context of the larger concern with the social impact of crime films. This concern was, of course, not confined to Britain, but it took on an especially intense form in contemporary discourses on the national cinema. On the one hand, the filmmakers came under pressure not to glamorize crime, as Hollywood films supposedly did. A reviewer praised *Brighton Rock* because it "relentlessly deglamourizes crime and the criminal," while a censor's report on the screenplay for *The Blue Lamp* warned against depicting "the dangerous subject of adolescent criminals with any glamour."[19] On the other hand, the refusal of glamour, signified by adopting the techniques of documentary realism, ran the risk of alienating audiences who enjoyed the Hollywood films.

The films incorporate this dilemma into their own structures by contrasting the behavior of young criminals, shaped by American popular culture, with British cultural traditions. While both films draw on the iconography of the American gangster film (the U.S. release title for *Brighton Rock* was *Young Scarface*), they clearly belong to the "spiv cycle," described by Peter

Wollen as a response to "the changing pattern of crime that grew up in war-time as a result of state regulation of the economy." Spivs were small-time crooks most noted for their flashy clothing, but they modeled themselves on the gangsters in Hollywood films. As Wollen notes, "official ideology portrayed the spiv as an enemy of the war effort (and hence the people)," and the films present them as villains who are, however, "frequently fascinating."[20]

The workings of "official ideology" are very apparent in the opening commentary in *The Blue Lamp,* which attributes the rise in crime to the unsettling effects of the war on young people. It soon becomes clear that one of the symptoms of this disturbance is the growing influence of U.S. popular culture. The delinquents frequently use American slang in contrast to the colloquial English used by the "coppers" and, in one pointed shot, we see Diana (Peggy Evans), Riley's girlfriend, asleep with a copy of a magazine called *Movie Life* beside her.

After the release of *Brighton Rock,* a writer in the *Daily Mirror* claimed that the Hollywood studios were now more responsible than their British counterparts because they had banned the production of gangster films that "give a false impression of life in America."[21] In a reply published the next day, Greene pointed out that "in fact, Hollywood has not banned the production of gangster films but only the production of films that hold the gangster up to the sympathy of the audience."[22] He thus implied that *Brighton Rock* does not evoke sympathy for Pinkie, but this is a matter of some controversy.

Some critics argue that Greene's screenplay adulterates the complex moral vision of his novel, which offers psychological and social explanations for Pinkie's behavior. According to Chibnall, the screenplay "stripped all sympathy" from Pinkie, "turning him from a damaged product of his environment into a psychopathic monster" and converting Ida into "a righteous heroine carrying the weight of audience identification."[23] Another critic suggests that, whatever the motives for the changes, the effect was in line with other films produced and directed by the Boulting brothers that deal with "the psychotic whose malevolence embodies a kind of evil which cannot be explained by social discourses."[24]

Although Pinkie is hardly an attractive figure, Attenborough's performance suggests that he is driven by the need to suppress his own fears about his masculinity. Even though the film omits most of the information about his childhood provided in the novel, he clearly comes from the same social (and religious) background as Rose (Carol Marsh), the young waitress whom he marries so that she cannot testify against him. His frequent expressions of hatred for her seem to cover an attraction that he dare not acknowledge. The film's moral effect is certainly more ambiguous than Greene implies in his letter to the *Mirror.* As Geoffrey Macnab has suggested, Attenborough makes the monstrous character "perversely sympathetic."[25]

In some ways, Riley is less of a monster than Pinkie simply because the social causes of his behavior are more clearly defined. Yet, while the commentator attributes juvenile delinquency to the broken families caused by the war, Riley's own family background is not revealed. Even if he is the product of a broken family, the film makes clear that this is not enough to explain his criminal behavior. Not all families have given way to the effects of the war: Police Constable Dixon (Jack Warner) and his wife (Gladys Henson) have lost their son in the war but welcome Andy Mitchell (Jimmy Hanley), who is the same age their son would have been and who has chosen to become a policeman, into their home.

After noting that Pinkie and Riley are alike in terms of their "age and appearance and ambivalence towards women," Murphy suggests that, whereas Pinkie is "a phenomenon – a boy so cold and ruthless that older men fall under his sway," Riley is a "'juvenile delinquent' whom the professionals despise and betray."[26] Pinkie is certainly the more powerful figure, perhaps "psychotic" while Riley is "neurotic," but both characters are distinguished from both the police and professional criminals by their immaturity.[27] Both are eventually brought to justice less by the efforts of the police than by their own efforts to avoid detection.

Pinkie tries to conceal the time of the murder by sending one of his gang to distribute the cards that the murdered man was supposed to hide around the resort as a publicity stunt for a newspaper. He then decides to retrieve one of the cards from a café in case the waitress finds it and remembers the man who left it, and this leads to his meeting with Rose and his decision to marry her to ensure her silence. All of this activity provides clues for Ida, after the police have closed the case, and it is when he tries to eliminate Rose that another member of the gang betrays him. Similarly, Riley goes to the police when he hears they are looking for Diana, because he thinks they have linked her to him and the killing of PC Dixon during a robbery. They are interested only in an earlier jewelry robbery at this point, but his actions provide the evidence they need to arrest him for murder.

Whereas Riley is a young "delinquent" who shoots the policeman in a moment of panic, Pinkie is the leader of a gang, but he is dismissed by a more professional gang leader who stays in a luxurious hotel and refers to himself as a "business man." The police are more concerned to keep the peace than to administer justice, and they do not want to antagonize the stronger gang. While the police in *The Blue Lamp* are supposedly trying to eradicate crime in general, the commentator implies that there is a relationship of mutual respect between the police and the professional criminals who help to trap Riley when he seeks refuge in a crowded greyhound racing stadium.

In both films, the issue of law and order and the figure of the criminal-monster are more complicated than they might at first seem. There is also an important contrast between the figures who represent normality in each film. As Chibnall and Murphy point out, "Pinkie's adversary, the loud, blowsy, cheerful Ida . . . is the opposite of a *femme fatale*."[28] Yet her function in the film is quite similar to that of the glamorous sirens of film noir in that she drives Pinkie to his death. Although the censor demanded the removal of most of the novel's religious references, Pinkie's Catholic sense of sin still contrasts with Ida's entirely secular idea of justice. She represents a certain kind of normality but is hardly a straightforward identification figure. Although the police are rather more helpful in the film than in the novel, the contrast between Pinkie and Ida carries the film's moral and renders it somewhat ambiguous.

In *The Blue Lamp,* the major moral opposition is between the highly unstable Riley and the stolid figure of PC Dixon, who was later resurrected to become the friendly neighborhood policeman in the BBC television series *Dixon of Dock Green* (1955-76). The robbery, during which Riley panics and shoots Dixon, takes place, appropriately enough, at a cinema, and sets the past (solid and silent) against the future (nervous and voluble), although the ending asserts that Mitchell becomes Dixon's true heir through imitating him. Yet, despite the narrative's efforts to marginalize Riley, Bogarde's performance creates an impact that challenges the ostensible moral logic of the film. As Jeffrey Richards puts it, the audience was expected to prefer Mitchell, but he now "looks rather bland, conventional and . . . sexless."[29]

At the end of both films, the monster is eliminated and normality apparently restored. In *The Blue Lamp,* Riley ends up in police custody, but the collaboration of the police and the underworld in his capture echoes Fritz Lang's *M* (1931) in which this convergence of legal and criminal interests carries distinct overtones of fascism. The ending of *Brighton Rock* was even more disturbing and proved much more controversial.

After Pinkie falls from the pier to his death while trying to escape from Ida and the police, Rose plays a recording that he made for her earlier, unaware that it contains an expression of hatred rather than love (Figure 53). However, the needle sticks just after he says, "you want me to say I love you," so that the last three words repeat over and over again. It seems like a miracle, but the stuck groove is the result of Pinkie's earlier attempt to destroy the record and, in any case, Greene thought the audience would realize that one day Rose would move the needle beyond the crack.[30] Many critics felt that the ending diluted the effect of the novel, in which Rose is left without consolation. For Murphy, it can be described simply as "a happy ending," but James Naremore claims that *Brighton Rock* has "one of the most unsettling conclusions of any thriller of the period."[31]

**Figure 53.** Rose (Carol Marsh) watches, but cannot hear, as Pinkie (Richard Attenborough) records his message of hate in *Brighton Rock.*

## THE VISIBILITY OF THE MONSTER:
## BRITISH HORROR FILMS

Criminal monsters continued to populate British cinema in the 1950s, but crime movies were soon replaced as objects of critical disdain by the horror films produced by Hammer Films and other even less reputable studios. In an essay published in *Sight and Sound* in 1959, Derek Hill proclaimed that "every horror film cycle has coincided with economic depression or war" and thus the new cycle of British horror films was a symptom of "a sick society."[32] His attempt to demonize these films sounds remarkably like Professor Van Helsing (Peter Cushing) in *The Satanic Rites of Dracula* (Alan Gibson, 1973) expounding the occult belief that the major disasters in world history – including both world wars – coincided with the dates on which Satan's power was at its height. The horror films erupted into the sedate world of British film culture much like the monsters in the films who shatter the peace of respectable society.

One of the few defenders of the genre at the time was the art critic Lawrence Alloway who, in a short article first published in 1960, took issue with Hill and claimed that the Hammer films were "the liveliest things in current British film production." He preferred the term "monster films" and insisted that "the reason for making and witnessing monster films is the visibility of the monster." They "play with death and disintegration, probing into the fearful territory around and below the healthy and intact human image," and the horror stems from their vision of "body as a package, which can be opened."

Monster films thus "exploit the ambiguities of repulsion and curiosity" provoked by "the fate of being a body," and in particular the fears and desires surrounding sexuality and death.[33]

The weight of critical opinion was on Hill's side, and there is still a widespread view that the Hammer horror films are tasteless and meretricious or that they pale in comparison to earlier and later works in the genre. An alternative critical position did emerge, building on Alloway's essay and David Pirie's claim, made in the early 1970s, that these films constitute "the only staple cinematic myth which Britain can claim as its own."[34] What is most surprising in the various critical response to the Hammer films, however, is the very different assessments of the kind of horror that they produce.

Andrew Tudor attributes the success of *The Curse of Frankenstein* (Terence Fisher, 1957), the first film in the cycle, to precisely those qualities that outraged the original critics, "its graphic display of 'gory' detail."[35] On the other hand, Pirie insists that, "contrary to popular assumption," Hammer "never really concentrated on *monsters* as such" because "their manifestations of evil" tended to be "intelligent and urbane."[36] Some critics argue that, "compared to modern exploitation movies, the Hammer films admittedly seem tame, but [they are] all the more remarkable for what they leave to the imagination."[37] Yet Ian Conrich suggests that, unlike previous British horror films that "relied on shadows, mysteries, suspense, passion, spectral figures and the viewer's imagination," the Hammer films "used excess, explicitness, sensuality and violence."[38]

The most convincing accounts of Hammer horror are those that stress the tension between restraint and excess. Thus Jonathan Coe declares that "Hammer films are . . . absolutely typical of English culture in the way they insist that extremes of violence and extremes of cosiness can and must coexist."[39] Similarly, Murphy describes the style as one in which "urbanity and restraint [are] only occasionally disrupted by shocking images of bodies pierced by wooden stakes, mouths dripping blood, naked brains, severed limbs."[40] Peter Hutchings suggests that it was through "a robust physicality, an insistence on the solid and corporeal nature of the conflict between the forces of good and evil . . . and the formal restraint that usually accompanied it, that Hammer horror distinguished itself from other types of horror."[41]

This tension is managed in most of the films through the use of period and foreign settings. Sue Harper points out that Fisher enjoyed making films set in the nineteenth century because the period offered a fruitful "combination of scientificity and the grotesque," and she argues that the "historical settings distance the audience from their own emotional habits."[42] Most of the early Hammer films use stylized central European settings in which, however, the actors make no attempt to conceal their national origins. The recurring faces and voices of what amounted to the Hammer repertory company produced an ambiguous blending of the strange–foreign and familiar–British, much like that found in some of the Gainsborough melodramas (see Chapter 4).

Although a number of directors produced distinctive variations on the formula, the classic Hammer style emerged in the films of Terence Fisher. After *The Curse of Frankenstein,* he was responsible for a string of films in which Hammer reclaimed monsters most familiar from their Hollywood versions, including *Dracula* (1958), *The Hound of the Baskervilles* and *The Mummy* (both 1959), *The Two Faces of Dr. Jekyll* (1960), *The Curse of the Werewolf* (1961), and *The Phantom of the Opera* (1962).[43] In these films, according to Pirie, Fisher revealed that he was "not essentially an expressionist film-maker" by his "persistent refusal to sacrifice continuity for strong dramatic emphasis" and by "his measured cinematic style."[44] Fisher himself described his approach in one of his notebooks in a way that suggests that Hammer horror may not be as remote from traditional accounts of the national character as it might seem: "Melodrama – overstatement of the natural. Mine – understatement of the supernatural."[45]

Pirie suggests that Fisher "emerges as a rational eccentric in the fundamental English tradition of Lewis Carroll, Wilkie Collins or Conan Doyle," not unlike the characters played by Peter Cushing in many of his films.[46] The ideological implications of this perspective divide the critics as much as the aesthetic issues. Whereas Vincent Porter refers to "the essential Victorian morality of the films," Marcia Landy argues that "many of the Hammer films appear to be on a crusade against narrow morality while espousing their own morality, which usually entails a more permissive view of sexual relations."[47] The social order depicted in the films is certainly rigid and patriarchal, but the focus on the body creates an entanglement of social and sexual relations that often disturbs the apparent ideological structure of the narrative. It is around the figure of the monster that these tensions become most visible.

The Frankenstein films play on the familiar confusion that often uses the scientist's name to refer to the monster. Technically, the grotesque beings that the baron constructs from assembled body parts are "creatures" rather than "monsters," since they have no will of their own, and their monstrous appearance and actions are the result of flaws in the experiments.[48] It is Cushing's Frankenstein who is, in his ruthless pursuit of the secret of life, the true monster, even if – especially in the later films – his activities are hindered or exploited by people who are often equally monstrous.

In *The Curse of Frankenstein,* the entire story may even be a figment of the baron's imagination. He tells it to a priest, while awaiting execution for murders which, he claims, were committed by the creature, whose existence he cannot prove because its grotesque body has been dissolved in an acid bath (Figure 54). Even on his own account, however, he murdered an old

**Figure 54.** "You don't believe me, do you?": Baron Frankenstein (Peter Cushing) fails to convince the priest (Alex Gallier) of the truth of his story at the end of *The Curse of Frankenstein.*

professor to obtain a brain for his creature. In the second film, *The Revenge of Frankenstein* (Fisher, 1958), the distinction between Frankenstein and the monster breaks down completely when, after he is severely beaten by the patients he has been exploiting for his experiments, the baron survives only because his assistant transplants his brain into another body. In the final sequence, he is working as a successful doctor in London.

In the Hammer version of *Dracula,* the monster is clearly the title character, played by Christopher Lee, who had appeared as the rather pathetic creature in the first Frankenstein film. Fisher claimed that his "greatest contribution to the Dracula myth was to bring out the underlying sexual element in the story."[49] His Dracula is unequivocally a monster, but he is also "fatally attractive" (Figure 55).[50] As Tudor points out, "there is no need for this Dracula to establish animal connections by metamorphosing into a bat . . . : it is quite clear that in his unrepressed physicality he *is* a beast as well as an apparently sophisticated human being."[51]

In the first film, Cushing plays Dracula's opponent Van Helsing as a much more benevolent version of the scientist than his Frankenstein. He is willing to accept the existence of the supernatural but is able to withstand the power of the seductive beast only because, as a dispassionate scientist, he seems to have no sexual desires of his own. Dracula's victims throughout the cycle (usually but not always women) are first hypnotized by his eyes and then submit to an embrace that starts as a kiss and becomes a bite, producing an ecstatic mixture of pleasure and pain. In this way, the monster's presence brings out the repressed sexual desires that lurk beneath the façade of respectable bourgeois society. Since Dracula is the "undead," the fatal attraction also links sexuality to mortality, and the restoration of order coincides with the physical crumbling of his body (only to be resurrected in the next film).

**Figure 55.** "I am Dracula, and I welcome you to my house": the urbane Count (Christopher Lee) greets Jonathan Harker at the beginning of *Dracula*.

In the later films, the clear moral framework, against which Frankenstein and Dracula are defined as monsters, becomes increasingly difficult to maintain. As Hutchings suggests, "the instability of the figure of Frankenstein in the late 1960s . . . results from an instability within generic structures as their ideological foundations begin to crumble."[52] The baron becomes even more monstrous but, at the same time, the people who oppose him often make his attacks on social hypocrisy quite convincing. When a priest smashes his laboratory in *The Evil of Frankenstein* (Freddie Francis, 1964), he laments that "they" always destroy anything they do not understand, and his assistant in *Frankenstein Created Woman* (Fisher, 1966) expresses contempt for people who think that the baron is "some sort of monster in league with the devil."

In *Frankenstein Must Be Destroyed* (Fisher, 1969), the baron speaks up in favor of "progress" before his fellow residents in a boardinghouse where he has taken refuge. Yet he first appears in the film after we have seen a bald old man with a scythe, who looks like the Dracula figure in Murnau's *Nosferatu,* stalk and murder a man in the streets of the city. When he pulls off his mask, the familiar features of Cushing/Frankenstein appear. He blackmails Carl, a young doctor who is involved in the drug trade, and first rapes and then kills Carl's fiancée. In the final film of the cycle, *Frankenstein and the Monster from Hell* (Fisher, 1973), he is confined in an asylum for the insane, where he is allowed by the corrupt governor to carry on his work with the assistance of a young scientist who has been inspired by his writing.

In the earlier *Horror of Frankenstein* (Jimmy Sangster, 1970), in which Ralph Bates temporarily replaced Cushing, Hammer had already tried to adapt the cycle to the new youth culture. This strategy of rejuvenation was taken even further in the Dracula cycle. In *Taste the Blood of Dracula* (Peter Sasdy, 1969), three apparently upright Victorian gentlemen resurrect Dracula in their search for new sensations but, when they lose their nerve, Dracula uses their children to take revenge on them. In *Scars of Dracula* (Roy Ward Baker, 1970), a young man, whose appearance defines him as a representative of contemporary youth culture despite the traditional period setting, finds himself involved in the ancient cult of the vampire.

The ambivalent relation between Dracula and contemporary youth culture is taken a stage further in the last two films in the Hammer Dracula cycle, in which the vampire legend is updated to the present.[53] Van Helsing had been missing since the first film, but Peter Cushing now returns to play the middle-aged grandson of the original vampire hunter who uses the family knowledge to protect the young people who fall into Dracula's clutches.

The precredits sequence of *Dracula A.D. 1972* (Alan Gibson, 1972) depicts what purports to be the "final confrontation" between Van Helsing and Dracula in 1872, in which both are killed. After a leap forward in time, accomplished by a pan up to the sky and a cut to a jet plane, the credits appear over shots of modern urban highways. A group of young people who spend their time in Chelsea looking for "kicks" are invited to participate in "something new but as old as the world" by their friend Johnny Alucard (Christopher Neame) – Dracula spelt backward. When he mentions the Devil, someone suggests it is "Sunday supplement stuff," but the ensuing events validate Van Helsing's claim that his grandfather was a scientist who collected "positive proof" that there is evil in the world. The professor assists a police officer who thinks they may be dealing with "cult murders" that are a sign of London's new status as a "cosmopolitan city," and who argues that the existence of evil shows the need for a police force.

In the following year's *The Satanic Rites of Dracula,* the desanctified church in which the count was revived and destroyed in the previous film has been torn down and replaced by a tall office block. This film illustrates the instability of genre boundaries, incorporating elements of occult horror, James Bond spy thriller, and soft-core sex film. Dracula himself becomes "that quintessential 1970s carnivore, the property developer," living at the top of the office tower where he plans his revenge on humanity, using the rites of the title to gain power over four establishment figures to develop and spread a new, more virulent form of bubonic plague.[54]

Although the monster is always defeated, the fragile state of moral authority in these late Hammer films involves a shift away from what Tudor calls "secure horror," which depicts "an ultimately successful struggle against disorder" toward "paranoid horror" in which "human actions are routinely unsuccessful, order far more precarious and boundaries between known and unknown rarely as clear as they might at first seem."[55] However, while it may be true that, as Landy suggests, "the horror film operates across the axis of inclusion and exclusion based on distinctions between the monstrous and the natural," horror ultimately stems not from "the *opposition* between the normal and the abnormal, the repressed and the legitimate, the human and the non-human, but rather the difficulties in defining and understanding what separates them."[56] The moral framework of the Hammer horror films depends on maintaining these distinctions but, even in the earlier films, there is a disturbing sense that they do not fully account for what we see.

David Sanjek argues that developments in the U.S. horror film that he traces back to George Romero's *Night of the Living Dead* (1968) accelerated the decline of British horror: "When monsters and human beings could no longer easily be distinguished, the tidy universe of the English horror film was in jeopardy."[57] Although this universe was never as tidy as Sanjek suggests, it is clear that the challenge to established authority in the 1960s did lead to major changes in the genre. Three British horror films that subsequently became cult movies represent distinct but related responses to this situation.

In *Witchfinder General* (1968), Michael Reeves eliminates the "fantastic, fairytale world which encloses even the most frightening of the Gothic horror films."[58] During the seventeenth-century English Civil War, Matthew Hopkins (Vincent Price) plays on the superstitious belief in witches to satisfy his own taste for cruelty.[59] The sexual openness of the young lovers, Sarah Lowes (Hilary Dwyer) and Richard Marshall (Ian Ogilvy), contrasts with the repressed emotions that drive the religious and political establishment. Hopkins persuades Sara to have sex with him in order to save her uncle, whom he has denounced, and then breaks his word. Marshall, a soldier in Cromwell's army, deserts in search of revenge, and he gradually loses his own humanity. The film ends with Sara screaming madly, after being tortured by Hopkins and then witnessing her lover brutally kill her tormentor with an ax.

Leon Hunt suggests that the films of Michael Reeves "helped to initiate the 'anti-authoritarian' generation gap strand in British horror."[60] A major contribution to this strand were Pete Walker's "antiestablishment paranoid narratives," of which the most compelling is probably *House of Whipcord* (1974).[61] It deals with the ordeal of Ann-Marie (Penny Irving), a young Frenchwoman living in London, who, after appearing naked in a news photograph, is kidnapped by a vigilante group opposed to the decline in moral standards in British society. She is taken to a prison run by a blind ex-judge (Patrick Barr) and his sadistic wife (Barbara Markham), a former prison matron, who punish the inmates with whips and hang them for repeated offences. The advocates of law and order emerge as self-deceiving hypocrites and more of a threat to the nation than the harmless sexual pleasures of those they persecute. Since the film generates its own hypocritical gaze at the abuse of the inmates, its bleak ending leaves the spectator to confront the contradictions that it provokes.

The other major film in this group is *The Wicker Man* (Robin Hardy, 1973), in which a highly moral policeman (Edward Woodward) investigates

**Figure 56.** *The Wicker Man:* Sergeant Howie (Edward Woodward) reminds Lord Summerisle (Christopher Lee) that he is "the subject of a Christian country."

the disappearance of a young girl on a remote Scottish island. He functions as our identification figure in discovering the pagan rituals practiced there, but his Christian righteousness is such an extreme version of a "normal" response that it distances us from his values. When it becomes clear that the investigation has been rigged by the local lord (Christopher Lee) so that the policeman will provide a needed human sacrifice, our position is further undermined (Figure 56). During the final sacrifice/murder, the camera is both inside and outside the wicker man in which the policeman is burned alive and, although Chibnall argues that the film is compromised by its "sympathy" for the policeman, it gains its power precisely from the difficulty in deciding where our sympathies should lie.[62]

## WHO DO YOU THINK YOU'RE LOOKING AT? TERROR AND THE CRIMINAL MONSTER

According to Alexander Walker, "public terrorism came to London in the first years of the Seventies" and was "reflected in films which put the emphasis of interest on the criminal anti-hero, stripped of political motives . . . and demonstrating his ugly skills with the verisimilitude of the psychopaths nurtured by Hollywood."[63] If the renewed interest in the crime film was provoked by new forms of political violence, the filmmakers drew extensively, as Walker also acknowledges, on the legends surrounding the Kray brothers, the twin monsters who terrorized the East End of London until they were sentenced to life imprisonment after a lengthy trial in 1969.[64] While the Krays and their entourage mixed with people from the show business world and provided ideas and information for many crime films, it was not until 1990 that a film tackled the legend directly.

**Figure 57.** *Get Carter:* Jack (Michael Caine) tells his dead brother's mistress (Dorothy White) that he is "the villain in the family" as he begins his ruthless quest for revenge.

Like most of the films discussed in this chapter, *The Krays* (Peter Medak) engages with the questions of whether monstrosity is innate or caused by the social and cultural environment. The film traces the brothers' villainy back to the disruption of family life in World War II (much like *The Blue Lamp*) but also to their intense relationship with their mother.[65] It begins and ends with the mother's dream, which heralds their birth and signals her death, in which the beauty of a bird in flight contrasts with the physical pain of the birth and the social reality of working-class life. The dream imagery displaces the film's biographical origins onto the level of myth, but it remains unclear to what extent these factors "explain" the brothers' aggression, Ronnie's homosexuality, and Reggie's possessive love that drives his wife to suicide.

Walker's coupling of terrorism and the Krays was provoked by three films released in 1971. The first of these was *Performance* (Donald Cammell and Nicolas Roeg), which was shot in 1968 and released only after lengthy delays caused by Warner Brothers' distaste for the film they had produced.[66] It used the Kray milieu for its first half during which a gangster (James Fox) runs into trouble with his own gang and takes refuge in the home of a reclusive rock singer (Mick Jagger). The film thus depicts the conjunction of the traditional criminal monster and a new folk devil produced by the youth and drug culture, and it ends with the unsettling merger of these two figures.

The other two films are more securely located within the gangster genre. *Get Carter* (Mike Hodges) is, in effect, a modern revenge tragedy in which Jack Carter (Michael Caine), a cockney gangster, travels to Newcastle to find out the truth about his brother's death and discovers that he was the victim of sordid underworld figures who live off prostitution and pornography (Figure 57). At first, Carter functions as an identification figure, seeking justice and protecting his family, but his pursuit of revenge makes him increasingly callous and brutal, a moral ambiguity virtually absent from the Hollywood remake (Stephen Kay, 2000) starring Sylvester Stallone. In the final sequence, he is gunned down by a mysterious and unseen sniper.

As the title suggests, there is little moral ambiguity in *Villain* (Michael Tuchner) in which Vic Dakin (Richard Burton) offers "the most compulsively creepy . . . interpretation yet derived from the Kray legend."[67] His one redeeming feature is his love for his mother, with whom he lives in their suburban home; otherwise he lives up to his title billing, but he operates in a society in which this has become a descriptive label rather than a forceful moral judgment. He is a misogynist, whose shame at his homosexual desire emerges in psychotic violence as he pursues his schemes of robbery and blackmail. A police officer tells him that he does not accept that "society is to blame" for the behavior of criminals, but when Vic is arrested at the end, he yells at the witnesses – and at us – "Who do you think you're looking at?"

The public fascination with the figure of the monster makes it difficult to see Vic and the underworld in which he operates as completely distinct from "normal" human feelings. In all three films, crime is linked to the sex industry and to social and political corruption, and they thus operate within the same terrain as the tabloid journalism of the period. Conservatives blamed the perceived decline in public morality on the new "permissiveness" associated with the 1960s, but the films also stressed the dangers of repression.

In 1979 Margaret Thatcher led the Conservative Party to electoral victory on a platform that placed great emphasis on law and order and used the discourse of crime to discredit political activists. In turn, some of the crime films of this period can be read as attempts to turn this strategy around by associating Thatcherist rhetoric with crime. This strategy is most fully realized in *The Long Good Friday* (John Mackenzie, 1979), in which, according to Walker, Harold Shand (Bob Hoskins), is "a monster because his hankering for the Conservative virtues is so wildly at variance with his practice of the terrorist ones."[68]

Harold sees himself as a "business man" and wants to turn the derelict port of London, a sign of the nation's economic and political decline, into a site for the Olympic Games. In an attempt to secure support from the U.S. Mafia, he takes Charlie, his "American friend" (Eddie Constantine), for a boat trip on the Thames and, framed by Tower Bridge, delivers a speech of which Thatcher would have been proud. He insists that Britain is now "a leading European state" and emphasizes "the global nature of this venture," which provides an "opportunity for profitable progress."

The film's opening sequences are extremely fragmented and, while we do see all the events that will lead to Harold's downfall, the absence of dialogue means that we lack the information to connect them. A shot of a Concorde jet taxiing along a runway heralds Harold's arrival and invests him with power and authority as he strides purposefully through the airport. The rest of the film depicts his attempts to make sense of the situation and to control

**Figure 58.** "Frost-bite or verbals": Harold (Bob Hoskins) tries to find out what is going on from the local gangsters hanging upside-down in an abattoir in *The Long Good Friday.*

it, while using his rhetorical skills to conceal the problem from the Americans. As the explosions and killings multiply, all images and relationships become potentially unstable. When Harold rounds up a group of petty criminals for questioning, he hangs them upside down in an abattoir (Figure 58), and several inverted point-of-view shots express the increasing sense of instability, as does the collision in a stock-car race when a car lands upside down with a sign that reads "this side up" now right side up.

Harold tries to make the best of things and describes his current problems as an exception that has made London seem "like Belfast on a bad night." Later Charlie likens the events to "a bad night in Vietnam," and the film thus reinstates the political context to which Walker saw the earlier films as an implicit response. Harold discovers that his operation has been targeted by the IRA because of a mistake made by a member of his gang. At the end, he is a powerless and speechless prisoner at the mercy of the IRA, whose political violence is seen as the logical outcome of a situation in which the boundaries between politics and crime have broken down.

As many science-fiction films have demonstrated, an unseen monster is often more frightening than a visible one, and Harold's monstrosity is thus softened by his transition into victim. It is also complicated by his concern for his mother and, unlike the other mother-fixated gangsters, by the warm relationship he shares with his wife, Victoria (Helen Mirren). Another mitigating factor is Hoskins's genial cockney persona, which became even more benign in later films like *Mona Lisa* (Neil Jordan, 1986), where he plays a small-time criminal saddened by his separation from his wife and daughter and forced to confront his prejudices when he is assigned as chauffeur to a black prostitute. The real monster in this film is the crime boss played by Michael Caine, who once again brings out the darker side of the cockney gangster.

In the following decade, a new cycle of British crime films exploited the "cool" postmodern violence they found in the films of Quentin Tarantino. In the British films, the most successful of which were Guy Ritchie's *Lock, Stock and Two Smoking Barrels* (1998) and *Snatch* (2000), the gangsters are rarely "lovable," but they seem more like adolescents playing (violent) games than true monsters. However, two extreme monsters appeared in crime films released in 2000, both based on stage plays by Louis Mellis and David Scinto and directed by filmmakers whose previous work was mainly in music videos and television commercials.

*Sexy Beast* (Jonathan Glazer) plays with the personas of its actors. It first introduces Gary Dove, a retired gangster living in Spain, played by Ray Winstone, who played the monstrous fathers in *Nil by Mouth* and *The War Zone* (see Chapter 3). He is not the film's monster, however, as his peace is shattered by the arrival of Don Logan, played by Ben Kingsley, an actor associated with restrained and thoughtful characters, most notably in the title role in *Gandhi* (Richard Attenborough, 1982). Don wants Gary to return to London to take part in a planned bank robbery and will not take no for an answer (Figure 59). He is "a spitting, bullying, foul-mouthed monster," an apparently elemental force, although Kingsley does manage to suggest an underlying insecurity that turns him into a monstrous version of a "playground bully."[69]

The opening of *Gangster No. 1* (Paul McGuigan) is also rather deceptive about who the monster will be. The first sequence takes place at a boxing match where the aging gangster (whose name we never learn) overhears news that Freddie Mays is about to be released from prison. This news seems to disturb the gangster, played by Malcolm McDowell, whose star persona is probably most influenced by his juvenile monster in Stanley Kubrick's *A Clockwork Orange* (1971); Freddie is played by David Thewlis, the monstrous angry young man in Mike Leigh's *Naked* (see Chapter 3). McDowell narrates the story of how he started to work for Freddie, who was Gangster No. 1 in London in the 1960s, and his iron rule over his gang suggests that Freddie will be the film's monster. But it is the narrator's younger self (Paul Bettany) who begins to imitate his boss and then savagely eliminates him and all his rivals so that he can take his place.

In both films, image and narrative are fractured, apparently to suggest the pressures caused by the intensity of the monster figures. The first sign of disturbance in *Sexy Beast* occurs when a huge boulder crashes down a hill, narrowly missing Gary and landing in his swimming pool. There are also several surreal shots involving a monstrous rabbit in the scrubland near his house. With the help of his wife, Gary kills Don and buries him under the swimming pool and then must participate in the robbery to conceal what he has done. As Glazer suggests, the film itself becomes something of a monster, combining elements that are "not immediately compatible with one another," includ-

**Figure 59.** *Sexy Beast:* Don Logan (Ben Kingsley) visits Gary (Ray Winstone) at his Spanish villa and tries to persuade him to take part in a heist.

ing "the heist, the love story, the psychodrama, and the macabre details and fantasy elements."[70] All of these elements relate to the monster at the center of the film, but they do not add up to a coherent explanation of his excesses.

As Mark Kermode suggests, *Gangster No. 1* offers "a chronically fractured vision of underworld London, split not only in the juxtaposition of its two alienated time zones (the sixties, the present day) but within the confines of the frame itself."[71] At moments of intensity, the image splits into fragments that recall a kaleidoscope or a cubist painting. The climax comes when the gangster allows Freddie to walk into a trap that leaves him and his girlfriend lying in the street, apparently bleeding to death, and then tortures and dismembers the rival gang leader who arranged the trap. In this bloody sequence, the gangster strips to avoid spoiling his clothes, and the killing is then shown from the dying man's point-of-view. As in *Sexy Beast,* there are possible social and psychological explanations for the gangster's behavior, but they seem inadequate in the face of the enormity of the evil he represents.

# CHAPTER TEN

# The Ruling Class

## Ideology and the School Movie

One of the most distinctive features of British society is the importance and persistence of class differences. It thus may seem rather strange to find Ernest Barker arguing that one of the "constants" in the "English" character is "social homogeneity" made possible because "England has had little class-feeling," even though he admits that "down to our own days, it has had, and has even cherished, a whole ladder of class-differences."[1] In this argument, the national character transcends "class-differences" and prevents them from becoming "class-feeling" that might threaten the social order.

Barker made these comments in 1947, in the aftermath of the People's War, but he does not see this state of society as a recent development. He seems to consider a long history of trade-union activity and events such as the General Strike of 1921 as insignificant compared with the interests that all citizens share in common. In more recent years, there have been claims that, although class was important in the past, Britain has developed into a classless society, a myth that Margaret Thatcher turned on its head by placing the blame for social breakdown and national decline on the loss of those traditions that enabled people to know their place in society.

Thatcher traced the problem back to the 1960s, when class differences and other kinds of inequality were challenged by new political movements. At that time, film theory and cultural studies became centrally concerned with a theory of "ideology" that sought to explain why people generally accepted the existing social hierarchy. The most influential expression of this theory was the work of Louis Althusser, who defined ideology as "the system of the ideas and representations which dominate the mind of a man or a social group."[2] Althusser's ideas were taken up in Britain by the writers for *Screen,* who sought to establish a more scientific approach to film criticism (as in Colin MacCabe's analysis of realism discussed in Chapter 3).

In his groundbreaking study of Ealing Studios, published in 1977, Charles Barr tried to bridge the gap between these new developments and more traditional approaches by suggesting that, "if national 'character' seems an old-fashioned impressionistic term, it is worth noting that it could perfectly well be replaced by 'ideology.'"[3] From an Althusserian perspective, Barr's suggestion would be acceptable only if did not imply that the two terms worked at the same level. According to Althusser, ideology makes social and cultural phenomena seem "natural," and this is exactly what happens when a psychological term like "character" is applied to a political institution like a nation. Since this theory also insisted that personal identity is a cultural construction rather than a genetic inheritance, the concept of ideology sets out to explain not only how a nation's social and cultural structures affect the behavior of its citizens but also how those citizens come to view themselves as conforming to an imaginary national character.

There were frequent objections to what became known as *Screen* theory on the grounds that it was alien to the national character. The critic and filmmaker Gavin Lambert was far from alone in insisting that "the English tend to be suspicious of theories and the French are very good at them."[4] Even within the realm of theory, however, there has been a strong reaction against Althusser, mainly because he saw ideology as such an all-pervasive and powerful phenomenon that there seems to be no possibility for resistance and change.

In effect, Althusser was trying to explain the failure of the student-led uprising against the French government in May 1968. He attempted to describe the mechanisms of the system that enabled the government to survive even though the students expected that the working class would support the cause of reform. In so doing, he distinguished between what he called Repressive and Ideological State Apparatuses (RSAs and ISAs). Whereas the RSAs (the army, the police) enforce the established order when it is under threat, the ISAs are far more effective because they circulate the dominant ideas in a society in such a way that most people take them for granted. In his most famous formula, Althusser defined ideology as representing "the imaginary relationship of individuals to their real conditions of existence."[5]

As his critics were quick to note, the main problem with this comprehensive definition is that, if human beings are always subject to ideology, and if indeed their subjectivity is produced by ideology, there seems little room for thoughts and actions that could effect radical change. Moreover, on this account, spectators passively absorb the ideological messages conveyed by popular films. Thus, in order to explain the popularity of the Ealing comedy *Whisky Galore!* (Alexander Mackendrick, 1949) in Scotland despite its allegedly demeaning view of Scottish culture, Scott Malcomson refers to "theories of ideology" that deal with the effects of "the incorporation by the oppressed of the cultural discourses of the oppressors."[6] Audiences who enjoy this film – or, in fact, any mainstream film – are thus cultural dupes who gain pleasure at the expense of their own best interests. Much the same explanation was of course often used to account for the popularity of Hollywood films in Britain.

It is easy to dismiss such arguments on the grounds that they do not allow for the complex and contradictory ways in which people actually engage with films. Cultural-studies methods and the recent turn to cognitive psychology in film theory stress the conscious activity of film spectators rather than their subordination to ideological discourses working at the level of the unconscious. Indeed, the reaction against Althusser had gone so far by 1994 that Christopher Williams (in an article published in *Screen*) could suggest that "ideology has become a hopelessly unusable term."[7]

However, Althusser's work did at least focus attention on the interaction of psychological and social processes in the production and reception of cultural texts and – even if he overstated the consequences – it did explain why social institutions are so resistant to change.

Although he referred to the "communications apparatus" and the "cultural apparatus," Althusser gave them less attention than he almost certainly would if he had been writing ten or fifteen years later. Instead, he insisted that "one ideological State apparatus certainly had the dominant role" and "this is the School." The function of the school is to drum into students "a certain amount of 'know-how' wrapped in the ruling ideology" and to equip them to become productive workers, technicians, or intellectuals. Althusser depicts a bleak situation in which even "those teachers who, in dreadful conditions, attempt to turn the few weapons they can find . . . against the ideology, the system and the practices in which they are trapped" find that "their own devotion contributes to the maintenance and nourishment" of the ideological function of the education system.[8]

In Britain the situation is complicated by a two-tiered school system: a state system of free education, whose condition varies according to where the school is situated, and "public" (actually private, fee-paying, and now often known as "independent") schools attended by a privileged minority. According to Althusser, it matters little whether the ISAs are publicly or privately owned since they all work to legitimate the power of the state and to reinforce its social structure. In Britain it is the private "public" schools whose classrooms traditionally produced the leading figures in public life.

## BUILDING CHARACTER: THE PUBLIC SCHOOL MOVIE

The literary genre of the school novel goes back to Thomas Hughes's *Tom Brown's Schooldays* (1857), and most of the classic examples deal with public schools. Most school movies belong to the same tradition and, as Jeffrey Richards notes, "it was not until the mid-1950s that a grammar school, let alone a secondary modern, was used as the setting for a film."[9] The genre certainly lends itself to ideological readings along the lines suggested by Althusser. The school movie typically raises problems whose origin is variously located in the teachers, the students, or the system, but the ending brings about some form of reconciliation and a sense that the system will survive

**Figure 60.** Mr. Chipping (Robert Donat) introduces his new wife (Greer Garson) to his astonished students in *Goodbye Mr. Chips*.

the test to which it has been put. Since the school readily functions as a microcosm of the nation, the films can also be viewed as allegories about the relevance of national traditions in the modern world.

*Goodbye Mr. Chips* (Sam Wood, 1939) is probably the best-known British school movie, but it was produced by MGM's British operation and directed by a veteran Hollywood director. In the opening sequence, two masters examine a statue of the school's founder and discuss England's historic traditions. Since the school was founded in 1492, it dates back to the discovery of America, setting up a contradictory relationship to the traditions depicted in the film for U.S. audiences, whose own national myths were founded on sweeping away those very traditions. The period covered by the extensive flashback that constitutes most of the narrative includes World War I, and there is an implicit sense throughout of the threat of another war that will once again test the values for which the school stands.

The film frames its narrative nostalgically as a flashback showing the development of Mr. Chipping (Robert Donat) from an awkward and unpopular young teacher to a beloved representative of the school spirit. Despite his difficulties, Chipping never questions the ideals that lie behind public school education and, in his retirement speech, as paraphrased by Richards, he defends "the old public school tradition of concentrating on the building of character, in order to turn out the gentleman all-rounder" who is "neither moneymad nor a snob."[10] He is able to change and succeed as a schoolmaster partly because he marries a woman (Greer Garson) whose feminine presence introduces a new warmth into the masculine school environment (Figure 60).

Although there were (and are) public schools for girls, the boys' schools

**Figure 61.** *The Guinea Pig*: The housemaster (Cecil Trouncer) who resents the presence of Jack (Richard Attenborough) at the school finds that the boy's parents (Bernard Miles, Joan Hickson) are decent people.

were most instrumental in maintaining an ideological framework in which their graduates "naturally" assumed positions of authority. These schools were engaged in the "construction of masculinity," producing "gentlemen [who] recognised each other through a shared repertoire of activity, gesture and idiom, including pronunciation."[11] School movies thus generally focus on the cultural implications of the "construction of masculinity" in an enclosed community of adolescents. The few women who appear in these films play a marginal role in the hierarchy of the school but are important as figures against whom the masculine code can be defined.

In *The Guinea Pig* (Roy Boulting, 1948), the main focus is on Jack (Richard Attenborough), a boy from a poor family who wins a scholarship to a public school, and on the effect of his presence on the teachers and his fellow pupils. However, two women play a prominent role in finally resolving the problems. The housemaster's wife (Edith Sharpe) tries to make the new boy feel at home, despite her husband's resentment at the threat to the school's traditions, and their daughter (Sheila Sim) becomes engaged to a progressive young master who takes over when her father retires. These women have a similar function to Mrs. Chipping, challenging the more rigid traditions but accepting a basically supportive role as wife and surrogate mother to the boys. The ending is also made possible by the housemaster's discovery that the boy's father, a shopkeeper, shares his conservative views and that the school charter includes a provision for teaching "charity boys" (Figure 61).

*The Guinea Pig* appeared at a time when public schools were under attack as an anachronism in the new postwar social order. Ideologically, it works

**Figure 62.** Crocker-Harris (Michael Redgrave) reflects on his situation, as he is watched by his wife (Jean Kent) and her lover (Nigel Patrick) in *The Browning Version.*

by voicing and validating many of the criticisms but then showing that the true public school spirit is flexible enough to accommodate change. *Goodbye Mr. Chips* works in much the same way, although the critical attitude is implicit rather than directly represented. Both films are thus examples of an ideological strategy that Roland Barthes calls "Operation Margarine": "take the established value which you want to restore or develop, and first lavishly display its pettiness, the injustices which it produces, the vexations to which it gives rise . . . ; then, at the last moment, save it *in spite of,* or rather *by* the heavy curse of its blemishes."[12] It is, of course, difficult to know the extent to which actual audiences accepted the films' ideological projects; nor is it clear that all school movies inevitably end up simply supporting the dominant ideology.

A case could be made that *The Browning Version* (Anthony Asquith, 1951) offers a more critical perspective on the education system and its own genre. It is certainly a complex ideological text. Based on a one-act play by Terence Rattigan, it deals with a public-school classics teacher whose retirement forces him to confront the failure of his teaching career and his marriage. The ordeal of Mr. Crocker-Harris (Michael Redgrave) unfolds against a series of allusions to the *Agamemnon* of Aeschylus (and to the translation by Robert Browning), a Greek tragedy whose hero returns home from the Trojan Wars only to be murdered by his wife and her lover. There are ironic parallels between this play and Crocker-Smith's marriage to a wife who is having an affair with another master, but he comes to realize that his situation lacks the tragic grandeur of the original (Figure 62).

Mrs. Crocker-Harris (Jean Kent) despises her husband and contrasts his expected ignominious departure from the school with what she envisages will happen when his successor retires. For him, she suggests, "it'll be roses, roses all the way, and tears and cheers and goodbye, Mr. Chips." *The Browning Version* thus becomes not only an ironic reworking of a Greek tragedy, but also a kind of anti-*Chips* in which a woman's presence produces coldness and failure rather than warmth and success. It is possible to read the public-school setting as merely a background to the personal story, but there is an inevitable association between the failure of human relationships and the ritual and politics of the educational system in which they are embedded. On the other hand, the blame for the situation may be displaced on to the adulterous woman, thus reinforcing the exclusive masculine codes of the public school.

In the final sequence, Crocker-Harris achieves a kind of redemption by deciding to leave his wife and by admitting his failure in his valedictory speech to the school, a speech that receives an enthusiastic ovation and avoids the anticlimax expected by the headmaster. As in *Goodbye Mr. Chips,* failure is transformed into success, although here the change comes too late.[13] The ideological effect remains ambiguous because it is unclear whether the teacher has failed the system or the system the teacher.

A similar uncertainty is apparent in the many comic versions of the school movie. In several comedies starring Will Hay, such as *Boys Will Be Boys* (William Beaudine, 1935) and *Good Morning, Boys* (Marcel Varnel, 1937), a bogus or conniving headmaster dismantles public-school traditions and creates what Marcia Landy calls "a carnival atmosphere in which everything that is considered respectable and predictable is turned upside down."[14] The endings restore order, but the pleasure of these films clearly comes from the mockery of traditional rituals, even if the school is seen as an aberration. The same audiences that enjoyed Hay's antics in these films probably also appreciated *Goodbye Mr. Chips* a few years later.

Whereas the serious school movies descend from *Tom Brown's Schooldays,* the comic treatments of school life draw on popular fiction but often also have their roots in Jean Vigo's film *Zéro de conduite* (1933), an anarchistic fantasy in which a revolt at a school denounces the hypocrisy of French society. Clear allusions to this film appear in several British film comedies of the 1950s.

The opening of *The Happiest Days of Your Life* (Frank Launder, 1950) visually recalls the opening of the French film, and the entire film has a similar anarchic spirit, adapted to a more complicated and farcical plot about a boys' school forced, as result of an error at the Ministry of Education, to share their premises with the pupils and mistresses of a girls' school. Both groups enter into a spirited struggle over space and resources, with the females proving more ruthless and resourceful. However, when the headmistress (Margaret Rutherford) receives a visit from several parents at the same time as the headmaster (Alastair Sim) has an appointment with representatives from a major public school considering him for a job, the male and female staff and students work together to create a good impression. However, the film concludes not with a return to order but with the arrival of busloads of screaming pupils from yet more schools.

*It's Great to Be Young!* (Cyril Frankel, 1955) is an attempt to blend the school movie with the musical through its depiction of a progressive school teacher, Mr. Dingle (John Mills), who encourages the members of the school orchestra in their love of classical, jazz, and pop music. When he loses his job for defying the new headmaster (Cecil Parker) who does not see music as an important part of the curriculum, the students protest by refusing to sing during assembly, and two boys on the roof drop leaflets and a tear-gas capsule. This is an allusion to the ending of *Zéro de conduite,* in which boys on the school roof throw stones at the staff and guests at an outdoor ceremony, but it is defused when Dingle tells the students that they are being irresponsible and the headmaster acknowledges that he was also wrong.

The schools in *The Happiest Days of Your Life* are all public schools, but the one in *It's Great to Be Young!* appears to be a state "grammar school," although most students come from affluent families. *Carry On Teacher* (Gerald Thomas, 1959) deals with a "secondary modern" school whose students are those who failed the entrance examinations for grammar school, but it conveys a similar message about the need for staff and students to work together. As in *The Happiest Days of Your Life,* the headmaster (Ted Ray) wants to put on a good show for inspectors so that he will be considered for the headship of a new progressive school. His rather inept staff, played by many of the *Carry On* regulars (see Chapter 8), try to help, but the pupils stage a campaign of disruption. When he learns that they have misbehaved because they do not want him to leave, the headmaster decides to stay at the school.

In this film, as in *It's Great to Be Young!,* the comedy stresses the conflict between staff and students, but the endings reveal the shared interests of both groups. These are comedies of consensus that promote the idea of a new Britain in which the class hierarchies of the past must be eliminated. This idea is treated more astringently in *The Happiest Days of Your Lives,* where the cooperation serves dubious ends, unleashing anarchic energies that become even more pronounced in the four comedies that it inspired about the monstrous girls of St. Trinian's school.

In the opening of the last of these, *The Great St. Trinian's Train Robbery* (Launder, 1966), officials at the Ministry of Education cheer the news of the Labour victory in the recent general election (much to the disgust of their cleaning woman) because they think it will mean the closure of public schools like St. Trinian's. Their jubilation ends when they discover that the new Labour minister refuses to close the school, supposedly because of his concern for deprived girls but actually because he is having an affair with the headmistress. In the St. Trinian's films, consensus is based on corruption, politics is detached from class, and tradition is a hollow mockery.

## ACTS OF CLASS VILLAINY: *IF. . . .* AND *KES*

The farce conventions of the St. Trinian's films cushion the impact of the satire. Two other films from the end of the 1960s offer a bleaker vision of a society in which political change seems impossible, at the same time that Althusser was producing his major theoretical works. The school in *If. . . .* (Lindsay Anderson, 1968) is a public school at the top of the education hierarchy; *Kes* (Ken Loach, 1969) deals with a state school in a northern industrial city. Both films use the school as a metaphor for the nation and both (like Althusser) came under attack for creating the impression that any effort to change the system was futile. Neither filmmaker is likely to have read Althusser at the time, so the question is not one of influence but of similar responses to a shared cultural context.

By the time he made *If. . . . ,* his second feature film, Lindsay Anderson, had already established himself as an outspoken critic of British culture and the national cinema. He had himself attended a public school, and he became a film critic at Oxford University, where he was one of the founders of *Sequence,* a film journal to which he contributed extensively between 1947 and 1952. During the 1950s, he continued to work as a critic and was the guiding spirit behind the Free Cinema movement. At the same time, he became a stage director at the Royal Court Theatre in London, and he made his first feature film in 1963: *This Sporting Life*, one of the final films of the British New Wave (see Chapter 3).

Like Anderson, Loach occupied a precarious position within British film culture at this time, but for somewhat different reasons. *Kes* was also his second feature film, and it was the beginning of his collaboration with Tony Garnett, a producer who encouraged Loach to develop his realist style as a tool for Marxist political analysis. Although *Kes* was made on a relatively low budget, with fewer concessions to the mainstream than *Poor Cow* (1967), Loach's previous film, it did achieve a modest commercial success. It proved popular with audiences in the north of England, but (after the accents had been somewhat toned down) it also did well in other parts of the country.

In a manifesto first published in 1957, Anderson declared that "the cinema reflects . . . the climate and spirit of a nation" and that British cinema was "dedicated to an out-of-date, exhausted national ideal," reflecting "one of the most class-conscious societies in the world." He placed the blame for this state of affairs largely on "our upper-class system of education."[15] *If. . . .* develops this idea, using the public school as "a metaphor . . . of life in Britain today – the image of the school as a reflection of a certain British tradition or . . . of a hierarchical society."[16]

Similarly, Loach called *Kes* a film about Britain, but the film focuses on a state school to expose "the colossal wastage of kids" as a result of "a national school system that educates them only for failure."[17] In an interview at the time of the film's release, Garnett attacked the 1944 Education Act, which established the principle of free education for all children, as "class villainy." In terms that closely resemble Althusser's, he argued that "education is a reflection of the needs of the ruling class," and its function is to produce workers willing to accept "factory discipline."[18] *Kes* thus represents the school as an ideological apparatus that perpetuates the class system that the Education Act was supposedly designed to dismantle.

As a Marxist, Loach was politically closer to Althusser than was Anderson, but he remained committed to a realist aesthetic as a means of promoting social change (see Chapter 3), casting many nonactors in *Kes* and shooting the film on location in the Yorkshire town of Barnsley. Anderson, on the other hand, described himself as an "anarchist," but he shared Althusser's interest in Brecht, especially the use of "distancing" devices in his plays to encourage the spectator to think about the ideological implications of the action. Accordingly, *If. . . .* uses a number of such devices that present the film as an allegory rather than a realistic depiction of school life. The most prominent of these are the chapter headings and the inclusion of black-and-white sequences in a predominantly color film.

A similar effect is created by the dense pattern of allusions to other texts, literary and cinematic, that is the basis of the film's style. It borrows its title from a poem by Rudyard Kipling, the author most associated with Britain's imperial past, that describes the challenges a boy must confront if he wants to become a man. The film also recalls Kipling's tales of schoolboy life in *Stalky & Co.* (1899), based on his own public-school experiences, in which, as in the film, three boys form a small gang (with one clearly the leader) that challenges the rules and traditions of the school. Whereas Kipling's boys are simply expressing a youthful resistance to adult authority before passing into manhood, Anderson's trio of outsiders eventually become revolutionaries who launch an attack with grenades and machine guns on the guests at a school ceremony (Figure 63).

The frequent allusions to other texts, like the distancing devices, constantly remind us that we are watching a film that belongs to a rich and complex cultural tradition. However, since many critics associated Brecht with a style based on a desire for "objectivity," they objected to several apparent fantasy sequences that seem to draw us into the subjective vision of the rebels. The

**Figure 63.** Mick (Malcolm McDowell) fires from the roof as the guests leave the Founder's Day ceremony at the end of *If. . . .*

most obtrusive of these is a sequence in which the boys shoot the school chaplain in a military exercise and are then asked to apologize to him when the headmaster pulls him from a drawer in his office (Figure 64).

Some critics have argued that "the indistinct border between what is reality and what is . . . fantasy tended to divert the audience, and so work against the film."[19] For others, the "subjective" moments support the overall Brechtian project of the film: "the symbolism, the irony, or the 'as if' quality produced by the chaplain being in the locker" invites "the viewer . . . to question the cinematic experience."[20] As Pam Cook suggests, however, there is no real contradiction in the film's apparent stylistic duality, because *If. . . .* is a film "concerned with the power of the imagination and its place in political action."[21]

The film's working title was *Crusaders,* an allusion to the tradition of "muscular Christianity" that helped to produce both public schools and the British Empire. This title remains as one of the chapter headings while, as Erik Hedling notes, another chapter called "Ritual and Romance" likens Mick (Malcolm McDowell) and his friends to "Grail Knights joined by their struggle for freedom."[22] The chaplain's active role in the school's Army Training Corps reinforces the conjunction of Christianity and militarism, and this tradition is linked to the national culture by the school motto, "I serve the nation," and by the Union Jack prominently displayed at the final assembly.

Although *Kes* adopts a more realist approach that largely avoids overt symbolism, it also deals with the stifling of imagination in modern British society and alludes to national traditions to suggest what is missing in the present. Billy Casper (David Bradley) is a small boy who is bullied at home and at school but reveals hidden capacities when he succeeds in training a kestrel

**Figure 64.** *If. . . . :* The headmaster (Peter Jeffrey) opens a drawer and asks the rebels to apologize to the chaplain (Geoffrey Chater) for shooting him.

("Kes"). The film was based on a novel by Barry Hines whose title, *A Kestrel for a Knave,* refers to a medieval law that designated the kestrel as the only hunting bird that a commoner could own. Billy reveals his suppressed desire for a fuller life through his relationship with the kestrel and, when he describes his experiences in the classroom, the engrossed faces of the other pupils suggest that they also have similar unacknowledged needs (Figure 65).

Falconry offers an escape, both in time and space, from the constraints of Billy's urban environment. Before he finds the kestrel, he takes time out from his newspaper round to read a "Desperate Dan" comic strip on a hill above a factory, suggesting that the mass media create a fantasy of potent masculinity as compensation for the bleak reality (Figure 66). After the gloomy opening that establishes the oppressiveness of Billy's daily life in the city, a haunting orchestral theme in the pastoral tradition of British classical music accompanies his journey into the woods. Later, a hymn sung at the school assembly provides an ironic counterpoint to shots of Billy's older stepbrother, Jud (Freddie Fletcher), and other miners descending into a coal mine. As in *If. . . . ,* these reminders of the past suggest a culture whose ideology masks the absence of those values on which it is supposedly based.

In both films, the effect of the appeal to the past is ambiguous, but in neither is it simply nostalgic. Their depiction of the headmasters exposes the ideological function through which the school system seeks to reconcile tradition and modernity. In *If. . . .* the headmaster speaks of the need for imagination to cope with technological advance and insists that the school adopts a critical attitude to the past; but the effect of his words is undercut by the old portraits by which he is surrounded. The headmaster in *Kes* lectures a

**Figure 65.** *Kes:* Billy (David Bradley) explains to the class how he trained the kestrel as his teacher (Colin Welland) looks on in surprise.

group of students, assembled in his office for punishment, on the merits of their predecessors and tells them that they will end up as "mere fodder for the mass media." He accuses them of not listening, but he himself fails to listen to a small boy who tries to explain that he is there not to receive punishment but with a message from a teacher.

There are also, in both films, younger masters who do their best to respond to the students' needs but who, like the well-meaning teachers described by Althusser, cannot make a significant difference. By including these figures, however, the films raise the question of their own effectiveness as oppositional texts. Their endings seem to confirm the power of the dominant ideology, although Anderson's attempt to avoid what Althusser saw as the pitfalls of realism proved far more ambiguous and controversial.

At the end of *If. . . .* Mick and his allies are on the roof of the school, shooting at students, teachers, parents, and dignitaries in the courtyard below. Although some critics saw the ending as a literal depiction of terrorist violence in which the spectator is asked to identify with the rebels, it functions (typically for Anderson) as a provocation: The rebels aim the machine guns at the spectators in the cinema as well as the people in the courtyard. The final outburst of violence is a logical response to the "muscular Christianity" of the establishment, but Anderson insisted that it works metaphorically and demands a more complex reading.

Many critics recognized the allusion to *Zéro de conduite,* but Pauline Kael objected that, while "Vigo's children were united by the high spirits that were bursting out of repression . . . Anderson devotes most of his energies to the

**Figure 66.** "Desperate Dan is stronger than all": Billy reads a comic strip above the city during a break in his newspaper round in *Kes*.

meanness of the students," and the rebellion is confined to "a self-chosen few."[23] Anderson was aware of this difference, noting that he had consciously modeled the film on "Vigo's poetic method, episodic, fragmentary, charged" but that "Vigo's children escape joyfully along the skyline, singing their . . . song of liberty," whereas "our Mick Travis is left firing desperately, trapped by the massed firepower of the establishment."[24]

The filmmakers were themselves divided about the effect of the ending. While Anderson stressed the impotence of the rebels, the screenwriter David Sherwin argued that Mick "becomes as evil and as terrible as the headmaster or the general."[25] In both interpretations, the ending hardly encourages a strong sense of the possibility of social change; but at least the rebels do act, however ambiguous their actions may be. In *Kes* Billy is more like Jute (Sean Bury), the new boy through whom we are introduced to the school in *If.* . . . and whose size and status make him the bewildered victim of the older boys. Though Jute will presumably find his place in the system, Billy's options are almost nonexistent, and the film ends with the shock of his discovery that Jud has killed the kestrel as an act of revenge because Billy did not place a bet that would have won him the equivalent of a week's wages.

*Kes* represents the possibility of breaking out of Billy's deadlocked situation, but the film ends with the burial of the kestrel. The point, in *If.* . . . as much as in *Kes,* is that the oppression has been internalized so that those who are trapped in the system resent those who try to change it, and those who try to change it are unable to envisage a satisfactory alternative. Although both films certainly stress the difficulty of getting outside ideology (in line with

Althusser's theory), the final effect is not simply a pessimistic recognition of cultural forces that block imagination and resistance. In very different ways, they represent the school as a place that enforces a dominant ideology that clearly works against the interests of the people caught up in it. The shock of their endings invites us to remember the sense of possibility that Mick and Billy briefly enjoyed.

## THE CHALLENGES OF A CHANGED WORLD: RECENT SCHOOL MOVIES

As these films suggest, British society had changed so much by the late 1960s that the ideological perspective of the traditional school movie had come under considerable pressure. The genre did not disappear, but it was largely displaced by youth films in which school life is less important than leisure activities. In terms of Althusser's ISAs, religion, the family, and the school are still major factors in the circulation of ideology, but it is arguable that the "communications apparatus" and the "cultural apparatus" are now more important. The fact that teachers often feel that they must counter the effect of the mass media on their students would suggest that the function of ideology in contemporary culture is rather more complex than Althusser's theory allows.

The relative handful of films dealing with state schools tend to be social-problem films that balance an implicit nostalgia for a past era, when students were supposedly less difficult to handle, with an awareness of the environmental causes of juvenile delinquency. In *To Sir with Love* (James Clavell, 1967), Mark Thackeray (Sidney Poitier), a black teacher in a multicultural school in the East End of London, wins the respect of his class when he discards the curriculum and encourages them to ask questions (Figure 67). His goal is to make education more relevant to their needs, but he also asks them to respect each other by referring to each other as Miss or by surname (for the males). His classes become focused on the skills and attitudes that they will need to survive when they leave school. He teaches them that they must try to change the world, but not by violent means.

Mark thus becomes one of Althusser's decent teachers whose efforts cannot really change the system, although the film ends with his decision not to give up teaching when he realizes what he has accomplished. The situation is even more dire in *The Class of Miss MacMichael* (Silvio Narizzano, 1978) in which Conor MacMichael, a liberal teacher (Glenda Jackson) in a school for "maladjusted students," is frustrated not only by the behavior of her students but also by the monstrous headmaster (Oliver Reed). There are many allusions to horror films, and the film explicitly raises the question of what might be considered "normal" in a world of hypocrisy and repression. While some students respond to creative teaching methods, it is not clear whether

**Figure 67.** *To Sir with Love:* Mark Thackeray (Sidney Poitier) confronts his hostile class before he has taught them the value of good manners.

they have a future, and the film ends inconclusively after the teacher goes berserk and ransacks the headmaster's office. In the final sequence, she looks down as he leaves, but there is no suggestion that her rebellion will actually make a difference.

When MacMichael returns home at the beginning of the film, she passes through a line of uniformed schoolboys who courteously make way for her. She smiles wryly, apparently recognizing that these are the "normal" students against whom the undirected vitality of her pupils will be judged. This image anticipates the nostalgia for a social order based on a clearly defined class hierarchy that became a major factor in the backlash against the "liberation" politics of the 1960s and the consequent loss of respect for traditional values. Although the school movie did not figure prominently among the nostalgic fictions produced by this development, the rather surprising remakes of *Goodbye Mr. Chips* (Herbert Ross, 1969) and *The Browning Version* (Mike Figgis, 1994) provide an opportunity to examine how generic conventions were adjusted (or not) to a new cultural context.

The second version of *Goodbye Mr. Chips* updates the action of James Hilton's short novel (published in 1934) not to the present but just enough to allow Chipping (Peter O'Toole) to make his retirement speech after guiding the school through the danger and disruption of World War II. He tells the boys they must face up to the challenges of "a changed world" that may lead to the end of the school as he and they have known it. Although he advises them to accept these changes, the final sequence shows the retired master benignly watching the traditional roll call of the boys that he himself conducted so many times in the past. Wartime shortages had forced the abandonment of school uniforms, but now the new boys are again wearing the old uniform.

Jeffrey Richards is very much in the minority when he claims that the remake is "even better" than the first film and "in fact one of the finest films the cinema has produced."[26] There is little in this semimusical version of the classic story that suggests the filmmakers intended the contradiction between word and image in the final sequence as a critical comment on the lack of real change in postwar Britain. Like the original, it was produced in Britain by MGM, with a Hollywood director, and the studio must have felt that there was still an American market for the story of a public schoolmaster who overcomes his weaknesses to earn the respect and affection of his students and colleagues.

During the 1980s, the British "heritage film" appealed to the same market (see Chapter 11), and the remake of *The Browning Version* turns the school into a large country house like those featured in many heritage films. However, it eliminates the sardonic allusion to *Goodbye Mr. Chips* in the original, and the story is updated to the present. According to the headmaster, Britain is now a "multicultural society," but the only visible evidence is that the class has one black student, who plays loud music in the washroom and turns out to be the son of a Nigerian diplomat. Unlike his earlier incarnation, this Crocker-Harris (Albert Finney) is a good teacher whose qualities are not appreciated by his pupils and colleagues, who all regard classics as irrelevant to a modern curriculum. At the end, there are hints that his wife (Greta Scacchi) may return, unlike the original in which the rupture is clearly final.

When Crocker-Harris shakes hands with a student and sees his wife waiting after the final assembly, a statue of Henry VIII is visible in the background. The figure of the king often associated with the founding of public schools (as in *The Guinea Pig*) watches over the apparent happy ending, a symbol of continuity, it would seem, rather than an ironic comment on the reunion of husband and wife from a monarch famed for his sexual appetite and changing wives to meet its needs. Like much of British culture since the 1960s, the film is caught between a recognition that the system is out of date and a nostalgia for its values.

# CHAPTER ELEVEN

# The Long Memory

## History and Heritage

The past is a highly visible presence in the British landscape. In his historical account of *The Making of the English Landscape,* first published in 1955, W. G. Hoskins described the signs of human settlement across the country dating back to pre-Roman times. Revisiting his work twenty years later, Hoskins noted that recent discoveries show that "everything is older than we think," and he went on to suggest that an attention to the historical landscape offers "refreshment and sanctuary from noise and meaningless movement."[1] Other historians have challenged this idea of the past as a refuge from the ravages of modernity, pointing out that many national traditions that seem to have their roots in the "deep past" are relatively recent fabrications. Eric Hobsbawm thus argues that the dominant myths of national identity depend on the "invention of tradition" and that it is "the very appearance of movements for the defence or revival of traditions" that provides evidence of a break with the past.[2]

In a discussion of Hobsbawm's argument, Robert Colls suggests that it tends to simplify the "complex and overlapping processes of invention, transformation and recovery."[3] The sense of "living in an old country" thus involves an intricate combination of historical awareness and mythmaking.[4] As Peter Miles and Malcolm Smith suggest, "the past is, in fact, simply dead and gone," but "assumptions about the lived experience of the past must form part of our lived culture in the here and now; history works for society as a whole as memory works for the individual."[5]

History thus provides a powerful but contested sense of tradition against which the present state of the nation is often judged. In the case of Britain, however, there have been many complaints, from across the political spectrum, that an obsession with the past has prevented the nation from fully exploiting modern technology and industrial advances. According to the Marxist historian Tom Nairn, for example, "the English national identity sags with the accumulated weight of its symbols and traditions,"[6] yet Martin Wiener develops a very similar argument in his book *English Culture and the Decline of the Industrial Spirit,* written from a perspective sympathetic to Margaret Thatcher's brand of conservatism.

Wiener analyzes the emergence and effects of a myth that he sees as a major factor in the "economic decline" that Thatcher was fighting at the time he was writing his book. He places the blame on "a conception of Englishness that virtually excluded industrialism," preventing Britain from fully exploiting its position as the "world's first industrial nation."[7] According to this argument, when power shifted from the upper to the middle classes during the Industrial Revolution, traditional aristocratic values retained their prestige and authority. However, Wiener pays little attention to the actuality of industrial life that made the myth attractive, and he does not really explain why its appeal is not limited to the classes in which it originated.

The appeal of the "heritage" movement can be seen as a product of what Jeffrey Richards calls "the widespread and deep-rooted hatred of modernity – the dehumanization, the exploitation and pollution that it has entailed."[8] The result would seem to be the construction of a version of the national past that has little relevance to most people's everyday experience and whose most potent image is the green rural landscape. Yet it is still possible for most Britons to enjoy such scenes by driving out of the urban areas in which the majority of them live, and the representation of this version of the past gains its strength from an awareness that it survives in the present, even though under threat and increasingly dependent on government protection.

Although Thatcher supported the principle of a free-market economy and sought to instill an entrepreneurial spirit into the nation, she also promoted a cultural vision of a return to supposedly Victorian family values. While the National Heritage Acts of 1980 and 1983 upheld the backward-looking tendencies deplored by Wiener, they also made good economic sense in view of the emergence of the "heritage industry" as a distinctive feature of the "postmodern" media environment. The idea of heritage thus offers a sense of continuity that masks cultural changes even while it draws on a nostalgic desire to reverse the effects of those changes. The result is a culture that uses the signs of history in highly contradictory ways.

There is, however, an important but difficult distinction to be made between history and heritage. Robert Hewison argues that "heritage is gradually effacing history, by substituting an image of the past for its reality," with the effect that "the open story of history has become the closed story of heritage."[9] This distinction depends on viewing history as an ongoing process, subject to reinterpretation in the light of new developments, whereas heritage stands for a nostalgic version of the past, seen as a fixed source of values against which the uncertain present is measured and found wanting. In practice, it is difficult to separate the two ways of seeing the past, and their interaction in British historical cinema is highly unstable. The meanings generated in these films depend partly on the attitudes of the filmmakers but also on those of the spectators, and both are shaped by the cultural contexts in which the films are made and viewed.

It might be better to distinguish among three kinds of film dealing with the past: *historical films,* based on actual events, in which the fictional elements are to some degree constrained by the historical record; *heritage films,* often adapted from literary classics, in which the plot and characters are fictional but located in a specific historical period; and *costume films,* set in a vaguely defined past, which show little respect for history or the national heritage.

Examples of the third category would include the Gainsborough costume melodramas of the 1940s and the Hammer horror films of a decade or so later (see Chapters 4 and 9, respectively). In this chapter, I focus on the first two categories.

## THE PLEASURES OF PROPERTY: *HOWARDS END* AND *MANSFIELD PARK*

Andrew Higson points out that "heritage cinema has since the 1910s been a vital plank in efforts to construct, maintain and reproduce a national cinema in this country."[10] Yet the term itself did not come into currency until the 1980s, at the time of the growth of the heritage industry. It was used to describe a cycle of films that looked back to an apparently less troubled past, with especial emphasis on upper-class society in the Edwardian age, the years preceding World War I. These films were often seen as the expression of a widespread discontent with the present state of the nation that also swept Thatcher to power.

In keeping with her free-market philosophy, Thatcher quickly dismantled the quota and subsidy systems designed to protect the film industry, and the international success of the heritage films without such assistance was often seen as a vindication of her policies. However, the relations between the vision of the nation in these films and the politics of Thatcherism became the subject of lively (and highly repetitive) debate. Rather than rehearse the theoretical arguments yet again, I focus on two films that illustrate many of the issues involved in the heritage debate. Like most of these films, *Howards End* (James Ivory, 1991) and *Mansfield Park* (Patricia Rozema, 1999) are adaptations of novels already established as part of the nation's literary heritage, and their central iconographic image is, as Higson describes it, "an imposing country house seen in an extreme long shot and set in a picturesque, verdant landscape."[11]

Both films also illustrate the international involvement in the production of many heritage films, which might seem surprising for "a genre which focuses on the English middle and upper classes at home and abroad before they were drowned by the flood of the First World War and the end of the Empire."[12] *Howards End* was made by Merchant Ivory Productions, a company whose main creative personnel were of Indian (producer Ismail Merchant), American (director James Ivory), and Polish–German-Jewish origins (screenwriter Ruth Prawer Jhabvala), and much of its budget came from Japanese sources. Patricia Rozema, who wrote and directed *Mansfield Park,* is a Canadian filmmaker of Dutch descent, working for an American company (Miramax).[13]

Forster was the preferred novelist of British heritage cinema during the 1980s, then Austen took over in the 1990s. The Austen novels depict a rather more stable society than Forster's, but both writers dealt with social and cultural issues that were very much part of contemporary experience for their first readers. In the film adaptations, the characters and events belong to the past, and their visual appeal depends heavily on the historical settings. According to Higson's influential argument, the films diluted the critical view of British society in the novels on which they were based and instead displayed "the past . . . as visually spectacular pastiche, inviting a nostalgic gaze that resists the ironies and social critiques so often suggested narratively."[14]

Ivory, the director most frequently identified with heritage cinema, denies that his films promote a nostalgic desire to return to a supposedly simpler past and insists that they "are fired as much by skepticism and indignation as by affection and admiration."[15] Admittedly, he makes this claim in a lavishly illustrated coffee-table book that also includes directions for tourists who wanted to visit the locations used in the films, but it does suggest the complex interaction of nostalgia, social criticism, and commodification at work in the films and in the spectators' responses to them. Claire Monk thus responded to Higson's argument by suggesting that the representation of "Englishness" in these films is "blatantly a *construct,* a product of cross-cultural masquerade, intrinsically impure" and that, "rather than involving any drive towards a unified or class identity, [they] are . . . concerned with division and uncertainty – of the characters' psyches as much as the social class to which they belong."[16]

Monk refers to recent critical work on the Gainsborough melodramas and likens the critics who dismiss the heritage films to earlier critics who attacked a cycle of films that appealed mainly to women (see Chapter 4).[17] According to Marcia Landy, however, the Gainsborough films refuse "to create a sense of 'actual' historical context" and thus enable "the spectator to appropriate events as contemporary to the viewer."[18] This strategy appears quite different from the heritage films, which situate their characters in a richly textured mise-en-scène in which, according to Higson, "objects, buildings, and landscapes become heritage fetishes, objects to be looked at, rather than to be used as narrative devices."[19] On the other hand, as Carl Freedman points out, for all their attention to detail, the heritage films provide few

**Figure 68.** "Even I know a good thing when I see it": Margaret (Emma Thompson) admires the house to which Henry (Anthony Hopkins) has invited her before making his proposal in *Howards End*.

"historically specific allusions" that would date the action for modern audiences.[20]

These conflicting critical responses suggest that the meanings generated by heritage films are far from stable. Indeed Higson's complaint that "mise-en-scène and drama . . . work against each other in their construction of the national past" implies a kind of divided attention that does not necessarily result in a simple nostalgic response.[21] In one sequence in *Howards End,* for example, Margaret Schlegel (Emma Thompson) visits Henry Wilcox (Anthony Hopkins) to discuss the possibility of renting one of his London properties. In the course of a strained and devious conversation on a staircase, Henry manages to propose and Margaret to accept him, with almost no direct reference to his loneliness after the death of his wife or her fear that she is destined never to marry. The luxurious setting, to which our attention is drawn visually and through the conversation, complicates our response to the strangled emotions, linking the couple's desires to the questions of property with which they are entangled (Figure 68).

Most of the dialogue in this sequence is taken from the novel and, as Forster's narrator comments, the proposal hardly ranks "among the world's great love scenes." The narrator makes a few more such remarks during the chapter devoted to the proposal, but the narration here depends mainly (as in much of the novel) on the blending of the narrator's voice with Margaret's inner thoughts. Thus, even before she goes to London, we are told that Margaret suspects that the invitation may be "a manoeuvre to get her to London, and result in an offer of marriage." When Henry does propose, we learn of her "immense joy" and her realization that she loves him. It is for his sake, we are told, that she keeps the conversation "in tints of the quietest gray" but, immediately after, "she thrilled with happiness."[22]

We also, in the novel, see the house through Margaret's eyes as Henry shows her around, and she draws conclusions about his character from his taste in furniture. Virginia Woolf described Forster as a novelist "who sees his people in close contact with their surroundings," but the descriptive passages in this chapter involve us in Margaret's inner life and help us to understand her response to the proposal.[23] In the film, on the other hand, we have to take in the surroundings while the characters are arranging their future lives. The film allows us to see the setting for ourselves, just as we see the actors and the costumes they are wearing, but we are in some ways more detached than a reader of the novel. We do not know whether Margaret is surprised by Henry's proposal or whether she accepts it out of love (as in the novel) or because she wants the security of marriage or because she feels a (perhaps unconscious) attraction to the dynamic modern ways that he represents.

Questions of property are certainly central to a narrative in which the ownership of the titular house is tied to the displacement of the landed gentry by a new class whose wealth comes from trade. Although Ruth Wilcox (Vanessa Redgrave) was born at Howards End, a relatively small country house, her husband's wealth comes from the Anglo-Imperial Rubber Company, which has its headquarters in London and business interests in many parts of the empire. Henry and his children suppress his wife's dying wish that Margaret should inherit Howards End and, when Margaret visits Henry in his office to seek help for her sister Helen (Helena Bonham Carter), his son Charles (James Wilby) stands in front of a map of Africa as he advises his father to "keep Howards End out of it." The ties between domestic property and imperial enterprise are subtly but clearly defined.

The novel uses the house as "the symbolic representation of civilised England" and raises the question of "who are its inheritors?"[24] In the course of the narrative, it passes from a woman whose family had lived there for centuries to an acquisitive businessman to a young woman whose "English" qualities are enriched by a cultural sensibility inherited from her German father. The values associated with Howards End, located as it is in a pastoral landscape shaped by folk customs, have a mystic power that set them apart from the philistine attitudes of the nouveau riche Wilcox family. It thus seems rather disingenuous for Monk, a critic generally sympathetic to heritage films, to claim that Merchant Ivory turned "Forster's most critical novel into a complacent Tory tract on the pleasures of property."[25] In the film, it is Henry who views Howards End as a property, but he gets no pleasure from it, and the film is at least as critical of him as the novel.

Indeed the film's plot follows the novel very closely. The story of Margaret's friendship with Ruth and her marriage to Henry is complicated by that of Helen, who has an illegitimate child by Leonard Bast (Samuel West), a poor office worker whom they have tried to help but who, thanks to bad advice from Henry, has lost his job. After Charles Wilcox kills Leonard in the name of the family honor, his father's health deteriorates, and the two sisters are united at Howards End where they care for Helen's child, who will eventually inherit the property.

At the end of novel, Margaret's awareness that "life's going to be melted down, all over the world" does not prevent her from hoping that "our house is the future as well as the past."[26] At the end of the film, the spectator's response must include an awareness that the characters' future is now our past and that, although Henry Wilcox is a broken man, it is his values rather than Margaret's that triumphed historically. The idyllic final shot in which a farmer follows his horse-drawn plough across a field in front of Howards End is shadowed by the exhaust fumes of the car on the adjacent road. While the appeal of this image is clearly nostalgic, moral and material issues have become hopelessly entangled in the course of the devious process by which the original bequest has been fulfilled.

Forster's novels themselves look back nostalgically to a more stable society that, if it ever existed, did so only in the circumscribed social arena in which Jane Austen set her novels. Writing almost a hundred years before Forster, Austen's assured and witty style is made possible by confining her narratives to the domestic lives of young women living in genteel society. The film adaptations generally respect this strategy of confinement, and they depend heavily – like the earlier heritage films – on the visual appeal of period costumes and settings. Inevitably, they allow their young lovers more physical intimacy than was possible according to the rules of social decorum by which the characters in the novels were bound, although the lovemaking is still very restrained by contemporary standards.

The film version of *Persuasion* (Roger Michell, 1995) draws on hints in the novel to open out the action to include sequences set on a ship that has been involved in the Napoleonic Wars. In *Mansfield Park,* Rozema went even further and created what John Wiltshire calls a heritage film that "seeks to modify, perhaps contest, the genre from within."[27] The two major changes entailed by this strategy were the incorporation of passages from Austen's letters and early fiction, as if Fanny Price (Frances O'Connor) was their author – thereby making her a much more lively and confident character than in the novel – and the development of the implications of the dependence of her uncle's wealth on slave labor.

As in *Howards End,* the title refers to a country house, and the plot similarly involves a devious process whereby the heroine eventually becomes its owner through marriage. Its first appearance in the film, however, makes it seem less like the luxurious mansions of heritage cinema and more like the haunted houses of Gothic fiction. The young Fanny travels by coach from her crowded and uncomfortable family home and passes a ship from which she hears singing that, the coachman tells her, comes from its "black cargo." She finally arrives at Mansfield Park at night, and it looms threateningly against the dark skies. Even when she is inside, it looks cold and empty, underlining the girl's discomfort in her new surroundings.

Rozema's Fanny quickly matures into a young woman who reads to the camera from her fantastic stories and from letters to her sister in which she comments caustically on what is going on around her. As Andy Richards puts it, she is "resolutely all the things the Fanny of the novel is not: vivacious, artistic, even sexy."[28] This is a major departure from the narrative technique of the novel in which there is a clear distinction between the narrator and the character. Wiltshire argues that it violates Austen's "mastery of techniques for the representation of inner life" because, while it invests Fanny with "private selfhood," it abolishes "interior depth" and trivializes her by representing her "in fragments taken only from burlesque."[29] Yet the effect is to give her a tremendous energy and, while this is clearly not Austen's Fanny, the film implies that she represents the vitality and independence that enabled the writer to achieve the assured tone of her mature work.

In any case, Austen's fictional world is not as remote from social and historical realities as critics often maintain. Raymond Williams points out that her focus on "the standards which govern human behaviour" involves "a direct preoccupation with estates, incomes and social position, which are seen as indispensable elements of all the relationships that are projected and formed."[30] In a discussion of the novel that seems to have had a major impact on Rozema's screenplay, Edward Said argues that *Mansfield Park* is "the most explicit in its ideological and moral affirmations of Austen's novels" and that it "steadily, if unobtrusively, opens up a broad expanse of domestic imperialist culture."[31] He points out that, while there are only a few direct references to the sugar plantations in Antigua, these would be enough for the contemporary reader to fill in the gaps and realize that the way of life at Mansfield Park depends on the slave trade.

Rather than allow the colonial context to remain in the background, as it does in *Howards End,* Rozema develops it in ways that will impress it on a modern film viewer. The opening sequence establishes a parallel between the slaves on the ship and Fanny confined in the coach that is taking her from her home. Although there is no suggestion that the two situations are the same, the treatment of Fanny stems from the logic that justifies slavery, and she feels trapped and homesick. The film also attributes the excessive behavior of Fanny's cousin Tom (James Purefoy), which results in a near-fatal illness, to his shock at what he saw on his father's plantation. When she is nursing him, Fanny discovers Tom's sketchbook in which he has depicted white men, including his father, beating and raping black slaves, the brutal imagery "rupturing . . . the film's predominantly genteel *mise en scène*" (Figure 69).[32]

The more explicit treatment of this theme in the film, like the feminist revisions to its heroine, thus represents a critical reading in the spirit of Said's

**Figure 69.** *Mansfield Park:* Mr. Bertram (Harold Pinter) insists that his son is "mad" when he catches Fanny (Frances O'Connor) with Tom's sketchbook depicting atrocities on the family's sugar plantation.

discussion to bring out issues already present in the novel in a way that recognizes historical and cultural changes since it was published. Rozema says that her approach draws on "the audience's knowledge about what kind of form we have entered here . . . , including their knowledge of the conventions of romance."[33] By making Fanny a storyteller, the film plays with its own narrative conventions and draws attention to the tension between romance and the laws of property. When her uncle (Harold Pinter) accuses her of reading too many novels, she admits that she is "an unabashed novel reader," but insists that this has not affected her judgment in rejecting an arranged marriage.

As in all good romances, the film's ending brings together the lovers, in this case Fanny and her cousin Edmund (Jonny Lee Miller), and thwarts those who have tried to prevent their union. It playfully draws attention to its conventionality by having Fanny narrate what happened to each character, and twice acknowledge that "it might have turned out different." Each time, the characters freeze for a moment, before Fanny adds, "but it didn't." According to Wiltshire, this ending is "a fantasy at odds with the very premises of Austen's art" that reveals the film's inability to "cope with the material it feels ideologically driven to contain."[34] However, Rozema again seems to be developing a hint from Said, who comments that Austen displays "a bit of metafictional impatience" in her own ending when the narrator declares that she is "impatient to restore every body, not greatly in fault with themselves, to tolerable comfort, and to have done with the rest."[35]

## THIS SCEPTRED ISLE: THREE RECENT ROYAL FILMS

According to Geoffrey Macnab, "British cinema has always enjoyed basking in the shadow of monarchy."[36] The pageantry of royalty is a major feature of the heritage industry, but the public role of the monarchy has come under scrutiny in recent years, mainly because of a series of scandals involving the private lives of members of the Royal Family. Many British historical films have depicted kings and queens, as major or minor characters, and, in effect, have charted the process by which the monarchy gradually evolved from an institution of absolute power (the object of the dynastic wars chronicled in Shakespeare's history plays) to its present purely ceremonial function. The representation of the monarchy in these films thus depends on the period in which the action takes place, but it also draws on public feelings toward royalty at the time the films were made.

The modern role of the monarchy as a force for stability and respectability in the nation dates back to the reign of Queen Victoria, and the first major challenge to this role came with the abdication crisis of 1936, when Edward VIII, who had been king for only a few months, decided to renounce the throne so that he could marry a divorced woman. Herbert Wilcox's two films about Victoria, *Victoria the Great* (1937) and *Sixty Glorious Years* (1938), thus functioned as a reaffirmation of the monarchy at a time of doubt and uncertainty, and perhaps also as a corrective to the irreverence of Korda's *The Private Life of Henry VIII* (see Chapter 2).

The crisis was effectively managed by the government, and George VI, with his wife and young family, not only restored confidence in the monarchy but adapted it to the demands of the People's War. In many wartime documentaries and newsreels, the king and queen are shown mingling with the people, viewing bomb damage or simply enjoying family life with their two young daughters.

The coronation of Elizabeth II in 1953 was a spectacular celebration of the end of postwar austerity, with the new monarch symbolizing continuity and the nation's ability to reconcile tradition and modernity. *A Queen Is Crowned* (Castleton Knight, 1953), a documentary record of the coronation, begins with images of white cliffs and green field as Laurence Olivier recites John of Gaunt's speech, from Shakespeare's *Richard II*, in praise of "this sceptred isle." After a brief fragment of "Jerusalem" is heard over shots of a rural village, the narration acknowledges that the nation is "no longer England only" and introduces images of Scotland, Wales, and Ireland, before noting that "the Commonwealth of nations" is also part of "the realms and territories of the Queen."

This brief opening sequence unites images of the landscape, rural life, and royal castles to suggest the natural and historical roots of the monarchy and the national traditions that it embodies. There is no reference to cities or to industry, but it does allude to modern conditions through the reference to the Commonwealth, an institution through which Britain hoped to maintain its status as a world power despite the loss of the empire. The coronation itself was also an event that combined the traditional spectacle of royalty with the popular culture of street parties throughout the nation, and it coincided with the emergence of television, the medium that enabled much of the population to see it and whose live coverage had more impact than the Technicolor images of the film that was released several days later.

The queen herself also functioned as a symbol for new times – a "new Elizabethan age" – through the ways in which her image circulated in discourses that sought to reconcile traditional gender roles with modern trends. Christine Geraghty argues that she personified "the mature woman of the 1950s with the emphasis on glamour as well as responsibility, on youth as well as maturity, on motherhood and public duty, on being a wife as well as a mother."[37] As the final items on this daunting list suggest, the monarchy articulates political and domestic issues primarily through the image of the Royal Family, both in the literal sense of the relations of the monarch and in the idea of the monarch as the head of the national family. It is hardly surprising, then, that historical films have tended to focus on the conflict between the monarch's private life and public role, with the result that they often intersect with broader concerns about personal rights and public responsibilities.

Pamela Church Gibson draws attention to this theme when she distinguishes between heritage films, in which "there is often a conflict between private longings and social expectations, with the protagonists invariably choosing personal freedom over stifling social convention," and "royal films," in which "no such escape is possible . . . , with potential solutions to personal problems often entailing a constitutional crisis."[38] Under George VI and Elizabeth II, it seemed that the conflict between public duty and personal fulfillment had been resolved, but it emerged again in scandals concerning the private life of Elizabeth's sister, Margaret, and then, in even stronger form, around the failure of the marriage of Prince Charles and Lady Diana Spencer. The "royal film" had been largely in abeyance since the 1930s (although royal fictions flourished on television), but three major films of the 1990s – *The Madness of King George* (Nicholas Hytner, 1994), *Mrs. Brown* (John Madden, 1997), and *Elizabeth* (Shekhar Kapur, 1998) – dealt with crises in the lives of monarchs in different historical periods but very much in the context of contemporary debates on the monarchy.

Commenting on attitudes to the Royal Family in the early 1990s, Rosalind Brunt claimed that "in Britain far from disappearing the monarchy has never been so popular." She described the wedding of Prince Charles and Lady Diana in 1981 as "a popular spectacle [that] offered a view of Britishness intended for export as well as home consumption," fulfilling "the requirement that royalty overcompensate for national inadequacy" and revealing an "aspiration for a myth of nationhood that could reverse decline and overcome social division."[39] The later breakdown of the royal marriage, and the Royal Family's undemonstrative response to Diana's gruesome death, placed great strain on the popular appeal of the monarchy while, at the same time, making highly visible the pressures of public life (and media publicity) on the members of the Royal Family. The three "royal films" of the 1990s adapted history to suit this new cultural context, each dealing with a personal crisis in the life of a monarch, who like Elizabeth II, had a long and eventful reign.

The monarch in *The Madness of King George*, adapted by Alan Bennett from his own stage play, is George III, who reigned from 1760 to 1820. In the course of a political crisis occasioned by the king's mental illness, the struggle between rival factions in Parliament confirms that the monarch no longer has any real power. As performed by Nigel Hawthorne, the king seems to be caught between a desire to assert his authority and a recognition of his mainly ceremonial function (he is especially troubled by the loss of the American colonies). His illness undermines the myth of the sanctity of the king's body, and much of the film deals with his treatment by a doctor/priest (Ian Holm) who uses his eyes to calm the king, breaking the taboo against looking at the monarch.

According to Craig Tepper, the king's eventual recovery brings about an ending that implies that, unlike the Americans and French, the British did not resort to revolution but instead reshaped "their national psyche" by "exorcising" from the king's "mind and body, through the newly devolving authority, vested in medicine and the law, the madness that therein resided God and England."[40] This idea needs to be qualified by the revelation, in a closing caption, that the king probably suffered from porphyria, a physical condition on which the medical practices depicted in the film could have had no effect, and by the film's depiction of the legal and political establishment as hardly more sane than the king. Since the caption also mentions that porphyria is a hereditary disease, it also hints that its effects may still be at work in the contemporary situation.

Some critics objected that the film suppresses the fact that George had later bouts of madness and that it seems to ask us to identify with a king who was historically repugnant. According to Jonathan Coe, *The Madness of King George* asks us "to accept that the return to power of someone who was (as the film cannot help making pretty clear) an intolerant despot should be regarded as some sort of happy ending."[41] Other critics agreed that "the audience's sympathy is firmly with the King" and that the ending is a "merely triumphalist finale."[42] However, these responses downplay the film's ironies and its double perspective on George, who is both a despot and a deeply troubled man. His "recovery" is also called into question when he is told that he seems to be more like himself and replies that he was always himself, even when he was ill, but has now learnt how to *seem* himself.

**Figure 70.** "We must be a model family for the nation to look to": George III (Nigel Hawthorne) and his family wave to the crowds after his recovery at the end of *The Madness of King George.*

The film ends with the Royal Family posing for what would later be called a "photo opportunity," as the king tells them that it is their job to be a "model family" (Figure 70). As David Cannadine makes clear in his study of the recent history of the monarchy, the image presented here does not conform to historical reality, in which "the lives, loves and morals of George III's children were such as to make them arguably the most unloved royal generation in English history."[43] The ending of *The Madness of King George* does, however, point to the emerging cultural order in which the symbolic power of the monarchy came to depend on the image. Cannadine quotes Walter Bagehot, who wrote in 1871 that "to be a symbol, and an effective symbol, you must be vividly and often seen," and he comments that "the nadir of royal grandeur and ceremonial presence was reached in those two decades following Albert's death" when Queen Victoria became known as Mrs. Brown.[44]

The reference is to an almost forgotten episode in the reign of a monarch who reigned from 1837 to 1901 and who gave her name to the values that Conservative politicians sought to restore in the 1980s. As depicted in *Mrs. Brown,* Victoria (Judi Dench) withdraws from public life until she gradually overcomes her grief with the help of John Brown, a bluff Scotsman (played by the comedian Billy Connolly). While her family and other members of the royal household have been urging her to resume her public duties, they are now scandalized by her personal relationship with a commoner. As critics were quick to notice, the historical situation depicted in the film could easily be applied to the contemporary crisis, "with the spectre of Diana invoked in the Queen's anger at being denied the love which she needs to sustain her."[45] One critic even suggested that Diana "showed Britain the same spirit that John Brown sought to instil in Victoria."[46]

**Figure 71.** "Don't even think it": The courtiers notice how "flushed" Queen Victoria (Judi Dench) is when she returns late from a trip with Brown (Billy Connolly) in *Mrs. Brown.*

Kara McKechnie argues that, "although the visual approach of the film is not overtly postmodern, the ways its love story is foregrounded over the 'demands' of history and biography take advantage of gaps in historical record-ing."[47] Earlier historical films also exploited such gaps, but "postmodern" his-torical films, like the three "royal films" of the 1990s, play with the uncertain boundaries between history and myth. In the case of *Mrs. Brown,* the film is careful not to offer "proof" that the queen's relationship with Brown is any-thing more than friendship but, when they return late from a visit to a family on her estate, one member of the household suggests that she looks flushed and may be drunk. Another insists she is not; but when the first tries to offer an alternative explanation, the second adds, "don't even think it" (Figure 71).

The film thus slyly undermines the traditional view of the queen, but its ideological implications are rather ambiguous. In the second half of the film, Victoria distances herself from Brown, who destroys himself through his al-coholism and paranoid care for her safety. Although Colin McArthur accuses the film of "operating an ideological con trick," it hardly functions as an un-problematic affirmation of the status quo.[48] The (qualified) sympathy that the film elicits for Victoria depends on a recognition that she does not live up to "Victorian" values.

The third "royal film" goes back further in time, to the reign of the first Queen Elizabeth (r., 1558–1603). This monarch had been the subject of many earlier films, which focused mainly on the period of the defeat of the Spanish Armada (in 1588). *Elizabeth* deals with the beginning of her reign and depicts "her change from a young political innocent – and a highly sexual woman – to a machiavellian and deliberately sexless stateswoman."[49] Kapur, an experi-enced Indian director, was best known internationally for his *Bandit Queen* (1994), a graphic, fact-based account of an abused woman who became the

**Figure 72.** "I have become a virgin": Queen Elizabeth (Cate Blanchett) appears before her court in her new image as the Virgin Queen at the end of *Elizabeth.*

leader of a gang of outlaws. In its violent opening sequence, the burning of "heretics" by the orders of the Catholic Queen Mary, *Elizabeth* declares its difference from the restraint associated with British heritage and history films.

Critics differ over the extent of the film's concern with the visual representation of the historical period. Church Gibson argues that "the fastidious attention to period detail which characterises the heritage film is conspicuously missing," but both Moya Luckett and Kara McKechnie find the film visually authentic.[50] The different perceptions here point to the difficulty of defining an accurate historical image when our sense of the period owes so much to media representations, but all these critics agree that the narrative shows "scant respect for actuality." McKechnie argues that it demonstrates "the postmodern approach to history" more forcefully than *The Madness of King George* or *Mrs. Brown.*[51]

Though all three films take liberties with the historical record, *Elizabeth* alludes to actuality primarily through a well-known portrait of the queen that celebrates the image of the Virgin Queen, which Elizabeth (Cate Blanchett) deliberately constructs at the end of the film (Figure 72). The film undermines this image, by showing Elizabeth's sexual relationship with the Earl of Leicester (Joseph Fiennes), but affirms its effectiveness. Elizabeth uses it to end the political intrigues over whom she should marry and thus appropriates the mythic power that the Virgin Mary formerly had over the people. While some critics felt that this trajectory turned her into "a kind of Elizabethan Princess Di," others emphasized the ways in which Kapur captures "the age's intensity and oddity . . . its otherness from us as well as him."[52] At the end, Elizabeth's transformation is accompanied first by Mozart's *Requiem* and then by Elgar's stately "Nimrod" variation as her acceptance of death-in-life turns her into an icon of the national culture.

It is the extremity of the tension between history and contemporaneity that distinguishes *Elizabeth* from the other two films, but the outcome is quite similar. If, as Church Gibson maintains, these outcomes were determined by history, the films all offer ironic endings in which the monarch overcomes difficulties but achieves success on terms that expose the moral hypocrisy of the public sphere. George III regains his sanity, Victoria returns to public life, and Elizabeth gains control of the nation, but they all must construct an image whose symbolic power depends on the suppression of their physical bodies and personal desires.

## THE MELODRAMA OF CONSCIOUSNESS: HENRY JAMES AND THE HERITAGE FILM

According to Church Gibson, these "cinematic representations of monarchy" – *Elizabeth,* in particular – "moved so far beyond the constraints of the heritage genre as to alter and destabilise it."[53] While it is not clear that these films count as heritage films, based on Church Gibson's own definition quoted above, there were already several films whose critical or ironic treatment of generic conventions had earned the label *postheritage.* Monk, for example, uses the term to describe films, like Sally Potter's *Orlando* (1992) and Christopher Hampton's *Carrington* (1995), that provided "the visual, literary and performative period pleasures associated with . . . the heritage film" while distancing themselves from "the conservatism those films were so often condemned for in the 80s and early 90s."[54]

Since Monk herself did not find heritage films conservative and argued that, in any case, the term was a critical construct used by "the academic/ intellectual left" as a political weapon, she did not see the need for postheritage strategies.[55] However, a rather different challenge to the idea of heritage emerged in four films based on novels by Henry James, a writer whose position in the nation's literary heritage was itself rather insecure. He wrote in English, and his novels are often discussed as contributions to English literature; but he was an American who, although he lived in England for many years, offered an outsider's perspective on British society. Many of his novels are set wholly or partly in England, although they also often contrast English manners with the warmer and less inhibited pleasures of Italy.

Set in the late nineteenth or early twentieth century, these novels share themes and settings with those of Forster (who also used Italy in a similar way), but they also provided the basis for adaptations that intensify the tension that Monk notes in the heritage films between "their supposed national character and their international address."[56] *The Portrait of a Lady* (Jane Campion, 1996), *Washington Square* (Agnieszka Holland, 1997), *The Wings of the Dove* (Iain Softley, 1997), and *The Golden Bowl* (James Ivory, 2000) were all funded by American companies and directed or written by filmmakers from different national backgrounds.[57] In the case of *Washington Square,* the only one set entirely in the United States, there was no British involvement in the production, although the film has much in common with the other three.

The other major challenge that James poses is that his prose style seems highly resistant to cinematic adaptation. As Kathleen Murphy puts it, "Henry James *works* every word, every phrase, every description or discourse, so that you must travel his narratives attuned to minute changes in social/spiritual weather and the moral and psychological reverberations of every bit of small talk."[58] In his discussion of the "melodramatic imagination," however, Peter Brooks shows that the plots of the novels have an underlying melodramatic structure that may explain their attraction for filmmakers. Since James internalizes the melodramatic conflicts, creating a "melodrama of consciousness" that involves "the heightening of experience and the intensification of choice," the films have to find what Robin Wood calls " objective correlatives . . . for inner states."[59]

Wood also points out that the four novels that inspired the James films of the 1990s share the same basic premise: "a young American heiress falls prey to the attractions and persuasions of a suitor . . . who is really after her money."[60] Like the Austen and Forster adaptations, they thus involve an entanglement of desire and property as the basis for personal relations, but James's narratives also focus on what J. A. Ward calls the problem of "improper intervention in the life of another."[61] While this is also an issue in many of the fictions of Austen and Forster, James's later novels in particular force us to see a parallel between characters who manipulate others and a writer who claims to have access to his characters' inner lives.

As Wood suggests, "*The Portrait of a Lady* is still firmly grounded in the nineteenth century: however complex the characters, James presumes to know them, and to communicate his knowledge of them to the reader; by *The Golden Bowl* (and via *The Wings of the Dove*) all confidence in such an undertaking has dissolved beyond the possibility of restoration."[62] Film would thus seem to be an unlikely medium to take over this concern, especially since these films reject the use of voice-over narration. However, they all set up tensions between the vividness of the visual image and the physical bodies of the actors, on the one hand, and a sense of inner struggles that cannot be clearly expressed and that lead to choices that the characters do not fully understand.

All four films open with striking sequences that confront audiences with the tensions and pressures that lie beneath the social manners depicted in the novels and beneath the surface of James's artful prose. *The Portrait of a Lady* begins with a prologue in which contemporary Australian women discuss their sex lives, setting up a contrast with the feelings of entrapment felt by Isabel (Nicole Kidman) in the past depicted in the film itself. *Washington Square* opens with a frantic and bloody childbirth in which the mother dies, an event that overshadows the life of Catherine (Jennifer Jason Leigh), whose physical awkwardness seems to be a product of her failure to live up to her father's idealized image of her mother. Both of these films draw out the feminist implications of the novels in complex and challenging ways, but it is the adaptations of the late novels that take the biggest risks.

*The Wings of the Dove* opens with a sequence set in the London Underground railway system. This setting itself situates the action during a period of transition to modern forms of communication. A young woman is sitting on a bench looking disconsolate. When she gets on a crowded train, she makes eye contact with a young man, who offers her his seat, and when she gets off, he follows her along the platform to the elevator (Figure 73). Once inside, they passionately embrace, until she starts to resist, and there is a sudden cut to an extreme close-up of her eyes to which makeup is being applied by an older woman. This cut succinctly introduces the relationship between Kate Croy (Helena Bonham Carter) and her Aunt Maud (Charlotte Rampling), on whom she is dependent and who has made her break off her relationship with the man on the train, Merton Densher (Linus Roache).

Most spectators will have immediately recognized the woman at the station as Bonham Carter, the actress most often associated with the heritage genre. The passionate embrace might come as something of a shock, although the characters played by Bonham Carter have always been more sexually adventurous than they might appear. At the beginning of *Howards End,* in the middle of *A Room with a View* (Ivory, 1986), and at the end of *Where Angels Fear to Tread* (Charles Sturridge, 1991), all based on Forster novels, a young woman played by Bonham Carter kisses a young man and sets off tensions that disturb the society in which she lives.

If the sexual charge of the opening of *The Wings of the Dove* is unexpected, the final sequence is even more so. It depicts the final meeting of Kate and Merton, after she has disturbed their relationship by using him to obtain the money of Milly Theale (Alison Elliott), an American heiress with a fatal disease. After leaving Merton and Milly together in Venice, Kate has sabotaged her own plan by revealing it to a man she knows will inform Milly. She now visits Merton in his apartment in London, to which he has returned after Milly's death, where she burns a letter that apparently contains the news of his inheritance, and then strips naked in his bedroom. They desperately attempt to make love, but she leaves when he is unable to reassure her that he is not in love with the memory of Milly (even though he apparently did not love her when she was alive).

Between these two sequences of charged sexuality, the adaptation is remarkably free, retaining "no more than half-a-dozen lines from the novel" and

**Figure 73.** Kate (Helena Bonham Carter) and Merton (Linus Roache) share a brief intimate moment behind bars in a railway station elevator at the beginning of *The Wings of the Dove*.

setting the action "amid the social instabilities of 1910 rather than the restrictions of the book's 1901."[63] However, as Wood shows in his monograph on the film, it remains very close to the spirit of the original even though "not one single scene in the film has a close counterpart in the novel."[64] It develops a series of binary oppositions: rich–poor, English–U.S., London–Venice, underground train–gondola, vitality–sickness, inside–outside, aristocratic receptions–carnival, restraint–sexuality, fashionable clothes–the naked bodies in the final sequence. Despite these seemingly melodramatic oppositions, the film emphasizes the "apparent discrepancy between motive and action, cause and effect" that Brooks finds characteristic of James's fiction.[65]

The opening sequence of *The Golden Bowl* also disrupts generic expectations to bring out the underlying passions at work in the polite society in which its main action takes place. In sixteenth-century Italy, a duke finds his young wife in bed with his son and brutally kills the offending couple. As Ginette Vincendeau suggests, this prologue "acts as a *mise en abyme* of the rest of the story," which takes place in the early years of the twentieth century and which also depicts the infidelity of a woman married to an older man.[66] Prince Amerigo (Jeremy Northam), whose ancestors were involved in the bloody events of the past, attends a ball in a costume that makes him look like a character in the prologue, and the film often alludes, directly and indirectly, to this historical atrocity.

The tensions in the main narrative center on Amerigo's marriage to Maggie Verver (Kate Beckinsale), an American heiress, despite his love for Charlotte Stant (Uma Thurman), another American, and despite Maggie's close relationship with her father, Adam (Nick Nolte), who eventually marries Charlotte. In the sequence following the prologue, Amerigo shows Charlotte around his palazzo and explains that his grandfather moved out because he was being poisoned by the arsenic in the gold leaf falling from the now ruined ceilings. A cut takes us to the perfect gold leaf on the ceiling of the English home of Adam Verver, described in a caption as "America's first billionaire." England thus becomes the site of the interaction between impoverished European heritage and modern American wealth, and the conflict is finally resolved not by the death of the lovers but by the departure of Adam and Charlotte for the United States.

The main metaphor in the film, as in the novel, is the golden bowl, a beautiful artifact from the past that has a barely discernible flaw. However, the adaptation also uses cinema itself as a metaphor. At one point, Charlotte imagines (or remembers) the United States, and we see flickering silent-film footage of an American city. The effect is jarring since it suddenly reminds us of the pastness of the events that have become very present to us in the film's sumptuous color images. A film that opened with the shadowy evocation of the sixteenth century then ends with black-and-white newsreel-style images that represent the arrival of Adam and Charlotte in the United States with all the art objects he has accumulated in Europe.

The casting of English actors as an Italian prince and an American heiress complicates the film's treatment of cultural stereotypes. Like the other James adaptations, it suggests that the complex interaction of history and fiction, of authenticity and artifice, at work in films that supposedly represent the national heritage, retains its appeal and may still evolve in new directions.

# CHAPTER TWELVE

# I'm British but . . . :

## Empire and After

The empire film constitutes one of the most distinctive British genres. Stories of British colonial endeavors were, however, themselves colonized by Hollywood in the 1930s in films like *The Charge of the Light Brigade* (Michael Curtiz, 1936) and *Gunga Din* (George Stevens, 1939), which exploited the opportunities for action and spectacle in exotic imperial settings (India in both these cases) and drew on the acting talents of Hollywood's British colony. Alexander Korda struck back with a series of lavish empire films, whose extensive location shooting was made possible by the cooperation of imperial authorities. The most successful of these were directed by his brother Zoltan, including *Sanders of the River* (1935), about the civilizing influence of a colonial administrator in Africa, and a trilogy of films set in India: *Elephant Boy* (1937, codirected by Robert Flaherty), *The Drum* (1938), and *The Four Feathers* (1939).[1]

The last two films were filmed in Technicolor to make the most of the exotic settings, while their stories of bravery and sacrifice stressed the scope and beneficence of British imperial rule. It was already becoming clear that the empire's days were numbered and, after World War II, the dismantling of the British Empire – as former colonies became independent states – was one of the most visible signs that the nation was no longer a major world power. In the 1960s Hollywood studios invested in several British-made "post-imperial" epics, including *Lawrence of Arabia* (David Lean, 1962), *Zulu* (Cy Endfield, 1963), and *Khartoum* (Basil Dearden, 1966), set in the past but expressing "a sense of the impending end of Empire or a more complex and ambivalent attitude towards it" (Figure 74).[2]

The loss of the empire was a theme frequently harped on by right-wing politicians in the postwar years and linked to the domestic changes brought about by the "socialist" welfare state. At the same time, many immigrants from the former colonies came to Britain to meet a demand for workers in mainly low-paying jobs. For the most part, these newcomers had little choice but to settle in already economically depressed areas in the larger cities, and they were often blamed for an increase in poverty and crime in these areas. There were recurring "race" riots, like those in the London borough of Notting Hill in 1958, and British culture had to deal with the consequences of "what happens when 'out there' becomes 'over here.'"[3]

While the empire films of the 1960s may reflect a nostalgia for the days when Britain was a world power, they also suggest that the roots of contemporary problems lay in the past misuse of colonial power. As such they need to be read alongside "social problem" films like *Sapphire* (Basil Dearden, 1959), in which London police uncover racial tensions as they investigate the murder of the title character, a woman of "mixed race" who passed as white. When the inspector discovers that the victim was "colored," he learns immediately afterward that she was pregnant. The film thus explicitly raises the issue of miscegenation that was a central, but usually unavowed, concern for the colonial ideology in the empire films. Since the police already know that Sapphire wore a red taffeta petticoat under her tweed skirt, the questions of "color" and "passing" become entangled in what amounts to an investigation of her sexual as well as racial identity.

Made a year after the Notting Hill riots and at the beginning of the British New Wave movement, the film sought to emphasize its topicality by its use of "authentic locations" and contemporary music.[4] Sapphire was a student at the Royal Academy of Music, but the film's score is played by John Dankworth's modern jazz band (soon to be heard playing Dankworth's own score in *Saturday Night and Sunday Morning*), and the students meet in a coffee bar where they listen to traditional jazz (also featured in the opening of *Look Back in Anger*).

A sequence set in a nightclub seems to subvert the film's antiracist intentions when the black owner claims that he can tell the "lilywhites" because their feet start tapping when they hear bongo drums, and his view seems to be confirmed by rapidly edited shots of a woman dancing. Since the murderer turns out to be the racially prejudiced and sexually frustrated sister of Sapphire's white boyfriend, it is easy to argue that the film "sidesteps any serious confrontation with the question of racism" by "locating it in individuals who are often already pathologized."[5]

Yet, after her body is dumped in a park in the opening sequence, Sapphire appears in the film only in a black-and-white photograph in which she is dancing ecstatically and, as Lola Young suggests, the film plays on the contrast between her present "deadness" and "the descriptions of her vivaciousness."[6] By bringing together contemporary discourses on race and sexuality, *Sapphire* may open itself up to regressive readings, but it does not close off the question of why such a vibrant young woman felt it necessary to conceal her racial background and why her sexual independence led to her death. It at least anticipates later films that will explore the relations between racial and sexual identities in ways that many critics have seen as more progressive.

**Figure 74.** *Khartoum:* General Gordon (Charlton Heston) seeks "peace in the Sudan" and offers the rebellious Mahdi (Laurence Olivier) a present from China.

## WE'RE LONDONERS YOU SEE:
### *SAMMY AND ROSIE GET LAID*

The tensions and anxieties that flared up in the "race" riots were, at least part-ly, the result of living conditions in the inner cities, but they were also foment-ed by discourses that stressed the need to maintain the purity of racial and national identities. As it turned out, the immigrants from the former colonies were an early instance of the large-scale shifts in populations through exile or migration, caused by rapid political and technological changes that soon became a global phenomenon and eventually turned Britain, like many other nations, into a multicultural society. As Stuart Hall has recently stated, "most definitions of 'Britishness' assume that the person who belongs is 'white,'" but the transformation of British society has encouraged a more hybrid con-cept of national identity and the development of new cultural forms.[7]

One sign of these changes emerged in Notting Hill, where residents at-tempted to overcome the prejudice that led to the riots of 1958 by establish-ing a local carnival that "offered a marked contrast to the drab conformism of Britain during the 1950s" and soon became "the largest street festival in Europe."[8] This trend has been widely contested, not least by the insular nation-alism associated with Margaret Thatcher's years of rule, and racist views are still to be found in British culture and British cinema. On the other hand, it has become increasingly difficult to sustain the notion of cultural purity in the context of the new global economy. According to Jan Nederveen Pieterse, globalization can be seen as "a process of hybridization which gives rise to a global mélange" so that the key question becomes "the *terms* of mixture, the conditions of mixing and mélange."[9]

Many people now live outside their "home" countries, but these changes have also resulted in new definitions of "home," in which global and local influences interact. Hanif Kureishi, who was born in London to an English mother and Pakistani father, describes the appeal of the "idea of 'home'" to

**Figure 75.** "We're Londoners you see": Sammy (Ayub Khan-Din) and Rosie (Frances Barber) enjoy a walk beside the Thames in *Sammy and Rosie Get Laid.*

"Pakistanis and Indians born and brought up here who consider their position to be the result of a diaspora" and are "awaiting return to a better place, where they belong, where they are welcome."[10] In Kureishi's short stories, novels, plays, film and television screenplays, and in the one film he has directed, he explores the need to develop a new sense of "home" in the spirit of Stuart Hall's insistence that "modern nations are all cultural hybrids."[11]

Kenneth Kaleta argues that Kureishi's nationalism is "neither Asian nor British, neither colonized nor assimilated; rather, it has assumed the global identity of post–World War II, twentieth-century urbanism."[12] The key to understanding this "global identity" is through the function of London in much of Kureishi's work. Kaleta quotes Kureishi on his "love and fascination for inner London" and claims that "London is an apt metaphor for the new national identity that Kureishi defines."[13]

This "metaphor" is central to Kureishi's screenplay for *Sammy and Rosie Get Laid* (Stephen Frears, 1987), in which Rafi (Shashi Kapoor) returns to London, where he lived as a youth, after retiring from a highly dubious political career in Pakistan. He is immediately confronted by riots in the streets provoked by the police shooting of a black woman. Whereas he remembers London as "the center of civilization," he now finds the city a "cesspit" and urges his son to "come home." Sammy (Ayub Khan-Din) replies that London is his home and launches into an account of the pleasures of life in the city. He insists that he and Rosie (Frances Barber), his white British lover, "love our city and we belong to it." It provides the basis for a new sense of identity that displaces their national and racial differences: "Neither of us are English, we're Londoners you see" (Figure 75).

**Figure 76.** "What's left for you in this country now?": Johnny (Daniel Day-Lewis) meets the family of Omar (Gordon Warnecke) in *My Beautiful Laundrette.*

Sammy's rapturous list of urban delights gains much of its impact from the contrast with the urbane ideal found in the contemporary heritage films (see Chapter 11). In the discourse of heritage, as David Morley describes it, "the countryside . . . is still largely represented as the essence of white English-ness – as a stable, culturally homogeneous, historically unchanging territory in which racial difference can only be seen as an uncomfortable and desta-bilising presence."[14] In *Howards End,* for example, Ruth Wilcox's love of the country house in which she was born illustrates the need for "belonging" that Kureishi refers to in speaking of the old sense of "home." When she (mistak-enly) declares that her son takes after her because "he truly loves England," she makes an exception of London, which they find "unstable" and "imper-manent" because buildings are being pulled down all the time.

It is precisely its instability that Sammy, like Kureishi, celebrates in his ode to London. In an essay on "London Films," Charlotte Brunsdon argues that, as depicted in contemporary British cinema, London is "a contradictory and plural place: deeply territorialized and local while also offering brief moments of utopian multiculturalism," most notably in Kureishi's films.[15] Kureishi him-self refers to "the fluidities and possibilities" that he finds there, and it is this quality that he and Frears sought to capture in the style of the film.[16] In the diary Kureishi kept during the production, he described it as "a film of juxta-positions and contrasts, of different scenes banging hard together," and he even hoped that it would not be "too diffuse."[17]

Many critics did indeed feel that the film dealt with too many topics and had too many characters, unlike his earlier collaboration with Stephen Frears, *My Beautiful Laundrette* (1985), which seemed rather more optimistic about the utopian possibilities of the new multicultural nation (Figure 76). The critics were even harder on *London Kills Me* (1991), Kureishi's first, and so far last, directorial effort, but all these films depict characters whose social situations, political beliefs, and sexual needs interact and often contradict each other. Kureishi refuses to idealize the victims of racism and intolerance and often depicts racist attitudes within the diasporic communities themselves. The effect is to unsettle the spectator through the collision of utopian and dystopian perspectives, using "irony" as "a way of commenting on bleakness and cruelty without falling into dourness and didacticism."[18]

The montage sequence in which Sammy describes his love for London is a good example of this technique. Sukhdev Sandhu points out that it is "didactic and provocative rather than merely descriptive" in its challenge to both isolationist and assimilationist approaches to the diasporic experience.[19] However, the overall effect depends on the coupling of a celebration of diversity with an ironic depiction of the superficial pursuit of the latest trends, including a "seminar in semiotics" in which an audience member asks the theorist Colin MacCabe to define "the relation between a bag of crisps and the self-enclosed unity of the linguistic sign."

The structure of the whole film depends on this tension between its didactic purpose and its ironic disavowal of political correctness. It reaches its utopian climax with a split-screen image of three unlikely couples making love – Sammy with Anna (Wendy Gazelle), a visiting American photographer, in her studio; Rosie with Danny (Roland Gift), a black youth, in his caravan on a patch of wasteland beneath a highway; and Rafi with Alice (Claire Bloom), a white woman he knew in the past, in her suburban home. This moment of shared passion is temporary, and the film's other climactic sequence is the eviction of the squatters from the wasteland that has been purchased by developers. In keeping with Kureishi's ironic strategies, Frears edits the images of the caravans leaving the site to the accompaniment of the hymn "I Vow to Thee My Country," recorded from a Conservative election broadcast.

*Sammy and Rosie Get Laid* was made at the time of Thatcher's third electoral victory, which, according to Kureishi at the time, marked "the death of the dream of the sixties, which was that our society would become more adjusted to the needs of all the people who live in it." He felt that "the anger and despair following the Election" gave the film "a hard political edge" that made it less popular than *My Beautiful Laundrette.*[20] In another of Frears's additions to the screenplay, the film opens with a shot of urban waste accompanied by the voice of Thatcher speaking of the urgent need to clean up the "inner cities." Her way of doing this is to put the needs of developers before those of the people, and Kureishi presents a much more ambivalent view of the messy realities of people's lives. The film ends with Sammy and Rosie silently embracing each other after Rafi's suicide, their complicated relationship offering a glimmer of hope that still retains some of the force of the film's earlier utopian moments.

## YOU TRY FUSION AND YOU GET CONFUSION: *BHAJI ON THE BEACH* AND *EAST IS EAST*

The darkly ironic tone in the films of Frears and Kureishi challenged what Sarita Malik calls "the unremitting politicization of discourse when reading a Black film [that] produced a focus on 'positive' and 'negative' images." As Malik suggests, this approach also encouraged the production of films, like *Young Soul Rebels* (Isaac Julien, 1991), *Wild West* (David Attwood, 1992), and *Bhaji on the Beach* (Gurinder Chadha, 1993), that "refuse a simple focus on racial politics and acknowledge other facets of identity," shifting the focus "from the 'politics of race' to the 'politics of the dance-floor,' the former inextricably linked to the latter."[21] These tactics made the films more complicated as ideological texts, but they made them more accessible, not only to audiences from the cultures that they depicted but also – at least potentially – to mainstream audiences gradually becoming more receptive to diasporic visions of cultural and national identity.

During this period, one of the major developments in the politics of "race" in Britain was the emergence of a coalition around the idea of "black culture," incorporating the shared experience of racism by Britons from African, Asian, and Caribbean backgrounds. There were, of course, differences among these groups, one of which, as explained by Cary Raginder Sawhney, is that, thanks largely to the influence of popular music, Afro-Caribbean influences have become part of British popular culture and "can be seen as inextricably linked with cultural notions of modernity, while Asian cultures have characteristically been seen as backward, fixed in a colonial past."[22] Yet, as far as British cinema is concerned, it is films dealing with Asian communities that have been most successful in crossing over into the mainstream, especially with *Bhaji on the Beach* and *East Is East* (Damien O'Donnell, 1999).

Gurinder Chadha, who was born in Kenya to Punjabi parents and has lived in Britain for most of her life, insists that *Bhaji on the Beach*, her first feature film, is "a very English film" but also that its style depends on "the pull between a very British film and being quite Indian on the other." She adds that this pull is "present in every single scene, every single character, every single frame of the film."[23] It deals with a group of British-Indian women who take a day trip from Birmingham, Britain's second-largest city, to the working-class seaside resort of Blackpool. The older women, or "aunties," still have their roots in traditional Indian culture, while the two teenagers, Ladhu (Nisha Nayar) and Madhu (Renu Kochar), are thoroughly assimilated and speak with broad Birmingham accents. In between are two young women with problems: Ginder (Kim Vithana), who travels with her son and has separated from her abusive husband, and Hashida (Sarita Khajuria), who has just discovered that she is pregnant by Oliver (Mo Sesay), her British-Caribbean boyfriend.

The film's seriocomic tone and the tension between realism and allegory resemble *Sammy and Rosie Get Laid*. Birmingham is a site of constraint and Blackpool one of excess, and the tensions that have developed in the former are worked out in the latter in a way that exposes both the racism of British society and the aunties' illusions of an authentic Indian culture. When the group assembles for the trip, their leader, Simi (Shaheen Khan), delivers a speech in which she refers to the "twin yoke" of sexism and racism that they must bear in "patriarchal" society, but all the women appear dismayed by her theoretical jargon. They quickly cheer up when she urges them to have "a female fun time," and the minibus leaves to the sounds of a lively Punjabi version of "Summer Holiday," the title song from a 1963 film starring Cliff Richard, an icon of white British popular culture (born in Lucknow, India).

Simi's speech sets the tone of the film as a tension between a recognition of the serious problems that the women face and the desire for "fun" to make life bearable for them – and to attract an audience for the film. The conjunction of racism and sexism is confirmed when the women attract the attention of a gang of "lager louts" at a highway rest area. When Simi tries to leave, one of the gang asks if she is a lesbian, and she retorts, "Are you the alternative?" However, racism and sexism also exist within the Indian community: Ginder rejects the subordinate role of women in the traditional Indian family (and her mother-in-law links her attitude to her dark skin); Hashida has not dared to tell her parents about her boyfriend. Racism and sexism are also very much part of the commercial pleasures of the Blackpool tourist industry, but the film suggests that even stereotypes can become a source of "fun" provided that people are willing to listen to each other.

The appropriation of the Cliff Richard song signals the film's commitment to cultural hybridity. Chadha argues that *Bhaji on the Beach* addresses "the sort of cross-referenced identities we all share," and she includes the *Carry On* comedies, with their "very constructed sense of Englishness," among the influences on her work, along with the colorful musicals of popular Indian cinema.[24] As Anne Ciecko suggests, the film "borrows, but it also hybridizes, inverts, and destabilizes" in a spirit that draws on traditions of the "carnivalesque" (see Chapter 8).[25] In the context of recent developments in British society, the idea of carnival must evoke Caribbean culture, but it also applies to the gaudy pleasures of Blackpool and Bollywood.

The cultural interactions that carnival encourages are highly ambiguous. In a sequence set in the college where Hashida met Oliver, Chadha relates this theme to the coalition around the idea of black British culture. Oliver's friend tries to dissuade him from following Hashida to Blackpool and, while Chinese students eat breakfast in the background, declares with exasperation, "you try fusion and you get confusion." In a sense, the film is on the side of

**Figure 77.** Asha (Lalita Ahmed) and Ambrose (Peter Cellier) enjoy the pleasures of Blackpool's Golden Mile in *Bhaji on the Beach.*

confusion, recognizing the appeal of secure cultural identities but also insisting that these are illusory.

The implications of the film's vision for the national culture emerge most clearly in the brief encounter between Asha (Lalita Ahmed), one of the "aunties," and Ambrose (Peter Cellier), a charming old actor, whom she meets on the beach (Figure 77). Asha suffers from headaches that bring on visions, such as the one that opens the film in which she is harangued by a god and surrounded by gigantic versions of the products she sells in the family store. Ambrose, who refers to Blackpool as "this fallen woman that I call home," once appeared in Indian roles in empire films but is now hoping for the role of Widow Twanky in the Christmas pantomime. He takes Asha to the theater, which he associates with "our popular culture," and tells her that he admires her because she has "hung on" to her traditions. However, her headaches derive from the pressures involved in hanging on to traditions that require her to sacrifice herself for the sake of her family.

Chadha uses the parallels between the situations of Asha and Ambrose to suggest a similar dynamic underlying cultural differences. When Rekha (Souad Faress), an Indian visitor who accompanies the group, first sees the Golden Mile, a stretch of outdoor attractions in Blackpool, she stops in astonishment and cries out, "Bombay!" She later tells the "aunties" that their view of India is hopelessly out-of-date, and the film draws attention to an emergent global popular culture. In some ways, its vision is close to the "mass culture" critique, especially with regard to the influence of U.S. popular culture in Britain: The two boys who spend the day with Ladhu and Mahdu work at a hot-dog stand and wear cowboy outfits, and the women meet up in the evening at the Manhattan Bar, where male strippers wear (and take off) U.S. Navy uniforms. On the other hand, the film stresses the differences within popular culture and its utopian potential (see Chapter 5). It ends when the spectacular illuminations are turned on, as the minibus passes along the Golden Mile past the reunited Hashida and Oliver, while the older women now understand Ginder's situation, having witnessed the violence of her husband, who pursued her to Blackpool.

If the "female fun time" in *Bhaji on the Beach* is eventually achieved, it is despite the social constraints, and the internalized guilt, from which the women suffer. The tone of *East Is East*, which proved to be even more popular, involves a similar seriocomic tension; but it proves to be both more farcical and less optimistic. Adapted from his own play by Ayub Khan-Din (who played Sammy in *Sammy and Rosie Get Laid*), the film is set in Salford, a working-class district of Manchester, in 1971. It deals with a mixed-race family, consisting of George Khan (Om Puri), his white wife Ella (Linda Bassett), and their seven children. George owns a fish-and-chip shop but wants to bring up his children as traditional Muslims. The comedy stems largely from their efforts to outwit him, but their opposition brings out the latent violence behind his patriarchal authority.

The period setting is important in that it makes possible a fairly conventional generational conflict in which the children rebel against the father's traditions. This plot had already been turned on its head two years earlier in *My Son the Fanatic* (Udayan Prasad, 1997), based on a screenplay by Kureishi, in which a taxi driver (also played by Om Puri), who has adapted comfortably to his new life in a northern city, is shocked to find that his son wants to go back to the old ways. In the entrepreneurial culture of the 1990s, the overt racism of 1970s Britain has receded, but the son tells his father that "some of us want something else besides muddle" and that he is seeking "belief, purity, belonging to the past."

Like the so-called heritage films, *East Is East* looks back to a simpler time when cultural politics were more clearly defined. Yet it is *My Son the Fanatic* that begins with a song celebrating the "green and pleasant land," accompanied by shots of a country house and cows beside a river. Whereas the earlier film established ironic parallels between British and Muslim nostalgia, *East Is East* "draws on the vocabulary of northern realism."[26] It opens with establishing shots of terraced houses that evoke the long-running television series *Coronation Street*, also set in Manchester, which, until recently, had not really acknowledged the large immigrant population in the industrial north. The series also did not draw attention to the politics of racism, as the film does in its newsreel footage of Enoch Powell advocating repatriation as a solution to the "race problem" and its depiction of one of the Khans' neighbors who shares Powell's views (Figure 78).

**Figure 78.** *East Is East:* George (Om Puri) stands in front of posters for Enoch Powell while his neighbor tries to get signatures for a petition on "repatriation."

Despite its engagement with white racism and the equally fanatical attitudes of the domestic tyrant, the film could still be described as a "funny, feel-good film [that] looks set to do for race relations what *The Full Monty* did for unemployment."[27] Its humor owes even more to the *Carry On* tradition than *Bhaji on the Beach* and often depends on pushing stereotypes to excess. When George arranges a marriage for his eldest son, he runs away in the middle of the ceremony and turns up later as a gay hairdresser; two other sons find their prospective brides physically repulsive; and a formal meeting with the patronizing family of these marriage prospects is disrupted by the arrival of yet another son, an art student, with his latest creation, a life-size replica of female sexual organs.

According to Malik, the farcical elements do not prevent the film from working as an "interrogation into identity, belonging and Britishness," but she stresses that it hinges on "the slippery line between laughing *at* and laughing *with* British-Pakistanis."[28] There are some quite uncomfortable moments, as in the invitation to laugh at the "ugliness" of the brides George has chosen for his sons, and the inclusion of a sequence in which he brutally beats his wife for taking the children's side. It is her patience and dignity that give the film its moral center, and it ends not with the utopian reconciliation of *Bhaji on the Beach* but with the couple quietly sitting in the fish-and-chip shop drinking tea.

### COMEDIES OF CHAOS AND CHANCE: *NOTTING HILL* AND *BEAUTIFUL PEOPLE*

Andrew Higson has recently argued that films like *My Beautiful Laundrette* and *Bhaji on the Beach* call into question the "national cinema" approach to contemporary cinema, and he suggests that they should rather be discussed in the context of "a new post-national cinema that resists the tendency to nationalise questions of community, culture and identity" and embraces "multiculturalism, difference and hybridity."[29] On the other hand, John Hill insists that we need not assume "the demise of a British national cinema" just because it "no longer reflects a unified national identity or culture"; instead we should "see this in terms of a growth of films prepared to engage with a more diverse and complex sense of national, regional, ethnic, social, and sexual identities within the U.K."[30]

Clearly, the idea of national identity is changing, partly because of the multicultural influences brought about by postwar immigration but also because of pressures caused by the "postmodern" global media environment. Mike Featherstone links "the unwillingness of migrants to passively inculcate the dominant cultural mythology of the nation or locality" to a more general sense of "the fragmentation of identity," and he then suggests that this is why characters in films like *My Beautiful Laundrette* "do not present positive unified identity images and are consequently not easy to identify with."[31] As we have seen, this is not an entirely new development in British cinema, but Paul Gilroy argues that, in the contemporary cultural context, the concept of "diaspora . . . offers new possibilities for understanding identity, not as something inevitably determined by place or nationality, and for visualizing a future where new bases for social solidarity are offered and joined, perhaps via the new technologies."[32]

In terms of the future of British cinema, the central tension would seem to be between the desire to find new forms of national identity along the lines of Tony Blair's vision of "cool Britannia" and a sense that Britain has been absorbed into a multinational global culture. On the one hand, as Claire Monk points out, "the notion of a new British identity – with its emphasis on youth, modernity, style, and urban energy – served to signal New Labour's repudiation of the 'heritage' version of national identity officially promoted by Thatcherite Conservatism in the 1980s."[33] On the other, this new identity has to function in a "a world in which everyone's identity has been thrown into question," and in which, according to Kobena Mercer, "the mixing and fusion of disparate elements to create new, hybridized identities point to ways of surviving, and thriving, in conditions of crisis and transition."[34]

Two British comedies from 1999 illustrate some of the issues involved in the new situation. *Notting Hill* (Roger Michell) was the much anticipated follow-up to *Four Weddings and a Funeral* (Mike Newell, 1994), with the same writer (Richard Curtis), producer (Duncan Kenworthy), and star (Hugh Grant), and produced by Working Title (one of Britain's most successful film companies in recent years) through the international conglomerate PolyGram Filmed Entertainment. *Beautiful People* (Jasmin Dizdar) was produced by an enterprising new company, Tall Stories, with the support of the British Film Institute and Channel Four, with additional funding coming from the Arts Council of England (using the proceeds of the National Lottery), the Merseyside Film Production Fund, BskyB, and British Screen. Its director became a British citizen in 1993, after leaving his native Bosnia before the collapse of former Yugoslavia and graduating from film school in Prague.

Economically, *Notting Hill* is clearly a product of the new global economy whose commercial success depends on its ability to appeal to audiences beyond the domestic market. It addresses the issue of national identity through the conflict between the "Englishness" of William Thacker (Grant), who owns a travel book shop but lives quietly in Notting Hill, which he calls "a little village within the city," and the glamorous jet-set lifestyle of the American film star Anna Scott (Julia Roberts). Their romance draws on the British fascination with Hollywood and the U.S. attraction to old English charm, and the film exploits the contrast between its stars' personas. It begins with a montage of images of Anna, making public appearances that could easily be stock footage of Roberts, and then introduces William, whose awkward modesty plays on an awareness that "Grant's public image and charm are inextricably tied to his unreliability."[35]

Like most medium-budget British films, *Beautiful People* was produced by piecing together funding from a number of sources. In this case, the budget was raised entirely from British sources, but it is culturally a more global film than *Notting Hill.* It develops several intertwining plot lines that confront characters from Britain and from former Yugoslavia. Andrew Horton claims that the film "rides a surprisingly successful line between Bosnian chaos and British order," but it also makes clear that Britain is not as ordered as the stereotype suggests.[36] In one of the plot lines, Doctor Mouldy (Nicholas Farrell) treats a Bosnian couple whose child was conceived after the wife was raped by Serbs, and he invites them to stay in his home. As they ride there in a taxi, Elgar's famous *Pomp and Circumstance March No. 1* celebrates their new life, but they arrive to find the messy reality of the house in which he has lived with his two sons since his wife left him.

Stella Bruzzi objects to "the film's use of implausible coincidences such as the Serb and the Croat adversaries finding themselves on the same ward, or Doctor Mouldy treating the pregnant Bosnian woman in the same hospital" and claims that this "falsifies the film's dominant realism." While this comment testifies to the endurance of the realist paradigm in British film culture, Bruzzi does go on to situate the film within "a distinctly European tradition of surrealism, irreverence and anarchic political commentary."[37] This tradition is clearly dominant in a film that includes such characters as Griffin (Danny Nussbaum), a London skinhead who is accidentally parachuted into Bosnia with relief supplies on which he has fallen asleep when drunk, and Jerry (Gilbert Martin), a Scottish journalist who contracts "Bosnia syndrome," in which he identifies with victims of the war and demands to have his leg amputated. As these examples suggest, *Beautiful People* is as much a fairy tale as *Notting Hill* but one with much darker overtones.[38]

As Horton indicates, *Beautiful People* depicts "the world of 'London' as a gumbo of nationalities, refugees and 'natives' who can also feel like aliens in their own land." He adds that "whenever Dizdar's camera travels through the streets of London, faces of all nationalities appear, suggesting multiple stories that could be told, lives that could be followed with similar results."[39] By contrast, Claire Monk complains of the "social cleansing" in *Notting Hill.*[40] A guest at the wedding of the Bosnian refugee and the daughter of a cabinet minister in *Beautiful People* declares that "here in England we're a mixed bunch too" but assures him that there is no likelihood of "ethnic cleansing." Yet black and ethnic inhabitants have virtually disappeared from *Notting Hill,* and while, as Nick James points out, this omission does correspond to the actual process of "urban gentrification" in which the "posh sections" have swallowed much of the area, it is still noticeable that most of the few nonwhite people glimpsed in the film belong to the media entourage surrounding Anna, not to William's "village."[41]

Both films have "utopian" endings, although, as might be expected, their implications are quite different. The misunderstandings that keep the couple apart in *Notting Hill* are overcome when William exploits the public rituals of a press conference to propose to Anna (Figure 79), but the final shot places them in a space that alludes to traditional myths of Deep England. William is sitting with a visibly pregnant Anna in a small fenced park reserved for affluent residents of the neighborhood. When they climbed into this park earlier, an inscription on a bench made Anna realize that there are couples who stay together, a significant moment underlined by the camera pulling up to look down on the green garden from on high, and the happy ending thus involves a reaffirmation of love and family in an idyllic image – although rural England is now reduced to a small, isolated park available only to the privileged few.

Robin Wood likens the ending of *Beautiful People* to that of a screwball comedy, but he notes that "the utopianism is qualified by a whole range of more or less subtle disturbances." He also argues that, "if one of the film's projects is the construction of the multicultural society, another (closely related) is its redefinition of the notion of 'family.'"[42] The doctor who cures Jerry convinces him that the world is beautiful – until the doctor mentions his bill – and reunites him with his family. Most of the other families that form at the end of the film are unconventional in some way, with the problem of their likely endurance more apparent than in *Notting Hill.*

According to Horton, the ending of *Beautiful People* offers a highly positive view of the prospects for the national identity: "the chaos and chance of

**Figure 79.** *Notting Hill:* The private life of William (Hugh Grant) and Anna (Julia Roberts) becomes a media event when he proposes at a press conference.

each relationship explored suggest the birth of new, potentially positive possibilities" and encourage a sense that "Britain has changed as it embraces – willingly or not – those who have taken up residence within her land."[43] Other critics are less optimistic, including Bruzzi, who concludes that, "in all the freneticism, there is no time to think, which makes its status as a political allegory a bit of a problem."[44] This judgment sounds very similar to James's concern that *Notting Hill* ignores the political reality of a time when "the English are redefining themselves against a background of Scots and Welsh devolution and the gradual European absorption of all the British," with the result that the film "enjoys only the confusion not the potential for change."[45]

It is a moot point whether comedies should provide political analysis of the kind these critics require, but they can provide allegorical representations of the nation as an imagined community. The difference between the two films in this respect is apparent in their treatment of the diasporic groups that do not fit easily into traditional versions of national identity, but it is also apparent in their depiction of cultural differences among citizens of the multinational nation.

In *Notting Hill,* William shares his home with Spike (Rhys Ifans), a scruffy Welshman whose obnoxious behavior and unreliability give him a "primitive" quality that contrasts with the diffidence of the Englishman (although there is a nagging sense that he represents a more extreme version of qualities inherent in William's character). He is a genial comic character who ends up engaged to William's sister (Emma Chambers), one of a group of eccentric English characters who cheerfully accept their own social and economic failure. As well as the Scottish journalist and his family, *Beautiful People* includes a Welsh Nationalist (Nicholas McGaughey), who specializes in bombing the holiday homes of English families and who occupies the same hospital room as the Bosnian Serb and Croat (Dado Jehan and Faruk Pruti) who brawl on a

**Figure 80.** Serb and Croat refugees (Dado Jehan and Faruk Pruti) meet on a bus and continue their fight in the streets of London in the opening sequence of *Beautiful People*.

London bus in the opening sequence (Figure 80). All three testify to the ongoing reality of political division, but they participate in the utopian ending as they play cards with the Sister (Linda Bassett) who has desperately tried to prevent violence in the ward.

Robert Murphy insists that the ending of *Notting Hill* is not nostalgic but celebrates "the pleasures of middle-class life."[46] It has to be admitted that this celebration depends on the exclusion of much that is included in *Beautiful People,* whose ending might be seen as a celebration of the pleasures of life in a world in which they are constantly threatened by ignorance and intolerance. The precarious pleasures that both films offer provide support for Ien Ang's claim that "this totalizing system of global capitalism in which we are all trapped, is nevertheless a profoundly unstable one, whose closure can never be completed."[47] If the position of British cinema within this system is often a very uncomfortable one, it seems that filmmakers will continue to produce films that engage with the evolving myths of national identity in varied and unpredictable ways that reinforce, criticize, or challenge these myths.

# Notes

## INTRODUCTION

1 Anderson, "Alfred Hitchcock," 48; Houston, *The Contemporary Cinema,* 124; Williams, "The Social Art Cinema," 193.
2 Truffaut, *Hitchcock,* 140.
3 Barr, "Introduction," 1. The publication of Barr's anthology *All Our Yesterdays* in 1986 was a key moment in the emergence of the new story of British cinema discussed later in this chapter. Whereas most previous references to Truffaut's notorious remarks expressed complete or qualified approval, later references tended to be more skeptical.
4 O'Regan, *Australian National Cinema,* 123.
5 Truffaut, *Hitchcock,* 140.
6 O'Regan refers to Australian cinema as "a messy affair"; *Australian National Cinema,* 2.
7 See Schatz, "The New Hollywood."
8 Welsh, "'Ill Met by Moonlight,'" 159; Flor, "Intertextuality in *Shadowlands,*" 97.
9 Hill, *British Cinema in the 1980s,* 64-5.
10 Blandford, Grant, and Hillier, *The Film Studies Dictionary,* 87. For a fuller account of European influences on British cinema in the 1990s, see Christie, "As Others See Us."
11 Schatz, "The New Hollywood," 30.
12 Kracauer, *From Caligari to Hitler,* 9.
13 Ibid., 8, 11.
14 Kennedy, "The Brits Have Gone Nuts," 51.
15 Barthes, *Mythologies,* 58-9.
16 Higson, *Waving the Flag,* 1.
17 Orr, "The Art of National Identity," 327.
18 Sinfield, *Literature, Politics, and Culture,* 3.
19 Higson, *Waving the Flag,* 1.
20 Jon Burrows argues that the panic over the "Big Film Slump" was partly orchestrated by the studios to provoke the government into action; "Big Studio Production," 25-6.
21 Wood, "Low-budget British Films," 53.
22 "British Not British," 3.
23 Falcon, "Last Tango in Lewisham," 23.

## CHAPTER ONE. THE NATIONAL HEALTH: GREAT BRITAIN / DEEP ENGLAND

1 Anderson, *Imagined Communities,* 6.
2 Luke, "New World Order," 94-5.
3 Barker, *Britain and the British People,* 6.

4   Richards, *Films and British National Identity*, 2.
5   Anderson, "Get Out and Push," 139.
6   Barr, *English Hitchcock*, 6.
7   From Wordsworth's "It Is Not to Be Thought Of" (1807); quoted in Barker, *Britain and the British People*, v.
8   The poster is reproduced in Ryall, *Alfred Hitchcock*, plate 3.
9   See Barr, "*Blackmail*: Silent and Sound."
10  *World Film News* (February 1937), quoted in Ryall, *Alfred Hitchcock*, 170-1.
11  Hitchcock, quoted in Gottlieb, ed., *Hitchcock on Hitchcock*, 178.
12  Whitebait, *New Statesman* (21 October 1944), quoted in Ellis, "Art, Culture and Quality," 40.
13  Sinfield, *Literature, Politics, and Culture*, 118.
14  Calder, *The Myth of the Blitz*, 182. In *This Is England*, Neil Rattigan makes use of this term, citing Calder, but notes that "Patrick Wright implies that he coined the term in . . . *On Living in an Old Country*": 320n.
15  Higson, "Re-presenting the National Past," 110.
16  Balcon, quoted in McFarlane and Mayer, *New Australian Cinema*, 202.
17  Caughie, with Rockett, *The Companion to British and Irish Cinema*, 25.
18  The social diversity of men fighting in a common cause is also a key element in many non-Ealing British war films. Neil Rattigan presents a nuanced account of the ideological implications of the treatment of class in these films and argues that most of them were unable to present a coherent and convincing representation of the war as the "People's War"; see *This is England*
19  Barr, *Ealing Studios*, 73.
20  Dixon, quoted in Brown and Kardish, *Michael Balcon*, 65.
21  Houston, *Went the Day Well?* 58.
22  Robbins, *Great Britain*, 329.
23  See, for example, the essays collected in Corner and Harvey, eds., *Enterprise and Heritage*.
24  See Carter, "*Chariots of Fire*."
25  See Johnston, "Charioteers and Ploughmen," 99.
26  Puttnam, quoted in Yule, *David Puttnam*, 166.
27  See ibid., 163-8, and Walker, *National Heroes*, 174-5.
28  Puttnam, quoted in Yule, *David Puttnam*, 174.
29  Kael, quoted in ibid., 183.
30  Park, *Learning to Dream*, 96; Johnston, "Charioteers and Ploughmen," 102.
31  Wollen, "Over Our Shoulders," 182.
32  Johnston, "Charioteers and Ploughmen," 101, 104.
33  Sarris, quoted in Yule, *David Puttnam*, 182.
34  Kael, quoted in ibid., 183.
35  Blake, *A Selection of Poems and Letters*, 162.
36  Peter Miles and Malcolm Smith note that "Blake's 'Jerusalem' has always remained a more potent anthem for British socialism than the 'Internationale'"; *Cinema, Literature and Society*, 41.
37  Blaydes and Bordinat, "Blake's 'Jerusalem,'" 214; see also Bowden, "Jerusalem," 96.
38  Cannadine, "Gilbert and Sullivan," 23.
39  Babington, *Launder and Gilliat*, 31.
40  Carter, "*Chariots of Fire*," 16.
41  Hill, *British Cinema in the 1980s*, 23.

## CHAPTER TWO. THE MAGIC BOX:
## WHAT IS BRITISH CINEMA?

1 From an article in *The Cinema Studio* (January 1951), quoted in Burton,"Seeing Is Believing," 157.
2 Durgnat, *A Mirror for England,* 17.
3 Truffaut, *Hitchcock,* 140.
4 Linda Wood discusses the beneficial effects of the quota system for young filmmakers ("Low-budget British Films," 57–8).The Cinematographic Act of 1927 was especially timely because of the increased costs caused by the conversion to sound that occurred in the following years. For a thorough account of British cinema before the act, see Gledhill, *Reframing British Cinema.*
5 Sorlin,"From *The Third Man* to *Shakespeare in Love,*" 81.
6 Grierson, quoted in Hardy, ed., *Grierson on the Movies,* 38, 114.
7 This comment appears in a question to Alberto Cavalcanti in Lovell (et al.) and Kitses,"Interview," 44.
8 Grierson, quoted in Hardy, ed., *Grierson on Documentary,* 139.
9 See Sussex, *The Rise and Fall of British Documentary,* 23–5. The budget was £2,500.
10 Grierson, quoted in ibid., 24.
11 Ibid.
12 Grierson, quoted in Hardy, ed., *Grierson on Documentary,* 143.
13 Corner, *The Art of Record,* 71.
14 Greene, *The Pleasure Dome,* 40.
15 Ibid., 79.
16 Hardy, *John Grierson,* 90.
17 Korda, quoted in Kulik, *Alexander Korda,* 60.
18 Ibid., 76.The foreigners involved in the production included the Germans O. F. Werndorff (set design) and Kurt Schroeder (music) and the Hungarians Lajos Biró (cowriter of the original story) and Korda's brother Vincent (who also worked on the set design). The editor was an American, Harold Young, with whom Korda had worked in Hollywood.
19 Ibid., 93.
20 Korda also directed *The Girl from Maxim's,* based on the Feydeau play, in Paris (in French and English versions) in 1932–3, but it was not released until 1934, after the success of *Henry VIII.*
21 Street,"Stepping Westward," 55.
22 Kulik, *Alexander Korda,* 99.
23 See Diemert, *Graham Greene's Thrillers,* 36.
24 Hitchcock, in an article originally published in *The Listener* (2 February 1938), quoted in Gottlieb, ed., *Hitchcock on Hitchcock,* 189.
25 Barr,"Before *Blackmail,*" 17.
26 Truffaut, *Hitchcock,* 159.The words quoted are Truffaut's.
27 Grierson, in an article originally published in *The Clarion* (October 1930), quoted in Hardy, ed., *Grierson on the Movies,* 108.
28 Greene, *The Pleasure Dome,* 75, 65.
29 Sarris, *The American Cinema,* 58.
30 Hitchcock, quoted in Gottlieb, ed., *Hitchcock on Hitchcock,* 198.
31 Elsaesser,"The Dandy in Hitchcock," 10–11.

32 Diemert, *Graham Greene's Thrillers,* 44.

33 See Phillips, *Graham Greene,* 6.

34 Greene, quoted in ibid., 20.

35 J. Danvers Williams, *Film Weekly* (5 November 1938), quoted in Gottlieb, ed., *Hitchcock on Hitchcock,* 196.

36 Yacowar, *Hitchcock's British Films,* 304n.

37 Thomson, *England in the Twentieth Century,* 175.

38 Chamberlain, quoted in Ibid., 175.

39 Barr, "Hitchcock's British Films Revisited," 15.

40 See Beckman, "Violent Vanishings."

41 Gilliat, quoted in Brown, *Launder and Gilliat,* 90.

## CHAPTER THREE. THE COMMON TOUCH: THE ART OF BEING REALISTIC

1 Lovell, *Pictures of Reality,* 65.

2 Richard Winnington (1947), quoted in Ellis, "Art, Culture and Quality," 33.

3 C. A. Lejeune (1947), quoted in ibid., 33.

4 Higson, *Waving the Flag,* 179.

5 Richards, *Films and British National Identity,* 123; Murphy, *Realism and Tinsel,* 111.

6 Dyer, *Brief Encounter,* 51.

7 Richards, *Films and British National Identity,* 125; Medhurst, "This Septic Isle," 29.

8 Barker, "An Attempt at Perspective," 553.

9 Truffaut, *Hitchcock,* 140.

10 Durgnat, *A Mirror for England,* 200n.

11 Truffaut, "A Certain Tendency of the French Cinema," 224-5. This is a (very poor) translation of an article that originally appeared in *Cahiers du cinéma* 31 (January 1954): 15-29.

12 Perkins, "The British Cinema," 3, 4, 7. The article was followed by the statement that Perkins wrote it "on behalf of the editorial board."

13 Houston, *The Contemporary Cinema,* 123.

14 Mass Observation was founded in 1935 by Humphrey Jennings, Charles Madge, and Tom Harrison, who recruited "mass observers" to record aspects of everyday life and public behavior. Although most of the observers were middle class, their diaries and surveys produced a wealth of material that has proved extremely useful to historians.

15 Rohdie, "Review," 135.

16 MacCabe, "Realism and the Cinema," 12, 9, 16.

17 MacCabe, "Theory and Film," 25.

18 MacCabe, "*Days of Hope,*" 100.

19 Bazin, *What Is Cinema?* 35-6. Bazin's examples included Flaherty, as well as Erich von Stroheim, Orson Welles, and the Italian neorealists.

20 Williams, "After the Classic," 277.

21 Ibid., 282.

22 Kumar, "The Social and Cultural Setting," 42.

23 McFarlane, "A Literary Cinema?" 138.

24 Eaton, "Not a Piccadilly Actor in Sight," 32.

25 Higson "Space, Place, Spectacle," 18.

26 Hill, *Sex, Class and Realism*, 132. As Hill points out the New Wave films directed by Tony Richardson, in particular, often include self-conscious "poetic" or "satiric" effects that seem to come from outside the world of the film.

27 Harper, *Women in British Cinema*, 95–6, 120.

28 Clayton, quoted in Sinyard, *Jack Clayton*, 44; Reisz, quoted in Taylor, "Tomorrow the World," 82.

29 Walker, *Hollywood, England*, 47; Murphy, *Sixties British Cinema*, 14.

30 The relatively new Independent (i.e., commercial) Television Network is also a target in *A Kind of Loving* (John Schlesinger) and *The Loneliness of the Long Distance Runner* (Tony Richardson), both released in 1962. In all these films, television viewing is associated mainly with the older generation.

31 Hill, *Sex, Class and Realism*, 133.

32 Murphy, *Sixties British Cinema*, 19.

33 Cook, ed., *The Dilys Powell Film Reader*, 20–1.

34 See Marwick, "*Room at the Top*," 132. For a fuller account of the negotiations with the censors, see Aldgate, *Censorship and the Permissive Society*.

35 Palmer, "What Was New in the British New Wave?" 135.

36 Hill, *Sex, Class and Realism*, 161.

37 Ibid., 160.

38 Eaton, "Not a Piccadilly Actor in Sight," 32.

39 McKnight, "Ken Loach's Domestic Morality Tales," 83.

40 Hill, *British Cinema in the 1980s*, 172; Brown, "Paradise Found and Lost," 253.

41 Leigh, *Naked and Other Screenplays*, xxxix, and in Movshovitz, ed., *Mike Leigh: Interviews*, 52.

42 Hill, "Every Fuckin' Choice Stinks," 20.

43 Hill, "Failure and Utopianism," 180; Hill, "From the New Wave to 'Brit-Grit,'" 252.

44 Carney and Quart, *The Films of Mike Leigh*, 8; Leigh, *Naked and Other Screenplays*, xxxvii.

45 Leigh, *Naked and Other Screenplays*, xii.

46 Turner, "*Raining Stones*," 51.

47 Lovell, "The British Cinema," 202.

48 Carney and Quart, *The Films of Mike Leigh*, 6.

49 Loach, quoted in Quart, "A Fidelity to the Real," 29.

50 Loach, quoted in Hill, "Interview with Ken Loach," 167.

51 Leigh, *Naked and Other Screenplays*, xxxii.

52 Leigh, quoted in Movshovitz, ed., *Mike Leigh: Interviews*, 18.

53 Williamson, "*My Name Is Joe*," 58.

54 Hill, *British Cinema in the 1980s*, 196.

55 Fuller, ed., *Loach on Loach*, ix.

56 Knight, "Naturalism, Narration and Critical Perspective," 71. For a discussion of the version of Althusser's theory of ideology to which Knight refers, see Chapter 10.

57 Turner, "*Raining Stones*," 51; Eaton, "Not a Piccadilly Actor in Sight," 33.

58 Hill, *British Cinema in the 1980s*, 195. For a comparison with Brecht, see Carney and Quart, *The Films of Mike Leigh*, 120.

59 Leigh, *Naked and Other Screenplays*, xxxiii; Carney and Quart, *The Films of Mike Leigh*, 47.

60 While both acknowledged the influence of Leigh, they have said that their commitment to realism came more from Alan Clarke, a director who worked mainly in television but whose most famous film, *Scum* (1979), about a prison for young offenders,

was given a theatrical release after it proved too intense for television; see Kelly, *Alan Clarke,* 228-9. Ray Winstone, the star of *Nil by Mouth* and *The War Zone,* also appeared in *Scum* and Loach's *Ladybird, Ladybird.*

61  James, "Being There," 6, 8. John Hill also noted that *Nil by Mouth* excludes "wider patterns of social life" ("From the New Wave to 'Brit-Grit,'" 253) and Leonard Quart that it "gives no political or social explanations for the family situation" ("*Nil by Mouth,*" 49).

62  Roth, quoted in Danielson, "Welcome to My Nightmare," 10.

63  See the front page of the October 1997 issue of *Sight and Sound;* inside, the heading for an interview with the film's designer refers to the setting as "desolate Deptford."

64  Roth, quoted in Lim, "Marching Off to War," 14.

## CHAPTER FOUR. THE MIRROR CRACK'D: BRITISH EXPRESSIONISM

1  Bazin, *What Is Cinema?* 28.
2  Gledhill, "The Melodramatic Field," 30.
3  Richards, "Gainsborough," 292.
4  Landy, *Film, Politics, and Gramsci,* 324.
5  Powell, quoted in Salwolke, *The Films of Michael Powell and the Archers,* 87-8.
6  Winnington, quoted in ibid., 133.
7  Winston Churchill hated the film and tried to stop its production and then its release; see Kennedy, *The Life and Death of Colonel Blimp,* 52-63. Kennedy suggests that "Clive Candy is an almost exact inversion of Winston Churchill" (52).
8  Christie, *Arrows of Desire,* 47.
9  The war is similarly absent in *Brief Encounter,* which, despite its contemporary costumes and location shooting, is apparently set before the war but contains no reference to the political uncertainty of the time. See also the discussion of *Brighton Rock* in Chapter 9.
10  Fuller, "*A Canterbury Tale,*" 36.
11  Lant, *Blackout,* 199.
12  The term "rogue talents" is taken from title of the chapter on Roeg and Russell in Walker, *The Once and Future Film.* Boorman is discussed in his previous chapter as a "visionary."
13  Kael, *Reeling,* 79; Feineman, *Nicolas Roeg,* 128.
14  Ciment, *John Boorman,* 36.
15  Hacker and Price, *Take Ten,* 232.
16  Gomez, "Russell's Images of Lawrence's Vision," 248-9.
17  Sinyard, *The Films of Nicolas Roeg,* 3.
18  Russell, *A British Picture,* 57; Boorman, quoted in Walker, *Hollywood, England,* 387.
19  Kael, *Reeling,* 79.
20  Jameson, "History and the Death Wish," 7.
21  Kolker, "The Open Texts of Nicolas Roeg," 83.
22  Gentry, "Ken Russell," 10.
23  Russell, quoted in Zambrano, "*Women in Love,*" 53, and in Gentry, "Ken Russell," 10.
24  Russell, *A British Picture,* 34.
25  Wood, "Ken Russell," 909.
26  Gomez, "Russell's Images of Lawrence's Vision," 249-50.
27  Zambrano, "*Women in Love,*" 50, 46.

28  Christie, "Women in Love," 50.
29  Paul Mayersburg, quoted in Izod, The Films of Nicolas Roeg, 15; Barker, "What the Detective Saw," 194; Kennedy, "The Illusions of Nicolas Roeg," 27.
30  Milne, "Don't Look Now," 238.
31  Kolker, "The Open Texts of Nicolas Roeg," 82.
32  Palmer and Riley, "Seeing, Believing, and 'Knowing' in Narrative Film," 18.
33  Sanderson, Don't Look Now, 41–2; Dick, "Desperation and Desire," 13.
34  Strick, "Zardoz and John Boorman," 76.
35  Boorman, quoted in Yakir, "The Sorcerer," 50.
36  Boorman, quoted in Kennedy, "The World of King Arthur," 31, 33.
37  Boorman, quoted in Ciment, John Boorman, 200.
38  Boorman, quoted in Kemp, "Gone to Earth," 24. It was also risky to take this subject seriously after Monty Python and the Holy Grail (see Chapter 8).
39  Kemp, "Gone to Earth," 24; Boorman, quoted in Ciment, John Boorman, 197.
40  Ciment, John Boorman, 180.
41  Wollen, "The Last New Wave," 41, 38, 40.
42  Jarman, quoted in Grundmann, "History and the Gay Viewfinder," 27.
43  Greenaway, quoted in Woods, Being Naked Playing Dead, 282.
44  Wollen, "The Last New Wave," 45.
45  Jarman, quoted in Hacker and Price, Take Ten, 255.
46  Driscoll, "'The Rose Revived,'" 78.
47  O'Pray, Derek Jarman, 95.
48  Higson, "Re-presenting the National Past," 123, 125.
49  Lippard and Johnson, "Private Practice, Public Health," 285; Jarman, quoted in Hacker and Price, Take Ten, 237.
50  Jarman, The Last of England, 188.
51  Ibid., 166.
52  Hewison, Future Tense, 103.
53  Kuhn, Family Secrets, 110.
54  Greenaway, quoted in Bergan, "Food for Thought," 29.
55  Boorman, quoted in Petrakis, "Blasphemy in Cinema," 172.
56  Greenaway, quoted in Pally, "Cinema as a Total Art Form," 6.
57  Greenaway, quoted in Hacker and Price, Take Ten, 190.
58  Park, Learning to Dream, 89.
59  Walsh, "Allegories of Thatcherism," 260; Gras, "Dramatizing the Failure to Jump," 124.
60  Woods, Being Naked Playing Dead, 198.
61  Pascoe, Peter Greenaway, 158.
62  Hacker and Price, Take Ten, 206.
63  Van Wert, "The Cook, The Thief," 49.
64  Greenaway, quoted in Bergan, "Food for Thought," 28.
65  Ibid.

## CHAPTER FIVE. MILLIONS LIKE US: NATIONAL CINEMA AS POPULAR CINEMA

1  Higson, "The Concept of National Cinema," 46.
2  Elsaesser, "Chronicle of a Death Retold," 166.
3  Ryall, "British Cinema and Genre," 23.
4  Kracauer, From Caligari to Hitler, 8.
5  Williams, The Politics of Modernism, 107.

6 Gramsci, *Selections from Cultural Writings,* 208.

7 Higson, *Waving the Flag,* 9.

8 Leavis, *Fiction and the Reading Public,* 85.

9 Quoted in Robbins, *Great Britain,* 310.

10 Hall, "Notes on Deconstructing 'The Popular,'" 233, 237.

11 Richards, *The Age of the Dream Palace,* 183, 186.

12 Greene, *The Pleasure Dome,* 78-9.

13 The early screenplays were for *21 Days* (Basil Dean) and *The Green Cockatoo* (William Cameron Menzies), both made in 1937 but not released until 1939-40. For Greene's attitude to these films, see Phillips, *Graham Greene,* 44-7.

14 Cotten had a long association with Welles, including *Citizen Kane* (1941), in which he also played the best friend of the powerful and unscrupulous Kane. There were suggestions that Welles took a hand in directing *The Third Man,* but there is no evidence that he did more than occasionally contribute to the dialogue. The bravura use of camera angles, lighting, and deep space all develop out of Reed's earlier work (which was certainly influenced by Welles).

15 Moss, *The Films of Carol Reed,* 186. Calloway is the narrator in Greene's prose version of the story, written as an aid to preparing the screenplay.

16 Greene, *The Pleasure Dome,* 39, 94.

17 Thomson, "Greene in the Dark," 22.

18 Diemert, *Graham Greene's Thrillers,* 133; Elsaesser, "The Dandy in Hitchcock," 11.

19 Greene, *The Pleasure Dome,* 227-8. He made this comment in his review of *Goodbye Mr. Chips* (a film discussed in Chapter 10).

20 Diemert, *Graham Greene's Thrillers,* 117.

21 DeVitis, *Graham Greene,* 29. DeVitis refers specifically to the novel *Stamboul Train* (1932), Greene's first thriller, and seems to be thinking of Hitchcock's use of the train in *The Lady Vanishes* - which was, of course, made several years later.

22 Greene, *The Pleasure Dome,* 65.

23 Ibid., 123.

24 Van Wert, "Narrative Structure in *The Third Man,*" 341; Shelden, *Graham Greene,* 328.

25 Quoted in Moss, *The Films of Carol Reed,* 179.

26 Armes, *A Critical History of British Cinema,* 207.

27 Driver, "A *Third Man* Cento," 41; Moss, *The Films of Carol Reed,* 180-1.

28 See Nolan, "Graham Greene's Films," 307.

29 See Gomez, "*The Third Man,*" 333.

30 Kael and Greene, quoted in Phillips, *Graham Greene,* 71-2.

31 See ibid., 73, and Moss, *The Films of Carol Reed,* 191.

32 The absurdity is both heightened and contained by the repetitive zither music (composed and played by Anton Karas) that Reed discovered and used throughout the film to create a jaunty but disturbing counterpoint to the action. The soundtrack music became a popular hit. See White, *The Third Man,* 33-5.

33 Greene, quoted in Phillips, *Graham Greene,* 73.

34 Naremore, *More than Night,* 79-80.

35 Phillips, *Graham Greene,* 19.

36 Fleming, quoted in Bennett and Woollacott, *Bond and Beyond,* 22.

37 Brosnan, *James Bond in the Cinema,* 12.

38 Richard Maibaum, quoted in McGilligan, *Backstory,* 287. Maibaum worked on the screenplays for many Bond films.

39 Wood, *Hitchcock's Films,* 100.

40  Ibid., 9; Chapman, *Licence to Thrill,* 1.

41  Houston, "*Dr. No,*" 197.

42  Whitehall, "*Dr. No,*" 36.

43  Sarne, "*Goldfinger,*" 26.

44  Houston, "007," 14-16.

45  When Fleming died in 1964, he had written twelve Bond novels and two collections of short stories. Other writers continued producing Bond novels, most notably John Gardner (sixteen novels from 1981 to 1996) and Raymond Benson (eleven novels from 1996 to the present). Some of these might be described as "novelizations," but the whole phenomenon has blurred the distinction among adaptations, novelizations, and original works.

46  Houston, "007," 16.

47  Bennett and Woollacott, *Bond and Beyond,* 229.

48  Brosnan, *James Bond in the Cinema,* 11.

49  Thompson, *Storytelling in the New Hollywood,* 305.

50  Chapman, *Licence to Thrill,* 270.

51  Bennett and Woollacott, *Bond and Beyond,* 11, 36.

52  Walker, *Hollywood, England,* 189-90. Although Fleming's Bond is often regarded as an English gentleman, and Fleming thought that David Niven would be the best actor for the role, Bond's father was Scottish (and his mother Swiss).

53  Moore took over the role in *Live and Let Die* (Guy Hamilton, 1973). He was best known for his starring role as a reformed English gentleman thief in the television series *The Saint* (1962-9), based on a character created by Leslie Charteris in the 1930s.

54  Chapman, *Licence to Thrill,* 38-9.

55  Amis, *The James Bond Dossier,* 74-5; Chapman, *Licence to Thrill,* 29.

56  Bennett and Woollacott, *Bond and Beyond,* 55.

57  Brosnan, *James Bond in the Cinema,* 11. For a fuller discussion of the political implications of recent Bond films, see my "'The World Has Changed.'"

58  Dyer, *Only Entertainment,* 18-26.

59  Hill, "Failure and Utopianism," 183.

60  Hallam, "Film, Class and National Identity," 270.

61  Howard, "Exhibition and Repression," 25.

62  Ibid., 28.

63  The same information is conveyed slightly differently in the U.S. release version. This version begins with with mock dictionary definitions of terms that might have puzzled U.S. audiences: "Tory," "colliery," "redundancy," and "brassed off." It ends with definitions of "closure" and "redundancy" and invites the audience to draw its own "conclusions."

64  Marris, "Northern Realism," 47; Monk, "*Billy Elliot,*" 40.

65  Monk, "*Billy Elliot,*" 40; Monk, "Projecting a 'New Britain,'" 34.

66  Dyer, *Only Entertainment,* 24.

## CHAPTER SIX. THE STARS LOOK DOWN: ACTING BRITISH

1  Richards, *Films and British National Identity,* 112.

2  McVay, "The Art of the Actor," 22.

3  Hill, *British Cinema in the 1980s,* 81-2.

4  Babington, "Introduction," 19.

5  Macnab, *Searching for Stars,* 61-2.
6  Richards, *The Age of the Dream Palace,* 209.
7  Greene, *The Pleasure Dome,* 101.
8  Richards, *The Age of the Dream Palace,* 236.
9  Debray, "Admirable England," 128.
10  Keleher, "Laurence Olivier," 24.
11  Greene, *The Pleasure Dome,* 171.
12  Schickel, "Olivier 1907-1989," 26.
13  Spoto, *Marilyn Monroe,* 370; Schickel, "Olivier 1907-1989," 24.
14  Olivier, quoted in Naremore, *Acting in the Cinema,* 51.
15  Olivier, quoted in Baty, *American Monroe,* 156, and Keleher, "Laurence Olivier," 24.
16  Kael, *Kiss Kiss Bang Bang,* 419; Thomson, "Our Lord of Danger," 29.
17  Schickel, "Olivier 1907-1989," 24.
18  Spoto, *Marilyn Monroe,* 379.
19  McCann, *Marilyn Monroe,* 103.
20  Olivier, quoted in Spoto, *Marilyn Monroe,* 378.
21  McCann, *Marilyn Monroe,* 104.
22  Chibnall, *J. Lee Thompson,* 75, 77.
23  Cook, "The Trouble with Sex," 176. It should be noted that Dors and the film's publicity team encouraged this response by the pinup photos used to promote the film; see Chibnall, *J. Lee Thompson,* 78-9, 97-8.
24  The story of Ruth Ellis later became the subject of *Dance with a Stranger* (Mike Newell, 1985).
25  Geraghty, "Diana Dors," 345.
26  Babington, "Introduction," 12, drawing on remarks made by Thomas Elsaesser in "Images for England," 267-8.
27  Kernan, "*Accident,*" 63.
28  For a detailed analysis of this transition, see Palmer and Riley, *The Films of Joseph Losey,* 68-71.
29  Losey, quoted in Ciment, *Conversations with Losey,* 264.
30  Houston and Kinder, "The Losey-Pinter Collaboration," 26.
31  Losey, quoted in Leahy, *The Cinema of Joseph Losey,* 156.
32  Palmer and Riley, *The Films of Joseph Losey,* 83.
33  For Losey's account of the problem with the dog, see Milne, *Losey on Losey,* 18.
34  Dixon, "The Eternal Summer of Joseph Losey and Harold Pinter's *Accident,*" 35.
35  Losey, quoted in Milne, *Losey on Losey,* 20.
36  Petley, "The Upright Houses," 71.
37  Hill, *British Cinema in the 1980s,* 188.
38  Bigsby, "The Politics of Anxiety," 294.
39  DeVinney. "Transmitting the Bildungsroman to the Small Screen," 92, 94; Hare, quoted in Oliva, *David Hare,* 179.
40  Petley, "The Upright Houses," 72.
41  Hare, *Writing Left-Handed,* 35, 26.
42  Giles, "History with Holes," 89.
43  Bate, *The Genius of Shakespeare,* 161.
44  Bloom, *Shakespeare,* 3, 10, 13.
45  Bate, *The Genius of Shakespeare,* 201, 214.
46  Terence Hawkes, quoted in Bennett, *Performing Nostalgia,* 21.
47  Richard E. Grant, one of the actors in the company, quoted in Hatchuel, *A Companion to the Shakespearean Films of Kenneth Branagh,* 17.

48  Rosenthal, "Kenneth Branagh," 21-2.
49  Michael Skovmand, quoted in Hatchuel, *A Companion to the Shakespearean Films of Kenneth Branagh*, 41.
50  Hatchuel, ibid., 95.
51  Simon, quoted in Lehmann, "Kenneth Branagh at the Quilting Point," 14.
52  Forbes, "*Henry V*," 259; MacCabe, "Throne of Blood," 13-14.
53  Manheim, "The English History Play on Screen," 129-30.
54  Branagh, quoted in Fuller, "Kenneth," 7, and in Quinn and Kingsley-Smith, "Kenneth Branagh's *Henry V*," 170-1.
55  Lehmann, "Kenneth Branagh at the Quilting Point," 7; Pursell, "Playing the Game," 274.
56  Light, "The Importance of Being Ordinary," 18-19.
57  Drakakis, "Shakespeare in Quotations," 170.
58  Rothwell, "*Elizabeth* and *Shakespeare in Love*," 79.

## CHAPTER SEVEN. NO SEX PLEASE – WE'RE BRITISH: SEX, GENDER, AND THE NATIONAL CHARACTER

1  Dors, quoted in Geraghty, "Diana Dors," 344.
2  Grierson, in an article originally published in 1929, quoted in Hardy, *Grierson on the Movies*, 33.
3  Bazin, "Hitchcock versus Hitchcock," 65.
4  Mulvey, "Visual Pleasure and Narrative Cinema," 11.
5  Huyssen, "Mass Culture as Woman," 194.
6  See Light, *Forever England*, and Sexton, "Grierson's Machines."
7  Quoted in Robbins, *Great Britain*, 310.
8  Macnab, *Searching for Stars*, 62.
9  Quoted in Costello, *Love, Sex and War*, 281.
10  Haste, *Rules of Desire*, 99.
11  Murphy, *Realism and Tinsel*, 103.
12  Costello, *Love, Sex and War*, 370.
13  Janni, quoted in Walker, *Hollywood, England*, 109. Janni produced John Schlesinger's New Wave film *A Kind of Loving* (1962) and worked with the same director on *Billy Liar* and *Darling* (see later in this section).
14  Macnab, *Searching for Stars*, 143, 153; see also Geraghty, "The Woman Between."
15  Haste, *Rules of Desire*, 185-6.
16  Halasz, "Great Britain," 30.
17  Haste, *Rules of Desire*, 150.
18  The parallels between the two films may have inspired the title of *Alfie Darling* (Ken Hughes, 1975), a rather odd sequel/remake of *Alfie* with singer Alan Price in the title role.
19  Tarr, "*Sapphire, Darling*," 64.
20  Geraghty, "Women and 60s British Cinema," 104; Luckett, "Travel and Mobility," 233.
21  French, "The Alphaville of Admass," 107.
22  Richards, *Films and British National Identity*, 158; Luckett, "Travel and Mobility," 243.
23  Geraghty, "Women and 60s British Cinema," 104.
24  Walker, *Hollywood, England*, 280.
25  Carson, "Comedy, Sexuality and 'Swinging London' Films," 49.
26  Ibid., 51.
27  Murphy, *Sixties British Cinema*, 144.

28 Walker, *Hollywood, England,* 307.
29 Richards, *Films and British National Identity,* 163.
30 Isabel Quigly, quoted in Richards, *Films and British National Identity,* 163.
31 Sheridan, *Keeping the British End Up,* 29.
32 Hunt, *British Low Culture,* 2.
33 Greene, *The Pleasure Dome,* 248.
34 The spelling of the name of the title character was changed ever so slightly to avoid copyright problems.
35 Conrich, "Forgotten Cinema," 87, 93.
36 Sheridan, *Keeping the British End Up,* 9.
37 Hunt, *British Low Culture,* 126.
38 Sheridan, *Keeping the British End Up,* 211.
39 McGillivray, "Horrible Things," 44, 47.
40 Hunt, *British Low Culture,* 101.
41 Chibnall, *Making Mischief,* 71.
42 Ibid., 77.
43 Merz, "The Tension of Genre," 122.
44 Monk, "*The Tango Lesson,*" 55.
45 Potter, "On Shows," 291.
46 Felber, "Capturing the Shadows of Ghosts," 31.
47 Brunsdon, "Not Having It All," 175.
48 Adler, quoted in Felperin, "Falling Angel," 15.
49 Brunsdon, "Not Having It All," 170, 174. Ackroyd became Ken Loach's regular cinematographer after working on *Riff-raff* (1991).
50 McGrath, "*Stella Does Tricks,*" 50.
51 Adler, quoted in Felperin, "Falling Angel," 15.
52 Cook, "*Under the Skin,*" 56.
53 Adler, quoted in Felperin, "Falling Angel," 16.

## CHAPTER EIGHT. CARRY ON REGARDLESS: THE BRITISH SENSE OF HUMOR

1 Richards, *The Age of the Dream Palace,* 234.
2 Garrod, "Humour," 350.
3 Higson, *Waving the Flag,* 111.
4 Hitchcock, quoted in Geduld, ed., *Film Makers on Film Making,* 127; Higson, *Waving the Flag,* 112.
5 Johnson, "Have the British a Sense of Humour?" 48.
6 Nuttall and Carmichael, *Common Factors/Vulgar Factions,* 23.
7 Green, "Ealing," 297.
8 Sobchack, "Bakhtin's 'Carnivalesque' in 1950s British Comedy," 180.
9 Mackendrick and Balcon, quoted in Ellis, "Made in Ealing," 113, 119.
10 These films were all released between April and June 1949; a fourth Ealing comedy, *A Run for Your Money* (Charles Frend) was released in November, but this film, about the misadventures of two Welsh miners in London, did not enjoy the success of the other films and is one of the few Ealing films not mentioned in the text of Charles Barr's book on the Studios.
11 Barr, *Ealing Studios,* 107.
12 Ibid., 110–11.
13 Ibid., 125.

14 Kemp, *Lethal Innocence,* 39.

15 Richards, *Films and British National Identity,* 175.

16 Kemp, *Lethal Innocence,* 46.

17 Porter, "The Context of Creativity," 190; Kemp, *Lethal Innocence,* 65.

18 Jean-Louis Tallenay, quoted in Kemp, *Lethal Innocence,* 66.

19 Mackendrick, quoted in ibid., 51.

20 Ibid.,

21 Kemp, *Lethal Innocence,* 51.

22 Ibid., 61.

23 Sinyard, "Film," 242.

24 Barr, *Ealing Studios,* 135.

25 An unnamed critic in the *New Yorker,* quoted in Medhurst, "Carry On Camp," 17.

26 Orwell, "The Art of Donald McGill," 191-3. See also Johnson, "Have the British a Sense of Humour?" 52, and Nuttall and Carmichael, *Common Factors/Vulgar Factions,* 37-8.

27 *Hancock's Half Hour* was an enormous success on BBC radio from 1954 to 1959 and equally successful on television from 1956 to 1961. Tony Hancock made several films, but his curmudgeonly persona did not prove so appealing on the large screen.

28 Orwell, "The Art of Donald McGill," 184.

29 Medhurst, "Carry On Camp," 17-18.

30 Jordan, "Carry On," 314-15.

31 Orwell, "The Art of Donald McGill," 186.

32 See Medhurst, "Carry On Camp," 19.

33 Gerald Thomas directed the much later *Carry On Columbus* (1992), which featured Jim Dale but few of the other *Carry On* stock company. Series producer Peter Rogers purportedly has a *Carry On London* in the works.

34 Gray, "Certain Liberties Have Been Taken," 94, 98, 102.

35 Orwell, "The Art of Donald McGill," 191n.

36 Gray, "Certain Liberties Have Been Taken," 106.

37 Ibid., 95.

38 Orwell, "The Art of Donald McGill," 188.

39 Medhurst, "Music Hall and British Cinema," 183.

40 Sterritt and Rhodes, "Monty Python," 22. Ellen Bishop also argues that "the Monty Python troupe is reinscribing the carnivalesque spirit in popular culture" ("Bakhtin, Carnival and Comedy," 54).

41 Hunt, *British Low Culture,* 36.

42 Whannel, "Boxed In," 190.

43 Palin, quoted in Rubenstein, "Monty Python Strikes Again," 7.

44 Glass, "Laugh at Obstacles," 12.

45 Ibid.

46 Walker, *The Once and Future Film,* 89.

47 Glass, "Laugh at Obstacles," 12.

48 Perry, *Life of Python,* 144.

## CHAPTER NINE. SEXY BEASTS: BRITISH MONSTERS

1 Wilson, quoted in Barr, "Introduction," 14.

2 Barr, "Introduction," 14.

3 Murphy, *Realism and Tinsel,* 146.

4 Street, *British Cinema in Documents*, 33.
5 There were many crime films, but most of these were "quota quickies" or similar low-budget productions. James Chapman calculates that "thrillers" accounted for about one-fifth of British feature films in the 1930s; "Celluloid Shockers," 75.
6 Petley, "The Lost Continent," 98.
7 Prince, *Movies and Meanings*, 44–5.
8 Ibid., 45.
9 Tudor, *Monsters and Mad Scientists*, 195.
10 Lowenstein, "'Under-the-Skin Horrors,'" 221–2, 227–8.
11 Haraway, *Simians, Cyborgs, and Women*, 180.
12 Ryall, "England's Dreaming," 33.
13 Chibnall and Murphy, "Parole Overdue," 2.
14 Arthur Vesselo, *Sight and Sound* (Autumn 1947), quoted in Murphy, *Realism and Tinsel*, 154.
15 James Naremore suggests that critics in the United States viewed *Brighton Rock* as "a cross between an unfashionable genre picture and a respectable literary adaptation" (*More than Night*, 76).
16 Spicer, "Misfits and the Marginalised," 75. Robert Murphy notes that gangs continued to operate in Brighton, which was "not the safest of places to be in 1947"; *Realism and Tinsel*, 158.
17 The "documentary" effect evokes the British documentary movement but also parallels contemporary developments in Hollywood crime films, such as *Call Northside 777* (Henry Hathaway, 1948). In *The Blue Lamp*, the commentator's voice is briefly replaced by what purports to be that of a judge reading from a recent judgment on young offenders, an effect that recalls the use of the councillor in *Housing Problems* (see Chapter 2).
18 Brunsdon, "Space and Time," 148.
19 Joan Lester, *The Reynold's News* (11 January 1948), quoted in Chibnall, "Purgatory at the End of the Pier," 138; censor's report, quoted in Robertson, "The Censors and British Gangland," 21.
20 Wollen, "Riff-raff Realism," 19.
21 Reg Whitley, quoted in Falk, *Travels in Greeneland*, 53.
22 Greene, quoted in ibid., 54.
23 Chibnall, "Purgatory at the End of the Pier," 138.
24 Spicer, "Misfits and the Marginalised," 74.
25 Macnab, "*Brighton Rock*," 53.
26 Murphy, *Realism and Tinsel*, 166.
27 The critical discourse around the films frequently, but imprecisely, uses psychological terminology to describe these juvenile criminals. Wollen refers to both Pinkie and Riley as "the psychotic young criminal" ("Riff-raff Realism," 21–2); Richards describes Riley as "neurotic" ("Basil Dearden at Ealing," 22); for Durgnat, he is "a hysteric teenage thug" (*A Mirror for England*, 137).
28 Chibnall and Murphy, "Parole Overdue," 5.
29 Richards, *Films and British National Identity*, 144–5. Compare Andy Medhurst: "Where Bogarde's performance stands as compelling, thrilling, and above all erotic, Hanley is drab, bland, and neutered" ("Dirk Bogarde," 347–8). However, Steve Chibnall argues that "in an age when bravery was so intimately linked to desire, Bogarde's sexual allure would have been defused by his cowardice" ("The Teenage Trilogy," 144).
30 Greene, quoted in Phillips, *Graham Greene*, 163.

31 Murphy, "Riff-raff," 304; Naremore, *More than Night*, 75.

32 Hill, "The Face of Horror," 6–7.

33 Alloway, "Monster Films," 121–2, 124.

34 Pirie, *A Heritage of Horror*, 9.

35 Tudor, *Monsters and Mad Scientists*, 40–1.

36 Pirie, *A Heritage of Horror*, 29–30.

37 Eyles, Adkison, and Fry, *House of Horror*, 117.

38 Conrich, "Traditions of the British Horror Film," 228.

39 Coe, "Hammer's Cosy Violence," 12.

40 Murphy, *Sixties British Cinema*, 163.

41 Hutchings, *Hammer and Beyond*, 57, 59.

42 Harper, "The Scent of Distant Blood," 116.

43 *Dracula* was released in the United States as *Horror of Dracula*.

44 Pirie, *A Heritage of Horror*, 50. In this respect Fisher is very unlike Ken Russell, who became the critics' whipping boy a decade later.

45 Fisher, quoted in Harper, "The Scent of Distant Blood," 125n.

46 Pirie, *A Heritage of Horror*, 50.

47 Porter, "The Context of Creativity," 202; Landy, *British Genres*, 406–7.

48 Mangravite, "The House of Hammer," 48.

49 Eyles et al., *House of Horror*, 17.

50 Ibid., 95.

51 Tudor, *Monsters and Mad Scientists*, 171–2.

52 Hutchings, *Hammer and Beyond*, 114.

53 Dracula (but not Christopher Lee) reappeared in the hybrid vampire–martial arts movie *The Legend of the 7 Golden Vampires* (Baker, 1974) made by Hammer in coproduction with the Hong Kong company Shaw Brothers.

54 Hunt, *British Low Culture*, 143.

55 Tudor, *Monsters and Mad Scientists*, 215.

56 Landy, *British Genres*, 392; Coubro, "The Appeal and Success of Hammer Film Productions," 176–7.

57 Sanjek, "Twilight of the Monsters," 196.

58 Murphy, *Sixties British Cinema*, 191.

59 Price had played villains with relish in the early 1960s in many of Roger Corman's U.S. horror films, often based on stories by Edgar Allan Poe. In the United States, *Witchfinder General* was released as *The Conqueror Worm*, with an added epigraph from Poe to cash in on the success of the earlier films.

60 Hunt, *British Low Culture*, 150. Reeves was only twenty-four when he directed *Witchfinder General*, his third film. He died of a drug overdose shortly after its release. For a full account of his short career, see Halligan, *Michael Reeves*.

61 Sanjek, "Twilight of the Monsters," 197.

62 Chibnall, "A Heritage of Evil," 160.

63 Walker, *National Heroes*, 25.

64 Ronnie Kray had appeared as an extra in *Brighton Rock*, and Iain Sinclair suggests that he would be perfectly cast as Pinkie ("Smart Guys," 22).

65 Mary Desjardins relates the treatment of the mother in the film to Margaret Thatcher's dismantling of the "nanny" state (see "Free from the Apron Strings").

66 The film was released in the Unied States in the fall of 1970 but was first shown in London in January 1971.

67 Sinclair, "Smart Guys," 22.

68 Walker, *Hollywood, England*, 252.

69 Armour, "Between a Rock and a Hard Place," 94; Brooks, *Sexy Beast,* 50.
70 Glazer, quoted in Olsen, "A Place in the Sun," 16.
71 Kermode, *Gangster No. 1,* 46.

## CHAPTER TEN. THE RULING CLASS: IDEOLOGY AND THE SCHOOL MOVIE

1 Barker, "An Attempt at Perspective," 563.
2 Althusser, *Lenin and Philosophy,* 158.
3 Barr, *Ealing Studios,* 108.
4 Lambert, quoted in Lovell (et al.) and Kitses, "Interview," 56.
5 Althusser, *Lenin and Philosophy,* 158, 162.
6 Malcomson, "Modernism Comes to the Cabbage Patch," 17.
7 Williams, "After the Classic," 276.
8 Althusser, *Lenin and Philosophy,* 155, 157.
9 Richards, *The Age of the Dream Palace,* 313.
10 Richards, *Visions of Yesterday,* 58.
11 Colls, "Englishness and the National Culture," 5-6.
12 Barthes, *Mythologies,* 41.
13 The film thus evokes the idea of the "heroic failure" found in other British films of the period, such as *Scott of the Antarctic* and *The Magic Box* (see Chapter 2).
14 Landy, *British Genres,* 350.
15 Anderson, "Get Out and Push," 139.
16 Robinson, "Anderson Shooting *If. . . . ,*" 131.
17 Loach, quoted in Stephenson, "*Kes* and the Press," 48-9.
18 Garnett, quoted in Bream, "Spreading Wings at Kestrel," 40.
19 Hacker and Price, eds., *Take Ten,* 36.
20 Hedling, *Lindsay Anderson,* 102.
21 Cook, "Auteur Theory and British Cinema," 148.
22 Hedling, *Lindsay Anderson,* 88.
23 Kael, *Going Steady,* 353.
24 Anderson, quoted in Hedling, *Lindsay Anderson,* 96.
25 Sherwin, quoted in ibid., 103.
26 Richards, *Visions of Yesterday,* 58.

## CHAPTER ELEVEN. THE LONG MEMORY: HISTORY AND HERITAGE

1 Hoskins, *The Making of the English Landscape,* 11, 16.
2 Hobsbawm, "Introduction," 7-8.
3 Colls, "Englishness and the National Culture," 1.
4 See Wright, *On Living in an Old Country.*
5 Miles and Smith, *Cinema, Literature and Society,* 2.
6 Nairn, *The Break-up of Britain,* 270.
7 Wiener, *English Culture,* ix, 5.
8 Richards, *Films and British National Identity,* 175.
9 Hewison, "Commerce and Culture," 175.
10 Higson, "The Heritage Film and British Cinema," 236.
11 Higson, "Re-presenting the National Past," 115.

12 Craig, "Rooms without a View," 10.
13 Douglas McGrath, the director of *Emma* (1996), was American, as was the star, Gwyneth Paltrow; *Sense and Sensibility* (1995) was based on a screenplay by Emma Thompson but directed by Ang Lee, who was born in Taiwan and became a film-maker in the United States.
14 Higson, "Re-presenting the National Past," 109.
15 Pym, *Merchant Ivory's English Landscape,* 9.
16 Monk, "The British 'Heritage Film' and Its Critics," 120.
17 Ibid., 122–3.
18 Landy, *Film, Politics, and Gramsci,* 107.
19 Higson, *Waving the Flag,* 61.
20 Freedman, "England as Ideology," 97–8.
21 Higson, "Re-presenting the National Past," 119. Higson explores this "divided response" more fully and rather more appreciatively in his latest work on the heritage film. See his *English Heritage, English Cinema,* especially the chapter on *Howards End,* 146–93.
22 Forster, *Howards End,* 150, 130, 145, 151.
23 Woolf, "The Novels of E. M. Forster," 342.
24 Brooker and Widdowson, "A Literature for England," 137.
25 Monk, "Sexuality and the Heritage," 34.
26 Forster, *Howards End,* 288.
27 Wiltshire, *Recreating Jane Austen,* 135.
28 Richards, "*Mansfield Park,*" 59.
29 Wiltshire, *Recreating Jane Austen,* 78, 96–7.
30 Williams, *The Country and the City,* 141.
31 Said, *Culture and Imperialism,* 100.
32 Richards, "*Mansfield Park,*" 59.
33 Rozema, quoted in Goslawski, "Patricia Rozema's *Mansfield Park,*" 37.
34 Wiltshire, *Recreating Jane Austen,* 136–7.
35 Said, *Culture and Imperialism,* 109; Austen, *Mansfield Park,* 420.
36 Macnab, "*The Madness of King George,*" 47.
37 Geraghty, *British Cinema in the Fifties,* 158–9.
38 Church Gibson, "From Dancing Queen to Plaster Virgin," 135.
39 Brunt, "A 'Divine Gift to Inspire'?" 285, 289–90.
40 Tepper, "*The Madness of King George,*" 50.
41 Coe, "Power Mad," 31.
42 McKechnie, "Taking Liberties with the Monarch," 223; Greenberg, "*The Madness of King George,*" 48.
43 Cannadine, "The Context, Performance and Meaning of Ritual," 109.
44 Ibid., 118–19.
45 Church Gibson, "From Dancing Queen to Plaster Virgin," 137.
46 J. Ellis, quoted in McKechnie, "Taking Liberties with the Monarch," 226.
47 Ibid., 228.
48 McArthur, "*Mrs. Brown,*" 50.
49 Church Gibson, "From Dancing Queen to Plaster Virgin," 137–8.
50 Ibid., 138; Luckett, "Image and Nation," 90; McKechnie, "Taking Liberties with the Monarch," 222.
51 Luckett, "Image and Nation," 90; McKechnie, "Taking Liberties with the Monarch," 234.
52 Rothwell, "*Elizabeth* and *Shakespeare in Love,*" 78; Bruzzi, "*Elizabeth,*" 48.

53 Church Gibson, "From Dancing Queen to Plaster Virgin," 133, 136.

54 Monk, "Sexuality and the Heritage," 33.

55 Monk, "The British Heritage-Film Debate Revisited," 177.

56 Ibid., 186.

57 Campion is Australian and Holland Polish. *The Golden Bowl* involved the international talents of the Merchant Ivory group discussed earlier.

58 Murphy, "Jane Campion's Shining," 29.

59 Brooks, *The Melodramatic Imagination,* 157, 159; Wood, *The Wings of the Dove,* 22.

60 Wood, *The Wings of the Dove,* 10. The film version of *The Golden Bowl* had not been released at the time Wood was writing, but he referred to a recent BBC television adaptation.

61 Ward, *The Imagination of Disaster,* 13.

62 Wood, *The Wings of the Dove,* 18.

63 Horne, "The James Gang," 19.

64 Wood, *The Wings of the Dove,* 21. Wood adds that "the closest is in fact the climactic scene between Kate and Merton, though in James they keep their clothes on."

65 Brooks, *The Melodramatic Imagination,* 170–1.

66 Vincendeau, "*The Golden Bowl,*" 52.

## CHAPTER TWELVE. I'M BRITISH BUT . . . :
## EMPIRE AND AFTER

1 The frequent remakes of A. E. W. Mason's tale, about a coward who redeems himself by rescuing his friends from Sudanese rebels, testifies to the enduring appeal of imperial adventure in Britain and the United States. *The Four Feathers* was originally published in 1902 and had been filmed at least three times (twice in Hollywood) before Korda's 1939 version. Since then, there have been a 1977 made-for-television adaptation, directed by Don Sharp, that received U.S. theatrical release and, most unexpectedly, a 2002 remake by Shekhar Kapur, the Indian director of *Elizabeth.* These later versions remain surprisingly faithful to the spirit of the original, although they proved much less popular than Korda's epic.

2 Hall, "Monkey Feathers," 118.

3 Young, *Fear of the Dark,* 21.

4 Publicity release, quoted in Tarr, "*Sapphire, Darling,*" 53.

5 Tarr, ibid., 56; Young, *Fear of the Dark,* 109.

6 Young, *Fear of the Dark,* 101.

7 Hall, "The Spectacle of the 'Other,'" 230.

8 Kushner, "Immigration and 'Race Relations,'" 415–16.

9 Pieterse, "Globalization as Hybridization," 45, 57.

10 Kureishi, *My Beautiful Laundrette,* 36.

11 Hall, "The Question of Cultural Identity," 297.

12 Kaleta, *Hanif Kureishi,* 217.

13 Ibid., 236, 239.

14 Morley, *Home Territories,* 146.

15 Brunsdon, "London Films," 44, 46.

16 Kureishi, quoted in Kaleta, *Hanif Kureishi,* 236.

17 Kureishi, *Sammy and Rosie Get Laid,* 109.

18 Kureishi, *My Beautiful Laundrette,* 43.

19 Sandhu, "Pop Goes the Centre," 142.

20 Kureishi, *Sammy and Rosie Get Laid,* 125–6.

21 Malik, "Beyond the Cinema of Duty?" 208, 210–11.

22 Sawhney, "'Another Kind of British,'" 60.

23 Chadha, quoted in Stuart, "Blackpool Illumination," 26–7, and in Malik, "Beyond 'the Cinema of Duty'?" 212.

24 Chadha, quoted in Stuart, "Blackpool Illumination," 26. Chadha achieved another, even greater, "cross-over" with *Bend It Like Beckham* (2002), about a young British-Asian woman who overcomes her family's opposition to her dream of playing soccer. Its North American release coincided with the emergence as an international superstar of English soccer player David Beckham, to whose celebrated free kicks the title alludes.

25 Ciecko, "Representing the Spaces of Diaspora," 76.

26 Marris, "Northern Realism," 50.

27 Spencer, "Hello Mr. Chips," 36.

28 Malik, "Money, Macpherson and Mind-Set," 96.

29 Higson, "The Instability of the National," 38.

30 Hill, "Contemporary British Cinema," 33.

31 Featherstone, "Localism, Globalism, and Cultural Identity," 66.

32 Gilroy, "Diaspora and the Detours of Identity," 304.

33 Monk, "Projecting a 'New Britain,'" 34.

34 Mercer, *Welcome to the Jungle,* 4–5.

35 O'Sullivan, "*Notting Hill,*" 50.

36 Horton, "*Beautiful People,*" 45.

37 Bruzzi, "*Beautiful People,*" 42.

38 Robert Murphy discusses *Notting Hill* as an urban fairy tale in "Citylife," 298–9.

39 Horton, "*Beautiful People,*" 45–6.

40 Monk, "Projecting a 'New Britain,'" 35.

41 James, "Farewell to Napoli," 21.

42 Wood, "*Beautiful People,*" 30, 33.

43 Horton, "*Beautiful People,*" 46.

44 Bruzzi, "*Beautiful People,*" 42.

45 James, "Farewell to Napoli," 22.

46 Murphy, "A Path through the Moral Maze," 11.

47 Ang, *Living Room Wars,* 176.

# Bibliography

Aldgate, Anthony. *Censorship and the Permissive Society: British Cinema and Theatre 1955-1965*. Oxford: Clarendon Press, 1995.

Alloway, Lawrence. "Monster Films." In *Focus on the Horror Film*, ed. Roy Huss and T. J. Huss. Englewood Cliffs, NJ: Prentice-Hall, 1972. 121-4.

Althusser, Louis. *Lenin and Philosophy and Other Essays*, trans. Ben Brewster. New York: Monthly Review Press, 1971.

Amis, Kingsley. *The James Bond Dossier*. New York: New American Library, 1965.

Anderson, Benedict. *Imagined Communities: Reflections on the Origins and Spread of Nationalism*, rev. ed. London: Verso, 1991.

Anderson, Lindsay. "Alfred Hitchcock." In *Focus on Hitchcock*, ed. Albert J. LaValley. Englewood Cliffs, NJ: Prentice-Hall, 1972. 48-59 [1949].

"Get Out and Push." In *Declaration*, ed. Tom Maschler. Port Washington, NY: Kenniket Press, 1972. 135-60.

Ang, Ien. *Living Room Wars: Rethinking Media Audiences for a Postmodern World*. London: Routledge, 1996.

Armes, Roy. *A Critical History of British Cinema*. London: Secker & Warburg, 1978.

Armour, Nicole. "Between a Rock and a Hard Place: *Sexy Beast*." *Cinema Scope* 6 (Winter 2001): 94-5.

Ashby, Justine, and Andrew Higson, eds. *British Cinema, Past and Present*. London: Routledge, 2000.

Austen, Jane. *Mansfield Park*, ed. John Lucas. London: Oxford University Press, 1970.

Babington, Bruce. "Introduction: British Stars and Stardom." In *British Stars and Stardom: From Alma Taylor to Sean Connery*, ed. Babington. Manchester: Manchester University Press, 2001. 1-28.

*Launder and Gilliat*. Manchester: Manchester University Press, 2002.

ed. *British Stars and Stardom: From Alma Taylor to Sean Connery*. Manchester: Manchester University Press, 2001.

Barker, Adam. "What the Detective Saw." *Monthly Film Bulletin* (July 1988): 193-5.

Barker, Ernest. "An Attempt at Perspective." In *The Character of England*, ed. Barker. Oxford: Clarendon Press, 1947. 550-75.

*Britain and the British People*, 2d ed. London: Oxford University Press, 1955.

Barr, Charles. *Ealing Studios*. London: Cameron & Tayleur, 1977.

"*Blackmail*: Silent and Sound." *Sight and Sound* 52, no. 2 (Spring 1983): 122-6.

"Introduction: Amnesia and Schizophrenia." In *All Our Yesterdays: 90 Years of British Cinema*, ed. Barr. London: British Film Institute, 1986. 1-29.

"Hitchcock's British Films Revisited." In *Dissolving Views: Key Writings on British Cinema*, ed. Andrew Higson. London: Cassell, 1996. 9-19.

*English Hitchcock*. Moffat: Cameron & Hollis, 1999.

"Before *Blackmail*: Silent British Cinema." In *The British Cinema Book*, 2d ed., ed. Robert Murphy. London: British Film Institute, 2001. 11-19.

ed. *All Our Yesterdays: 90 Years of British Cinema*. London: British Film Institute, 1986.

Barthes, Roland. *Mythologies,* trans. Annette Lavers. London: Jonathan Cape, 1972.

Bate, Jonathan. *The Genius of Shakespeare.* New York: Oxford University Press, 1998.

Baty, S. Paige. *American Monroe: The Making of a Body Politic.* Berkeley: University of California Press, 1995.

Bazin, André. *What Is Cinema?* trans. Hugh Gray. Berkeley: University of California Press, 1967.

   "Hitchcock versus Hitchcock." In *Focus on Hitchcock,* ed. Albert J. LaValley. Englewood Cliffs, NJ: Prentice-Hall, 1972. 60-9.

Beckman, Karen. "Violent Vanishings: Hitchcock, Harlan, and the Disappearing Woman." *Camera Obscura* 39 (September 1996): 79-103.

Bennett, Susan. *Performing Nostalgia: Shifting Shakespeare and the Contemporary Past.* London: Routledge, 1996.

Bennett, Tony, and Janet Woollacott. *Bond and Beyond: The Political Career of a Popular Hero.* New York: Methuen, 1987.

Bergan, Ronald. "Food for Thought." *Films and Filming* (October 1989): 27-9.

Bigsby, C. W. E. "The Politics of Anxiety: Contemporary Socialist Theatre in England." In *Contemporary British Drama 1970-90,* ed. Hersh Zeifman and Cynthia Zimmerman. Toronto: University of Toronto Press, 1993. 282-94.

Bishop, Ellen. "Bakhtin, Carnival and Comedy: The New Grotesque in *Monty Python and the Holy Grail.*" *Film Criticism* 15, no. 1 (Fall 1990): 49-64.

Blake, William. *A Selection of Poems and Letters,* ed. J. Bronowski. Harmondsworth, Middlesex: Penguin Books, 1958.

Blandford, Steve, Barry Keith Grant, and Jim Hillier. *The Film Studies Dictionary.* London: Arnold, 2001.

Blaydes, Sophie B., and Philip Bordinat. "Blake's 'Jerusalem' and Popular Culture." *Literature/Film Quarterly* 11, no. 4 (1983): 211-14.

Bloom, Harold. *Shakespeare: The Invention of the Human.* New York: Riverhead Books, 1998.

Bowden, Martyn J. "Jerusalem, Dover Beach, and Kings Cross: Imagined Places as Metaphors of the British Class Struggle in *Chariots of Fire* and *The Loneliness of the Long Distance Runner.*" In *Place, Power, Situation and Spectacle: A Geography of Film,* ed. Stuart C. Aitken and Leo E. Zonn. Lanham, MD: Rowman & Littlefield, 1994. 69-100.

Bream, Paul. "Spreading Wings at Kestrel." *Films and Filming* 18, no. 6 (March 1972): 36-40.

"British Not British." *Sight and Sound* n.s., 13, no. 6 (June 2003): 3.

Brooker, Peter, and Peter Widdowson. "A Literature for England." In *Englishness: Politics and Culture 1880-1920,* ed. Robert Colls and Philip Dodd. London: Croom Helm, 1986. 116-63.

Brooks, Peter. *The Melodramatic Imagination: Balzac, Henry James, Melodrama, and the Mode of Excess.* New Haven: Yale University Press, 1976.

Brooks, Xan. "*Sexy Beast.*" *Sight and Sound* n.s., 11, no. 2 (February 2001): 49-50.

Brosnan, John. *James Bond in the Cinema.* London: Tantivy Press, 1972.

Brown, Geoff. *Launder and Gilliat.* London: British Film Institute, 1977.

   "Paradise Found and Lost: The Course of British Realism." In *The British Cinema Book,* 2d ed,, ed. Robert Murphy. London: British Film Institute, 2001. 248-55.

Brown, Geoff, and Laurence Kardish. *Michael Balcon: The Pursuit of British Cinema.* New York: Museum of Modern Art, 1984.

Brunsdon, Charlotte. "Space and Time in the British Crime Film." In *British Crime Cinema,* ed. Steve Chibnall and Robert Murphy. London: Routledge, 1999. 148-59.

"Not Having It All: Women and Film in the 1990s." In *British Cinema of the 90s*, ed. Robert Murphy. London: British Film Institute, 2000. 167-77.

"London Films: From Private Gardens to Utopian Moments." *Cineaste* 26, no. 4 (September 2001): 43-6.

Brunt, Rosalind. "A 'Divine Gift to Inspire'?: Popular Cultural Representation, Nationhood and the British Monarchy." In *Come On Down?: Popular Media Culture in Post-War Britain,* ed. Dominic Strinati and Stephen Wagg. London: Routledge, 1992. 285-301.

Bruzzi, Stella. "*Elizabeth.*" *Sight and Sound* n.s., 8, no. 11 (November 1998): 47-8.

"*Beautiful People.*" *Sight and Sound* n.s., 9, no. 9 (September 1999): 42.

Burrows, Jon. "Big Studio Production in the Pre-Quota Years." In *The British Cinema Book,* 2d ed., ed. Robert Murphy. London: British Film Institute, 2001. 20-7.

Burton, Alan. "Seeing Is Believing: *The Magic Box.*" In *The Family Way: The Boulting Brothers and British Film Culture,* ed. Burton et al. Trowbridge, Wiltshire: Flicks Books, 2000. 155-74.

Burton, Alan, Tim O'Sullivan, and Paul Wells, eds. *Liberal Directions: Basil Dearden and Postwar British Film Culture.* Trowbridge, Wiltshire: Flicks Books, 1997.

*The Family Way: The Boulting Brothers and British Film Culture.* Trowbridge, Wiltshire: Flicks Books, 2000.

Calder, Angus. *The Myth of the Blitz.* London: Jonathan Cape, 1991.

Cannadine, David. "The Context, Performance and Meaning of Ritual: The British Monarchy and the 'Invention of Tradition,' c. 1820-1977." In *The Invention of Tradition,* ed. Eric Hobsbawm and Terence Ranger. Cambridge: Cambridge University Press, 1983. 101-64.

"Gilbert and Sullivan: The Making and Un-Making of a British 'Tradition.'" In *Myths of the English,* ed. Roy Porter. Cambridge: Polity Press, 1992. 12-32.

Carney, Ray, and Leonard Quart. *The Films of Mike Leigh: Embracing the World.* Cambridge: Cambridge University Press, 2000.

Carson, Bruce. "Comedy, Sexuality and 'Swinging London' Films." *Journal of Popular British Cinema* 1 (1998): 48-62.

Carter, Ed. "*Chariots of Fire:* Traditional Values/False History." *Jump Cut* 28 (1983): 14-17.

Caughie, John, with Kevin Rockett. *The Companion to British and Irish Cinema.* London: British Film Institute, 1996.

Chapman, James. "Celluloid Shockers." In *The Unknown 1930s: An Alternative History of the British Cinema 1929-39,* ed. Jeffrey Richards. London: I. B. Tauris, 1998. 75-97.

*Licence to Thrill: A Cultural History of the James Bond Films.* New York: Columbia University Press, 2000.

Chibnall, Steve. "The Teenage Trilogy: *The Blue Lamp, I Believe in You* and *Violent Playground.*" In *Liberal Directions: Basil Dearden and Postwar British Film Culture,* ed. Alan Burton et al. Trowbridge, Wiltshire: Flicks Books, 1997. 137-53.

*Making Mischief: The Cult Films of Pete Walker.* Guildford: Fab Press, 1998.

*J. Lee Thompson.* Manchester: Manchester University Press, 2000.

"Purgatory at the End of the Pier: Imprinting a Sense of Place through *Brighton Rock.*" In *The Family Way: The Boulting Brothers and British Film Culture,* ed. Alan Burton et al. Trowbridge, Wiltshire: Flicks Books, 2000. 134-42.

"A Heritage of Evil: Pete Walker and the Politics of Gothic Revisionism." In *British Horror Cinema,* ed. Chibnall and Julian Petley. London: Routledge, 2002. 156-71.

Chibnall, Steve, and Robert Murphy. "Parole Overdue: Releasing the British Crime Film into the Critical Community." In *British Crime Cinema,* ed. Chibnall and Murphy. London: Routledge, 1999. 1–15.

eds. *British Crime Cinema.* London: Routledge, 1999.

Christie, Ian. *Arrows of Desire: The Films of Michael Powell and Emeric Pressburger.* London: Faber & Faber, 1994.

"As Others See Us: British Film-making and Europe in the 90s." In *British Cinema of the 90s,* ed. Robert Murphy. London: British Film Institute, 2000. 68–79.

Christie, Ian Leslie. "*Women in Love.*" *Sight and Sound* 39, no. 1 (Winter 1969–70): 49–50.

Church Gibson, Pamela. "From Dancing Queen to Plaster Virgin: *Elizabeth* and the End of English Heritage?" *Journal of Popular British Cinema* 5 (2002): 133–41.

Ciecko, Anne. "Representing the Spaces of Diaspora in Contemporary British Films by Women Directors." *Cinema Journal* 38, no. 3 (1999): 67–90.

Ciment, Michel. *Conversations with Losey.* London: Methuen, 1985.

*John Boorman,* trans. Gilbert Adair. London: Faber & Faber, 1986.

Coe, Jonathan. "Power Mad." *Sight and Sound* n.s., 5, no. 4 (April 1995): 30–3.

"Hammer's Cosy Violence." *Sight and Sound* n.s., 6, no. 8 (August 1996): 10–13.

Colls, Robert. "Englishness and the National Culture." In *Englishness: Politics and Culture 1880–1920,* ed. Colls and Philip Dodd. London: Croom Helm, 1986. 1–28.

Colls, Robert, and Philip Dodd, eds. *Englishness: Politics and Culture 1880–1920.* London: Croom Helm, 1986.

Conrich, Ian. "Forgotten Cinema: The British Style of Sexploitation." *Journal of Popular British Cinema* 1 (1998): 87–100.

"Traditions of the British Horror Film." In *The British Cinema Book,* 2d ed., ed. Robert Murphy. London: British Film Institute, 2001. 226–32.

Cook, Christopher, ed. *The Dilys Powell Film Reader.* Oxford: Oxford University Press, 1992.

Cook, Pam. "Auteur Theory and British Cinema." In *The Cinema Book,* ed. Cook. New York: Pantheon Books, 1985. 147–65.

"*Under the Skin.*" *Sight and Sound* n.s., 7, no. 12 (December 1997): 56.

"The Trouble with Sex: Diana Dors and the Blonde Bombshell Phenomenon." In *British Stars and Stardom: From Alma Taylor to Sean Connery,* ed. Bruce Babington. Manchester: Manchester University Press, 2001. 167–78.

Corner, John. *The Art of Record: A Critical Introduction to Documentary.* Manchester: Manchester University Press, 1996.

Corner, John, and Sylvia Harvey, eds. *Enterprise and Heritage: Crosscurrents of National Culture.* London: Routledge, 1991.

Costello, John. *Love, Sex and War: Changing Values 1939–45.* London: Collins, 1985.

Coubro, Gerry. "The Appeal and Success of Hammer Film Productions." In *Studies in Communication,* ed. Asher Cashdan and Martin Jordan. Oxford: Blackwell, 1987. 166–78.

Craig, Cairns. "Rooms without a View." *Sight and Sound* n.s., 1, no. 2 (June 1991): 10–13.

Curran, James, and Vincent Porter, eds. *British Cinema History.* London: Weidenfeld & Nicolson, 1983.

Danielson, Shane. "Welcome to My Nightmare." *Sight and Sound* n.s., 9, no. 8 (August 1999): 8–10.

Debray, Régis. "Admirable England." In *After Diana: Irreverent Elegies,* ed. Mandy Merck. London: Verso, 1998. 127–30.

Desjardins, Mary. "Free from the Apron Strings: Representations of Mothers in the Maternal British State." In *Fires Were Started: British Cinema and Thatcherism,* ed. Lester Friedman. Minneapolis: University of Minnesota Press, 1993. 130–44.

DeVinney, Karen. "Transmitting the Bildungsroman to the Small Screen: David Hare's *Dreams of Leaving* and *Heading Home." Literature/Film Quarterly* 24, no. 1 (1996): 92–8.

DeVitis, A. A. *Graham Greene,* rev. ed. Boston: Twayne, 1986.

Dick, Leslie. "Desperation and Desire." *Sight and Sound* n.s., 7, no. 1 (January 1997): 11–13.

Diemert, Brian. *Graham Greene's Thrillers and the 1930s.* Montreal: McGill–Queen's University Press, 1996.

Dixon, Wheeler Winston. "The Eternal Summer of Joseph Losey and Harold Pinter's *Accident."* In *The Films of Harold Pinter,* ed. Steven H. Gale. Albany: State University of New York Press, 2001. 27–37.

ed. *Re-Viewing British Cinema, 1900–1992: Essays and Interviews.* Albany: State University of New York Press, 1994.

Drakakis, John. "Shakespeare in Quotations." In *Studying British Cultures,* ed. Susan Bassnett. London: Routledge, 1997. 152–72.

Driscoll, Lawrence. "'The Rose Revived': Derek Jarman and the British Tradition." In *By Angels Driven: The Films of Derek Jarman,* ed. Chris Lippard. Trowbridge, Wiltshire: Flicks Books, 1996. 65–83.

Driver, Paul. "A *Third Man* Cento." *Sight and Sound* 59, no. 1 (Winter 1989–90): 36–41.

Durgnat, Raymond. *A Mirror for England: British Movies from Austerity to Affluence.* London: Faber & Faber, 1970.

Dyer, Richard. *Only Entertainment.* London: Routledge, 1992.

*Brief Encounter.* London: British Film Institute, 1993.

Eaton, Michael. "Not a Piccadilly Actor in Sight." *Sight and Sound* n.s., 3, no. 12 (December 1993): 32–3.

Ellis, John. "Made in Ealing." *Screen* 16, no. 1 (Spring 1975): 78–127.

"Art, Culture and Quality: Terms for a Cinema in the Forties and Seventies." *Screen* 19, no. 3 (Autumn 1978): 9–66.

Elsaesser, Thomas. "Images for England (and Scotland, Ireland, Wales . . .)." *Monthly Film Bulletin* (September 1984): 267–9.

"Chronicle of a Death Retold." *Monthly Film Bulletin* 54 (June 1987): 164–7.

"The Dandy in Hitchcock." In *Alfred Hitchcock: Centenary Essays,* ed. Richard Allen and S. Ishi Gonzalès. London: British Film Institute, 1999. 3–13.

Eyles, Allen, Robert Adkison, and Nicholas Fry, eds. *House of Horror: The Complete Hammer Films Story,* rev. ed. London: Creation Books, 1994.

Falcon, Richard. "Last Tango in Lewisham." *Sight and Sound* n.s., 11, no. 7 (July 2001): 20–4.

Falk, Quentin. *Travels in Greeneland: The Cinema of Graham Greene.* London: Quartet Books, 1984.

Featherstone, Mike. "Localism, Globalism, and Cultural Identity." In *Global/Local: Cultural Production and the Transnational Imaginary,* ed. Rob Wilson and Wimal Dissanayake. Durham, NC: Duke University Press, 1996. 46–77.

Featherstone, Mike, Scott Lash, and Roland Robertson, eds. *Global Modernities.* London: Sage, 1995.

Feineman, Neil. *Nicolas Roeg.* Boston: Twayne, 1978.

Felber, Lynette. "Capturing the Shadows of Ghosts: Mixed Media and the Female Gaze in *The Women on the Roof* and *The Governess." Film Quarterly* 54, no. 4 (Summer 2001): 27–37.

Felperin, Leslie. "Falling Angel." *Sight and Sound* n.s., 7, no. 12 (December 1997): 14–17.

Flor, Carlos Villar. "Intertextuality in *Shadowlands:* From the Essay to the Love Story." *Literature/Film Quarterly* 27, no. 2 (1999): 97–102.

Forbes, Jill. "*Henry V.*" *Sight and Sound* 58, no. 4 (Autumn 1989): 258–9.

Forster, E. M. *Howards End,* ed. Alistair M. Duckworth. Boston: Bedford Books, 1997.

Freedman, Carl. "England as Ideology: From 'Upstairs, Downstairs' to *A Room with a View.*" *Cultural Critique* 17 (Winter 1990–91): 79–106.

French, Philip. "The Alphaville of Admass; or, How We Learned to Stop Worrying and Love the Boom." *Sight and Sound* 35, no. 3 (Summer 1966): 106–11.

Friedman, Lester, ed. *Fires Were Started: British Cinema and Thatcherism.* Minneapolis: University of Minnesota Press, 1993.

Fuller, Graham. "Kenneth." *Film Comment* 25, no. 6 (November–December 1989): 2–7.

"*A Canterbury Tale.*" *Film Comment* 31, no. 2 (March–April 1995): 33–6.

ed. *Loach on Loach.* London: Faber & Faber, 1998.

Garrod, H. W. "Humour." In *The Character of England,* ed. Ernest Barker. Oxford: Clarendon Press, 1947. 340–51.

Geduld, Harry M., ed. *Film Makers on Film Making.* Bloomington: Indiana University Press, 1969.

Gentry, Ric. "Ken Russell: An Interview." *Post Script* 2, no. 3 (Spring–Summer 1983): 2–23.

Geraghty, Christine. "Diana Dors." In *All Our Yesterdays: 90 Years of British Cinema,* ed. Charles Barr. London: British Film Institute, 1986. 341–5.

"The Woman Between: The European Woman in Post-War British Cinema." *European Journal of Cultural Studies* 2, no. 2 (May 1999): 147–62.

*British Cinema in the Fifties: Gender, Genre and the 'New Look.'* London: Routledge, 2000.

"Women and 60s British Cinema: The Development of the '*Darling*' Girl." In *The British Cinema Book,* 2d ed., ed. Robert Murphy. London: British Film Institute, 2001. 100–15.

Giles, Paul. "History with Holes: Channel Four Television Films of the 1980s." In *Fires Were Started: British Cinema and Thatcherism,* ed. Lester Friedman. Minneapolis: University of Minnesota Press, 1993. 70–91.

Gilroy, Paul. "Diaspora and the Detours of Identity." In *Identity and Difference,* ed. Kathryn Woodward. Milton Keynes, Buckinghamshire: Open University Press, 1997. 301–43.

Glass, Fred. "Laugh at Obstacles: *The Meaning of Life.*" *Jump Cut* 29 (February 1984): 12–13.

Gledhill, Christine. "The Melodramatic Field: An Investigation." In *Home Is Where the Heart Is: Studies in Melodrama and the Woman's Film,* ed. Gledhill. London: British Film Institute, 1987. 5–39.

*Reframing British Cinema 1918–1928: Between Restraint and Passion.* London: British Film Institute, 2003.

Gomez, Joseph A. "*The Third Man:* Capturing the Visual Essence of Literary Conception." *Literature/Film Quarterly* 2, no. 4 (Fall 1974): 332–40.

"Russell's Images of Lawrence's Vision." In *The English Novel and the Movies,* ed. Michael Klein and Gillian Parker (New York: Frederick Ungar, 1981). 248–56.

Goslawski, Barbara. "Patricia Rozema's *Mansfield Park.*" *Take One* 26 (Winter 2000): 34–7.

Gottlieb, Sidney, ed. *Hitchcock on Hitchcock: Selected Writings and Interviews.* Berkeley: University of California Press, 1997.

Gramsci, Antonio. *Selections from Cultural Writings,* ed. David Forgacs and Geoffrey Nowell-Smith. Cambridge, MA: Harvard University Press, 1985.

Gras, Vernon. "Dramatizing the Failure to Jump the Culture/Nature Gap: The Films of Peter Greenaway." *New Literary History* 26 (1995): 123-43.

Gray, Frances. "Certain Liberties Have Been Taken with Cleopatra: Female Performance in the *Carry On* Films." In *Because I Tell a Joke or Two: Comedy, Politics and Social Difference*, ed. Stephen Wagg. London: Routledge, 1998. 94-110.

Green, Ian. "Ealing: In the Comedy Frame." In *British Cinema History*, ed. James Curran and Vincent Porter. London: Weidenfeld & Nelson, 1983. 294-302.

Greenberg, Harvey Roy. "*The Madness of King George*." *Cineaste* 21, no. 3 (1995): 47-8.

Greene, Graham. *The Pleasure Dome: The Collected Film Criticism 1935-40*, ed. John Russell Taylor. Oxford: Oxford University Press, 1980.

Grundmann, Roy. "History and the Gay Viewfinder: An Interview with Derek Jarman." *Cineaste* 18, no. 4 (1991): 24-7.

Hacker, Jonathan, and David Price. *Take Ten: Contemporary British Film Directors*. Oxford: Oxford University Press, 1991.

Halasz, Piri. "Great Britain: You Can Walk across It on the Grass." *Time* (15 April 1966): 30-4.

Hall, Sheldon. "Monkey Feathers: Defending *Zulu*." In *British Historical Cinema*, ed. Claire Monk and Amy Sargeant. London: Routledge, 2002. 110-28.

Hall, Stuart. "Notes on Deconstructing 'The Popular.'" In *People's History and Socialist Theory*, ed. Raphael Samuel. London: Routledge & Kegan Paul, 1981. 227-39.

"The Question of Cultural Identity." In *Modernity and Its Futures*, ed. Stuart Hall, David Held, and Tony McGrew. Cambridge: Polity Press, 1992. 274-316.

"The Spectacle of the 'Other.'" In *Representation: Cultural Representations and Signifying Practices*, ed. Hall. London: Sage, 1997. 223-90.

Hallam, Julia. "Film, Class and National Identity: Re-imagining Communities in the Age of Devolution." In *British Cinema, Past and Present*, ed. Justine Ashby and Andrew Higson. London: Routledge, 2000. 261-73.

Halligan, Benjamin. *Michael Reeves*. Manchester: Manchester University Press, 2003.

Haraway, Donna. *Simians, Cyborgs, and Women: The Reinvention of Nature*. New York: Routledge, 1991.

Hardy, Forsyth. *John Grierson: A Documentary Biography*. London: Faber & Faber, 1979.

ed. *Grierson on Documentary*. London: Faber & Faber, 1979.

ed. *Grierson on the Movies*. London: Faber & Faber, 1981.

Hare, David. *Writing Left-Handed*. London: Faber & Faber, 1991.

Harper, Sue. "The Scent of Distant Blood: Hammer Films and History." In *Screening the Past: Film and the Representation of History*, ed. Tony Barta. Westport, CT: Praeger, 1998. 109-25.

*Women in British Cinema: Mad, Bad and Dangerous to Know*. London: Continuum, 2000.

Haste, Cate. *Rules of Desire: Sex in Britain: World War I to the Present*. London: Chatto & Windus, 1992.

Hatchuel, Sarah. *A Companion to the Shakespearean Films of Kenneth Branagh*. Winnipeg: Blizzard Publishing, 2000.

Hedling, Erik. *Lindsay Anderson: Maverick Film-Maker*. London: Cassell, 1998.

Hewison, Robert. *Future Tense: A New Art for the Nineties*. London: Methuen, 1990.

"Commerce and Culture." In *Enterprise and Heritage: Crosscurrents of National Culture*. ed. John Corner and Sylvia Harvey. London: Routledge, 1991. 162-77.

Higson, Andrew. "Space, Place, Spectacle: Landscape and Townscape in the 'Kitchen Sink' Film." *Screen* 25, nos. 4-5 (July-October 1984): 2-21.

"The Concept of National Cinema." *Screen* 30, no. 4 (Autumn 1989): 36-46.

"Re-presenting the National Past: Nostalgia and Pastiche in the Heritage Film." In *Fires Were Started: British Cinema and Thatcherism,* ed. Lester Friedman. Minneapolis: University of Minnesota Press, 1993. 109–29.

*Waving the Flag: Constructing a National Cinema in Britain.* Oxford: Clarendon Press, 1995.

"The Heritage Film and British Cinema." In *Dissolving Views: Key Writings on British Cinema,* ed. Higson. London: Cassell, 1996. 232–48.

"The Instability of the National." In *British Cinema, Past and Present,* ed. Justine Ashby and Higson. London: Routledge, 2000. 35–47.

*English Heritage, English Cinema: Costume Drama since 1980.* Oxford: Oxford University Press, 2003.

ed. *Dissolving Views: Key Writings on British Cinema.* London: Cassell, 1996.

Hill, Derek. "The Face of Horror." *Sight and Sound* 28, no. 1 (Winter 1958–59): 6–11.

Hill, John. *Sex, Class and Realism: British Cinema 1956–1963.* London: British Film Institute, 1986.

"Interview with Ken Loach." In *Agent of Challenge and Defiance: The Films of Ken Loach,* ed. George McKnight. Trowbridge, Wiltshire: Flicks Books, 1997. 160–76.

"Every Fuckin' Choice Stinks." *Sight and Sound* n.s., 8, no. 11 (November 1998): 18–21.

*British Cinema in the 1980s.* Oxford: Clarendon Press, 1999.

"Failure and Utopianism: Representations of the Working Class in British Cinema of the 1990s." In *British Cinema of the 90s,* ed. Robert Murphy. London: British Film Institute, 2000. 178–87.

"From the New Wave to 'Brit-Grit': Continuity and Difference in Working-Class Realism." In *British Cinema, Past and Present,* ed. Justine Ashby and Andrew Higson. London: Routledge, 2000. 249–60.

"Contemporary British Cinema: Industry, Policy, Identity." *Cineaste* 26, no. 4 (September 2001): 30–3.

Hobsbawm, Eric. "Introduction: Inventing Traditions." In *The Invention of Tradition,* ed. Hobsbawm and Terence Ranger. Cambridge: Cambridge University Press, 1983. 1–14.

Hobsbawm, Eric, and Terence Ranger, eds. *The Invention of Tradition.* Cambridge: Cambridge University Press, 1983.

Hoggart, Richard. *The Uses of Literacy: Aspects of Working Class Life with Special Reference to Publications and Entertainments.* Harmondsworth, Middlesex: Penguin, 1957.

Horne, Philip. "The James Gang." *Sight and Sound* n.s., 8, no. 1 (January 1998): 16–19.

Horton, Andrew. "*Beautiful People.*" *Cineaste* 25, no. 3 (June 2000): 45–6.

Hoskins, W. G. *The Making of the English Landscape.* London: Penguin, 1985 [1955].

Houston, Beverle, and Marsha Kinder. "The Losey–Pinter Collaboration." *Film Quarterly* 32, no. 1 (Fall 1978): 17–30.

Houston, Penelope. "*Dr. No.*" *Sight and Sound* 31, no. 4 (Autumn 1962): 197.

*The Contemporary Cinema.* Harmondsworth, Middlesex: Penguin, 1963.

"007." *Sight and Sound* 34, no. 1 (Winter 1964–5): 14–16.

*Went the Day Well?* London: British Film Institute, 1992.

Howard, Greg. "Exhibition and Repression in *The Full Monty.*" *Film Criticism* 24, no. 1 (Fall 1999): 22–38.

Hunt, Leon. *British Low Culture: From Safari Suits to Sexploitation.* London: Routledge, 1998.

Hutchings, Peter. *Hammer and Beyond: The British Horror Film.* Manchester: Manchester University Press, 1993.

Huyssen, Andreas. "Mass Culture as Woman: Modernism's Other." In *Studies in Entertainment: Critical Approaches to Mass Culture,* ed. Tania Modleski. Bloomington: Indiana University Press, 1986. 188-207.

Izod, John. *The Films of Nicolas Roeg: Myth and Mind.* New York: St. Martin's Press, 1992.

James, Nick. "Being There." *Sight and Sound* n.s., 7, no. 10 (October 1997): 6-9.

"Farewell to Napoli." *Sight and Sound* n.s., 9, no. 5 (May 1999): 20-2.

Jameson, Fredric. "History and the Death Wish: *Zardoz* as Open Form." *Jump Cut* 3 (September-October 1974): 5-8.

Jarman, Derek. *The Last of England,* ed. David L. Hirst. London: Constable, 1987.

Johnson, Ian. "Have the British a Sense of Humour?" *Films and Filming* 9, no. 6 (March 1963): 48-53.

Johnston, Sheila. "Charioteers and Ploughmen." In *British Cinema Now,* ed. Martyn Auty and Nick Roddick. London: British Film Institute, 1985. 99-110.

Jordan, Marion. "Carry On . . . Follow that Stereotype." In *British Cinema History,* ed. James Curran and Vincent Porter. London: Weidenfeld & Nelson, 1983. 312-27.

Kael, Pauline. *Kiss Kiss Bang Bang.* New York: Bantam, 1969.

*Going Steady.* New York: Bantam, 1971.

*Reeling.* New York: Warner Books, 1977.

Kaleta, Kenneth A. *Hanif Kureishi: Postcolonial Storyteller.* Austin: University of Texas Press, 1998.

Keleher, Leroy. "Laurence Olivier: Getting On with It." *Take One* 6, no. 8 (July 1978): 24-5.

Kelly, Richard, ed. *Alan Clarke.* London: Faber & Faber, 1998.

Kemp, Philip. *Lethal Innocence: The Cinema of Alexander Mackendrick.* London: Methuen, 1991.

"Gone to Earth." *Sight and Sound* n.s., 11, no. 1 (January 2001): 22-4.

Kennedy, A. L. *The Life and Death of Colonel Blimp.* London: British Film Institute, 1997.

Kennedy, Harlan. "The Illusions of Nicolas Roeg." *American Film* 5, no. 4 (January-February 1980): 22-7.

"The World of King Arthur According to John Boorman." *American Film* 6, no. 5 (March 1981): 30-7.

"The Brits Have Gone Nuts." *Film Comment* 21, no. 4 (July-August 1985): 51-5.

Kermode, Mark. "*Gangster No. 1.*" *Sight and Sound* n.s., 10, no. 7 (July 2000): 45-6.

Kernan, Margot S. "*Accident.*" *Film Quarterly* 20, no. 4 (Summer 1967): 60-3.

Knight, Deborah. "Naturalism, Narration and Critical Perspective: Ken Loach and the Experimental Method." In *Agent of Challenge and Defiance: The Films of Ken Loach,* ed. George McKnight. Trowbridge, Wiltshire: Flicks Books, 1997. 60-81.

Kolker, Robert Phillip. "The Open Texts of Nicolas Roeg." *Sight and Sound* 46, no. 2 (Spring 1977): 82-4, 113.

Kracauer, Siegfried. *From Caligari to Hitler: A Psychological History of the German Film.* Princeton: Princeton University Press, 1947.

Kuhn, Annette. *Family Secrets: Acts of Memory and Imagination.* London: Verso, 1995.

Kulik, Karol. *Alexander Korda: The Man Who Could Work Miracles.* London: Virgin Books, 1990.

Kumar, Krishan. "The Social and Cultural Setting." In *The Present,* ed. Boris Ford. Harmondsworth, Middlesex: Penguin, 1983. 15-61.

Kureishi, Hanif. *My Beautiful Laundrette and The Rainbow Sign.* London: Faber & Faber, 1986.

*Sammy and Rosie Get Laid.* London: Faber & Faber, 1988.

Kushner, Tony. "Immigration and 'Race Relations' in Postwar British Society." In *Twentieth-Century Britain: Economic, Social and Cultural Change,* ed. Paul Johnson. London: Longman, 1994. 411-26.

Landy, Marcia. *British Genres: Cinema and Society, 1930-1960.* Princeton: Princeton University Press, 1991.

*Film, Politics, and Gramsci.* Minneapolis: University of Minnesota Press, 1994.

Lant, Antonia. *Blackout: Reinventing Women in Wartime British Cinema.* Princeton: Princeton University Press, 1991.

LaValley, Albert J., ed. *Focus on Hitchcock.* Englewood Cliffs, NJ: Prentice-Hall, 1972.

Leach, Jim. "'The World Has Changed': Bond in the 1990s and Beyond?" In *The James Bond Phenomenon: A Critical Reader,* ed. Christoph Lindner. Manchester: Manchester University Press, 2003. 248-58.

Leahy, James. *The Cinema of Joseph Losey.* London: Zwemmer, 1967.

Leavis, Q. D. *Fiction and the Reading Public.* London: Chatto & Windus, 1964 [1932].

Lehmann, Courtney. "Kenneth Branagh at the Quilting Point: Shakespearean Adaptation, Postmodern Auteurism, and the (Schizophrenic) Fabric of 'Everyday Life.'" *Post Script* 17, no. 1 (Fall 1997): 6-27.

Leigh, Mike. *Naked and Other Screenplays.* London: Faber & Faber, 1995.

Light, Alison. *Forever England: Femininity, Literature and Conservatism between the Wars.* London: Routledge, 1991.

"The Importance of Being Ordinary." *Sight and Sound* n.s., 3, no. 9 (September 1993): 16-19.

Lim, Dennis. "Marching Off to War." *Cinema Scope* 1 (1999): 12-15.

Lippard, Chris, and Guy Johnson. "Private Practice, Public Health: 'The Politics of Sickness and the Films of Derek Jarman." In *Fires Were Started: British Cinema and Thatcherism,* ed. Lester Friedman. Minneapolis: University of Minnesota Press, 1993. 278-93.

Lovell, Alan. "The British Cinema: The Known Cinema?" In *The British Cinema Book,* 2d ed., ed. Robert Murphy. London: British Film Institute, 2001. 200-5.

Lovell, Alan (with Jim Hillier, Sam Rohdie, and Kevin Glover), and Jim Kitses. "Interview: Alberto Cavalcanti and Gavin Lambert." *Screen* 13, no. 2 (Summer 1972): 33-78.

Lovell, Terry. *Pictures of Reality: Aesthetics, Politics and Pleasure.* London: British Film Institute, 1980.

"Landscapes and Stories in 1960s British Realism." *Screen* 31, no. 4 (Winter 1990): 357-76.

Lowenstein, Adam. "'Under-the-Skin Horrors': Social Realism and Classlessness in *Peeping Tom* and the British New Wave." In *British Cinema, Past and Present,* ed. Justine Ashby and Andrew Higson. London: Routledge, 2000. 221-32.

Luckett, Moya. "Image and Nation in 1990s British Cinema." In *British Cinema of the 90s,* ed. Robert Murphy. London: British Film Institute, 2000. 88-99.

"Travel and Mobility: Femininity and National Identity in Swinging London Films." In *British Cinema, Past and Present,* ed. Justine Ashby and Andrew Higson. London: Routledge, 2000. 233-45.

Luke, Timothy W. "New World Order or Neo-World Orders: Power, Politics and Ideology in Informationalizing Glocalities." In *Global Modernities,* ed. Mike Featherstone et al. London: Sage, 1995. 91-107.

McArthur, Colin. "*Mrs. Brown.*" *Sight and Sound* n.s., 7, no. 9 (September 1997): 50.

MacCabe, Colin. "Realism and the Cinema: Notes on Some Brechtian Theses." *Screen* 15, no. 2 (Summer 1974): 7-27.

"*Days of Hope:* A Response to Colin McArthur." *Screen* 17, no. 1 (Spring 1976): 98-101.

"Theory and Film: The Principles of Realism and Pleasure." *Screen* 17, no. 3 (Autumn 1976): 7-27.

"Throne of Blood." *Sight and Sound* n.s., 1, no. 6 (October 1991): 12-14.

McCann, Graham. *Marilyn Monroe.* New Brunswick: Rutgers University Press, 1988.

McFarlane, Brian. "A Literary Cinema? British Films and British Novels." In *All Our Yesterdays: 90 Years of British Cinema,* ed. Charles Barr. London: British Film Institute, 1986. 120-42.

McFarlane, Brian, and Geoff Mayer. *New Australian Cinema: Sources and Parallels in American and British Film.* Cambridge: Cambridge University Press, 1992.

McGilligan, Pat. *Backstory: Interviews with Screenwriters of Hollywood's Golden Age.* Berkeley: University of California Press, 1986.

McGillivray, David. "Horrible Things." *Films and Filming* 21, no. 3 (December 1974): 44-8.

McGrath, Melanie. "*Stella Does Tricks.*" *Sight and Sound* n.s., 8, no. 2 (February 1998): 50.

McKechnie, Kara. "Taking Liberties with the Monarch: The Royal Bio-Pic in the 1990s." In *British Historical Cinema,* ed. Claire Monk and Amy Sargeant. London: Routledge, 2002. 217-36.

McKnight, George. "Ken Loach's Domestic Morality Tales." In *Agent of Challenge and Defiance: The Films of Ken Loach,* ed. McKnight. Trowbridge, Wiltshire: Flicks Books, 1997. 82-98.

Macnab, Geoffrey. "*Brighton Rock.*" *Sight and Sound* n.s., 4, no. 4 (April 1994): 53.

"*The Madness of King George.*" *Sight and Sound* n.s., 5, no. 4 (April 1995): 47.

*Searching for Stars: Stardom and Screen Acting in British Cinema.* London: Cassell, 2000.

McVay, Douglas. "The Art of the Actor." *Films and Filming* 12, no. 10 (July 1966): 19-25.

Malcomson, Scott. "Modernism Comes to the Cabbage Patch: Bill Forsyth and the 'Scottish Cinema.'" *Film Quarterly* 38, no. 3 (Spring 1985): 16-21.

Malik, Sarita. "Beyond 'the Cinema of Duty'? The Pleasures of Hybridity: Black British Film of the 1980s and 1990s." In *Dissolving Views: Key Writings on British Cinema,* ed. Andrew Higson. London: Cassell, 1996. 202-15.

"Money, Macpherson and Mind-Set: The Competing Cultural and Commercial Demands on Black and Asian British Films in the 1990s." *Journal of Popular British Cinema* 5 (2002): 90-103.

Mangravite, Andrew. "The House of Hammer." *Film Comment* 28, no. 3 (May-June 1992): 46-53.

Manheim, Michael. "The English History Play on Screen." In *Shakespeare and the Moving Image: The Plays on Film and Television,* ed. Anthony Davies and Stanley Wells. Cambridge: Cambridge University Press, 1994. 121-45.

Marris, Paul. "Northern Realism: An Exhausted Tradition?" *Cineaste* 26, no. 4 (September 2001): 47-50.

Marwick, Arthur. "*Room at the Top, Saturday Night and Sunday Morning,* and the 'Cultural Revolution' in Britain." *Journal of Contemporary History* 19 (1984): 127-52.

Medhurst, Andy. "Dirk Bogarde." In *All Our Yesterdays: 90 Years of British Cinema,* ed. Charles Barr. London: British Film Institute, 1986. 346-54.

"Music Hall and British Cinema." In *All Our Yesterdays: 90 Years of British Cinema,* ed. Charles Barr. London: British Film Institute, 1986. 168–88.

"Carry On Camp." *Sight and Sound* n.s., 2, no. 4 (August 1992): 16–19.

"This Septic Isle." *Sight and Sound* n.s., 8, no. 2 (February 1998): 28–9.

Mercer, Kobena. *Welcome to the Jungle: New Positions in Black Cultural Studies.* New York: Routledge, 1994.

Merz, Caroline. "The Tension of Genre: Wendy Toye and Muriel Box." In *Re-Viewing British Cinema, 1900–1992: Essays and Interviews,* ed. Wheeler Winston Dixon. Albany: State University of New York Press, 1994. 121–31.

Miles, Peter, and Malcolm Smith. *Cinema, Literature and Society.* London: Croom Helm, 1987.

Milne, Tom. *Losey on Losey.* London: Secker & Warburg, 1967.

"*Don't Look Now.*" *Sight and Sound* 42, no. 4 (Autumn 1973): 237–8.

Monk, Claire. "The British 'Heritage Film' and Its Critics." *Critical Survey* 7, no. 2 (1995): 116–24.

"Sexuality and the Heritage." *Sight and Sound* n.s., 5, no. 10 (October 1995): 32–4.

"*The Tango Lesson.*" *Sight and Sound* n.s., 7, no. 12 (December 1997): 54–5.

"*Billy Elliot.*" *Sight and Sound* n.s., 10, no. 10 (October 2000): 40.

"Projecting a 'New Britain.'" *Cineaste* 26, no. 4 (September 2001): 34–7, 42.

"The British Heritage-Film Debate Revisited." In *British Historical Cinema,* ed. Monk and Amy Sargeant. London: Routledge, 2002. 176–98.

Monk, Claire, and Amy Sargeant, eds. *British Historical Cinema.* London: Routledge, 2002.

Morley, David. *Home Territories: Media, Mobility and Identity.* London: Routledge, 2000.

Moss, Robert F. *The Films of Carol Reed.* New York: Columbia University Press, 1987.

Movshovitz, Howie, ed. *Mike Leigh: Interviews.* Jackson: University Press of Mississippi, 2000.

Mulvey, Laura. "Visual Pleasure and Narrative Cinema." *Screen* 16, no. 3 (Autumn 1975): 6–18.

Murphy, Kathleen. "Jane Campion's Shining: Portrait of a Director." *Film Comment* 32, no. 6 (November–December 1996): 29–33.

Murphy, Robert. "Riff-raff: British Cinema and the Underworld." In *All Our Yesterdays: 90 Years of British Cinema,* ed. Charles Barr. London: British Film Institute, 1986. 286–305.

*Realism and Tinsel: Cinema and Society in Britain 1939–49.* London: Routledge, 1989.

*Sixties British Cinema.* London: British Film Institute, 1992.

"A Path through the Moral Maze." In *British Cinema of the 90s,* ed. Murphy. London: British Film Institute, 2000. 1–16.

"Citylife: Urban Fairy-tales in Late 90s British Cinema." In *The British Cinema Book,* 2d ed., ed. Murphy. London: British Film Institute, 2001. 292–300.

ed. *British Cinema of the 90s.* London: British Film Institute, 2000.

ed. *The British Cinema Book,* 2d ed. London: British Film Institute, 2001.

Nairn, Tom. *The Break-up of Britain: Crisis and Neo-Nationalism.* London: New Left Books, 1977.

Naremore, James. *Acting in the Cinema.* Berkeley: University of California Press, 1988.

*More than Night: Film Noir in Its Contexts.* Berkeley: University of California Press, 1998.

Nolan, Jack Edmund. "Graham Greene's Films." *Literature/Film Quarterly* 2, no. 4 (Fall 1974): 302–9.

Nuttall, Jeff, and Rodick Carmichael. *Common Factors/Vulgar Factions.* London: Routledge & Kegan Paul, 1977.

Oliva, Judy Lee. *David Hare: Theatricalizing Politics.* Ann Arbor: UMI Research Press, 1990.

Olsen, Mark. "A Place in the Sun." *Film Comment* 37, no. 2 (March–April 2001): 16–17.

O'Pray, Michael. *Derek Jarman: Dreams of England.* London: British Film Institute, 1996.

O'Regan, Tom. *Australian National Cinema.* London: Routledge, 1996.

Orr, John. "The Art of National Identity: Peter Greenaway and Derek Jarman." In *British Cinema, Past and Present,* ed. Justine Ashby and Andrew Higson. London: Routledge, 2000. 327–38.

Orwell, George. "The Art of Donald McGill." In *The Collected Essays, Journalism and Letters of George Orwell,* vol. 2: *My Country Right or Left 1940–1943,* ed. Sonia Orwell and Ian Angus. Harmondsworth, Middlesex: Penguin, 1970. 183–95.

O'Sullivan, Charlotte. "*Notting Hill.*" *Sight and Sound* n.s., 9, no. 6 (June 1999): 49–50.

Pally, Marcia. "Cinema as a Total Art Form: An Interview with Peter Greenaway." *Cineaste* 18, no. 3 (1991): 6–11, 45.

Palmer, James, and Michael Riley. *The Films of Joseph Losey.* Cambridge: Cambridge University Press, 1993.

"Seeing, Believing, and 'Knowing' in Narrative Film: *Don't Look Now* Revisited." *Literature/Film Quarterly* 23, no. 1 (1995): 14–25.

Palmer, R. Barton. "What Was New in the British New Wave? Re-viewing *Room at the Top.*" *Journal of Popular Film and Television* 14, no. 3 (Fall 1986): 125–35.

Park, James. *Learning to Dream: The New British Cinema.* London: Faber & Faber, 1984.

Pascoe, David. *Peter Greenaway: Museums and Moving Images.* London: Reaktion Books, 1997.

Perkins, V. F. "The British Cinema." *Movie* 1 (June 1962): 2–7.

Perry, George. *Life of Python.* London: Michael Joseph, 1983.

Petley, Julian. "The Upright Houses: A Guide to the Political Theatre of David Hare." *Monthly Film Bulletin* 52 (March 1985): 71–2.

"The Lost Continent." In *All Our Yesterdays: 90 Years of British Cinema,* ed. Charles Barr. London: British Film Institute, 1986. 98–119.

Petrakis, John. "Blasphemy in Cinema: An Interview with Peter Greenaway." In *Peter Greenaway: Interviews,* ed. Vernon Gras and Marguerite Gras. Jackson: University Press of Mississippi, 2000. 172–5.

Phillips, Gene D. *Graham Greene: The Films of His Fictions.* New York: Teachers College Press, 1974.

Pieterse, Jan Nederveen. "Globalization as Hybridization." In *Global Modernities,* ed. Mike Featherstone et al. London: Sage, 1995. 45–68.

Pirie, David. *A Heritage of Horror: The English Gothic Cinema 1946–1972.* London: Gordon Fraser, 1973.

Porter, Vincent. "The Context of Creativity: Ealing Studios and Hammer Films." In *British Cinema History,* ed. James Curran and Porter. London: Weidenfeld & Nelson, 1983. 179–207.

Potter, Sally. "On Shows." In *Framing Feminism: Art and the Women's Movement 1970–1985,* ed. Rozsika Parker and Griselda Pollock. London: Pandora, 1987. 290–2.

Prince, Stephen. *Movies and Meaning: An Introduction to Film,* 2d ed. Boston: Allyn & Bacon, 2001.

Pursell, Michael. "Playing the Game: Branagh's *Henry V.*" *Literature/Film Quarterly* 20, no. 4 (1992): 268-75.

Pym, John. *Merchant Ivory's English Landscape.* London: Pavilion Books, 1995.

Quart, Leonard. "A Fidelity to the Real: An Interview with Ken Loach and Tony Garnett." *Cineaste* 10, no. 4 (Fall 1980): 26-9.

"*Nil By Mouth.*" *Cineaste* 23, no. 4 (July 1998): 49-50.

Quinn, James, and Jane Kingsley-Smith, "Kenneth Branagh's *Henry V:* Genre and Interpretation." In *British Historical Cinema,* ed. Claire Monk and Amy Sargeant. London: Routledge, 2002. 163-75.

Rattigan, Neil. *This Is England: British Film and the People's War, 1939-1945.* London: Associated University Presses, 2001.

Richards, Andy. "*Mansfield Park.*" *Sight and Sound* n.s., 10, no. 4 (April 2000): 58-9.

Richards, Jeffrey. *Visions of Yesterday.* London: Routledge & Kegan Paul, 1973.

*The Age of the Dream Palace: Cinema and Society in Britain 1930-1939.* London: Routledge & Kegan Paul, 1984.

"Gainsborough: Maniac in the Cellar." *Monthly Film Bulletin* 52, no. 9 (September 1985): 291-3.

"Basil Dearden at Ealing." In *Liberal Directions: Basil Dearden and Postwar British Film Culture,* ed. Alan Burton et al. Trowbridge, Wiltshire: Flicks Books, 1997. 14-35.

*Films and British National Identity: From Dickens to Dad's Army.* Manchester: Manchester University Press, 1997.

Robbins, Keith. *Great Britain: Identities, Institutions and the Idea of Britishness.* London: Longman, 1998.

Robertson, James C. "The Censors and British Gangland." In *British Crime Cinema,* ed. Steve Chibnall and Robert Murphy. London: Routledge, 1999. 16-26.

Robinson, David. "Anderson Shooting *If. . . .*" *Sight and Sound* 37, no. 3 (Summer 1968): 130-1.

Rohdie, Sam. "Review: *Movie Reader, Film as Film.*" *Screen* 13, no. 4 (Winter 1972-3): 135-45.

Rosenthal, Daniel. "Kenneth Branagh." *International Film Guide* (1998): 21-6.

Rothwell, Kenneth S. "*Elizabeth* and *Shakespeare in Love.*" *Cineaste* 24, nos. 2-3 (1999): 78-80.

Rubenstein, Lenny. "Monty Python Strikes Again: An Interview with Michael Palin." *Cineaste* 14, no. 2 (1985): 6-9.

Russell, Ken. *A British Picture: An Autobiography.* London: Heinemann, 1989.

Ryall, Tom. *Alfred Hitchcock and the British Cinema.* Urbana: University of Illinois Press, 1986.

"British Cinema and Genre." *Journal of Popular British Cinema* 1 (1998): 18-24.

"England's Dreaming." *Sight and Sound* n.s., 11, no. 8 (August 2001): 30-3.

Said, Edward W. *Culture and Imperialism.* London: Vintage, 1994.

Salwolke, Scott. *The Films of Michael Powell and the Archers.* Lanham, MD: Scarecrow Press, 1997.

Sanderson, Mark. *Don't Look Now.* London: British Film Institute, 1996.

Sandhu, Sukhdev. "Pop Goes the Centre: Hanif Kureishi's London." In *Postcolonial Theory and Criticism,* ed. Laura Chrisman and Benita Parry. Cambridge: D. S. Brewer, 2000. 133-54.

Sanjek, David. "Twilight of the Monsters: The English Horror Film 1968-1975." In *Re-Viewing British Cinema, 1900-1992,* ed. Wheeler Winston Dixon. Albany: State University of New York Press, 1994. 195-209.

Sarne, Mike. "*Goldfinger.*" *Films and Filming* 11, no. 2 (November 1964): 26.

Sarris, Andrew. *The American Cinema: Directors and Directions 1929-1968.* New York: E. P. Dutton, 1968.

Sawhney, Cary Rajinder. "'Another Kind of British': An Exploration of British Asian Films." *Cineaste* 26, no. 4 (September 2001): 58-61.

Schatz, Thomas. "The New Hollywood." In *Film Theory Goes to the Movies,* ed. Jim Collins, Hilary Radner, and Ava Preacher Collins. New York: Routledge, 1993. 8-36.

Schickel, Richard. "Olivier 1907-1989." *Film Comment* 25, no. 5 (September-October 1989): 22-6.

Sexton, Jamie. "Grierson's Machines: *Drifters,* the Documentary Film Movement and the Negotiation of Modernity." *Canadian Journal of Film Studies* 11, no. 1 (Spring 2002): 40-59.

Shelden, Michael. *Graham Greene: The Man Within.* London: Minerva, 1995.

Sheridan, Simon. *Keeping the British End Up: Four Decades of Saucy Cinema.* London: Reynolds & Hearn, 2001.

Sinclair, Iain. "Smart Guys." *Sight and Sound* n.s., 6, no. 8 (August 1996): 22-4.

Sinfield, Alan. *Literature, Politics, and Culture in Postwar Britain.* Berkeley: University of California Press, 1989.

Sinyard, Neil. "Film." In *The Cambridge Guide to the Arts in Britain,* vol. 9: *Since the Second World War,* ed. Boris Ford. Cambridge: Cambridge University Press, 1988. 238-51.

*The Films of Nicolas Roeg.* London: Charles Letts, 1991.

*Jack Clayton.* Manchester: Manchester University Press, 2000.

Sobchack, Tom. "Bakhtin's 'Carnivalesque' in 1950s British Comedy." *Journal of Popular Film and Television* 23, no. 4 (Winter 1996): 179-85.

Sorlin, Pierre. "From *The Third Man* to *Shakespeare in Love:* Fifty Years of British Success on Continental Screens." In *British Cinema, Past and Present,* ed. Justine Ashby and Andrew Higson. London: Routledge, 2000. 80-91.

Spencer, Liese. "Hello Mr. Chips." *Sight and Sound* n.s., 9, no. 11 (November 1999): 36-7.

Spicer, Andrew. "Misfits and the Marginalised: Gender in the Boultings' Feature Films." In *The Family Way: The Boulting Brothers and British Film Culture,* ed. Alan Burton et al. Trowbridge, Wiltshire: Flicks Books, 2000. 66-80.

Spoto, Donald. *Marilyn Monroe: The Biography.* New York: HarperCollins, 1993.

Stephenson, William. "*Kes* and the Press." *Cinema Journal* 12, no. 2 (Spring 1973): 48-55.

Sterritt, David, and Lucille Rhodes. "Monty Python: Lust for Glory." *Cineaste* 26, no. 4 (September 2001): 18-23.

Street, Sarah. *British Cinema in Documents.* London: Routledge, 2000.

"Stepping Westward: The Distribution of British Feature Films in America, and the Case of *The Private Life of Henry VIII.*" In *British Cinema, Past and Present,* ed. Justine Ashby and Andrew Higson. London: Routledge, 2000. 51-62.

Strick, Philip. "*Zardoz* and John Boorman." *Sight and Sound* 43, no. 2 (Spring 1974): 73-7.

Stuart, Andrea. "Blackpool Illumination." *Sight and Sound* n.s., 4, no. 2 (February 1994): 26-7.

Sussex, Elizabeth. *The Rise and Fall of British Documentary: The Story of the Film Movement Founded by John Grierson.* Berkeley: University of California Press, 1975.

Tarr, Carrie. "*Sapphire, Darling* and the Boundaries of Permitted Pleasure." *Screen* 26, no. 1 (January-February 1985): 50-65.

Taylor, John Russell. "Tomorrow the World: Some Reflections on the UnEnglishness of English Films." *Sight and Sound* 43, no. 2 (Spring 1974): 80–3.

Tepper, Craig. "*The Madness of King George.*" *Film Quarterly* 49, no. 3 (Spring 1996): 46–50.

Thompson, Kristin. *Storytelling in the New Hollywood: Understanding Classical Narrative Technique.* Cambridge, MA: Harvard University Press, 1999.

Thomson, David. *England in the Twentieth Century,* 2d ed. Harmondsworth, Middlesex: Penguin, 1981.

"Our Lord of Danger." *Film Comment* 19, no. 2 (March–April 1983): 24–30.

"Greene in the Dark." *Film Comment* 27, no. 4 (July–August 1991): 18–25.

Truffaut, François. *Hitchcock.* London: Secker & Warburg, 1968.

"A Certain Tendency of the French Cinema." In *Movies and Methods,* ed. Bill Nichols. Berkeley: University of California Press, 1976. 224–37. [Trans. of "Une Certaine Tendance du cinéma francais" (1954).]

Tudor, Andrew. *Monsters and Mad Scientists: A Cultural History of the Horror Movie.* Oxford: Blackwell, 1989.

Turner, Jenny. "*Raining Stones.*" *Sight and Sound* n.s., 3, no. 10 (October 1993): 50–1.

Van Wert, William F. "Narrative Structure in *The Third Man.*" *Literature/Film Quarterly* 2, no. 4 (Fall 1974): 341–6.

"*The Cook, The Thief, His Wife and Her Lover.*" *Film Quarterly* 44, no. 2 (Winter 1990–1): 42–50.

Vincendeau, Ginette. "*The Golden Bowl.*" *Sight and Sound* n.s., 10, no. 11 (November 2000): 52.

Walker, Alexander. *Hollywood, England: The British Film Industry in the Sixties.* London: Michael Joseph, 1974.

*National Heroes: British Cinema in the Seventies and Eighties.* London: Harrap, 1985.

Walker, John. *The Once and Future Film: British Cinema in the Seventies and Eighties.* London: Methuen, 1985.

Walsh, Michael. "Allegories of Thatcherism: The Films of Peter Greenaway." In *Fires Were Started: British Cinema and Thatcherism,* ed. Lester Friedman. Minneapolis: University of Minnesota Press, 1993. 255–77.

Ward, J. A. *The Imagination of Disaster: Evil in the Fiction of Henry James.* Lincoln: University of Nebraska Press, 1961.

Welsh, Jim. "'Ill Met By Moonlight': Michael Hoffman's *Dream.*" *Literature/Film Quarterly* 27, no. 2 (1999): 159–61.

Whannel, Garry. "Boxed In: Television in the 1970s." In *The Arts in the 1970s: Cultural Closure?* ed. Bart Moore-Gilbert. London: Routledge, 1994. 176–97.

White, Rob. *The Third Man.* London: British Film Institute, 2003.

Whitehall, Richard. "*Dr. No.*" *Films and Filming* 9, no. 2 (November 1962): 36.

Wiener, Martin J. *English Culture and the Decline of the Industrial Spirit, 1850–1980.* Cambridge: Cambridge University Press, 1981.

Williams, Christopher. "After the Classic, the Classical and Ideology: The Differences of Realism." *Screen* 35, no. 3 (Autumn 1994): 275–92.

"The Social Art Cinema: A Moment in the History of British Film and Television Culture." In *Cinema: The Beginnings and the Future,* ed. Williams. London: University of Westminster Press, 1996. 190–200.

Williams, Raymond. *The Country and the City.* St. Albans, Hertfordshire: Paladin, 1975.

*The Politics of Modernism: Against the New Conformists.* London: Verso, 1989.

Williamson, Judith. "*My Name Is Joe.*" *Sight and Sound* n.s., 8, no. 11 (November 1998): 58.

Wiltshire, John. *Recreating Jane Austen*. Cambridge: Cambridge University Press, 2001.

Wollen, Peter. "The Last New Wave: Modernism in the British Films of the Thatcher Era." In *Fires Were Started: British Cinema and Thatcherism*, ed. Lester Friedman. Minneapolis: University of Minnesota Press, 1993. 35-51.

"Riff-raff Realism." *Sight and Sound* n.s., 8, no. 4 (April 1998): 18-22.

Wollen, Tana. "Over Our Shoulders: Nostalgic Screen Fictions for the 1980s." In *Enterprise and Heritage: Crosscurrents of National Culture*, ed. John Corner and Sylvia Harvey. London: Routledge, 1991. 178-93.

Wood, Linda. "Low-budget British Films in the 1930s." In *The British Cinema Book*, 2d ed., ed. Robert Murphy. London: British Film Institute, 2001. 53-9.

Wood, Robin. *Hitchcock's Films*. London: Zwemmer, 1965.

"Ken Russell." In *Cinema: A Critical Dictionary*, vol. 2, ed. Richard Roud. New York: Viking Press, 1980. 909-10.

*The Wings of the Dove*. London: British Film Institute, 1999.

"*Beautiful People.*" *CineAction* 54 (January 2001): 28-39.

Woods, Alan. *Being Naked Playing Dead: The Art of Peter Greenaway*. Manchester: Manchester University Press, 1996.

Woolf, Virginia. "The Novels of E. M. Forster." In *Collected Essays*, vol. 1. London: Chatto & Windus, 1966. 342-51.

Wright, Patrick. *On Living in an Old Country: The National Past in Contemporary Britain*. London: Verso, 1985.

Yacowar, Maurice. *Hitchcock's British Films*. Hamden, CT: Archon Press, 1977.

Yakir, Dan. "The Sorcerer." *Film Comment* 17, no. 3 (May-June 1981): 49-53.

Young, Lola. *Fear of the Dark: "Race," Gender and Sexuality in the Cinema*. London: Routledge, 1996.

Yule, Andrew. *David Puttnam: The Story So Far*. London: Sphere Books, 1988.

Zambrano, Ana Laura. "*Women in Love:* Counterpoint on Film." *Literature/Film Quarterly* 1, no. 1 (January 1973): 46-54.

# Filmography

*Note*: This filmography lists first all the British films mentioned in the text, although a case could be made that some of these are not British films (just as at least one film in the list of non-British films that follows might have been listed here). The dates shown are the copyright dates given in the films themselves, which may or may not coincide with their release dates.

## BRITISH FILMS CITED

*Accident,* dir. Joseph Losey (London Independent Producers, 1967)
*Adventures of a Taxi Driver,* dir. Stanley Long (Alpha/Salon, 1975)
*Alfie,* dir. Lewis Gilbert (Paramount/Sheldrake, 1966)
*Alfie Darling* (aka *Oh Alfie*), dir. Ken Hughes (Signal, 1975)
*And Now for Something Completely Different,* dir. Ian McNaughton (Columbia/Kettle-drum/Python, 1971)
*Au Pair Girls,* dir. Val Guest (Kenneth Shipman, 1972)
*Beautiful People,* dir. Jasmin Dizdar (Tall Stories/British Film Institute/Channel 4/Arts Council of England/Merseyside Film Production Fund/BSkyB/British Screen, 1999)
*Bend It Like Beckham,* dir. Gurinder Chadha (Kintop Pictures/The Film Council/Film-förderung Hamburg/BskyB/British Screen, 2002)
*Bhaji on the Beach,* dir. Gurinder Chadha (First Independent/Umbi/Channel 4, 1993)
*Billy Elliot,* dir. Stephen Daldry (Arts Council of England/BBC/Tiger Aspect/WT2, 2000)
*Billy Liar,* dir. John Schlesinger (Vic Films, 1963)
*The Bitch,* dir. Gerry O'Hara (Brent Walker, 1979)
*Blackmail,* dir. Alfred Hitchcock (British Independent Pictures, 1929)
*The Blue Lamp,* dir. Basil Dearden (Ealing, 1949)
*Boys Will Be Boys,* dir. William Beaudine (Gainsborough, 1935)
*Brassed Off,* dir. Mark Herman (Film Four/Miramax/Prominent Features, 1996)
*Brazil,* dir. Terry Gilliam (Embassy, 1985)
*Brief Encounter,* dir. David Lean (Eagle–Lion/Cineguild, 1945)
*Brighton Rock* (U.S. title: *Young Scarface*), dir. John Boulting (Associated British/Charter Films, 1947)
*The Browning Version,* dir. Anthony Asquith (General Film Distributors, 1951)
*The Browning Version,* dir. Mike Figgis (UPI/Percy Main, 1994)
*A Canterbury Tale,* dir. Anthony Powell and Emeric Pressburger (Rank/Archers, 1944)
*The Captive Heart,* dir. Basil Dearden (Ealing, 1946)
*Caravaggio,* dir. Derek Jarman (British Film Institute/Channel 4, 1986)
*Carrington,* dir. Christopher Hampton (Polygram/Freeway/Sheldo/Dora, 1995)
*Carry On Abroad,* dir. Gerald Thomas (Fox–Rank, 1972)
*Carry On Again Doctor,* dir. Gerald Thomas (Rank/Adder, 1969)
*Carry On at Your Convenience,* dir. Gerald Thomas (Rank, 1971)
*Carry On Cabby,* dir. Gerald Thomas (Anglo-Amalgamated, 1963)
*Carry On Camping,* dir. Gerald Thomas (Rank/Adder, 1968)

*Carry On Cleo,* dir. Gerald Thomas (Anglo-Amalgamated, 1964)

*Carry On Columbus,* dir. Gerald Thomas (Comedy House/Island World, 1992)

*Carry On Constable,* dir. Gerald Thomas (Anglo-Amalgamated, 1957)

*Carry On Doctor,* dir. Gerald Thomas (Rank, 1967)

*Carry On Emmannuelle,* dir. Gerald Thomas (Hemdale, 1978)

*Carry On England,* dir. Gerald Thomas (Rank, 1976)

*Carry On Girls,* dir. Gerald Thomas (Fox–Rank, 1973)

*Carry On Matron,* dir. Gerald Thomas (Rank, 1971)

*Carry On Nurse,* dir. Gerald Thomas (Anglo-Amalgamated, 1958)

*Carry On Sergeant,* dir. Gerald Thomas (Anglo-Amalgamated/Insignia, 1958)

*Carry On Spying,* dir. Gerald Thomas (Anglo-Amalgamated, 1964)

*Carry On Teacher,* dir. Gerald Thomas (Anglo-Amalgamated, 1959)

*Carry On . . . Up the Khyber,* dir. Gerald Thomas (Rank/Adder, 1968)

*Chariots of Fire,* dir. Hugh Hudson (Twentieth Century–Fox/Allied Stars/Enigma, 1981)

*The Class of Miss MacMichael,* dir. Silvio Narizzano (Brut/Kettledrum, 1978)

*A Clockwork Orange,* dir. Stanley Kubrick (Warner/Polaris, 1971)

*Coalface,* dir. Alberto Cavalcanti (GPO Film Unit, 1935)

*Come Play with Me,* dir. George Harrison Marks (Roldvale/Tigon, 1977)

*Confessions of a Window Cleaner,* dir. Val Guest (Columbia-Warner/Swiftdown, 1974)

*Cool It Carol!* dir. Pete Walker (Miracle, 1970)

*The Cook, the Thief, His Wife & Her Lover,* dir. Peter Greenaway (Palace/Allarts Cook/Erato Films, 1989)

*The Curse of Frankenstein,* dir. Terence Fisher (Warner/Hammer, 1957)

*The Curse of the Werewolf,* dir. Terence Fisher (Universal International/Hotspur/Hammer, 1961)

*Dance with a Stranger,* dir. Mike Newell (Channel 4/First Film/Goldcrest Films/NFFC, 1985)

*Darling,* dir. John Schlesinger (Anglo-Amalgamated/Vic Films/Appia, 1965)

*The Devils,* dir. Ken Russell (Warner/Russo, 1971)

*Diamonds Are Forever,* dir. Guy Hamilton (United Artists/Eon/Danjaq, 1971)

*Dr. No,* dir. Terence Young (United Artist/Eon, 1962)

*Doctor Zhivago,* dir. David Lean (MGM, 1965)

*Don't Look Now,* dir. Nicolas Roeg (British Lion/Casey/Eldorado, 1973)

*Dracula* (U.S. title: *Horror of Dracula*), dir. Terence Fisher (Rank/Hammer, 1958)

*Dracula* A.D. *1972,* dir. Alan Gibson (Warner/Hammer, 1972)

*The Draughtsman's Contract,* dir. Peter Greenaway (British Film Institute/Channel 4, 1982)

*Drifters,* dir. John Grierson (Empire Marketing Board, 1929)

*Drowning by Numbers,* dir. Peter Greenaway (Film Four International/Elsevier Vendex, 1988)

*The Drum* (U.S. title: *Drums*), dir. Zoltan Korda (United Artists/London Films, 1938)

*East Is East,* dir. Damien O'Donnell (Assassin Films/BBC, 1999)

*Edward II,* dir. Derek Jarman (Palace/Working Title/British Screen/BBC, 1991)

*Elephant Boy,* dir. Robert Flaherty and Zoltan Korda (London Films, 1937)

*Elizabeth,* dir. Shekhar Kapur (Channel 4/Gramercy/Polygram/Working Title, 1998)

*Emma,* dir. Douglas McGrath (Haft Entertainment/Matchmaker Films/Miramax, 1996)

*The Entertainer,* dir. Tony Richardson (British Lion/Bryanston/Woodfall/Holly, 1960)

*Evergreen,* dir. Victor Saville (Gaumont, 1934)

*Excalibur,* dir. John Boorman (Warner/Orion, 1981)

*The Evil of Frankenstein,* dir. Freddie Francis (Rank/Hammer, 1964)

*The Fallen Idol,* dir. Carol Reed (British Lion/London Films, 1948)

*Family Life,* dir. Ken Loach (EMI/Kestrel, 1971)

*Fanny By Gaslight* (U.S. title: *Man of Evil*), dir. Anthony Asquith (Gainsborough, 1944)

*Fire over England,* dir. William K. Howard (London Films/Pendennis, 1937)

*First a Girl,* dir. Victor Saville (Gaumont, 1935)

*The Four Feathers,* dir. Zoltan Korda (London Films, 1939)

*The Four Feathers,* dir. Don Sharp (Norman Rosemont Productions/Trident Films, 1977)

*The Four Feathers,* dir. Shekhar Kapur (Belhaven Limited/Dune Films/Jaffilms, 2002)

*Four Weddings and a Funeral,* dir. Mike Newell (Rank/Polygram/Channel 4/Working Title, 1994)

*Frankenstein and the Monster from Hell,* dir. Terence Fisher (Hammer/Avco, 1973)

*Frankenstein Created Woman,* dir. Terence Fisher (Warner/Hammer–Seven Arts, 1966)

*Frankenstein Must Be Destroyed,* dir. Terence Fisher (Warner-Pathé/Hammer, 1969)

*From Russia with Love,* dir. Terence Young (United Artists/Eon, 1963)

*The Full Monty,* dir. Peter Cattaneo (Twentieth Century–Fox, 1997)

*Gandhi,* dir. Richard Attenborough (Columbia/Goldcrest/Indo-British/International Film Investors/National Film Development Corporation of India, 1982)

*Gangster No. 1,* dir. Paul McGuigan (British Screen/BSkyB/Filmboard Berlin–Brandenburg/Little Bird/NFH/Pagoda/Road Movies, 2000)

*Get Carter,* dir. Mike Hodges (MGM, 1971)

*The Girl from Maxim's,* dir. Alexander Korda (London Films, 1933)

*The Go-Between,* dir. Joseph Losey (EMI/World Film Services, 1971)

*The Golden Bowl,* dir. James Ivory (Merchant Ivory/Miramax/TFI Films, 2000)

*Goldfinger,* dir. Guy Hamilton (United Artists/Eon, 1964)

*Good Morning, Boys* (U.S. title: *Where There's a Will*), dir. Marcel Varnel (Gainsborough, 1937)

*Good Time Girl,* dir. David MacDonald (Triton/Rank, 1948)

*Goodbye Mr. Chips,* dir. Sam Wood (MGM, 1939)

*Goodbye Mr. Chips,* dir. Herbert Ross (MGM, 1969)

*The Governess,* dir. Sandra Goldbacher (Arts Council of England/BBC/British Screen/Pandora/Parallax/Sony Classics, 1997)

*Great Expectations,* dir. David Lean (Rank/Cineguild, 1946)

*The Great St. Trinian's Train Robbery,* dir. Frank Launder (British Lion/Braywild, 1966)

*The Green Cockatoo* (U.S. title: *Four Dark Hours*), dir. William Cameron Menzies (New World/Fox British, 1937)

*The Guinea Pig* (U.S. title: *The Outsider*), dir. Roy Boulting (Pilgrim, 1948)

*Hamlet,* dir. Kenneth Branagh (Rank/Castle Rock, 1996)

*The Happiest Days of Your Life,* dir. Frank Launder (British Lion/Individual, 1950)

*Henry V,* dir. Laurence Olivier (Rank/Two Cities, 1945)

*Henry V,* dir. Kenneth Branagh (Curzon/Renaissance Films, 1989)

*Hidden City,* dir. Stephen Poliakoff (Other Cinema/Film Four/ZDF, 1987)

*Hindle Wakes,* dir. Victor Saville (Gaumont, 1931)

*Horror of Frankenstein,* dir. Jimmy Sangster (EMI/Hammer, 1970)

*The Hound of the Baskervilles,* dir. Terence Fisher (United Artists/Hammer, 1959)

*House of Whipcord,* dir. Pete Walker (Miracle, 1974)

*Housing Problems,* dir. Arthur Elton and Edgar Anstey (British Commercial Gas Association, 1935)

*Howards End,* dir. James Ivory (Merchant Ivory/Film Four, 1991)

*If. . . . ,* dir. Lindsay Anderson (Paramount/Memorial, 1968)

*Industrial Britain,* dir. Robert Flaherty and John Grierson (Empire Marketing Board, 1932)

*Intimacy,* dir. Patrice Chéreau (Arte/Azor/Canal Plus/France 2/Mikado/Telema/WDR, 2000)

*The Ipcress File,* dir. Sidney Furie (Rank/Steven/Lowndes, 1965)

*It's Great to Be Young!* dir. Cyril Frankel (Associated British-Pathé/Marble Arch, 1955)

*Jubilee,* dir. Derek Jarman (Whaley–Malin/Megalovision, 1977)

*Kes,* dir. Ken Loach (United Artists/Woodfall, 1969)

*Khartoum,* dir. Basil Dearden (United Artists, 1966)

*Kind Hearts and Coronets,* dir. Robert Hamer (Ealing, 1949)

*A Kind of Loving,* dir. John Schlesinger (Anglo-Amalgamated, 1962)

*Knight without Armour,* dir. Jacques Feyder (London Films, 1937)

*The Krays,* dir. Peter Medak (Rank/Parkfield, 1990)

*The Lady Vanishes,* dir. Alfred Hitchcock (Gaumont-British/Gainsborough, 1938)

*Ladybird, Ladybird,* dir. Ken Loach (Film Four International, 1994)

*The Ladykillers,* dir. Alexander Mackendrick (Ealing, 1955)

*The Last of England,* dir. Derek Jarman (Blue Dolphin/Anglo International/British Screen/Channel 4/ZDF/Tartan Films, 1987)

*The Lavender Hill Mob,* dir. Charles Crichton (Ealing, 1951)

*Lawrence of Arabia,* dir. David Lean (Columbia/Horizon, 1962)

*The Legend of the 7 Golden Vampires* (U.S. title: *The Seven Brothers Meet Dracula*), dir. Roy Ward Baker (Hammer/Shaw Brothers, 1974).

*The Life and Death of Colonel Blimp* (U.S. title: *Colonel Blimp*), dir. Anthony Powell and Emeric Pressburger (GFD/Archers, 1943)

*Life Is Sweet,* dir. Mike Leigh (Palace/Thin Man/Film Four International/British Screen, 1993)

*Lock, Stock and Two Smoking Barrels,* dir. Guy Ritchie (SKA Films/Steve Tisch, 1998)

*The Lodger,* dir. Alfred Hitchcock (Gainsborough, 1926)

*London Kills Me,* dir. Hanif Kureishi (Rank/Working Title/Polygram/Film Four, 1991)

*The Loneliness of the Long Distance Runner,* dir. Tony Richardson (British Lion/Bryanston/Woodfall, 1962)

*The Long Good Friday,* dir. John Mackenzie (Black Lion/Calendar, 1979)

*Look Back in Anger,* dir. Tony Richardson (Associated British/Woodfall, 1959)

*Love's Labours Lost,* dir. Kenneth Branagh (Intermedia, 2000)

*The Madness of King George,* dir. Nicholas Hytner (Rank/Samuel Goldwyn/Channel 4/Close Call, 1994)

*Madonna of the Seven Moons,* dir. Arthur Crabtree (Gainsborough, 1944)

*The Maggie,* dir. Alexander Mackendrick (Ealing, 1954)

*The Magic Box,* dir. John Boulting (Festival Films, 1951)

*The Man in Grey,* dir. Leslie Arliss (GFD/Gainsborough, 1943)

*The Man in the White Suit,* dir. Alexander Mackendrick (Ealing, 1951)

*The Man Who Knew Too Much,* dir. Alfred Hitchcock (Gaumont-British, 1934)

*Mandy,* dir. Alexander Mackendrick (Ealing, 1952)

*Mansfield Park,* dir. Patricia Rozema (BBC/Miramax, 1999)

*The Manxman,* dir. Alfred Hitchcock (British International, 1929)

*Meantime,* dir. Mike Leigh (Central/Mostpoint, 1981)

*Mrs. Brown* (U.S. title: *Her Majesty, Mrs. Brown*), dir. John Madden (Ecosse Films/Miramax, 1997)

*Momma Don't Allow,* dir. Karel Reisz and Tony Richardson (British Film Institute Experimental Fund, 1956)

*Mona Lisa,* dir. Neil Jordan (Hand Made/Palace, 1986)

*Monique,* dir. John Bown (Tigon, 1969)

*Monty Python and the Holy Grail,* dir. Terry Jones and Terry Gilliam (EMI/Python, 1974)

*Monty Python's Life of Brian,* dir. Terry Jones (Hand Made, 1979)

*Monty Python's The Meaning of Life,* dir. Terry Jones (Universal/Celandine/Monty Python Partnership, 1983)

*Moonraker,* dir. Lewis Gilbert (United Artists/Eon, 1979)

*Much Ado about Nothing,* dir. Kenneth Branagh (Samuel Goldwyn/Renaissance, 1993)

*The Mummy,* dir. Terence Fisher (Hammer, 1959)

*My Beautiful Laundrette,* dir. Stephen Frears (Working Title/Channel 4, 1985)

*My Son the Fanatic,* dir. Udayan Prasad (Arts Council of England/BBC/Union General Cinématographique/Zephyr, 1997)

*Naked,* dir. Mike Leigh (First Independent/Thin Man/Film Four, 1993)

*Night Mail,* dir. Harry Watt and Basil Wright (GPO Film Unit, 1936)

*Night Train to Munich,* dir. Carol Reed (Twentieth Century–Fox, 1940)

*Nil by Mouth,* dir. Gary Oldman (Twentieth Century–Fox/SE8 Group/Sony Classics, 1997)

*No Sex Please – We're British,* dir. Cliff Owen (Columbia, 1973)

*Notting Hill,* dir. Roger Michell (Polygram/Working Title, 1999)

*On Her Majesty's Secret Service,* dir. Peter Hunt (United Artists/Eon/Danjaq, 1969)

*Orlando,* dir. Sally Potter (Electric/Adventure Pictures/Lenfilm/Mikado/Sigma/British Screen, 1992)

*Passport to Pimlico,* dir. Henry Cornelius (Ealing, 1949)

*Peeping Tom,* dir. Michael Powell (Anglo-Amalgamated, 1959)

*Perfect Strangers* (U.S. title: *Vacation from Marriage*), dir. Alexander Korda (MGM/London Films, 1945)

*Performance,* dir. Donald Cammell and Nicolas Roeg (Warner/Goodtimes, 1968)

*Persuasion,* dir. Roger Michell (BBC/WGBH/Millesime/France 2, 1995)

*The Phantom of the Opera,* dir. Terence Fisher (Universal/Hammer, 1962)

*The Pillow Book,* dir. Peter Greenaway (Film Four/Kasander & Wagman/Alpha/Woodline, 1995)

*Pimpernel Smith,* dir. Leslie Howard (British National, 1941)

*Poor Cow,* dir. Ken Loach (Anglo-Amalgamated/Vic Films/Fenchurch, 1967)

*The Portrait of a Lady,* dir. Jane Campion (Polygram/Propaganda, 1996)

*The Prince and the Showgirl,* dir. Laurence Olivier (Warner/Marilyn Monroe Productions, 1957)

*The Private Life of Don Juan,* dir. Alexander Korda (London Films, 1934)

*The Private Life of Henry VIII,* dir. Alexander Korda (London Films, 1933)

*Prospero's Books,* dir. Peter Greenaway (Palace/Allarts/Cinea/Camera One/Penta/Elsevier Vendex/Film Four/VPRO/Canal Plus/NHK, 1991)

*A Queen Is Crowned,* dir. Castleton Knight (Rank/Universal International, 1953)

*The Rainbow,* dir. Ken Russell (Vestron, 1989)

*Raining Stones,* dir. Ken Loach (First Independent/Parallax/Channel 4, 1993)

*Rembrandt,* dir. Alexander Korda (London Films, 1936)

*The Revenge of Frankenstein,* dir. Terence Fisher (Columbia/Hammer, 1958)

*Riddles of the Sphinx,* dir. Laura Mulvey and Peter Wollen (British Film Institute, 1977)

*Riff-Raff,* dir. Ken Loach (British Film Institute/Parallax, 1991)

*Room at the Top,* dir. Jack Clayton (Remus, 1958)

*A Room with a View,* dir. James Ivory (Merchant Ivory/Goldcrest, 1986)

*Rosencrantz and Guildenstern Are Dead,* dir. Tom Stoppard (Hobo/Brandenburg, 1990)

*A Run for Your Money,* dir. Charles Frend (Ealing, 1949)

*Sabotage* (U.S. title: *The Woman Alone*), dir. Alfred Hitchcock (Gaumont-British, 1936)

*Sammy and Rosie Get Laid,* dir. Stephen Frears (Cinecom/Film Four, 1987)

*San Demetrio London,* dir. Charles Frend (Ealing, 1943)

*Sanders of the River* (U.S. title: *Bosambo*), dir. Zoltan Korda (London Films, 1935)

*Sapphire,* dir. Basil Dearden (Rank/Artna, 1959)

*The Satanic Rites of Dracula,* dir. Alan Gibson (Hammer, 1973)

*Saturday Night and Sunday Morning,* dir. Karel Reisz (Bryanston/Woodfall, 1960)

*Savage Messiah,* dir. Ken Russell (MGM/Russ-Arts, 1972)

*The Scarlet Pimpernel,* dir. Harold Young (London Films, 1934)

*Scars of Dracula,* dir. Roy Ward Baker (Hammer/EMI, 1970)

*Scott of the Antarctic,* dir. Charles Frend (Ealing, 1948)

*Scum,* dir. Alan Clarke (Berwick Street Productions/Boyd's Company, 1979)

*Secret Agent,* dir. Alfred Hitchcock (Gaumont-British, 1936)

*Secrets & Lies,* dir. Mike Leigh (Film Four/CIBY 2000/Thin Man, 1995)

*Sense and Sensibility,* dir. Ang Lee (Columbia/Mirage, 1995)

*The Servant,* dir. Joseph Losey (Elstree/Springbok, 1963)

*Sexy Beast,* dir. Jonathan Glazer (Film Four International/Fox Searchlight/Kanzeman/ Recorded Picture Co., 2000)

*Shadowlands,* dir. Richard Attenborough (Savoy, 1993)

*Shakespeare in Love,* dir. John Madden (Bedford Falls, 1998)

*Sing as We Go!* dir. Basil Dean (Associated Talking Pictures, 1934)

*Sixty Glorious Years,* dir. Herbert Wilcox (Imperator, 1938)

*Snatch,* dir. Guy Ritchie (Columbia/SKA Films, 2000)

*Sons and Lovers,* dir. Jack Cardiff (Twentieth Century–Fox/Company of Artists, 1960)

*The Spy in Black,* dir. Michael Powell (Harefield, 1939)

*Stella Does Tricks,* dir. Coky Giedroyc (British Film Institute, 1996)

*Strapless,* dir. David Hare (Virgin/Granada/Film Four International, 1988)

*Summer Holiday,* dir. Peter Yates (Associated British/Ivy, 1963)

*The Tango Lesson,* dir. Sally Potter (Adventure/Cinema Projects/Imagica/OKCK Films/ Pandors/PIE/Sigma/Sony Classics, 1997)

*Taste the Blood of Dracula,* dir. Peter Sasdy (Warner/Hammer, 1969)

*The Tempest,* dir. Derek Jarman (Boyd's Company, 1979)

*The Third Man,* dir. Carol Reed (British Lion/London Films/Selznick, 1949)

*The 39 Steps,* dir. Alfred Hitchcock (Gaumont-British, 1935)

*This Sporting Life,* dir. Lindsay Anderson (Rank/Independent Artists, 1963)

*Time Bandits,* dir. Terry Gilliam (Hand Made, 1981)

*The Titfield Thunderbolt,* dir. Charles Crichton (Ealing, 1953)

*To Sir with Love,* dir. James Clavell (Columbia, 1967)

*Tom Jones,* dir. Tony Richardson (United Artists/Woodfall, 1963)

*Tomorrow Never Dies,* dir. Roger Spottiswoode (United Artists/Eon/Danjaq, 1997)

*21 Days,* dir. Basil Dean (London Films/Denham Films, 1937)

*The Two Faces of Dr. Jekyll,* dir. Terence Fisher (Hammer, 1960)

*Under the Skin,* dir. Carine Adler (British Film Institute/Channel 4/Merseyside Film Production Fund/Rouge/Strange Days, 1997)

*Ups and Downs of a Handyman,* dir. John Sealey (KFR/Target, 1975)

*Victoria the Great,* dir. Herbert Wilcox (British Lion/Imperator, 1937)

*Villain,* dir. Michael Tuchner (EMI/Kastner, 1971)

*The War Zone,* dir. Tim Roth (Fandango/Film Four International/Mikado/Portobello/ Sarah Radclyffe Productions, 1998)

*The Weak and the Wicked,* dir. J. Lee Thompson (Associated British/Marble Arch, 1953)

*Wedding Rehearsal,* dir. Alexander Korda (Ideal/London Films, 1932)

*Went the Day Well?* dir. Alberto Cavalcanti (Ealing, 1942)

*Wetherby,* dir. David Hare (Greenpoint/Film Four/Zenith, 1985)

*Where Angels Fear to Tread,* dir. Charles Sturridge (Rank/Sovereign/London Weekend/ Stagescreen/Compact, 1991)

*Whisky Galore!* (U.S. title: *Tight Little Island*), dir. Alexander Mackendrick (Ealing, 1949)

*The Wicked Lady,* dir. Leslie Arliss (GFD/Gainsborough, 1945)

*The Wicker Man,* dir. Robin Hardy (British Lion, 1973)

*Wild West,* dir. David Attwood (Initial/Channel 4/British Screen, 1992)

*The Wings of the Dove,* dir. Iain Softley (Miramax/Renaissance Films, 1997)

*Witchfinder General* (U.S. title: *The Conqueror Worm*), dir. Michael Reeves (Tigon/ American International, 1968)

*Women in Love,* dir. Ken Russell (United Artists/Brandywine, 1969)

*The World Is Not Enough,* dir. Michael Apted (Eon, 1999)

*Yield to the Night* (U.S. title: *Blonde Sinner*), dir. J. Lee Thompson (Associated British, 1956)

*You Only Live Twice,* dir. Lewis Gilbert (United Artists/Eon, 1967)

*Young Soul Rebels,* dir. Isaac Julien (British Film Institute/Film Four/Sankofa/La Sept/ Iberoamericana, 1991)

*Zardoz,* dir. John Boorman (Twentieth Century-Fox, 1974)

*Zulu,* dir. Cy Endfield (Paramount/Diamond, 1963)

## NON-BRITISH FILMS CITED

*Bandit Queen,* dir. Shekhar Kapur (India, Mainline/Kaleidoscope/Channel 4, 1994)

*Bicycle Thieves* (*Ladri di Biciclette*), dir. Vittorio de Sica (Italy, Produzione de Sica, 1948)

*The Birds,* dir. Alfred Hitchcock (USA, Universal, 1963)

*The Cabinet of Dr. Caligari* (*Das Cabinet des Dr. Caligari*), dir. Robert Wiene (Germany, Decla-Bioscop, 1919)

*Call Northside 777,* dir. Henry Hathaway (USA, Twentieth Century-Fox, 1948)

*The Charge of the Light Brigade,* dir. Michael Curtiz (USA, Warner, 1936)

*Citizen Kane,* dir. Orson Welles (USA, RKO, 1941)

*Cleopatra,* dir. Joseph L. Mankiewicz (USA, Twentieth Century-Fox, 1963)

*Deliverance,* dir. John Boorman (USA, Warner/Elmer Enterprises, 1972)

*Emmanuelle,* dir. Just Jaeckin (France, Trinacra/Orphée, 1974)

*Get Carter,* dir. Stephen Kay (USA, Canton/Franchise, 2000)

*Gunga Din,* dir. George Stevens (USA, RKO, 1939)

*Last Tango in Paris* (*Le Dernier tango à Paris*), dir. Bernardo Bertolucci (France, Les Artistes Associés/United Artists, 1972)

*M,* dir. Fritz Lang (Germany, Nero-Film AG, 1931)

*Moana,* dir. Robert Flaherty (USA, Famous Players, 1925)

*Nanook of the North,* dir. Robert Flaherty (USA, Revillon Frères, 1922)

*Night of the Living Dead,* dir. George Romero (USA, Image Ten, 1968)

*North by Northwest,* dir. Alfred Hitchcock (USA, MGM, 1959)

*Nosferatu, a Symphony of Horror* (*Nosferatu - Eine Symphonie des Grauens*), dir. F. W. Murnau (Germany, Prana, 1922)

*Orient Express,* dir. Paul Martin (USA, Fox, 1934)

*The Pawnbroker,* dir. Sidney Lumet (USA, Landau-Unger, 1965)

*Point Blank,* dir. John Boorman (USA, MGM, 1967)

*Psycho,* dir. Alfred Hitchcock (USA, Shamley, 1960)

*Red Desert* (*Il deserto rosso*), dir. Michelangelo Antonioni (Italy–France, Cinematografica Federiz/Francoriz, 1964)

*The Silence* (*Tynstaden*), dir. Ingmar Bergman (Sweden, Svensk Filmindustri, 1963)

*2001: A Space Odyssey,* dir. Stanley Kubrick (USA, MGM, 1968)

*Washington Square,* dir. Agnieszka Holland (USA, Alchemy Filmowrk/Buena Vista/Caravan/Hollywood Pictures, 1997)

*Wuthering Heights,* dir. William Wyler (USA, Samuel Goldwyn, 1939)

*Zéro de conduite* (*Zero for Conduct*), dir. Jean Vigo (France, Gaumont/Franco Film/Aubert, 1933)

# Index